MARRIAGE ANALYSIS

FOUNDATIONS FOR SUCCESSFUL FAMILY LIFE

By

HAROLD T. CHRISTENSEN

CHAIRMAN OF SOCIOLOGY AND PROFESSOR IN THE DEPARTMENT
OF FAMILY LIFE, PURDUE UNIVERSITY

THE RONALD PRESS COMPANY · NEW YORK

4

TO MY FAMILY

PARENTS
Nettie Taylor and Henry Oswald Christensen

BROTHERS
Leland, Cornell, Arlond, Ross, Grant, Lyle

WIFE
Alice Spencer Christensen

CHILDREN
Carl, Boyd, Janice, Larry, Gayle

PREFACE

This book grows out of the realization that all is not well with marriage and family life today, and the belief that understanding, which can come from study and discussion, is a first step in overcoming the difficulty. Successful marriage is not automatic; nor does it result from mere wishful thinking or hocus-pocus manipulation. There are principles which underlie success here, just as there are in other segments of life.

By emphasizing *analysis* we have tried to approach marriage as a scientist would any other phenomenon—being systematic rather than eclectic, rational more than emotional. This is not an encyclopedia of factual information, nor a marriage manual, nor a source book, in the sense of having something on all subjects pertaining to marriage. Neither does it pretend to treat any one subject exhaustively, nor to have all the answers. Rather, it is an attempt at synthesis, through logical analysis, of some of the core problems of marriage.

The approach is what might be called functional, in contrast to institutional; person-centered, in contrast to group-centered. The focus, therefore, is upon the interpersonal relationships of men and women during courtship and marriage. Treatment of the family as a social institution is but incidental.

It is our reasoned conviction that marriage and family life are good, that they are productive of things worth while. This is the basic assumption of the book. Once accepting this as a premise, we have tried to remain objective—analyzing rather than dogmatizing, seeking truth rather than proof, teaching rather than preaching. But we are interested in welfare and improvement; and we have tried, therefore, to stimulate readers in the direction of greater effort. Our reach has been for both information and motivation.

From the group or social point of view, we believe that marital success is dependent upon the degree of public attention and encouragement given to it. Sometimes the culture is at fault, by understressing family values. As a result, many people enter marriage entirely unprepared for the obligations entailed, and unconvinced concerning the seriousness and importance of what is involved. There is need for a greater "family-mindedness" in society, for an enlightened and motivated public opinion concerning marriage. And it is to this broader end, also, that the book is directed.

Student and teacher aids are provided at the end of each chapter. These are intended to carry the reader farther than the material of the book. The *Problems and Projects* are more than a review of what has gone before; by dealing mainly with controversial issues and unsolved problems, they can provide stimulation for further thinking, discussion, and research. The lists of *Selected Readings* represent some of the best sources available on the subjects treated.

The author wishes to acknowledge the following sources of help: (1) Virgil Hurlburt, Reuben Hill, Evelyn Millis Duvall, A. Kimball Romney, Dwight W. Culver, Elizabeth K. Wilson, Hanna Meissner, Margaret Nesbitt, John M. Hadley, E. J. Asher, Evelyn S. Wigent, Phyllis Elwood, Lorna Davis, Milton Tew, Rebecca Nelson, Ruth C. Bundy, Lucile Spencer, Reed Bradford, Ariel S. Ballif, Wesley P. Lloyd, Ralph Britsch, and Harold G. Clark—these have read and criticized one or more chapters of the manuscript. Though in no way responsible for the opinions herein expressed, or the shortcomings still contained, their suggestions along the way have been invaluable. (2) Recognition is due the six hundred or more Purdue University students who first used this material in mimeographed form. Their lively discussions and frankly expressed reactions have provided a basis for pre-publication revision. (3) Special mention is made of the fact that certain sentences and paragraphs have been used, in adapted form, from an earlier published work by the author, *The Latter-day Saint Family*. For permission, appreciation is expressed to Milton Bennion.

H. T. C.

Purdue University
    February, 1950

CONTENTS

PART I

Dimensions

PART II

Factors

PART III

Processes

PART IV

Programs

PART I
DIMENSIONS

Chapter 1

INTRODUCTION AND ORIENTATION

It was the wise man, Solomon, who said: "There be three things which are too wonderful for me, yea, four which I know not: The way of an eagle in the air; the way of a serpent upon a rock; the way of a ship in the midst of the sea; and *the way of a man with a maid*." [1]

Since Solomon's day, man has learned much concerning these problems, and others. Yet, there is much that remains to be learned. Human behavior, especially, is complex; and, although man has never ceased extending the boundaries of knowledge concerning himself, there has always remained a residue not completely understood—problems to be solved, challenges in man's continuous quest.

Our concern throughout this writing will be with but one thing, "the way of a man with a maid." We move forward in humility and in confidence; humility in the realization that we do not have all of the answers but confidence in the knowledge that we are on the way, and that out of serious study can come both better understanding and richer living.

THE MEANING OF MARRIAGE

There is general agreement among students of society that the family is the most central and basic of all human groupings. The family is the child's first contact with the outside world; it receives him when he is more impressionable, interacts with him in a more intimate manner, and often holds him longer than any other group. It is there that attitudes and habits are first formed, that personality takes shape. The family is the seedbed of character and the workshop of social progress.

---

[1] Proverbs 30:18-19. Italics not in the original.

3

Social Functions of the Family.—Marriage and family life have proved themselves throughout the ages. So far as is known, no society has ever been without these institutions; they have both antiquity and universality. Societies vary regarding details of custom; but always, in all ages and all cultures, some sort of family life has been the norm. Love and procreation outside of marriage have been exceptions in the history of mankind, never the rule.

There must be a reason. Is it that man is born with the urge to marry, that family life is instinctive? Anthropologists, sociologists, and psychologists say not; for while the drive to mate is a part of one's original nature, the institutions for realizing and controlling this urge are a part of man's culture, and are learned. Why, then, are marriage and family life so ubiquitous? It is likely that the answer to this question lies in the similarity of needs among men and the apparent tendency of man everywhere to organize like institutions to meet these common needs. Institutions are promoted and perpetuated for the sake of specific functions they can perform in the light of recognized human needs. Major purposes of marriage and the family, therefore, those that justify their existence and explain their universality, are the personal and social functions they perform. Here is what they do.

1. They supply an affectional interaction between husband and wife, permitting, thereby, a satisfying of the sexual and emotional needs of each. Isolated living often leads to loneliness, and promiscuous loving lacks security. Both leave one short of the happiness goal. Because of this, marriage and family life make possible some of man's greatest personal satisfactions.

2. They set up a socially accepted means for the procreation of the human race. While reproduction is entirely possible outside of marriage, it in that way lacks control and dodges responsibility. Societies everywhere have deemed it important to safeguard reproduction with responsibility; marriage does that.

3. They make possible the protection and care of the human infant, which is about the most helpless of all infants in the

animal world. Without the responsibility that accompanies marriage, and the detailed care that family life affords, the human baby would find it very difficult to survive. His period of infancy is longer and he is less well equipped with hereditary behavior mechanisms (instincts) than are other animals. These differences are an advantage to the human in that they make possible greater learning and development, but they are a disadvantage in that they make him more helpless and dependent upon others in the early years.

4. They provide for the education, socialization, and emotional needs of the child. Since the human infant depends less upon instinct and more upon training, it is important to have institutions that will look after this need, in the early impressionable years especially. Procreation and protection are but first functions that the family can perform with reference to the child; attitude formation and habit training are also essential.

Complementary Nature of the Sexes.—It is a well-known and accepted fact that neither man nor woman is complete without the other. Apparently, nature intended it that way, for nearly everyone is endowed with strong biological and psychological attractions toward the opposite sex.

The complementary nature of male-female relationships is illustrated by various creation accounts. In the Bible, for example, God is said to have remarked, after He finished with the creation of man, "It is not good that the man should be alone," and then He created woman to be man's "help meet" and companion. Later He added, "Therefore shall a man leave his father and his mother, and shall cleave unto his wife: and they shall be one flesh." [2]

Non-Christian accounts are similar. Somewhat typical of them is the following, taken from a beautiful Hindu story:

In the beginning, when Twashtri came to the creation of woman, he found that he had exhausted his materials in the making of man, and that no solid elements were left. In this dilemma, after profound meditation, he did as follows. He took the rotundity of the moon, and the

----

[2] Genesis 2:18, 24.

curves of creepers, and the clinging of tendrils, and the trembling of grass, and the slenderness of the reed, and the bloom of flowers, and the lightness of leaves, and the tapering of the elephant's trunk, and the glances of deer, and the clustering of rows of bees, and the joyous gaiety of sunbeams, and the weeping of clouds, and the fickleness of the winds, and the timidity of the hare, and the vanity of the peacock, and the softness of the parrot's bosom, and the hardness of adamant, and the sweetness of honey, and the cruelty of the tiger, and the warm glow of fire, and the coldness of snow, and the chattering of jays, and the cooing of the kokila, and the hypocrisy of the crane, and the fidelity of the chakrawaka; and compounding all these together he made woman, and gave her to man. But after one week, man came to him, and said: "Lord, this creature that you have given me makes my life miserable. She chatters incessantly and teases me beyond endurance, never leaving me alone; and she requires incessant attention, and takes all my time up, and cries about nothing, and is always idle; and so I have come to give her back again, as I cannot live with her." So Twashtri said: "Very well"; and he took her back. Then after another week, man came again to him and said: "Lord, I find that my life is very lonely, since I gave you back that creature. I remember how she used to dance and sing to me, and look at me out of the corner of her eye, and play with me, and cling to me; and her laughter was music, and she was beautiful to look at, and soft to touch; so give her back to me again." So Twashtri said: "Very well"; and gave her back again. Then after only three days, man came back to him again and said: "Lord, I know not how it is; but after all I have come to the conclusion that she is more of a trouble than a pleasure to me; so please take her back again." But Twashtri said: "Out on you! Be off! I will have no more of this. You must manage how you can." Then man said: "But I cannot live with her." And Twashtri replied: "Neither could you live without her." And he turned his back on man, and went on with his work. Then man said: "What is to be done! for I cannot live either with her or without her." [3]

It may not be entirely facetious to add that man has been in this dilemma ever since. But, if this be true with man, so is it with woman—though in a lesser degree, perhaps, for woman has needed to adjust to man, more than he to her.

---

[3] F. W. Bain, *A Digit of the Moon,* pp. 13-15; as quoted by Ernest Crawley *The Mystic Rose* (London: Methuen & Co., Ltd., 1927), pp. 42-43.

Potentially, associations between the sexes are productive of a great deal of satisfaction. Nature and society have combined to make courtship and marriage seem attractive. Someone put it this way:

> It takes two for a kiss, only one for a sigh;
> Twain by twain we marry, one by one we die;
> Joy is a partnership, grief weeps alone.

But dissatisfactions are also potential, or possible, within the love relationships of men and women. These associations are of such a nature—personal, intimate, highly emotionalized, long continuing—as to permit misunderstanding and misery as well as harmony and happiness. They are highly intensive and extensive both at the same time, which means that satisfactions tend toward the extremes. Where marriage is successful, some of the greatest joy that is possible for man or woman is experienced there, but some of the deepest misery and suffering are known when it fails.

Support for this view is found in a study by Hornell Hart, professor of sociology at Duke University. He constructed a scale device, called a Euphorimeter, for measuring happiness under varying conditions. It was arranged so that a score of plus one hundred would indicate an average happiness. Applying the test to groups differing by marital status, he found the following: Married people who had never contemplated divorce or separation had a score of 213; young persons engaged to be married, 173; unmarried persons never yet engaged, 75; young persons with broken and unreplaced engagements, 62; and married persons who were on the verge of divorce, minus 160. It will be noted that the married individuals constituted both those groups that were most happy and most unhappy.[4]

No two individuals are just alike, especially if one is male and the other female; but neither are men and women entirely different. There is enough affinity between the sexes to give each a lift in the presence of the other, and enough antipathy

---

[4] Hornell Hart, *Chart for Happiness* (The Macmillan Co., New York, 1940), p. 33.

to make understanding and self-sacrifice necessary if unity is to be realized.

Happiness as a Measure of Success.—Marriage, then, has a purpose and a meaning for the mates who embrace it, for the offspring who result from it, and for the society that encourages it. Family life is basic in personality and central in society. It facilitates both the perpetuation of the race and the personal happiness of individuals.

There is no single criterion for successful marriage. One approach would be to measure success in terms of how well it meets the needs and expectations of society; a second would be to view the degree to which it facilitates personality development in husband and wife; a third would be to judge success on the basis of permanence or endurance of the marriage; a fourth would be to see how well the mates adjust and develop unity in their relationship; a fifth would be to consider marital satisfactions, or the amount of happiness mates derive from the union.[5] Each of these has certain advantages, and other disadvantages. Taken alone, no one is entirely satisfactory for it covers only part of the picture. A composite criterion, containing elements from each of these, might be preferable. Up to date, however, nothing like this has been developed.

In our culture, happiness is most widely accepted as the standard; people tend to interpret their marriages as being successful when they find them satisfying, and unsuccessful when unsatisfying. A major objection to using happiness as the criterion is that it is subjective and difficult to measure. This objection needn't cause too much concern, though, for the following reasons: (1) People usually agree on how happy or unhappy a given marriage should be rated. Studies show that husbands and wives generally agree between themselves with reference to their own marriage, and that these views line up rather closely with opinions or ratings from the outside. This means that happiness is something that can be recognized in a reasonably reliable manner, even if it is subjective. (2) Happi-

---

[5] Cf. Ernest W. Burgess and Harvey J. Locke, *The Family: From Institution to Companionship* (New York: American Book Co., 1945), pp. 432-49.

ness is known to correlate with other types of success criteria. Generally speaking, those mates are most happy who are best adjusted to each other and to society, who are able to make personal advancement, and who don't separate or get a divorce —exceptions admitted. This means that happiness can serve fairly well as a composite index of success.

It should be made clear, however, that we are not seeking to glorify personal pleasure in marriage at the expense of others or without considering the welfare of society. Satisfactions can be experienced on many levels, and it is the "higher" ones that interest us here. By contenting themselves with mere thrills and passing pleasures, people frequently deprive themselves of the more complete and permanent satisfactions that marriage can bring. Too many persons interpret happiness in an impatient and selfish manner, expecting it without sacrifice, and then wanting to turn away from marriage at the least provocation. There may be unhappy experiences within the marriage relationship, some of which cannot be avoided— such as loss of a job, sudden or prolonged illness, enforced separation in wartime, and death in the family. But these can be better met when the relationship is basically a happy one than when it is not. When we say that marriage is successful if it is happy, we mean long-range or total happiness, the kind that comes by understanding, cooperation, and self-effort directed toward adjustment.

A successful family is one in which all members are privileged to share in the common bond of happiness, made possible by intelligent and cooperative living, and where each is able to reinforce the individual happiness of each of the others. Marriage does not insure complete happiness, but it does open a way. With greater opportunity comes greater responsibility, however, which if not accepted may mean misery in place of joy.

Trouble Symptoms

If the purposes of marriage outlined above were always realized, if family life were generally successful, there would be little need for the discussions that are to follow. Unfortunately, such is not the case; the family today is in trouble.

To admit this is not being pessimistic, only realistic. Failure to recognize or acknowledge the true condition would only blind us to the problems the family faces, with the resulting complacency dragging heavily upon progress. There is room for optimism if men and women first have understanding and then are willing to exert the necessary effort.

It is not our contention that all, or even the majority, of marriages fail. Yet, one has but to look around to see abundant evidence of family breakdown and of the human suffering that follows. Misunderstandings, bewilderments, heartaches, tears, bitternesses, jealousies, hatreds—all of these, and more, are common in the family experience; too common. In spite of this, people still marry, and at an increasing rate (see Figure 1). Furthermore, nearly all who marry find some satisfaction in the relationship, and many experience supreme and continuous happiness. We must not lose sight of the positive side of the picture. Our purpose in turning briefly to the darker side now is to give a better understanding of the dimensions of the problem, to lay out the challenge.

Neither is it our position that failure is wholly the fault of those who marry. Society and the individual are jointly responsible. It is true that personal inadequacy is usually an underlying factor when marriage fails; but it is equally true that the person is partially the product of his society. Furthermore, there are elements in modern culture which make marital success more difficult of attainment than formerly. (1) This is a time of rapid change and almost infinite variety and stimulation; it is a day of great transition and confusion. Both the tempo and the complexity of modern civilization have been unparalleled in history, which explains some of the insecurity, bewilderment, and frustration so prevalent today. Our values are in conflict, as are also our institutions. Part of the problem of the modern family, therefore, lies in the unsettled nature of the transitional period it is in. (2) Not only is modern life extremely transitional, it is also much more "artificial" than in an earlier day. The natural environment has been replaced, or nearly so, by a man-made cultural environment. This is

especially true in the city where modern "cliff dwellers" live
their lives of mechanical convenience. Contraception artificially
limits the size of families. When children are born they are so
often raised as hothouse plants, denied the opportunity of performing little family tasks as well as the socializing development that comes from normal sibling interaction. We are not
reacting against technological culture as such, only pointing
out that its "unnaturalness" creates problems in family preparation and family living. (3) A third reason for the greater
difficulty attached to success in this field today is that we expect
more of marriage than formerly. Our sights have been lifted.
Since success or failure must always be measured against one's
definition of the situation, it follows that more effort is needed
now for the reason that success today is defined in terms of
higher goals. In a day when convention and duty were the
prime controls, people could accept marriage somewhat stoically
but without too much hope for freedom, personal development,
or happiness. Now, however, people in marrying expect happiness and will more readily separate when disappointed.

Some Facts about Divorce.—The most obvious and convincing evidence of failure in family relationships is where
husband and wife cease to live together. We do not mean that
a marriage can be called successful just because the mates stay
"hitched"; but if maladjustment has proceeded to the point of
divorce, certainly the relationship can be regarded as unsuccessful. It will be profitable, therefore, to take a quick examination of the divorce problem.

1. Judged by number of divorces alone, the marriage picture
in contemporary America is not at all bright. This country has
one of the highest divorce rates in the world, and one that
continues to increase (long-time trend—see Figure 1). During
the decade prior to World War II there were around 200,000
divorces annually in the United States, which was one for
every five or six marriages. This was a ratio twice as high
as that which existed at the beginning of the century. With
the war came social and personal disturbances which shot the
rate higher yet, and in the postwar years there have been about

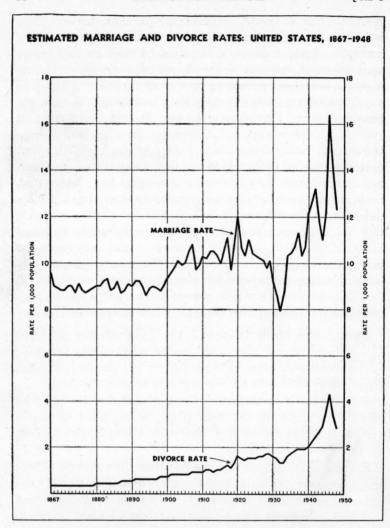

FIG. 1.—Marriage and divorce rates for the United States. Since the beginning of the century, marriage and divorce rates have both been going up. They were disproportionately low in periods of depression, and high during and following wars. Nineteen forty-six showed the highest marriage and divorce rates in the history of the Nation. (Adapted from Federal Security Agency, *Provisional Marriage and Divorce Statistics, United States, 1948,* Volume 31, Number 16, November 4, 1949, p. 230.)

500,000 divorces yearly, or about one for every three or four marriages. Nineteen forty-six saw an all-time high point in number and rate of divorces.[6] The peak in breakdowns of hasty war marriages has apparently passed. Nevertheless the long-time divorce trend is still upward, and there are authorities who estimate that within a decade or so it will be normal for more than half of all marriages to end in divorce.

2. If divorce is going to take place at all, it will usually happen within the first few years following marriage. Most divorces are asked for in the third and fourth years. Approximately two thirds of all divorces materialize before the tenth wedding anniversary. The average duration of marriage, for those that end in divorce, is about seven years. Significant also, though disturbing, is the fact that the trend is toward a shorter duration of marriage prior to divorce.[7] This has been especially true during and following the war, and it parallels the increase in the number of divorces noted above.

3. About three times as many wives ask for and secure divorces as do husbands. This is due to several factors, chief of which are these: state laws give wives more legal grounds upon which a divorce can be obtained; husbands more frequently offend or give cause for divorce; and chivalry plus social pressure inclines the husband to let the wife take the lead.

4. Divorce rates are known to be higher in the city than they are in rural areas; in the Western states than in the East; among actors and commercial travelers than in the more stable occupations; among Negroes than whites; among the uneducated than those who have college degrees; among those married by a justice of the peace than those having a church wedding; among childless couples than those with a family.

5. Legal grounds for divorce are often not the same as actual causes, and state laws on the subject vary greatly.

[6] The Federal Security Agency reports an estimated 405,000 divorces for 1948 as compared with 1,802,895 marriages. Respective figures were 483,000 and 1,991,878 for 1947; 610,000 and 2,291,045 for 1946; and 485,000 and 1,612,992 for 1945. Source: *Provisional Marriage and Divorce Statistics, United States,* 1948, Vol. 31, No. 16, November 4, 1949, pp. 228-29.

[7] See, for example, *Family Life Education,* 6:12, June, 1946. The American Institute of Family Relations found that before getting a divorce people wait only two thirds as long now as they did twelve years ago.

Legally, the three most commonly used reasons for divorce are cruelty, desertion, and adultery. Actually, this tells almost nothing. It is probable that most divorces are by mutual agreement, as evidenced by the fact that very few divorce suits are ever contested by the defendant. Since state laws require that there be some reason, with the implication of guilt, married mates wanting a divorce will very frequently resort to collusion, hatching up a case that will get them by the law. Of all real causes, incompatibility is the most basic, and behind that usually lie personality inadequacies. Authorities agree that successful marriage is one of the best evidences of a good adjustment to life, and unsuccessful marriage of a poor adjustment.

6. Divorce usually presents a crisis to members of the family: husband, wife, and children. The divorcees themselves will have experienced all the sorrows and frustrations that come from disillusionment in love, intimate conflict in the home, the ordeal of a public airing in the divorce court, an injured self-respect, and all the rest. These things alone are disorganizing. In addition the divorcee must reorganize his or her entire life, from some of the most personal of habit patterns to relationships with the public in general. No longer can he or she depend upon someone else for support, comfort, and the thousand and one little services that husband and wife normally perform for each other. No longer can he or she associate socially with all the same people, or in the same ways as formerly. Loneliness may creep in. Temptation may become strong. Because of all this, more divorcees turn antisocial, become psychopathic, or even commit suicide, than is proportionately true of the normal population. While all do not go to these extremes, many experience a period of severe stress before life again becomes normal, and some indulge in a holiday of unconventional living.[8]

Children of the divorced are frequently forced into a life of tension and strain. Their affections are torn between the two parents, who are in conflict. If the court decrees that they are to spend some time with each parent, as is often done, they may

---

8 Post-divorce adjustments are to be treated more extensively in Chapter 13.

be made the buffer to that conflict, the victim of jealousy and hate. Being young and immature they do not understand. Conflict comes to be normal in their way of life. No wonder juvenile delinquency is higher than average among children of divorced parents. No wonder, also, that these children have a higher than average chance of becoming divorced themselves later on.

7. However tragic in its consequences, divorce is only a symptom of deeper trouble; and, unless the real source of the trouble can itself be removed, divorce seems sometimes justified. It is unfortunate that people put so little into their preparing for marriage, that they err in mate selection and the like. Once a mistake has been made, nonetheless, it had better be recognized, and rectified, in favor of a new start. This is not to justify any lack of effort within the marriage process itself, but only to admit that "sometimes people get married for the wrong reasons and get divorced for the right ones." [9] The first and most important step toward the solution of difficulties should be a reconciliation of feelings and a readjustment of the relationships themselves. Failing this, after a long and honest effort, there is no point in perpetuating a "living hell" by forcing the marriage to stay formally intact long after love and harmony are gone. Sometimes husbands, wives, and children are better off by having a divorce. Though the breaking up of a family is unfortunate, the real evil is that which produces it; though it should be used only as a last resort, divorce should nevertheless be retained as a safety valve, as a way out when there is no other.

Separation Short of Divorce.—Desertion, sometimes referred to as "the poor man's divorce," is one way of escaping the expense and the ordeal of formal court proceedings. Yet the causes and consequences are essentially the same as for divorce. More poor people desert than do those who are economically well off; more urban residents than rural; more Negroes than whites; more men than women; more from mixed mar-

---

[9] From a speech by the Judge in Moss Hart's *Christopher Blake* (New York: Random House, 1947), p. 109.

riages than where the backgrounds of husband and wife are
similar. There is no way of knowing accurately the prevalence
of desertion, for a large number of cases are never reported
and many others are handled privately by social work agencies
of various kinds; there is no national reporting, and many
cases never get to the courts. It is estimated, however, that
there are probably one fourth as many desertions each year in
this country as there are divorces.[10]

Separation proper may be either voluntary or (in some
states) legal. Voluntary separation differs from desertion in
that both parties agree to the life apart, and from both legal
separation and divorce in that no legal proceedings are involved. Husband and wife simply agree to remain apart. Legal
separation, on the other hand, requires a court decree and it
leaves both spouses in a state of legal marital suspension—in
one sense they are neither married nor unmarried, for although
they do not live together they cannot marry anyone else. This
is sometimes called "limited divorce," or "separation from bed
and board," or "separate maintenance." It is not very popular
with those seeking to separate, and, although approximately
half the states have laws permitting it, some of the laws are
now being changed to provide that, after a certain length of
time, legal separation can become grounds for absolute divorce.
It is impossible to estimate the annual numbers of voluntary
and legal separations in this country, but it would seem that
these figures might easily run into the tens of thousands. Whatever they are, they are a part of the total picture of family
breakdown.

Incompatibility in the Home.—Sometimes family members
are incompatible in one degree or another without the formali-
ties of a break; that is, they continue to live together, though
unhappy. Why, then, don't they dissolve the union? There are
many reasons: religious scruples; a sense of duty; the social
stigma that sometimes follows a separation; the expense of
divorce; fear of financial dependence; consideration for the

---

[10] Ray E. Baber, *Marriage and the Family* (New York: McGraw-Hill Book
Co., 1939), pp. 480-83.

welfare of children; hope for a reconciliation or for an improvement in family satisfactions; and others. These are sufficient to hold some families together even after cooperation and real happiness have fled.

Happiness is a matter of degree. There are families that, though remaining intact, nevertheless have their satisfactions blunted and their purposes dissipated by habitual bickering, quarreling, and even open fighting. All of these fall far short of the goal, are evidences of family failure.

Fortunately, many marriages seem to be at least reasonably happy. Burgess and Cottrell, for example, from their sample of 526 middle-class American families, found that: [11]

> 42.6 per cent were very happy
> 20.5 per cent were happy
> 14.4 per cent were average
> 13.5 per cent were unhappy
> 8.0 per cent were very unhappy
> 1.0 per cent failed to reply

This is both encouraging and discouraging at the same time; it is encouraging that over three fifths of the couples sampled said that they were happy in marriage, but it is disconcerting that less than half claimed to be very happy, and that unhappiness should dominate in as many as a fifth of all cases. Furthermore, one needs to keep in mind that this sample was not representative of the entire population and that it did not take into account many who had already secured divorces at the time the study was made.

While accurate measures for determining the amount of marital incompatibility in America are not available, we can be rather certain that it is extensive. Adding this fact to the half million or more annual divorces, and to the many desertions and other separations, one gets a fairly good picture of the magnitude of the marriage problem.

By-Products of Family Breakdown.—Yet divorce, desertion, separation, and incompatibility do not tell the whole story.

---

[11] E. W. Burgess and L. S. Cottrell, *Predicting Success or Failure in Marriage* (New York: Prentice-Hall, Inc., 1939), pp. 32 ff. The authors also cite other studies which show marital happiness ratings that are not far different.

Marriage and family life are so intricately related to the character and conduct of men that, where these institutions fail, living in general sinks low. There are antisocial patterns of conduct extant, by-products of unhealthy homes, which well reflect the trouble encountered by the family.

One of these patterns is sexual indulgence outside of marriage, a subject to be treated in more detail in a later chapter. It shows itself through prostitution, venereal disease, premarital pregnancy, and the like. Both family breakdown and extramarital sex expression are on the increase, and it is no mere accident that the two trends run parallel. As will be seen, unchastity is probably both a cause and an effect of maladjusted home life.

Among the many evidences which show that a relationship does exist between sexual morality and family stability is a recent study on unmarried motherhood. From a random sample of 100 cases supplied by an unmarried mother agency, the author of the study found that 43 were from broken homes, 36 from homes in which the mother was overly dominating, 15 from homes where the father's personality was harmfully dominating, and the remaining 6 from homes in which there were other unwholesome conditions. She concluded, "Most conspicuous is the fact that none of them had happy, healthy relationships with their parents." [12]

Common observation and court records both testify to the fact that delinquency and crime are greatest among those individuals who have been neglected, abused, or immorally influenced as children within their own homes. So well accepted are the facts that chief responsibility for misconduct among children rests with the home, and that antisocial habits of youth tend to persist and to express themselves in adult crime, that J. Edgar Hoover and many others who have to do with the problem have started to refer to juvenile delinquency as "parent delinquency." Elliott and Merrill say this:

When we come to assign responsibility for delinquent behavior and delinquent attitudes, we see that the family must assume the primary

---

[12] Leontine R. Young, "Personality Patterns in Unmarried Mothers," *The Family*, 26:296-303, December, 1945.

burden. In one way or another the parents have been unequal to their task.[13]

It is from homes that are either underprivileged or broken, from parents that are either ignorant, neglectful, or abusive, that most of our criminals come.

Were it possible to isolate the various factors responsible for all the conflict and suffering existing in the world today, it seems probable that inadequate and maladjusted family life would be among the more prominent of the causes. This is so because of the profound influence that the home has over both character and conduct. In a broad sense, then, but a very real one, much of the disorganization of society is reflective of family imperfection. (Social disorganization is also a cause of family breakdown, as will be demonstrated in the next chapter.)

We do not want to exaggerate these social conditions and conflict situations that are indicative of marital difficulty. On the other hand, neither do we want to minimize them, for to do so would be both to shift responsibility and to lose an opportunity for correction.

CHANGE AND CHALLENGE

Thus it is that the most basic of all human groupings, the one that permits a realization of man's deepest satisfactions, is in trouble and seemingly losing ground. Part of the explanation lies in the disturbed and changing nature of contemporary society (see Chapter 2). Change means challenge.

Unless one chooses to ignore the situation entirely, letting nature take its course, there are mainly two alternatives. One of these is to blame marriage itself, and to seek a solution to the problem by finding substitutes or asking for fundamental modifications in the marriage system. The other is to accept the system, and then to seek to save it by changing those personal and social factors which are regarded as responsible for the trouble. We hold to this second approach.

---

[13] Mabel A. Elliott and Francis E. Merrill, *Social Disorganization* (New York: Harper & Bros., 1941), p. 115 and *passim*.

Radical Proposals.—There have been a number of theories and experiments regarding love and marriage which tend to pull away from long-established cultural norms. Their wide departure from the usual and the expected causes such schemes to be regarded as radical. Most serious students of society view these trends with caution, believing that they are productive of more problems than solutions.

One such proposal is trial marriage. Advocated early in the present century by Elsie Parsons, it claims that many marriage breakups could be avoided if couples would live together intimately before marrying permanently in order to try each other out and test the adjustment together. It is not the same thing as either promiscuity or prostitution, for with it, as proposed, the marriage goal is definitely in mind. What its proponents forget is that the system could be too easily abused; marriage intentions might be professed without being meant, as a device for sexual experimentation. This would be about the same thing as promiscuity, with all the attendant consequences—overemphasis upon sex, unprotected pregnancy, emotional exploitation, and the like. It seems doubtful that trial marriage could perform any needed function as well as these could be performed by sound education and personality testing well within the bounds of chastity. And, as will be shown later, marriages are more usually successful where premarital chastity has been maintained.

Closely related to the idea of trial marriage, though somewhat different, is so-called companionate marriage. It was proposed in all seriousness by Judge Ben B. Lindsey, of the Denver Juvenile Court, about a quarter of a century ago. It caused considerable debate throughout the country but failed to find sufficient support to be adopted in any state. As proposed, it would establish the first few years of marriage as the trial period, with an avoidance of childbearing during that time and the privilege of divorce by mutual consent if there should be no children. Chief objections to this idea are its unavoidable emphasis upon experimentation and temporizing in the marriage relationship, and its lengthy postponement of childbearing, both of which might handicap the marriage from the start.

Term marriage, though practiced on a small scale in some parts of the world, is not legal in America. It was advocated in this country by E. D. Cope about a half century ago, but the idea did not catch hold. It would legalize marriage for a period of time, say five years, with the couple having the option of either renewing or abandoning the enterprise after the contract period was up. Like other schemes of this sort, it would tend to precondition marriage for failure by encouraging experimentation and emphasizing impermanence. Furthermore, it would work great hardships upon many wives and children by leaving them desolate and unprotected at the end of the term. Although such an arrangement is nowhere legal here, easy divorce accomplishes about the same end.

Free love has been advocated in one form or another by such persons as Ellen Key, Bertrand Russell, and Aldous Huxley. The essential idea back of it is that sex behavior is entirely a private matter and should follow the dictates of love rather than those of the marriage convention. While only a small minority of our social thinkers actually advocate such a removal of controls from the field of sex, their influence has undoubtedly been great. This, unfortunately, coupled with the lessening of religious controls, the influence of modern sex novels, and other cultural changes, is causing many to practice it.

There are other deviant practices and alternative proposals pertaining to marriage as we know it. Communist Russia, for example, made divorce astonishingly easy, requiring only that it be requested, without submitting a reason, by either member of the contract. Other features of marriage and morals were radicalized there too. But more recent trends, it is encouraging to note, are toward the tightening of divorce and the encouragement of stable family life. Nazi Germany promoted procreation outside of marriage and was almost successful in removing the social stigma connected with illegitimacy. Its eugenic program, with its baby farms and the like, threatened to make family reproduction secondary to state breeding. Some people would have it that way here. Another proposal, sometimes heard, is the legalizing of so-called virgin hospitals, whereby unmarried women, through artificial impregnation, would be allowed to have and rear children. There are others, and much more might be said about these mentioned, but this is sufficient for illustrative purposes.

Our Point of View.—The thing to be done when marriage falters, as it does today, is not to abandon it but to discover what is causing the breakdown and then adjust those individuals and outside circumstances that are responsible. Marriage is too important an institution to be discarded lightly; its antiquity and universality demonstrate that it is needed by society. Furthermore, some of man's greatest satisfactions are rooted in family group life.

Some people claim that it is our divorce laws that are at fault, and that they should be tightened, making it difficult if not impossible for individuals once married to find a legal way out. This would be attacking a symptom rather than a cause, and, though it undoubtedly would reduce the number of divorces, it would likely not reduce the real trouble to any appreciable extent. How would advocates of this supposed cure-all stop mates from separating in spite of the law or from making mockery of marriage after love had turned to hate?

Others argue that the contemporary family is but a victim of social trends and conditions, and that the way to right it is to straighten out society—eliminate poverty and unemployment, provide adequate housing, establish permanent peace, and so on. There is virtue in this reasoning, for, as we shall see, institutions do feel the impact of social forces about them.

Yet, this is not the entire picture. Institutions also respond according to the kinds of people involved. It is true that a family can be most successful in the society that is most "healthy," but it is likewise true that mature and intelligent personalities can make a success of marriage under extremely adverse circumstances. The processes of marital interaction are multiple and circular—society affects the individual; the individual affects society; and both affect the family.

Koos observed that society is doing very little to prepare its people for marriage, though many of the family troubles studied by him were cultural in origin:

A further challenge to our culture lies in the head-in-the-sand attitude toward education for family life. We operate, apparently, on the theory that marriages are made in heaven—we unfortunately disregard the necessity for their operating on earth. As one analyzes the training for family life available to these families (and, in general, to all families), it becomes increasingly clear that with the exception of some factual information on sex given to a few of the youth, and some isolated, ill-planned and tedious lectures on subjects such as "How to Prevent Bed Wetting," the culture does little in preparing individuals for carrying on in adequate fashion the most fundamental group in society.[14]

When marriage fails, does major responsibility lie with the culture or with the people? The question is largely an academic one, for society and the individual are not separate entities; rather, each is a part of the other. Nevertheless, initiative for strengthening the family must invariably rest with individuals: if society is to provide a setting more encouraging to family relationships, it will be up to the people to see that necessary changes are brought about; if the culture is to become more family-minded, so as to better prepare people for marriage, it is the people themselves that must first establish the programs; if married mates are to be able to rise above circumstances, by adjusting to them, it will be because as individuals they have learned to face life.

Trouble signals from the family are heard today on every hand. Whether these turn out to be death pangs of a decadent institution or birth pains of new adjustments is yet to be seen. The answer lies in how well individuals are able both to strengthen their own personalities and to reorganize society in terms of family values.

Prelude to Analysis.—It is assumed that by now the reader will have become oriented to the general nature of the problem under discussion. He has seen how marriage has meaning in terms of human happiness. He has examined, though but briefly, major trouble symptoms which give evidence of marriage and family breakdown, of frustrated goals. He has come

---

[14] Earl L. Koos, *Families in Trouble* (New York: King's Crown Press, 1946), pp. 126-27.

to understand that some would have us scrap these institutions altogether, or nearly so, but that the real solution lies in the direction of improvement rather than abandonment, of adjustment rather than license and chaos.

These, then, are the dimensions.

Chapters that follow are designed to lay bare some of the most important factors involved and processes operating in this great adventure called marriage. Our aim is for fuller understanding as background for happier love relationships within the family framework.

Problems and Projects

1. Do you agree with the statement that marriage usually results in the extremes of either happiness or unhappiness?

2. "The family is the seedbed of character and the workshop of social progress." Discuss.

3. Is happiness the ultimate goal of marriage or is it a part of a number of goals? Are there other, and better, criteria of marital success? Discuss.

4. Consider each of the family functions listed in this chapter and decide whether or not you think they could be performed as well under some other system, without marriage. Give reasons for your answer.

5. Does the increasing divorce rate prove that there is more family trouble than formerly, or only that divorce is more accepted? Discuss pro and con.

6. Most divorces involve childless couples. Noting this, some have claimed that "a good way to save a disintegrating marriage is to have a child." What do you think?

7. Why do some couples refrain from divorce after marriage has failed? Are these sound reasons? What effects will continuation of marriage, without love, have upon the various family members?

8. In considering the substitutes for marriage mentioned in this chapter, decide what would be gained and lost by each family member under each of these arrangements.

9. Examine further the question of "free love" versus monoga-

mous marriage. This could be used for a special class report or panel discussion.

10. Arrange for a few class reports on marriage and family customs in other cultures.

11. List as many causes of divorce as you can. Rank these in the order of their assumed influence. Compare your list with those of other members of the class.

SELECTED READINGS

ANSHEN, RUTH NANDA (ed.). *The Family: Its Function and Destiny.* New York: Harper & Bros., 1949.

BABER, RAY E. *Marriage and the Family.* New York: McGraw-Hill Book Co., 1939. Chaps. i, "The Family in Transition"; xvii, "Conflicting Sex Patterns."

BECKER, HOWARD, and HILL, REUBEN (eds.). *Family, Marriage, and Parenthood.* Boston: D. C. Heath & Co., 1948. Chap. xxiii, "The Scope and Meaning of Divorce."

ELLIOTT, MABEL A., and MERRILL, FRANCIS E. *Social Disorganization.* New York: Harper & Bros., 1941. Part III, "Family Disorganization."

GROVES, ERNEST R. *Marriage.* New York: Henry Holt & Co., Inc., 1941. Chaps. i, "The Study of Marriage"; ii, "The Purpose of Marriage."

HARPER, ROBERT A. *Marriage.* New York: Appleton-Century-Crofts, Inc. 1949. Chaps. i, "Marriage in Modern Society: Romance and Realism"; ii, "Why People Do and Don't Marry"; xii, "Divorce."

HART, HORNELL, and HART, ELLA B. *Personality and the Family.* Boston: D. C. Heath & Co., 1941. Chap. i, "Past and Present Sexual Behavior."

LANDIS, JUDSON T., and LANDIS, MARY G. *Building a Successful Marriage.* New York: Prentice-Hall, Inc., 1948. Chaps. i, "Successful Marriage"; iii, "Why People Marry Or Do Not Marry."

NIMKOFF, MEYER F. *Marriage and the Family.* Boston: Houghton Mifflin Co., 1947. Chap. i, "Organization of the Family."

TRUXAL, ANDREW G., and MERRILL, FRANCIS E. *The Family in American Culture.* New York: Prentice-Hall, Inc., 1947. Chap. i, "The Nature of the Family."

PART II
FACTORS

Chapter 2

SOCIETY AND SUCCESSFUL MARRIAGE

Diagnosis, as every scientist knows, must precede both prognosis and prescription. If we would meet the challenge that faces modern marriage, we shall first of all need to understand what forces are operating and how they operate.

Viewed broadly, marital success can be regarded as contingent upon two interrelated factors: (1) society, and (2) personality. Though these overlap and express themselves in an infinite variety of combinations, they can nevertheless be separated for purposes of analysis. In later chapters we shall deal with the personal elements. Here our focus is to be upon society as a factor in marriage and family stability.

Social institutions are in large part the products of their cultural environments. They are usually organized around certain biologically determined needs, it is true, which explains their universality. But they develop along a variety of lines according to the cultural and interactional patterns of the societies that provide their settings. Thus, every institution represents both unity and diversity, unity as to broad outline or general characteristics, and diversity as to detail. Furthermore, as circumstances change, institutions alter—either that or lose their functional usefulness and in time perish.

To all of this the family is no exception. It arose in response to basic and universal human needs (see Chapter 1); it has assumed a variety of culturally imposed forms; and it changes as society changes, though not always at the same rate or without disturbance.

The following case study of a day in the life of an urban family reveals something of the nature and problems of modern marriage. Though not entirely typical, it illustrates how different family life can be from an earlier day when families were large, father was the boss, and mother devoted most of her time to care of children and the home.[1]

Husband (talking to wife at 6:30 A.M.) : Won't be home for dinner tonight. Dinner meeting at the lodge and installation later. You're invited. Will you be there?

Wife: Don't know. If I go downtown after school, read in the library, and go to my class, I'm too dirty and broken down to break in on a social affair.

Husband: Jane, I want to get to work. Shall I expect you or not? You never can make up your mind.

Wife: No—yes, I'll be there at 9:30. (Wife lies in bed until the housekeeper notifies her that it is 7:45.)

Daughter (eleven years old) : Will you write me a note why I was absent Friday?

Mother: Why didn't you ask me last night, honey? I'll be late, I can't.

Daughter: What are you a mother for if you never have time to do anything for me?

Mother writes the note hurriedly; grabs a glass of orange juice and a cup of coffee; runs around a bed to give her eight-year-old daughter a good-by kiss.

Mother: Get your hair combed there, young lady, and wear knee-length socks today.

Mother (to Housekeeper) : Order what you want from the butcher and send one of the kids to the store. Won't be home. Tom won't be home either.

Both Daughters: Out again! Why don't you come home?

Mother: Angels, I'll be home all tomorrow evening.

Mother changes her mind about going downtown directly from school. She is tired, conscience-stricken about the children's righteous complaint, and dirty. She goes home after school. As she walks around the back of the house she hears the high-pitched preaching of the housekeeper. "You two are spoiled. Your mother thinks you are so good."

Daughters and housekeeper are surprised to see the mother, who calls the children outside, hugs them, talks about cooperation with and respect for the housekeeper, and tries to be soothing and com-

---

[1] By permission, from Ernest W. Burgess and Harvey J. Locke, *The Family: From Institution to Companionship* (New York: American Book Co., 1945), pp. 113-14.

panionable. She is exhausted and weary with the endless coaxing, cajoling, and encouraging necessary in her job of teaching school.

Supper is a sketchy, poorly balanced meal. It is unconventional to cook a decent meal when the man of the house is absent. After supper the children settle down to their books. They love to read.

Housekeeper: You didn't practice your piano today, Helen. Helen barely flicks an eyelid. You didn't change your dress, Helen. You didn't put your coat away, Ann.

Children sigh, get up, and do suggested chores, and settle down to read in their bedroom. The housekeeper returns to mother who is trying to read.

Housekeeper: The children are careless about everything. Now when I was a child . . .

Mother notes time, grabs her hat, notebook, and purse and hurries off to class. She meets husband at 9:30 at the lodge.

He smiles a big smile. He is glad to see her, glad—not thrilled. Husband makes a speech to his group. He uses "come" for "came" and "was" for "were." Husband and wife have a dance or two, and a drink.

Husband (on the way home): How was my talk, Jane?

Wife: Fine, Tom. You talked well, but you used "come" for "came" and "was" for "were."

Husband: You damn school teachers. You never listen to what a fellow really says. You only sit and watch for grammatical errors. You sure do cramp my style when I talk.

TRANSITIONAL TENSIONS

Society is in a state of flux. It has always been so, for that matter, but the changes that have been affecting it in recent decades have been particularly violent. Most of these stem from the Industrial Revolution and the new mode of life it has ushered in. Gone are the days of isolation, self-sufficient economy, and hand production. Gone also are the simplicity and the slow tempo of living that were a part of the preindustrial age. Nearly everything is mass production now, and living in general has become more accelerated and complicated as a result.

Change itself is never bad, nor good, only inevitable. But it does require adjustment. Institutions quite naturally receive the impact of the social currents about them, and where they are

able to adjust adequately they survive. Otherwise they may
pass out of existence.

There is no implication here that society has been in a state
of retrogression, or that man should return to the "good old
days" when life was simple and almost everyone was sup-
posedly happy. There is no reason why man should be less
happy today than formerly; quite the opposite. Times are not
worse, just different. The suggestion is that man and his institutions must adjust, always adjust, or they will lag and may
be thrown off balance. Though there are special difficulties in
the complexity and the unsettled nature of this transitional
period, opportunities are probably greater for genuine accomplishment and satisfaction today, because knowledge is widespread, than in any other period of time. The potentials are
here; it is now up to man to turn them into actualities.

Population on the Move.—The machine age has brought
with it a great many social innovations. One change has had
to do with the ecology of populations, their spatial distributions
and movements in relation to resources and culture. Another
has had to do with the natural increase of populations, the balance of births over deaths. We shall be interested to see how
each of these factors has reflected itself upon the family
pattern.

Urbanization has been an inevitable concomitant of the industrial revolution. Production by power machinery brought
about the factory system which in turn required that large
numbers of workers live close to the plants where they were
employed. Not only was the city, in this way, made necessary
by the machine age, but it was made possible as well; for without modern methods of transportation, communication, sani-
tation, and the like no large metropolitan center could long
survive. So rapid has been the urbanward trend in this country
that at the present time approximately three fifths of the entire population live in cities (centers of 2,500 or over). A bare
century ago it was less than one fifth.

As America has moved from a predominantly agricultural
to a predominantly industrialized economy, from a rural to an

urban nation, it has seen its family structure grow weaker and weaker. There are reasons for this. Life in the city is complex, and its tempo rapid; apartment dwellings there are small and crowded; people's nerves are irritated by the noise, crowding, and speed around them; anonymity furnishes greater opportunity for infidelity; children often are in the way and are not wanted. City life is not as conducive to healthy marriage relationships as is the more natural and quiet life of the country, and as a result more city families are broken by divorce, desertion, and separation.

Mobility of population is another characteristic of an urban, industrial, secular society, and it, too, is having an unstabilizing influence upon the family. Where a family group transplants itself from one culture to another, whether this be from Europe to America, rural to urban, or any other change that involves a fundamental gap in types of culture or shift in types of association, there is often a period of disorganization sufficient in duration and intensity to have lasting effects. This is because of the conflict between cultures and the disequal rates with which family members assimilate or absorb the new. An illustration of family conflict in which children are rebelling against their immigrant parents, who were trying to preserve the old-world customs, has been recorded by Koos:

Pop and mom always want us to go to their parties and dance the old dances. Nuts! We'd look silly, wouldn't we? None of our friends do that sort of thing, and they only laugh at us if we do them. That's the trouble, you can't be like other kids and do what your parents want, too.[2]

Where the pattern is one of constant mobility, such as with the actor, the traveling salesman, or the migratory worker, other tension and conflict factors are brought into play. One of these is the separation of family members which frequently causes them to grow apart rather than together. Solidarity in family relationships comes best when there is intimate and continual association of family members, seldom when they are

---

[2] By permission, from Earl L. Koos, *Families in Trouble* (New York: King's Crown Press, 1946), p. 37.

separated either frequently or for long periods of time. Another is the uprooting of community ties and the releasing of social controls, which leaves those who are on the move free to disregard the traditional folkways and mores, and confused by the great variability of cultural stimuli to which they are exposed. Family organization is most stable where it is integrated into the life of the community. When mobility is great, integration becomes difficult.

Urbanization and mobility are only two aspects of population change, the recent accentuation of which has had a disorganizing effect upon marriage and family life. Another is the trend toward childlessness, which is a common accompaniment of these other two. The crowding of cities and the constant movement of peoples both add to the expense and inconvenience of rearing children. Contraception, a technological product of the industrial age, has made possible family limitation on a mass scale. The death rate has been going down, too, though recently not so rapidly as has the birth rate, with the net effect being a decline in size of family and an increase in number of childless marriages. More detail will be given concerning this trend and its implications in a later chapter. It is important for present purposes, however, to observe that divorce and childlessness have been increasing together. Approximately two thirds of all divorces take place with childless couples, and while childlessness is in some cases a result of incompatibility, it is undoubtedly in other cases a cause. Children, when present in the family, often seem to supply a common focus of attention, interaction, and affection for parents, and in this way they help to cement the marriage relationship. It seems logical, then, that at least part of the explanation for the advancing divorce rate is to be found in the lowering birth rate.

From Familism to Individualism.—Population changes are being paralleled by functional shifts within society, which are likewise reflecting themselves upon the family. Most important of these is the rise of individualism.

Familism might be defined as the opposite of individualism; it is a form of social organization in which all primary interests and values focus about the family rather than the person. Early societies were like that, as are also some of the more agricultural ones today—China, for instance. Under such a system kinship bonds are strong and interpersonal loyalties among family members are great. The emphasis, in familistic societies, is always upon group solidarity, never upon individual prerogatives. Child discipline is relatively easy, therefore, and divorce between mates exceptionally rare.

Mechanization and urbanization have tended to make difficult the familistic way of life. Factory work usually takes people outside of homes. Specialization decreases the number of interests that people have in common. New vistas are opened up and many start to chafe under the old restraints. Thus it is that, with the Industrial Revolution, came a new and growing emphasis upon the rights and powers of the individual. There came to be a cult of individualism, as a matter of fact, which found its political expression in democracy, its economic expression in *laissez faire,* and its philosophical expression in various theories of progress. While technological specialization has practically eliminated economic self-sufficiency, and in that sense made people more dependent upon society, it has made them more individualistic so far as the family is concerned.

In familistic cultures the family is strong because it is central in society and is consequently given a large number of useful functions to perform. In individualistic cultures, on the other hand, the family is made weaker by reason of its not being accorded such a central position and of its having been robbed of many of its original functions. The modern family, by coming into competition with newer secular agencies, has had to give up many of the tasks that it formerly performed. The educational function has been taken over largely by the schools, and, while there are advantages in the greater efficiency that has resulted, it is unfortunate that in many homes there is now felt little or no responsibility for child teaching. The religious function has been almost completely given over to the churches or thrown out entirely. This is unfortunate also, for the interrelationship between religion and character is well established, and the home has proved to be one of the best places for both to be promoted. The recreational function has been usurped by commercial agencies to such an extent that it has become common thought that to have a good time one must go out of the home and spend money. A countertrend, however, is home recreation built around movie, radio, and television sets. The governmental or protective function has been passed on to the state for the most part; in fact, the state now will even protect a child against its parents when they are overly neglectful or abusive. The economic function has also been largely removed from the home. The consumption of economic goods is still there, to be sure, although not so much as formerly. Income and production, however, have been highly individualized, as is shown by the fact that each adult family member will usually have his own job and separate source of income, and also that such businesses as dry cleaning, laundering, and baking are increasing in volume much more rapidly than the population, proving that some activities are actually leaving the home. With the decreasing birth rate it becomes evident that the reproductive function of the family is at least suffering a decline and in an increasingly large number of cases it has left completely. All in all, there isn't much left to hold many modern families together.

The affectional function, that which serves the sexual and emotional needs of husband and wife, is about all there is for many present-day families to stand upon. This puts considerable strain on affection alone, and where the pressure becomes great, marriage bonds sometimes break.

Burgess and Locke point to the shift from institution to companionship as being the most significant recent trend in marriage and family relationships.

In the past the important factors unifying the family have been external, formal, and authoritarian, as the law, the mores, public opinion, tradition, the authority of the family head, rigid discipline, and elaborate ritual. At present, in the new emerging form of the companionship family, its unity inheres less and less in community pressures and more and more in such interpersonal relations as the mutual affection, the sympathetic understanding, and the comradeship of its members.[3]

Though affection and companionship are highly important family functions, they are sometimes difficult to attain, and especially to retain, when other functions are lacking. It is not so easy now for the family to succeed as in a day when it had more to do and when necessity, tradition, and community pressure gave it more support. To give but one example, a wife in colonial times would ordinarily think twice before seeking a divorce, for marriage to her meant economic security. Now, however, the wife is often as well prepared for the making of a living as is her husband, and fear of financial dependency is no longer such a deterrent. Furthermore, divorce is more widely accepted today. We are not suggesting that the family be strengthened by reloading it with its earlier functions, however, or by surrounding it with restrictions. Even if desirable, such a course would be possible only if there could be a complete cultural reversal away from technology; this seems neither desirable nor practical.

Lewis Mumford points out that the family has been gaining some functions while losing others, and he expresses the opinion that certain of the earlier home tasks need to be turned over to other agencies. He says:

. . . Certain functions, domestic in origin, require more ample space or special facilities; these should be taken out of the house even further than they are today: childbirth and infectious illnesses, weddings and funerals, need their communal buildings.

With the return of entertainment to the house, through the phonograph, the radio and the motion picture—with the near prospect of television—the modern house has gained in recreational facilities what it lost through the disappearance of many of the earlier household industries. The radio and the telephone, moreover, have made the house no less a center of communication than was the old market-place. So if certain functions have diminished, others have gained. . . .[4]

---

[3] Burgess and Locke, *op. cit.*, p. vii.
[4] Lewis Mumford, *The Culture of Cities* (New York: Harcourt, Brace & Co., 1938), p. 467.

It may well be that the family will gain by the interchange, after becoming adjusted to the difference. Certain it is that many of the drudgeries are being taken out of the home, thus leaving more time for companionable experiences. We can expect further developments along this line, not only in labor-saving devices within the home, but in special services from the outside—hospitals, laundries, bakeries, precooked-food dispensaries, dishwashing establishments, nursery schools, diaper services, and the like. With less drudgery involved in housework, more cultural and recreational conveniences within the home, and more time for members to be together, family life ought to find new meaning and strength. The newer emphasis is upon satisfying personal needs of family members; once burdened down with the necessity of producing goods, families can now turn attention to developing personalities. Unless, or until, the companionship element is made to fill the gap left by other departing functions, however, the family will remain weakened by the loss.

Historically considered, the patriarchal pattern of family organization was most common, but lately this has been giving way and a newer equalitarian or democratic type is emerging. Patriarchal families are those in which the authority of the husband and father is supreme; wife and children alike obey him as their lord and master. In some societies, such as the early Roman, this power of the male family head went so far as to permit him to beat, torture, or even take the life of a wife or child. Usually, however, it did not go this far, and in many cases control was mixed with genuine affection. Yet, by the very nature of the system, it was autocratic. The newer individualism of our day is changing all this; democracy in the home is struggling to supplant autocracy, consideration is taking the place of patriarchal dictation.

Though the end in view seems highly desirable, the processes required for attaining it are somewhat disturbing. Transitions are always disorganizing, and what has happened here is that patriarchal sanctions have in some cases been released before democratic patterns and procedures within the family have been adequately established to take their place. Then, too, love is

always harder to apply than force, real democracy more difficult than autocracy. But, to us, the results seem worth the effort
required.

One aspect of this emerging democracy in family relationships is a new set of conflicts between male and female. The
traditional roles are being disturbed: woman is becoming emancipated from the lowly status that has been hers, with few exceptions, throughout the ages; man's ego and assumed superiority are being challenged, forcing him to "move over"; the
sexes are coming to be more nearly equal in opportunity. This
is as it should be in a democracy; but the process is disorganizing nevertheless. For example, woman sometimes mistakes
license for freedom, and identity for equality, with the result
that her emancipation may mean the loss of both femininity
and virtue. Furthermore, with the traditional roles upset, and
without new ones of a democratic nature yet established, she
and man are both left confused and are thus forced with the
necessity of maneuvering with each other for personal advantage or for the establishment of new roles that can be accepted
and understood. More of this in a later chapter. Here it can
be observed that sex equality, while likely beneficial as an end
result, is disorganizing as a process.

Another disquieting, though promising, aspect of individualism in family relationships is the independence of youth.
Children in the home, school, and community are less manage-
able than formerly. Though disturbing to the elders, this tendency toward self-assertion, unless entirely undisciplined and
irresponsible, may be the spark of initiative that is needed for
the full realization of personality. Modern youth, as a rule,
cannot be frightened or beaten into submission. Nor should
they be. It is within the folkways of this age that young people
are to be more aggressive and more inclined to resist arbitrary
authority than formerly. It is only when undirected or perverted that this becomes a problem. Democracy means freedom,
and freedom without confusion or license requires great effort.
In the home, as in the nation, freedom ought to be capitalized
upon for the benefit of progress, never suppressed for the sake
of expediency in control.

Familism, then, has been yielding to individualism. It seems probable that both extremes are undesirable, that the most healthy condition for family survival and personality realization is where both family and individuality are valued, but each in balance with the other. Individualism has brought problems which challenge the family. Properly met, however, these can prove to be opportunities, extending toward increasingly higher levels of adjustment.

Our Schizoid Culture.—There are a great many contradictions within our culture which reflect upon personality and upon family behavior. Modern life is complex, fast-moving, and transitional. There have been innovations coming in so fast and with such magnitude that certain cultural segments remain undigested and society suffers from a "stomach-ache." Values are in conflict.

Bain has pointed out that when an individual exhibits similar tendencies toward irrational and unintegrated behavior, he is labeled as neurotic or psychotic. Not only are cultural contradictions analogous to those within the individual, Bain believes, but they are actually productive of personality difficulties. This means that psychiatry may not be able to get very far in its work with individuals until a societal mental hygiene has been developed; personality integration is to a large extent dependent upon cultural consistency. Bain's study illustrates various types of confusion extending over many sides of our culture—the familial, economic, political, legal, democratic, philanthropic, artistic, recreational, medical, religious, educational, and scientific. Regarding the first mentioned, he said:

The confusion in our culture on sex is notorious. There is scarcely any official recognition of the reproductive system by church, school, or home. Birth control is widely condemned but more widely practiced. Venereal disease is still more of a moral than medical problem. The "double standard" still flourishes. Sex-attitudes oscillate from the "romantic-holy" to the "prosaic-evil." We eulogize sex and love in the abstract, but there is a great deal of furtiveness, shame, and sense of sin connected with the facts and acts of sex.

We glorify parenthood, but provide little education for prospective parents. Declining birth rate, child care outside the home, and technological specialism have largely defunctionalized woman. Monogamous marriage is our ideal, but infidelity, marital maladjustment, and divorce abound. Marriage and divorce laws are anarchic and are frequently violated with impunity. Legal grounds for divorce are seldom the "real" reasons and the courts wink at collusion.

Our reliance upon mother love and maternal "instinct" results in personality distortions of both parents and children. If we would, we could cut maternal and infant death rates in half. We still control children by fear and force, but many parents, fearful of Freudian complexes and repressions, abjure all discipline and control. This is the age of the child, but we still have child labor, malnutrition, remediable defects, and preventable diseases. We have school health examinations but little treatment. We "love" children too much and too little; frequently the same child is a victim of this emotional polarity, indulged and frightened in almost the same breath.[5]

These contradictions of culture cause disturbances in both the individual and the marriage relationship. Personality integration is made more difficult because of the confusion that exists within and among various groups and ideologies to which the individual is exposed. Marriage solidarity is less easily attained than in cultures that are more consistent because of the greater likelihood of role conflicts. In simpler societies, where culture is more ordered and integrated, there is greater likelihood that husband and wife would see alike and accept the marital roles that the culture prescribes for them. But in modern American society, which is highly complex and unsettled, there is a wide and changing variety of permissible roles for the mates. Some of these patterns are on the way out, others are coming in; some are held to by certain families and groups but are not universal. It should be clear, therefore, that our culture is imposing a number of conflicts upon the marriage relationship; today, husbands and wives are less likely to agree concerning family roles than was true in other times and places. Tensions and frictions over such questions as who is to be boss, are wives to work, how large is the family to be, and what philosophy of discipline is to be

[5] Read Bain, "Our Schizoid Culture," *Sociology and Social Research,* **19**: 266-76, 1935.

used, must inevitably be greater in a culture that is full of unorganized roles and values.

The Zimmerman Thesis.—Zimmerman of Harvard has recently propounded the theory that the family in Western society, having gone through two great crises in the process of its history, is now soon to reach the maximum development of a third crisis.[6] The first of these breakdowns, according to Zimmerman, was in Greece around 300 B.C., the second in Rome about 300 A.D., and the third is best typified by the United States at the present time. Manifestations of the crisis have been essentially the same in all three of these periods: increased divorce rates, decreases in fertility, a revolt of youth against parents, a rise in juvenile delinquency, a growing sensualism, and a general forsaking of the familistic virtues of the past. Family disintegration is seen as paralleling the decline of states; this was true in both Greece and Rome, and, by implication, it could easily come to be true in the United States. Relating to the decline of states, family breakdown is regarded as part cause and part effect. Solution to the problem is not considered possible through any kind of a "patching job," but only by a clan or church sponsored return to familism.

Zimmerman, then, would have us undertake a sort of cultural reversal, almost desperately, in an attempt to recapture some of the virtues of familism. The alternative to this, he claims, is further chaos and the decline of civilization. Believing that the chances for such a reversal are slight, he sees an impending crisis as almost inevitable.

We would agree with this analysis on some points, but disagree on others. Certainly the family and society are interrelated. Certainly, also, does our modern family face a crisis, comparable in some respects to the family crises experienced in Greece and Rome during earlier periods. We think, too, that the materialism, hedonism, and individualism of this age are often excessive and that they may imperil both the family and civilization. However, we regard divorce more as a symp-

6 Carle C. Zimmerman, "The Developing Family Crisis," *Rural Sociology*, 11:319-30, December, 1946. See also his *Family and Civilization* (New York: Harper & Bros., 1947), *passim*.

tom of trouble than as an intrinsic evil, we think that technology is not only inevitable but desirable in many ways, and
we do not subscribe to the inference that there is always virtue
in a high birth rate. Some of these points will receive further
discussion in later chapters. Here we can only say that the
proper attack on the problem seems not to be in either denying or decrying the innovations of this age but in adjusting
to them. There is developing a new kind of family unity, one
based more upon equality and companionship than upon mere
duty and social pressure.[7] Change creates problems but it also
opens up new opportunity. The way out is seldom back, but
ahead.

Catastrophic Disturbances

There are certain social crises, catastrophic in nature, that
have impact upon marriage and the family. Adjustment difficulties are greater during times of crisis than at other times
for the reason that changes then are more sudden and more
extensive; catastrophe confronts the family with problems of
great magnitude which call for immediate adjustment and for
which its members are frequently unprepared. To be discussed
here are depression and war.

Depression.[8]—The business cycle, involving as it does periodic fluctuations between prosperity and depression, seems to
be a characteristic of modern industrialized society. It may
be that someday science will have developed far enough to
permit control of these economic irregularities but it hasn't
done that yet. Business depressions are always disorganizing
to society, the great one starting in 1929 and extending
through the early thirties having been particularly so. What
are their effects upon the family?

First of all, we can note relationships between depression
and certain statistical rates. (1) In times of depression the
marriage rate goes down. This is particularly true of the mid-

---

[7] Burgess and Locke, *loc. cit.*
[8] Most of what follows in this section is based upon the pioneer study of
Ruth S. Cavan and Katherine H. Ranck, *The Family and the Depression* (Chicago: University of Chicago Press, 1938).

dle and upper classes, and its reason is the expense of marriage, plus a desire to maintain previous standards of living. With the poor, however, including those on relief, depression seems to make very little difference in the rate at which they marry. As society starts its upward swing toward prosperity, the marriage rate increases rapidly as if to make up for lost time. (2) The divorce rate during depression is likewise low, and, as with the marriage rate, it picks up again when prosperity shows itself. Studies reveal, however, that more years of married life are lost through delayed marriage in a depression than are gained through delayed divorce. In both cases the phenomenon is merely, or largely, one of postponement and the reason is economic. Depression does not remove the causes of divorce, in other words, but simply delays it because of the expense involved. (3) Similar in behavior to both the marriage and divorce rates during depression is the birth rate; it is low while the depression lasts, but climbs rapidly as the cycle pulls the other way. Reasons are fewer marriages and an attempt to maintain the traditional living standard by saving the expense that additional children at that time would involve. (4) Depression also affects sex practices outside of marriage. Illegitimacy increases considerably, which suggests an increase in premarital relations as a substitute, probably, for marriage. Commercialized prostitution, on the other hand, actually declines during times of depression. It is commercialized, and, like most other businesses, must suffer when money is scarce.

While depression may have some effects that might occasionally be beneficial to a family, such as checking the trend toward extreme individualism by forcing the family to assume greater responsibility for its members, it is mostly disorganizing. Here are some of the reasons and ways: (1) It increases illicit sex behavior, as indicated above, which in turn weakens or undermines the very foundations of a happy home life both for the present and the future. (2) It requires that the family lower its sights or in other ways adjust its economic way of life. Loss of employment or decrease of income will usually mean curtailed expenditures. Plans for a new car or for a child's education may have to be abandoned. It may even be necessary to change the place of residence and to live under crowded and substandard conditions. This causes nervousness and irritability, especially when privacy is lacking, such as when two or more families move in together. (3) It leads to tensions and conflicts of one sort or another. Worry over where the next dollar is coming from, humiliation and shame at the loss of status or the necessity of accepting relief, the sense of failure and inadequacy, fear of the future, all tend to disorganize. As a result, the nerves of family members are on edge and quarreling is frequent. Discontent, rebellion, and an increase of delinquency and crime often result. (4) It disrupts the roles and blocks the goals of various family members, thus making for frustration and despair. Though the father could in no way change the situation, he may be blamed by other family members for not having work and be humiliated because of it. The son, who normally would find employment and settle down in marriage, now finds these avenues blocked and himself forced to a period of idleness.

In general, depression is hardest on the middle-class families of America. Except when the rich lose nearly everything, they are not so reduced in wealth but what they can draw upon savings and continue with a level of living not much different from before. The poor are accustomed to low standards anyway. But the middle class is laid low by depression and the emotional stresses that accompany its readjustment are not very easy to take.

War.[9]—In many ways war has the same effect upon family stability as does depression. Certainly both are disrupting. There are some situations, however, that are peculiar to war alone.

War has just the opposite effect upon marriage, birth, and divorce rates as does depression; in wartime, in other words, they are all high. One reason for this difference is the changed financial condition; for marriage, child rearing, and divorce all cost money, and there is more money in time of war. As

---

[9] An excellent and more extended treatment of this subject can be found in Burgess and Locke, *op. cit.,* chap. xxi, pp. 663-707.

will be seen presently, however, this is only part of the explanation.

Marriage and birth rates are related to each other and to the various circumstances of war. The year 1942 had the highest marriage rate in our national history up to that time, and 1943, as might be expected, saw a new peak in the birth rate. Marriages increased in the early war years for a number of reasons, chief of which were these: first, the heightened emotionalism or hysteria of the war period coupled with such things as the glamour of the uniform and a newly stimulated desire for adventure; second, the feeling of desperation in the face of separation and possible death, motivated by the thought that marriage might have to come "now or never"; and finally, the fact that everyone else was doing it. Births increased as a natural consequence of more marriages, plus a conscious motivation in some instances, such as draft evasion, the desire on the part of the husband to leave progeny in case of death, or on the part of the wife to have something by which to remember her husband. Both marriages and births sagged from their peak rates as the war progressed, but then rose again with peace and the return of men. In the long run we can expect the birth rate to continue its downward trend.

Related to an increase in divorce is the general relaxing of morals that took place during the war period and extended into the postwar years. While depression seems to stimulate sexual promiscuity, war goes even farther. Morals tend to take a holiday during times of war, and as a result illegitimacy, prostitution, and venereal disease rates all go up. With the separation of the sexes for military service, there comes an increased sex hunger and a tendency on the part of girls to let down standards in order to compete for male companionship. Another reason is the brutalizing and animalizing experiences of military life, coupled with the feeling on the part of some girls that it is patriotic to cater to the man in uniform. A third is the revived philosophy "eat, drink, and be merry, for tomorrow we may die." Finally, there is the fact that many young and immature persons are neglected by parents or, through separation, are denied the primary group controls that formerly held them in line. In connection with this last we should observe that sexual immorality is frequently both a cause and an effect of broken family life (see Chapter 5).

The divorce rate took an upward swing during World War II and then rose even higher after the war was over. This parallels what has taken place in other war periods. Reasons for an increased divorce rate during and following a war are essentially two: (1) defense-working wives have more money which can be used to finance a divorce; and (2) the stresses and strains of war tend to increase the frictions and conflicts that cause divorce. This last-named is the more significant of the two, and in connection with it we would name the following contributing factors: (1) the letdown in morals referred to above; (2) the fact that many war marriages were inadvisable in the first place because the parties entering them were too young, their choice too impetuous, their acquaintance too short; (3) the fact of a much too brief time together after marriage, followed by long separations with differing experiences that make them grow apart; (4) the new financial independence that some wives find in defense work and that many are reluctant to yield later; and (5) the strains that come from overwork, irregular hours, crowded living, frequent moving, war casualties, the rising costs of living, and the like. All in all it becomes evident that war does not add strength to family relationships; the opposite is more commonly true.

In addition to the above, some have the problem of adjusting to a mate from a foreign land. It is estimated that about 100,000 service men married girls from other countries while abroad. Some of these marriages will work out very well, to be sure, but the "casualty list" will be high. This is because of cultural differences, together with the fact that many of the fellows were not serious or only halfhearted about it in the first place. A great many of these foreign wives have been deserted or divorced without even a chance to come to this country and give it a try. Others have come and found difficulty once here.

Nevertheless, what is, is. There is no point in growing gloomy over the situation and then leaving it at that. The postwar era has its special problems but with insight and effort they can be solved.

War is a social earthquake and the family, like other institutional structures, has been shaken severely by its impact. By and large, those families that were strongest to start with are the ones that have survived best. Family solidarity requires long-time building and continuous effort. We must start from where we are, make the best of what we have.

Someone has suggested that there is only one way of overcoming the effects of total war and that is by "total living."

Miscellany.—While depression and war are not the only social situations that disturb the family, they are probably the greatest in terms of magnitude and are somewhat representative of the problem as a whole. Floods, droughts, earthquakes, and other natural calamities likewise put people and families under tension. So also do epidemics, severe community conflicts, and numerous other social happenings that change the "climate" under which people interact and institutions operate. In general, the effects of all of these upon the family are the same—they create crises which, in turn, require adjustments.

SUSTENANCE AND SHELTER

In saying that lower-level families are generally better able to withstand economic depression than are those from the middle class, we do not mean to imply that marital adjustment is aided by poverty. The reverse seems more likely to be correct. Unemployment and impoverishment are especially difficult when brought on suddenly, it is true. Nevertheless, for some, inadequacy of income is a very real condition that must be lived with continually whether there is a depression or not.

A frequent cause of tension and friction within the home is lack of money. Since low-income families have less of that, they might be expected to have more than their share of trouble. Research by Koos bears this out; he found his below-average families to have more internal troubles and to suffer more lastingly from these disturbances than his better-than-average families. There was a kind of vicious-circle effect, with the poor and unfortunate becoming progressively more lost as they encountered succeeding misfortunes.[10]

Some insight into the problem can be gained by examining the following cases which will demonstrate three different trouble situations—worry over debt, injured pride in not being able to keep up, and disappointment over failure to get ahead.

1. Owing money doesn't bother Jim a bit, but I get so mixed up inside I can't stand it. I don't feel that I dare answer the door buzzer, because it'll be some collector with a court notice. Jim's been in court ever so often, but it doesn't bother him a bit. I get so I can't stand it, and then I raise the devil around here. Then he straightens out a while, but we're always right back again. We'd be all right if it wasn't for that.[11]

2. The children see all of these nice new things, furniture and all the rest, and then come home and nag for us to have things like them. Mary says she can't get a boy friend because we are laughed at for being behind the times. When the children talk about these things, it upsets the mister and then he gets mad at them and at me, and we have trouble. I try to keep the children from talking about how other people's tenements are fixed up, but I guess it's pretty hard not to see the difference.[12]

3. [*Wife*]: The thing that makes me so mad is how John just lies down and lets the world walk over him. When he came [to the United States] he was going to be so much—we would get somewhere. Now look at where we are, at this tenement. I try to stand it most of the time, but I get mad because he won't get ahead, and then I boil over and spoil things.

[*Husband*]: Caroline is a good wife, but she gets disappointed with me because I'm just about where I was when we came to America. We came right after we got married so we could better ourselves. Well, things don't always work out the way you think they are going to. America takes more education to get along than I had. We had some sickness and got behind (and on wages like mine you never catch up), the depression made us take relief, so you are just where you started from. Women don't understand such big things, and she gets

---

10 Koos, *op. cit.*, p. 121 and *passim*.
11 *Ibid.*, p. 76.
12 *Ibid.*, p. 38.

mad because she says I won't get ahead like I said I would. You just can't get ahead in a place like this—it's too big a problem.[13]

Perhaps it isn't amount of income so much as the discrepancy between one's expectation and realization regarding it that causes the conflict. When people grow accustomed to a given level of living and then have it greatly lowered, as in a depression, they are likely to feel frustrated and resentful. Similarly, people are likely to become uncomfortable and irritable whenever they are forced to live on a lower level than they had anticipated, or regard as adequate, or that their neighbors or competitors are able to maintain. It is the gap between what a person desires and what he is able to get that brings on the tension. When this gap gets too wide, people grow unhappy and hard to live with. Adjustment would require either that the income be increased or that the desires and expectations be lowered.

With many lower-class families, income stays substantially below what is actually needed, as well as expected. This adds an extra handicap. Family life cannot be kept healthy so long as family members are deprived of means for a decent living. People are more likely to be quarrelsome when hungry, or ill, or without cultural opportunity.

Any number of studies have shown correlations between poverty and disorganization. It is in the blighted areas of cities that the various indices of personal and social breakdown are found to be highest; for example, crime and delinquency, unemployment and public assistance, illiteracy, alcoholism, gambling, suicide, venereal disease, illegitimacy, sex offenses, divorce rates. For partial substantiation we quote the following:

In city after city—Birmingham, Buffalo, Cleveland, Denver, Detroit, Hartford, Indianapolis, Los Angeles, Milwaukee, Newark, Washington, and others—slum areas correspond to the areas of poorest health, of greatest personal and social disorganization. Digestive diseases occur more often in households without private flush toilets; home accidents are more frequent in homes of lower rental (and,

---

[13] *Ibid.*, p. 45.

therefore, presumably in the more dilapidated structures) ; children in overcrowded families have contagious diseases at earlier ages—and these correlations apparently hold true even if income is held constant.[14]

There have been a few studies which have attempted to test the health and social adjustments of families in public housing projects as compared with slum areas. It has been found that the better housed families have superior health, less delinquency, and that they make greater gains in social status and participation.[15] This would seem to be an endorsement of slum clearance and public housing. More research is needed, however, before these conclusions can be taken as wholly reliable and before all of the effects of housing upon family and social welfare are understood. Certainly we know that it isn't as simple as, "Clear the slums and you remove social ills"; housing is only one of the factors. To be successful, any housing reform program will need to take into account the values and habits of people and will need to deal with the over-all problem of community organization.[16]

The unsatisfactory condition of housing for millions of American families in this day is recognized and well known. During the war years building construction almost ceased, while the demand for dwellings increased enormously, due to a continued and rising marriage rate. The results are many: (1) Building and purchasing costs have about tripled the pre-war figure. (2) This has caused owners and real-estate dealers to promote sales, rather than rentals, so that a great many families have been forced to purchase against their will, beyond their means, and at exorbitant prices. (3) Many who refused to purchase, or couldn't, have been evicted. (4) Many of the new constructions are small, flimsy, and makeshift. (5) Some families have had to split up, with part of the members going one place and the others elsewhere, in order to have

---

[14] Charles Abrams and John P. Dean, "Housing and the Family," chap. xv in *The Family: Its Function and Destiny,* ed. Ruth Nanda Anshen (New York: Harper & Bros., 1949), p. 304.

[15] For a summary of important studies, see *ibid.,* pp. 304-6.

[16] Cf. John P. Dean, "The Myths of Housing Reform," *American Sociological Review,* 14 :281-88, April, 1949.

roofs over their heads. (6) A more common necessity has been for doubling up where two or more families occupy one dwelling unit. It is estimated that about two and one-half million married couples, or 7 per cent of the total, live that way now.[17]

It is almost inevitable that these unstable conditions and inadequate facilities in housing will affect the relationships of marriage and the family. In many instances people are being permitted to live under arrangements that are unsafe and indecent. Overcrowding and lack of privacy create tensions and conflict, to say nothing of the moral problem. There is frequent worrying over the financing of the mortgage and resentment concerning the price paid or the inconveniences endured. Recognition of the importance of good housing to family welfare was given by the National Conference on Family Life held in Washington, D. C., during the spring of 1948. Granting some progress since that time, adequate housing nevertheless remains one of the great needs facing the American family.

CONCLUSIONS

It should be clear by now that marital success is partially dependent upon a stable society. Families simply do not operate in isolation. No thinking person will deny that social change has repercussions upon the marriage and family institutions. Nor will he dispute the claim that these are sensitive to the pulse of society at large, and that the transitional and confused character of our contemporary culture leaves them dangling, so to speak, and somewhat insecure.

Changes affecting the family have been both technological and ideological in nature. In the first category would fall such events as the invention of the automobile, the vacuum cleaner, the radio, contraceptives, and a thousand or more other devices and processes which have revolutionized housekeeping and homemaking. Technological advance has increased the comforts and conveniences of man, has raised his level of living, given him more leisure, enlarged his knowledge and power

---

[17] Bureau of the Census, *Current Population Reports*, Series P-20, No. 21 December 19, 1948, p. 1.

to control the forces of nature. But it has also made life more
hurried, crowded, and insecure. In the second category would
be placed such things as the continuing shift in the direction
of greater sex freedom, the growing social acceptance of divorce, and the recent emphasis upon individual rights and personal pleasure. This newer freedom in thought has probably
made people more restless, but it has also opened the way
for a better realization of the democratic goals; it has both
created problems and opened up opportunities at the same time.

No solution to the marriage problem will come by way of
retreat. Technology undoubtedly is here to stay. So also are
the urban mode of life, a high mobility of population, and
many other innovations that have been temporarily disturbing
to marriage and the family. A certain amount of disorganization is inevitable to change, and change is always a necessary
prerequisite to progress, whatever the field. Hill tells us that,
though there are many cultural paradoxes in our present family
culture, "disorganization necessarily precedes reorganization
as familistic-patriarchal forms give way to smaller, more personalized family associations." [18] An acceptance of the technological age and a willingness to adjust to it are the only
attitudes that can make modern marriage succeed.

The same cannot be said for the "problem" aspects of society, however. By urging that people accept technology we do
not mean that they should embrace it in all of its present manifestations. The unfortunate effects of depression and war have
already been analyzed. There are other conditions and happenings that plague society, too, problems ranging all the way
from the distribution of obscene literature to poverty and bad
housing. All of these have their impact upon the family. One
way to improve marriage, therefore, is to build a better world,
to work for security, justice, and peace.

Also, it should be pointed out that not only is society a factor
in successful family life, but that the family is a factor in
maintaining a stable society. The two are interrelated and
interacting. Just as society, by providing the setting, influences

---

[18] Reuben Hill, "The American Family: Problem or Solution," *American
Journal of Sociology*, September, 1947, p. 125.

the growth and development of the family, so the family, by establishing attitudes and habits in young citizens, sets the stage for local, national, and world affairs. Such mutual inter-stimulation will incline us to one of two patterns: either (1) a vicious circle of disorganization as each adds weakness to the other, or (2) a constructive cycle moving forward as each contributes reinforcement to the other. Which shall it be?

Throughout the remainder of the book major attention will be given to personality factors. It should constantly be kept in mind, however, that back of personality lies society. The immediate responsibility for marriage rests with those who marry, it is true. But people are to a large extent the products of the world in which they live. The answer to family failure is better marriage, which depends upon better adjusted individuals, which in turn depends upon a better integrated and compatible social and cultural environment.

Problems and Projects

1. Is it correct to believe that almost everyone was happily married in the "good old days"? What evidence can you suggest to support or contradict this theory?
2. It has been demonstrated that family unity is more difficult under the urban way of life. Some have used this fact to argue for a general movement "back to the land." Do you agree or disagree? Why?
3. Draw a parallel between the early Roman family and the modern American family. From these comparisons would you say that the "Zimmerman thesis" is valid?
4. As the companionship family has emerged, certain family functions have been taken over by other agencies. Which of these losses of function do you consider most serious for the family? Are any of these losses beneficial? Give reasons.
5. Discuss the relative virtues of familism and individualism; of the institutional family as compared with the companionship family. Is the answer to family trouble a return to familism? Defend your answer.

6. What new responsibilities does the companionship family entail for men? For women?

7. What do you consider the promising aspects of the modern independence of youth? Of women?

8. Has the automobile weakened or strengthened family relationships? What about the picture show? The radio? Television?

9. How have the many inventions which reduce work in the home affected the family? Give several illustrations.

10. What possible relationships exist between kind of housing and degree of family unity? Cite cases from your experience or observation.

11. Since the divorce rate is lower during depression, why may we not conclude that depression has a strengthening influence upon marriage and family life? What is the true picture?

12. Study the conditions under which many marriages took place during the last war. Which of these do you feel contributed in considerable measure to the high divorce rate following the war? Explain.

Selected Readings

Angell, Robert C. *The Family Encounters the Depression.* New York: Charles Scribner's Sons, 1936.

Anshen, Ruth Nanda (ed.). *The Family: Its Function and Destiny.* New York: Harper & Bros., 1949. Chap. xv, "Housing and the Family."

Becker, Howard, and Hill, Reuben (eds.). *Family, Marriage, and Parenthood.* Boston: D. C. Heath & Co., 1948. Chap. xxiv, "What War Is Still Doing to the Family."

Burgess, Ernest W., and Locke, Harvey J. *The Family: From Institution to Companionship.* New York: American Book Co., 1945. Chaps. xvi, "The American Family in Transition"; xvii, "Mobility and The Family"; xxi, "War and The Family."

Cavan, Ruth S., and Ranck, Katherine H. *The Family and the Depression.* Chicago: University of Chicago Press, 1938.

Duvall, Evelyn Millis, and Hill, Reuben. *When You Marry.* Boston: D. C. Heath & Co., 1945. Chaps. xix, "Marriage Isn't What It Used To Be"; xx, "War and Postwar Problems."

Folsom, Joseph K. *The Family and Democratic Society.* New York: John Wiley & Sons, 1943. Chap. v, "Modern Social Changes Affecting the Family."

FRANK, LAWRENCE K. *Society As the Patient: Essays on Culture and Personality.* New Brunswick: Rutgers University Press, 1948.

HILL, REUBEN. *Families Under Stress.* New York: Harper & Bros., 1949.

KOOS, EARL LOMON. *Families in Trouble.* New York: King's Crown Press, 1946.

TRUXAL, ANDREW G., and MERRILL, FRANCIS E. *The Family in American Culture.* New York: Prentice-Hall, Inc., 1947.

Chapter 3

PERSONALITY BACKGROUNDS

The foundations for successful marriage do not start with
the marriage ceremony itself; they reach back into the courtships, into the childhoods, and into the hereditary backgrounds
of those involved. Happiness in marriage is the product of
years of preparation, conscious or unconscious, whereby the
infant is first formed and then molded gradually into a mature
personality capable of the loves and joys of married life. The
roots of successful marriage for every man and woman reach
deep into his past. Parents should realize that by giving birth
to normal healthy children, and by caring for these children
and training them properly, they not only secure greater happiness in their own lives but they also lay foundations for
successful marriages and families in the generations to come.

Chapter 3 turns directly to the human element in marriage,
to the personality backgrounds and tendencies which make or
mar the family relationship. Not only are these the most important of all forces operating to affect the success or failure
of marriage, but they are formed largely in the home and
they have continuity from generation to generation. "As the
twig is bent, the tree is inclined."

Basic Factors in Human Behavior

What makes people behave the way they do? Although
research has not moved far enough for a complete or final
answer to this question, the following factors seem basic: (1)
biological heredity, (2) physical environment, (3) social environment, and (4) cultural environment. The problem is to
determine, as best one can, how these several factors converge
upon the individual, how they shape his personality and in-

fluence his behavior. Before that, however, it will be well to briefly examine the nature of each.

Heredity refers to the biological process of transmitting traits from parents to offspring. It comes about through the union of male and female cells, and it manifests itself in such things as eye color, body shape, mental capacity, and numerous other physical and psychological tendencies which characterize the newborn child. Heredity sets the stage, so to speak; provides the "stuff" out of which human behavior emerges; establishes the potentials. Heredity plays its last hand at the time of conception, and though the product may be modified after that, environment can never completely change what nature has done.

The physical environment consists of various material elements and energies that at all times surround the human organism, influencing both development and behavior. Before birth it is made up of chemicals, temperatures, and other conditions within the mother. It is affected by such things as diet and exercise; and it, in turn, affects the growth rates, survival chances, and general health conditions of the child not yet born. After birth it consists of the many geographic factors—temperature, rainfall, sunshine, wind, soil, mineral resources, elevation, topography, and the like. During the prenatal stage this physical environment is the only one operating. In the postnatal, however, there are competitive influences along with it —the social and the cultural. Culture, particularly in the Western world, has developed nearly far enough to supersede geography in influence. To some extent man has learned how to control temperature, remove mountains, and in other ways harness the forces of nature to his advantage. Modern man is not nearly so dependent upon the elements as were his ancestors. Yet, neither is he independent of them.[1] Though the physical is perhaps the least important of man's postnatal environments today, it is nevertheless there and it has influence. To give but one example, soil compositions in the Great

---

[1] An interesting, though sobering, account of man's wrestle with nature, and his relative helplessness in the face of natural events is given in George Stewart's novel based on the science of meteorology, *Storm* (New York: Random House, 1941), 349 pp.

Basin area of the West result in iodine deficiencies in diets
built from foods grown there. This condition, in turn, produces a higher rate of goiter in that area, with some ill health
and personality tensions as end results.

The social environment comes from the presence of other
human beings and one's interaction with them. This is sometimes referred to as the "group situation." It starts with birth
and continues normally throughout the lifetime of the individual. "Man is a social animal" said Aristotle many years
ago. By this he meant that society, or the interaction of peoples
in groups, has a great deal to do with man's behavior. There
have been rare instances of men's being deprived of this social
or group environment and/or remaining undeveloped or "wild"
because of it. Such individuals, those growing up or living for
long periods of time without or with little human association,
are called feral men.[2] They are odd because they have not had
an opportunity to become socialized through normal contact
with others. No personality can develop normally and completely in isolation. Everyone is influenced by, and also influences, those around him.

The cultural environment is made up of the multitude of
man-made objects, customs, understandings, and skills that one
is born to accept. Culture is sometimes defined as man's "social
inheritance," for just as individuals are different, depending
upon the kind of biological inheritance that is theirs, so they are
also different, depending upon the kind of society into which
they are born.

Someone born to live in the heart of New York City, for
example, would have a far different social heritage, and therefore a different personality, from another on the upper reaches
of the Amazon. Culture, though not the same as society, is
one of society's products. It consists of all that is created
by man in interaction, deposited or retained by society, and
passed down from generation to generation.

Thus it is that man is the product of a number of forces,
all interrelated. Biology starts him off, lays down the raw

---

2 For an account of such individuals see A. L. Singh and Robert M. Zingg
Wolf-Children and Feral Man (New York: Harper & Bros., 1942).

materials out of which he can grow, establishes tendencies, sets limits. The physical environment, operating both before and after birth, influences his general health and, in some cases, also sets limits upon his development and activity. Starting soon after birth, both the social and the cultural environments come into strong play, the first by an inter-stimulation and interresponse of persons in contact with one another, and the second through an exposure to the traditional ways of thinking and acting that the group has built up. Personality is the outgrowth of them all.

It isn't really a question of nature *versus* nurture, as some would have it, but nature *and* nurture, operating jointly and with interactional effects. Heredity makes the start by providing materials out of which personality is to be built. But it is to the environments, mainly those social and cultural, that we must turn if we would understand the dynamics of personal action and the variability in directions of development. The age-old argument on the relative importance of heredity versus environment is fruitless, for both are absolutely essential and it is only through the interaction of one with the other that personality comes about. Science has not progressed far enough to give exact proportions for the various components of human behavior, nor is it likely that it will ever be able to do this. The important thing is to know what these components are, how they operate, and that they function in unison.

Heredity and Marriage

Although personality is more than biology, as has been seen, its roots do lead back into the inheritance streams of the ancestral generations that have gone before. The start comes from being born. While heredity can in no way determine personality singlehanded, it does lay out potentials and set up tendencies.

Principles of Human Genetics.[3]—No two persons are at any time exactly alike. Neither nature nor nurture is capable,

---

[3] For a popular but authentic treatment of heredity and its problems see Amram Scheinfeld, *You and Heredity* (New York: Frederick A. Stokes Co.,

seemingly, of throwing up exact duplicates. Each situation is unique. Variability is the only constant.

Peoples related by blood are more nearly alike than are those unrelated. Variability is therefore partially offset by continuity and similarity. In nature, each of the species tends to reproduce its kind, never exactly, but always approximately. Forces making for long-range variabilities in biological organisms are called evolution. Forces making for similarities in lines of descent are called heredity. Genetics is the science back of them both.

In addition to the body cells, every normal individual carries within him certain *germ cells* (sperms in the male and eggs or ova in the female), which become active at the time of puberty and upon which reproduction and heredity depend. Within each germ cell there are twenty-four pairs of string-like objects called *chromosomes,* and within or upon each chromosome there are numerous protein bodies called *genes.* It is these genes that determine the various hereditary traits of the individual—hair color, nose shape, body build, mental level, and the like. The genes are originally in pairs, but each pair separates as the chromosomes split longitudinally at the time of cell division prior to fertilization. There are both *dominant* and *recessive* attributes in the genes; those that are dominant always show up in the offspring, but the recessive traits appear only when they are matched with similar recessive traits from the other sex. This, together with the facts of multiple gene combination at the time of cell division, and chance sperm selection at the time of fertilization, explains how children in a family can be so different from their parents and from one another. The number of combinations that genes can take in forming the new offspring is almost infinite. By carrying traits recessively, parents of similar tendencies can pass on to their children characteristics which were not apparent in themselves. It should be clear from this that one's heredity depends primarily upon the kind of genes present in

1939), 434 pp. If a more technical and extended treatment is desired, see R. Ruggles Gates, *Human Genetics* (New York: The Macmillan Co., 1946), 2 vols., 1,518 pp.

both parents and the particular gene combination that happens to result from the processes of cell division and fertilization.

Another factor in biological variability is what geneticists call *mutation*. Sudden changes occasionally occur within the internal structures of the germ cells which affect heredity and which breed true. Exact causes of mutations are not known, nor are their results predictable. It is known that new traits are set up in this way, however, and that these tend to perpetuate themselves from generation to generation. Experimentation with the fruit fly has demonstrated that mutations can be induced by the application of X-ray radiations. For this reason medical technicians working around this kind of equipment are urged to exercise care. Results of atomic bomb radiations are still being studied. Some authorities now believe that the explosions at Hiroshima and Nagasaki may have caused mutations in the germ cells of survivors which could be carried recessively and crop out to plague the human race for many years to come.

Children can inherit only that which is found in the germ cells of their parents. They can be different from their parents, of course, for reasons given above—the possibility of infinite gene combinations from the union of the two family lines, and the possibility of recessive traits, not showing in parents, being thrown up in the offspring. But they cannot be so different as to defy the laws of heredity. Science, for example, has disproved the old superstition of an apparently white couple (but with the wife having some hidden Negro blood) being able to give birth to a coal-black baby. If a Negro baby is born to such a couple, one can be sure either that both parents have Negro ancestry or that the paternity of the child is in doubt.[4]

Acquired characteristics cannot be inherited. There is no known way by which changes in the body cells can be transferred to the germ cells and thereby show up in the offspring. Experiments with rats, for example, have shown that the offspring are invariably born with tails, though those of their parents and ancestors for generations had been cut off. Like-

---

[4] Scheinfeld, *op. cit.*, pp. 66-69.

wise, from common observation, we know that the child of a parent who has acquired a sun tan will be just as light in color as though the parent had not. The child of a watchmaker, to use still another illustration, will be born without any skills or predispositions in that direction. Should he become a watchmaker later it will be because of learning, not heredity. This is not to say that the genes are entirely independent of their environment; quite the contrary. We have already observed how mutations can be produced by the X-ray, an environmental medium. Scientists also know that genes express themselves differently in different environments, proving again that heredity and environment are cooperating interdependent forces.

Also, it should be pointed out, there is no scientific support for popular superstitions regarding predisposition through prenatal influence. It is true that the health of the mother during pregnancy can and will affect the general health or condition of the developing child, but not in any specialized way. By practicing music during pregnancy, for example, the mother cannot predispose the child to this art, nor can frights and other incidents on the part of the mother result in specific birthmarks.

Twinning is a tendency that seems to be inherited, although the laws by which it operates are not completely understood. Twins are of two kinds, *identical* and *fraternal*. Identical twins come from one egg which has been fertilized by one sperm, a dividing or splitting of the egg taking place after fertilization. That is why identical twins are so much alike; the same genes go into the making of them both. Fraternal twins, on the other hand, may be as different as ordinary brother and sister; indeed, they are often of opposite sexes, while identical twins must be either both males or both females. Fraternal twins result from the fertilization of two different eggs by two different sperms. Multiple births of a higher order, such as triplets, quadruplets, and quintuplets, may be of either the identical or the fraternal variety.[5]

---

[5] Most known facts concerning multiple births are summarized by H. H. Newman, *Multiple Human Births* (New York: Doubleday & Co., Inc., 1940), 214 pp.

One of the twenty-four pairs of chromosomes in the human germ cell has to do with sex determination. Geneticists represent this in the female with the symbol XX and in the male with XY. During cell division these pairs split. If an X sperm then unites with the egg during the process of fertilization, the result will be XX, or female; but if a Y sperm, an XY, or male, will be produced. It will be seen from this that the sex of the child is determined through the father, not the mother. Let it be clear, however, that there is no willful determination on the part of either father or mother; though the determining factors lie within man's nature they are beyond his control.

Genes located on the sex chromosomes sometimes produce what is known as sex-linkage. Thus, color blindness and hemophilia, where they exist in heredity, are known to be carried recessively by females but occasionally to skip generations and to show up only in males.

Problems in Eugenics.—Eugenics is a movement to improve the quality of the human stock. It is based upon the science of genetics and is impelled by the realization that many of the most capable in society are having the fewest children, and the least capable, the most children. Hence comes the fear that if this tendency is left unchecked there will be a qualitative deterioration of mankind. There are two programs: (1) positive eugenics which, through education and legislation giving economic inducements, attempts to increase the birth rate of the genetically fit; and (2) negative eugenics which, through sterilization mainly, attempts to limit the birth rate of the genetically unfit. Although the positive approach is the more constructive and hopeful of the two, it has been less developed.

Before we evaluate these programs it will be well to examine some of the factual data upon which they are based. Which of the many peculiarities and abnormalities in personality are inherited? Whom is it safe to marry?

A word of caution is in order. Human inheritance is extremely complicated, and no man, scientist or otherwise, has all the answers. Evidence is often scanty, and many of the important questions, therefore, remain controversial. Yet there is much that is known, and with continued research more is almost daily being discovered.

Intelligence, of course, is related to the genes. The two extremes of mental capacity, genius and feeble-mindedness, tend to perpetuate themselves in family lines. This is true particularly when like marries like. Some feeble-mindedness is brought about through such conditions as birth injury, malnutrition, and glandular trouble. Where the deficiency is so acquired, it is not inherited. But such cases represent only part of the total; it is probable that the majority of all idiots, imbeciles, and morons are that way because of bad heredity. Likewise, though environment is important to attainment, and the I.Q. can and does change moderately with development, it seems safe to assume that genius also depends primarily upon the genes. Capacity for achievement is inherited; an Edison, a Wagner, a Chopin is *born* before he is made.

The question of psychosis, or insanity as it is popularly called, is not so easily settled. Certain ailments of the mind are probably entirely independent of heredity. Of these, one is a type of paresis caused by syphilis. Another is traumatic psychosis due to an injury of the brain. There are other mental difficulties that seem definitely to run in families and to be at least partially hereditary; certain kinds of epilepsy, for example. Still others are in doubt, and claims are contradictory regarding these matters. The likely thing is that both heredity and environment are involved, that heredity determines the weaknesses or susceptibilities to some of these nervous and mental disorders, and that environment then supplies the inciting factors incident to the breakdown.

Constitutional vigor, which makes one resistant to disease and helps determine his length of life, is claimed by many to be hereditary. Longevity, we know, varies with families. Part of this, of course, is due to the way people live; but another and very important part is the kind of biological material they started with. Nature has a way of partially protecting itself— feeble-minded and other genetically deficient individuals have disproportionately high death rates, while the well-endowed tend to live for a long time.

One may inherit a susceptibility or predisposition for disease but never the disease itself. Tuberculosis is a good example. The tendency is for it to be in some families more than in others, and for two reasons: first, because of an inherited susceptibility; and second, because of unfavorable living conditions and greater contagion possibilities due to close family contacts. A child may become infected from some other member of the family, though this of course is not heredity. Yet where the predisposition is present, disease germs are resisted less easily and contagion becomes more likely.

Students of the subject are generally agreed that predispositions are also provided by heredity for such things as congenital deafness, glandular disturbances, diabetes, certain allergies, and possibly alcoholism and cancer. The riddle of cancer, as with many of these others, is still unsolved though there is considerable evidence that families differ in susceptibility to its various forms. Research continues.

Contrary to some popular misconceptions, the venereal diseases are not hereditary. There is the possibility of prenatal contagion, of course, as in the case of congenital syphilis or of infection at the time of birth, as in the case of blindness due to gonorrhea germs. Premarital physical examinations, including blood tests for the venereal diseases, are recognized as very important from the standpoint of health and are now required by law in more than half the states. Also important is early and competent prenatal care through which it is generally possible to protect the fetus against diseases and other abnormalities as it develops. Furthermore, as a safeguard against congenital blindness, most laws require that the baby's eyes be treated immediately after birth; silver nitrate has been widely used for this purpose, but there are recent claims that this weakens the eyes, and the newest practice is to use penicillin. Though extremely important, all of these are health measures only; they do not affect the genes and therefore have nothing to do with heredity.

A great many of the personality traits and behavior patterns that are characteristic of people are related to heredity only remotely and indirectly. If, for example, there is a tendency for redheads to be hotheads, as has been claimed, it is only because of conditioning through teasing and other types of role-defining by society. There is no scientific evidence that redheaded people are by nature temperamentally different from any others. Yet, as is true also of the midget, the cripple, or anyone who is significantly different or handicapped, such factors derived from nature do help create situations that tend to influence learning and shape personality. Similarly, criminality is not inherited in any biological way, though certain handicaps and tendencies originating in nature may be real factors contributing to its development.

The Right to Marry.—From the standpoint of eugenics there are some persons who should be denied parenthood and others that should be given special inducements to become parents. Furthermore, genetic considerations should be high on the list of all who choose a mate for marriage. No one has a "natural right" to marry or to procreate; these are privileges that ought to be contingent upon the fitness of those who would participate. Society needs to be protected from the blights of biological weakness which are passed from generation to generation.

There are good reasons why some people should not marry. Every right carries with it an equal responsibility, and marriage is no exception. For those who are either mentally or physically incapacitated, marriage would be both foolish and unkind, for it would force them to assume adult roles that they are totally incapable of handling. Consider the lowest grade of feeble-minded individuals, for example, those who are not even able to take care of themselves or to assume the most elementary responsibilities. Mentally, they are as infants, and there is no hope of their ever becoming self-sustaining. Consider the violently and permanently insane or extreme cases of chronic invalidism. Where persons like this can recover, marriage should be held as a real possibility; but it should wait upon recovery. For those either immature, or morally or socially inadequate, marriage should be delayed until there has been time for development and/or reform to take place. Unless ready and able to assume the necessary responsibilities, no one should marry.

The low-grade feeble-minded cannot be permitted either marriage or parenthood for the reason that they are custodial cases, unable to take care of their own needs, let alone those of a family. These are usually kept in institutions. They are incapable of responsible marriage even where their condition is known to be nongenetic.

Certain persons should probably be denied parenthood, though permitted marriage. These are those known to be defective in hereditary capacity, though themselves capable of a reasonable amount of self-support and social adjustment. High-grade feeble-minded individuals probably fall into this category. They should be denied parenthood for at least two reasons: (1) so that they will not pass on their defects to future generations, and (2) so that they will not give birth to children they cannot support—their lesser ability making them incapable of that much responsibility.

There is no simple or commonly accepted eugenic standard for judging when a marriage should remain childless. It seems questionable that most couples would consider clubfeet as a sufficient reason, or a harelip, or any one of a number of physical handicaps that may be related to the genes. Mental deficiency generally presents a greater problem. Each case is a matter for separate decision. Society ought to take a hand only in those cases that are quite serious and are known to be hereditary.

Sterilization is probably the most effective means for preventing parenthood. Other approaches are institutional segregation, which is expensive and therefore impractical except for the most extreme cases, and birth control which, to be effective, requires more intelligence and skill than mentally handicapped individuals ordinarily possess.

Modern sterilization is accomplished by a rather simple operation in which the tubes that carry the germ cells are cut and tied. It in no way desexes the individual, and the only way it alters his normal life is in the prevention of parenthood. About two thirds of the states have laws permitting sterilization for

defective strains and to date more than forty thousand opera-
tions have been performed. The question is still a controversial
one, however. Certainly it cannot be said that sterilization is a
panacea. Chief difficulties are these: (1) the impossibility of
determining accurately, in the light of present knowledge, just
which defects are hereditary, to what extent, and in which
cases; (2) the subjective and politically dangerous nature of
deciding where to draw the line, who shall be sterilized; and
(3) the fact that many defects are carried recessively, not
showing in the individual, which makes them impossible of
being reached in that generation. But when used cautiously,
and only on those cases which are somewhat extreme and have
been carefully diagnosed as to their hereditary nature, sterilization seems definitely to have a place.

Special attention has been given recently to the so-called Rh
factor in human blood types, so named because of its discovery
in Rhesus monkeys. Approximately 85 per cent of the white
population is known to possess this factor. These are labeled
Rh-positive; the remaining 15 per cent, rh-negative. The factor is hereditary, with Rh-positive being dominant over rh-
negative. Complications can develop whenever the wife is rh-
negative and the husband Rh-positive, which is true in about
one out of every dozen marriages. In such cases the fetus is
apt to be Rh-positive (will definitely be if the father is homo-
zygous, Rh Rh, and may be if he is heterozygous, Rh rh).
Antigens from an Rh-positive fetus will sometimes pass into
the blood stream of the rh-negative mother. This takes place
rather rarely, however, there being no direct connection between the blood streams of mother and infant. When it does
happen, antibodies are produced in the mother's blood, which
can pass back into the blood stream of the fetus, combine
with the Rh-positive cells there, and destroy them. The condition is characterized by anemia and is known as *erythroblas-
tosis fetalis* or hemolytic disease. It frequently causes stillbirth. Most of those born alive are now saved by means of
rh-negative blood transfusions. Fortunately the antibodies produced in the mother's blood accumulate slowly, and as a consequence the first child of a marriage is usually not affected—

unless previously there has been an aborted pregnancy or unless the mother has at some time had an Rh-positive blood transfusion. The possibility of a child's developing this disease increases with each succeeding pregnancy. It is estimated that only about one out of every thirty or forty children of rh-negative women are affected by the hemolytic conditions.

Over half of the states have laws forbidding first cousins to marry, and some carry the prohibition to second cousins. This is because of an incest horror, a feeling on the part of society that close blood unions are not good. Stockbreeders, however, have long used the principle of inbreeding to advantage. What inbreeding does is to bring out the recessive traits; it can be called good if these traits are good, but bad if the traits it brings to the front are undesirable. Eugenists tell us that there is nothing wrong with cousin marriage so long as the ancestries of the mates are good; in such a case it may even result in superior offspring. But if there are hereditary weaknesses, such as feeble-mindedness in the family lines, cousin marriage is extremely dangerous. It is much safer for cousins to avoid each other so far as marriage is concerned, but where the question does come up both law observance and genetic purity should be factors in making the decision.

In all instances, those considering marriage will want to concern themselves seriously over family backgrounds, realizing that heredity cannot be ignored and that the right to parenthood carries with it certain obligations. One way of meeting these obligations is to marry into a family that gives evidence of native normality, that seems to be free from the blights of major hereditary weaknesses. Unfortunately there is no absolutely certain way of determining this, though if one were to examine carefully the backgrounds of his own and the other family in question he should not go far wrong. Family doctors and old-timers in the community can often assist in this process. If a defect is found to repeat itself generation after generation, one can be rather certain that it is in the genes. If this same defect shows itself in the two family lines, it can be considered to be all the more likely to show up in the offspring. Where there is a question or doubt it is well to consult a geneticist or other qualified expert. It must be remembered, however, that no one has all the answers and that in every marriage there will be some risks. The main thing, and all that can be hoped for, is to reduce these risks to the smallest possible minimum. There will always be the problem of judgment, of deciding how much risk one is willing to assume, of determining whether a given defect is serious enough to matter.

Finally, it should be re-emphasized that the positive approach in eugenics needs more stress—by both society and the individual. Sterilization as applied to the unfit undoubtedly has some beneficial effects. So also do eugenic birth control and segregation, though in a more limited fashion. On the personal side there is value in avoiding anyone whose family history shows defective germ plasm. But these are all negative, designed to reduce an evil rather than promote a good. In the words of a once popular song, we should learn to "accentuate the positive." Population trends become dysgenic, not only when the genetically handicapped are allowed to breed or reproduce too rapidly, but also when those better endowed by nature fail to breed fast enough. Both conditions seem to exist. It is a well-known fact, for example, that relief clients have large families and continue with high birth rates, while college graduates often fail to reproduce their own numbers.[6] We are not implying that people are genetically inferior just because they are poor, or genetically superior just because they have made money or graduated from college. Circumstances enter in; to a considerable extent individuals are products of their environment. Furthermore, it seems logical to assume that in some families high fertility is a cause of poverty, rather than a result. Nevertheless, society is competitive and, to some extent, selective; the general tendency is for those of greater ability to move into the upper strata—exceptions conceded. Since this is true, failure of the upper classes to adequately reproduce themselves is possibly meaning a gradual lowering of genetic qualities in the entire population.

---

[6] One proof of this is found in Paul H. Landis, *Population Problems* (New York: American Book Co., 1948), pp. 115-19; 174-77.

There is another part to the picture, also. Child-rearing is more easily financed by families that are economically well to do. The children of educated parents are the ones most likely to receive training and cultural advantages comparable to their needs. Yet it is the rich and the well-educated that are having the smallest families. Aside from eugenic considerations, therefore, it is the ones most able to care for children that are having the fewest.

Society will need to find new and better ways of encouraging the genetically fit to reproduce at a proportionately faster rate. This is not to say that the average family should necessarily be larger, but that the quality of population should be better, that the breeding should come more from the top. America as yet has no systematic policy or program for accomplishing this. When developed, such a program may possibly and profitably follow the lead of Sweden by offering certain subsidies or economic inducements for fertility among the "right" families. If it is to be effective, however, it will need to go further than this and, by the educative process, change people's attitudes so that having a fair-sized family (for those genetically and economically fortunate) becomes the expected and the normal thing. In the meantime, healthy and well-endowed individuals can do their part by seeking other high-quality persons for marriage and by considering offspring partially in the light of social duty.

PERSONALITY DEVELOPMENT

Personality consists of all the traits, habits, ideas, and attitudes acquired by the individual in association with others and superimposed upon what nature at first provided. Said differently, personality is the sum total of all that you are. Back of it lie both heredity and environment; it is the product of these interacting forces. Every adult has personality, for with contact and interaction come learning and change along specialized lines. Some have immature personalities, others well-developed ones; some maladjusted, others poised and balanced; some show aggressive tendencies, others submissive; some are disagreeable and repulsive, others pleasing and inviting. We differ rather widely as to our personable characteristics, it is true, but all have these characteristics and together in each of us they make up personality.

Socialization.—At birth man is little more than animal. He has a biological equipment provided in large part by his ancestors. He has certain capacities that seek development, tendencies that want expression, and needs that must be satisfied. His prenatal existence has seen him grow biologically along patterns largely prescribed by nature. He has not yet had the experience of learning. Potentially he is human, but actually, at this stage, he is but a bundle of organized protoplasm.

It was Robert E. Park who first pointed out that "Man is not born human." [7] While one's original nature results almost entirely from biological factors, human nature develops gradually by processes that are largely sociological. The newborn infant, though an individual, does not as yet have personality; this he will shortly start developing. It is only through group interaction and cultural exposure that original nature changes into human nature and the biological individual becomes a social person.

The process by which this takes place is called "socialization." It is nurture operating to modify nature. It consists of "denaturalizing" the individual, of altering his original patterns in the direction of social acceptance, of making him a mature and responsible member of society.

Psychiatrists point out that patterns of disorganization in the adult personality are frequently traceable to early traumatic experiences wherein the child is denied free expression of his primary needs. Socialization requires some blocking of natural tendencies through discipline and adjustment. Improperly handled, this can be frustrating to the individual and result in feelings of guilt, anxiety, and hostility. Stokes says:

In the past we have tyrannized over our children from a combination of causes; we ignorantly failed to understand their natural and

---

[7] Robert E. Park and Ernest W. Burgess, *Introduction to the Science of Sociology* (Chicago: University of Chicago Press, 1921), p. 76.

inescapable personality needs; we attempted to force upon them adult ideals and standards that could not be comprehended and were often cruelly harsh and stupid; and finally we were accustomed to impose our will upon children by a show of overwhelming righteous anger and violence. That is more than the natural dignity and good feeling of a child can take. His fine qualities are destroyed and replaced by fear and hatred. Potential respect for law and order is undermined and friendly, responsible social growth is turned into fearful dependence and suspicion. In brief, a neurotic character is created.[8]

There is disagreement in deciding how much of the culture should be imposed upon the child as against letting him follow his natural bent. One school of thought argues for "self-regulation," claiming that the culture is contradictory anyway, that many of its prescriptions are inconsistent with personality needs, and that repression of these needs often acts to build up feelings of guilt and fear within the individual, causing him to be insecure and to develop aggressive tendencies. Though the argument seems to be correct, it can be carried too far. So long as man lives within groups and has a culture, it will be necessary for him to train his offspring in the ways of that culture; otherwise he will be producing social misfits. Of course this does not require that culture be left unimproved, that it remain inconsistent and incompatible with personality needs. Neither does it excuse adults from approaching the socialization of their children in an understanding and considerate manner (see Chapter 11).

Early Home Influences.—Socialization begins in the home. While personality, as has been seen, is the product of a multitude of forces extending throughout the lifetime of the individual, its first, most basic, and most lasting traits are formed in the family. On this virtually all authorities are agreed.

The reason is, of course, that the family gets the individual first, when he is most pliable; then it keeps him longest and interacts with him most intimately.

Not only is the human infant one of the most helpless at birth, but its period of infancy is longer than the correspond-

---

[8] Walter R. Stokes, *Modern Pattern for Marriage* (New York: Rinehart & Co., Inc., 1948), pp. 90-91.

ing period for other living creatures. These differences between men and animals present to man both a challenge and an opportunity. The challenge lies in the responsibility of caring for and training the young, and the opportunity lies in the possibility of learning and developing and advancing far beyond the animals. Animals are controlled largely by instincts and are unable to go much beyond them; man, on the other hand, is controlled largely by habits, and through the formation and reformation of these habits he is able to develop continually. The helpless and plastic condition of the human baby, together with its relatively long period of infancy, requires the existence of the family and makes possible the molding and building of personality. It also places a tremendous responsibility upon the home, for unless proper attitudes and habits are instilled into the lives of children during the early formative years when they are in the home, handicapping tendencies will become established in their places and the children will start through life with personalities that are warped.

There is a kind of "social osmosis" taking place in every home whereby the inclinations and mannerisms of parents are unconsciously picked up by the children.) Home atmosphere or "spirit" plays a large part in this, and is contagious to the highest degree. Absorption is more important in the establishment of personality inclinations than is formal instruction, though both have a place. As someone has pointed out, one teaches more by what he is than by what he says. The impressionability of children and the informality and intimacy of intrafamilial contacts make the home the primary agency in the building of personality. Some persons are lifted up and motivated to greater things by a healthy home life, while others, unfortunately, become maladjusted and antisocial by a similar process though opposite situation.

In connection with home atmosphere and informal learning we should like to present the following quotations from Bossard:

Underlying all the other factors in family interaction is the spirit or atmosphere of family life. This is one of the intangibles of life which students, preoccupied with scientific analysis and measurement, tend to avoid. And yet it is far too important a reality to pass by.[9]

The spirit of family life is compounded of many ingredients, some obvious and clear in the consciousness of the members of the family, but others buried in the unawareness of a deep mental hinterland. The turned-up nose of daughter Sue, the son's mischievous brown eyes, the mother's forgotten experience with a brown-eyed lover, the deepness of father's voice, sister Kay's lilting laughter, the wiggling stump of the tail of the family's cocker spaniel, the peaceful glow of candlelight at the evening dinner table, a roaring fire in the grate, father's deep satisfaction with his work, and mother's patent satisfaction with daddy—to some these may appear as incidental minutiae of family life. Clearer insight may recognize them as of the greatest importance.[10]

The greater part of the family's role in child-rearing, however, is achieved through indirection, in ways that are subtle and devious, for the most part unconscious, and as a by-product [of] the family routine. The family might be spoken of as a conditioning agency, and what happens to the child is by way of absorption from the life of the family as a whole. In other words, the family lives its collective life— it eats, talks, laughs, argues, wrangles, its members go about their allotted tasks—and in this life the young child grows and learns to live.[11]

Earlier it was shown how juvenile delinquency and adult criminality are related to unfortunate home conditions. Neither of these can be said to be inherited in any biological sense, but in a social sense they are, for attitudes and habits are highly contagious and the groups and culture one is born into help to shape the destiny that is to be his. Antisocial conduct comes from more than bad example, however; it also springs from such things as role conflicts, feelings of insecurity, and other situations which may produce emotional disturbances of one sort or another.

Sibling rivalry within the home is a natural and normal phenomenon. It is a part of the process of socialization, of growing up by learning to live with others. As brothers and sisters

[9] James H. S. Bossard, *The Sociology of Child Development* (New York: Harper & Bros., 1948), p. 93.
[10] *Ibid.*, p. 94.
[11] *Ibid.*, p. 162.

come to compete with one another for the attention and affection of parents, and for favor and power within the home, certain jealousies and conflicts are almost certain to develop. A usual pattern is for a child to feel hurt and jealous when a new baby comes into the family. This is a crisis for him, for until that time he has more or less been the center of attention and now he must learn to "move over" and share these favors. Typical reactions in this adjustment process are three: (1) reverting to baby talk or other infantile mannerisms so as to compete better with the intruder; (2) becoming aggressive or mean in one's treatment of the new baby brother or sister; and (3) ignoring the situation as long as possible by refusing to pay attention or have anything to do with the little one. Wise parents can guide children through these difficulties with enough love and consideration for all and without the process leaving serious personality imprints.

Child "spoiling" can only be mentioned at this point. It may result from one or more of many family situations which impede the socialization process and leave the child immature and self-centered. Ordinal position within the family may have something to do with it, though research regarding the matter is not yet conclusive. Some authorities suggest, for example, that the first and the last children in a fair-sized family are the ones most likely to be handicapped; the first because he is somewhat experimental with parents and may be overindulged, and the last because his parents are often inclined to give him an added share of attention and affection—the other children having married, leaving parents more time and money to spend upon this one, plus the conscious or unconscious reluctance of parents to be left alone. "Only children," may likewise be "spoiled," for the reason that they are the center of attention within the home, without competition, and may thereby be deprived of certain opportunities in social adjustment. Sometimes "spoiling" comes to a single boy among a number of sisters or to a single girl among a number of brothers. Occasionally an invalid in the family will become habituated to the special considerations that are given him while incapacitated, and so come to expect these favors to continue. Or it may be a child that is overprotected because of other reasons, or one that is neglected and allowed to go his own way. There are exceptions to all of these, for many parents understand the problem and are able to recognize and cope with these various situations when they arise. Whenever conditions within the home result in either neglect or favoritism, "spoiling" is likely to develop. And the "spoiled" child makes a very poor marriage risk.

The Ways of Learning.—Learning implies a modification of original traits and tendencies in the direction of acquired knowledge and skill; it is habit formation. While psychologists recognize a number of techniques in the learning process, the one known to have widest application is the so-called conditioned response. This means that original responses to given stimuli can, by association and repetition, be changed into something quite different. The process can be best illustrated by Pavlov's famous experiment: He found that by continually associating the ringing of a bell with the presenting of meat to a hungry dog, and then gradually leaving off the meat as the bell was rung, the saliva which originally would flow in the dog's mouth only at the showing of meat could be made to flow with the ringing of the bell alone; the dog, in other words, had learned to associate food with the ringing of a bell and to respond to this new stimulus. Man learns in much this same way.

Conditioning on the human level takes place through exposure to the three environments: the physical, the cultural, and the social. An example of physical conditioning would be that of the barefoot boy who learned to run around all thistle patches because of his experiences with a few of them. Cultural conditioning can be illustrated by noting how ministers as a class tend to be pious, or how Germans as a people tend to respect authority; cultural patterns, in other words, reflect themselves through the personalities of those who participate. Social conditioning (frequently referred to in such terms as common-human, personal-social, and psychogenic) results from person to person contacts in group situations. It is the least understood of the three but probably the most influential. Students of personality are more and more coming to recognize the extreme importance of early interactional experiences within the home. It is very generally recognized that people both influence others and are influenced by them, and this aside from and in addition to those physical and cultural settings within which all interaction takes place. Psychiatrists and psychoanalysts, in searching for answers to personality difficulties, attempt to reach back into the early lives of their clients. Frights, frustrations, affectional reactions, and other such experience patterns of early childhood are often found to be causes for maladjustments in later life. Though there are many theories regarding it, details of this conditioning process are not well known. It is usually considered that one's general emotional sets and temperamental tendencies are established in this way. Though heredity undoubtedly has something to do with it, such traits as extroversion or introversion, dominance or submission, optimism or pessimism, emotional independence or dependence, self-confidence or lack of confidence, and egocentrism or sociocentrism are determined by this early social conditioning—and once established cannot greatly be altered.[12]

Cooley, in describing personality from the standpoint of its social determinants, used the term "looking-glass self."[13] By this he meant that one's conception of himself comes from the way others react toward him, that each person sees himself reflected in the interactional processes around him, and that this reflection then makes up his self-image which becomes the core of his personality. Sometimes this process of learning within the social matrix is described in terms of *role-taking* and *social expectancy,* the idea being that personality growth comes about by the individual's seeing what others expect of him and then accepting these roles as a part of himself. Society, in other words, helps define the situation for the individual; social

---

[12] Cf. Ernest W. Burgess and Harvey J. Locke, *The Family: From Institution to Companionship* (New York: American Book Co., 1945), p. 244.

[13] Charles H. Cooley, *Human Nature and the Social Order* (rev. ed.; New York: Charles Scribner's Sons, 1922). Recent proponents of this same theory, that personality develops mainly through communication with other persons, include such notable thinkers as John Dewey, George H. Mead, and Ellsworth Faris.

images become internalized and made a part of personality; people tend to play the roles of social expectancy. All of this has some rather profound implications for teaching and learning within the home. Parents must realize that, within limits, their children may be made either "good" or "bad" according to what they come to feel is expected of them; many a boy or girl has become ill-behaved by being continually told that he is naughty or treated as if he were of no account, for example, just as others have become honorable and responsible by receiving trust and respect.

As the personality matures it is a common process for the many natural tendencies, conditioned responses, and internalized images to become integrated around some system of values that has been adopted by the individual. In this way there is formed within each personality what is known as a *life organization* which tends to give unity and meaning to the whole.

Motivation.—Human motivation is a very complex and relatively unsettled field. Current theories hold that man is endowed by nature with a set of reflexes and prepotent tendencies connected with food-getting, elimination, sleep, exercise, and other simple needs of the biological organism; that these are much more elementary than are the rather complex behavior mechanisms, called instincts, which other animals have; and that through conditioning and role-taking these early urges give way or become modified in favor of new and socially acquired drives.

W. I. Thomas named four fundamental incentives or drives which were thought to be back of all human behavior. Known widely as "The Four Wishes," these are: recognition, response, security, and new experience.[14] There was no claim that man is born with each of these fully developed; only that they have become common to all men everywhere.

The wish for recognition shows itself in an almost universal struggle for approval or praise from one's fellow men. It is

---

[14] W. I. Thomas, *The Unadjusted Girl* (Boston: Little, Brown & Co., 1923), chaps. i, ii.

illustrated by the pressure of social expectancy discussed above; for, to gain approval, people will usually conform. Everyone, seemingly, is in need of a certain amount of ego satisfaction, or self-esteem, obtained by being well thought of by others. Where children within the home are not given a proper amount of respect and approval they may, and often do, resort to mischievous and destructive acts in order to gain attention.

The wish for response reflects itself in the desire to love and to be loved. Affectional drives are common to all mankind. Nothing will so drive a person to despair, or give him such a deep sense of worthlessness, as the feeling that he is not loved or wanted. Parental demonstrations of affection are needed by every child. Kissing and caressing within the home have their place. Emotional disturbances in children can frequently be traced to the frustration of this basic wish.

The wish for security finds expression in man's inclination to play safe, to avoid the new and the hazardous. Physical security is found by the newborn infant when the mother holds it and protects it. Financial security is a concern of most adults. Emotional security is also of importance, equal to, or even greater than, these others. It is found through belonging to groups whose behavior is consistent and can be anticipated. Changeable and unpredictable discipline patterns by parents, to give but one example, can unnerve and greatly worry a child. Everyone wants to have the security of knowing what to expect.

The wish for new experience is exactly opposite to the security drive just discussed. In addition to the emotional support that comes from belonging to groups and from anticipating behavior, every normal person also wants to explore and seek after the new. Man, it would seem, is curious and adventurous by nature; he needs the stimulation that comes from experiencing that which is novel and different. Families differ considerably in the amount of new experiences they provide or permit for their members. Where the patterns of the family are too routinized, or where the parental discipline is too exacting or unyielding, children sometimes rebel for the sake of new experience.

Personalities differ greatly as to the relative emphasis placed upon these various wishes. Some, for example, will do almost anything for recognition, with all other drives made secondary or even ignored for the sake of this one goal. Response may be overemphasized in much the same way, as may security also, and new experience. Usually the personality will emphasize some combination of these wishes, such as where response and recognition are combined to form a strong motive for social service, or where response and new experience go together to produce a Don Juan seeking after a life of many loves.[15] With motivations, just as with all other aspects of personality, people get their start from heredity but take their functional direction from socialization within the framework of the physical, cultural, and social environments.

A similar but more recent, and in some ways superior, theory of motivation has been developed by A. H. Maslow.[16] According to this view, man is dominated by at least five sets of goals or basic needs, organized into a "hierarchy of relative prepotency." The first of these is the physiological. It is the most elementary need and, unless satisfied, will dominate the personality to the exclusion of all others; "man lives by bread alone—when there is no bread." The second need is for safety. Man wants to feel that he is living in an orderly and predictable world, that he is safe from danger, that he is secure. If wants of the body are first taken care of, safety and security seem extremely important. The third need is for love. After the physiological and safety needs have been fairly well gratified, man turns to affection. It is then that he feels the absence of companionship, that he craves a wife, or children. He "may even forget that once, when he was hungry, he sneered at love." The fourth need is for esteem. Beyond love, and safety, and physical comfort lies the common desire for attention and

---

15 Cf. Burgess and Locke, *op. cit.*, pp. 318-23.
16 A. H. Maslow, "A Theory of Human Motivation," *Psychological Review,* 50:370-96, July, 1943. The reader will note a similarity between these goals and the four wishes of W. I. Thomas: safety is about the same thing as security; love is roughly comparable to response; esteem includes the idea of recognition; and self-actualization is at least partly parallel with new experience. In addition to the five basic needs listed above, Maslow pointed to man's common desire to preserve the preconditions of need satisfaction (e.g., freedom), and to a possible need for knowledge or intellectual satisfaction.

recognition. Man needs to feel a certain sense of importance, needs to have his ego satisfied, needs to know that he is appreciated. The fifth basic need is for self-actualization. This means that man wants to do the kind of thing for which he is fitted, to express himself as he is, to realize his capacities, to be creative. As with the others, the emergence of this need depends upon how well satisfied one has become on the "lower" need levels. These five categories are not regarded as being mutually exclusive; ordinarily a person will be partially satisfied on all of them at the same time, though satisfactions on the "upper" levels will be less complete because the others will be taken care of first.

Occasionally one or more of these needs or drives in man remains unmet. What happens then? Lack of adequate gratification on a "lower" level of the hierarchy has the effect of holding one down, so to speak, of denying him achievement on one or more of the "upper" levels. More than that, unmet needs are the source of frustration and disorganization within the personality. Maslow concluded his analysis with the following, in part:

> Any thwarting or possibility of thwarting of these basic human goals, or danger to the defenses which protect them, or to the conditions upon which they rest, is considered to be a psychological threat. With a few exceptions, all psychopathology may be partially traced to such threats. A basically thwarted man may actually be defined as a "sick" man, if we wish.[17]

EMOTIONAL MATURITY

Terman [18] conducted an intensive study of psychological factors affecting marital happiness among 792 couples. His point of view is expressed as follows:

> Our theory is that what comes out of a marriage depends upon what goes into it and that among the most important things going

---

[17] *Ibid.,* p. 395. By permission of the *Psychological Review* and the American Psychological Association.
[18] From *Psychological Factors in Marital Happiness,* by Lewis M. Terman. 1938. Courtesy of McGraw-Hill Book Co., p. 110.

into it are the attitudes, preferences, aversions, habit patterns, and emotional-response patterns which give or deny to one the aptitude for compatibility.) In other words, we believe that a large proportion of incompatible marriages are so because of a predisposition to unhappiness in one or both of the spouses. Whether by nature or by nurture, there are persons so lacking in the qualities which make for compatibility that they would be incapable of finding happiness in any marriage. There are others, less extreme, who could find it only under the most favorable circumstances; and still others whose dispositions and outlooks upon life would preserve them from acute unhappiness however unfortunately they were mated.

We might add to this last statement by saying that mature individuals are able to find a reasonable amount of happiness in marriage, not only when ill-mated, but also when confronted with social situations that are highly unfavorable. This does not lessen the importance of either good matching or a favorable culture; it does stress the primary importance of personal maturity.

An excellent picture of the traits in personality which make for happiness or unhappiness in marriage is obtained from Terman's summary descriptions: [19]

Happily married women, as a group, are characterized by kindly attitudes toward others and by the expectation of kindly attitudes in return. They do not easily take offense and are not unduly concerned about the impressions they make upon others. They do not look upon social relationships as rivalry situations. They are cooperative, do not object to subordinate roles, and are not annoyed by advice from others. Missionary and ministering attitudes are frequently evidenced in their responses. They enjoy activities that bring educational or pleasurable opportunities to others and like to do things for the dependent or underprivileged. They are methodical and painstaking in their work, attentive to detail, and careful in regard to money. In religion, morals, and politics they tend to be conservative and conventional. Their expressed attitudes imply a quiet self-assurance and a decidedly optimistic outlook upon life.

Unhappily married women, on the other hand, are characterized by emotional tenseness and by ups and downs of moods. They give evi-

19 From *Psychological Factors in Marital Happiness,* by Lewis M. Terman. 1938. Courtesy of McGraw-Hill Book Co., pp. 145-46, 155.

dence of deep-seated inferiority feelings to which they react by aggressive attitudes rather than by timidity. They are inclined to be irritable and dictatorial. Compensatory mechanisms resulting in restive striving are common. These are seen in the tendency of the unhappy wives to be active "joiners," aggressive in business, and overanxious in social life. They strive for wide circles of acquaintances but are more concerned with being important than with being liked. They are egocentric and little interested in benevolent and welfare activities, except in so far as these offer opportunities for personal recognition. They also like activities that are fraught with opportunities for romance. They are more inclined to be conciliatory in their attitudes toward men than toward women and show little of the sex antagonism that unhappily married men exhibit. They are impatient and fitful workers, dislike cautious or methodical people, and dislike types of work that require methodical and painstaking effort. In politics, religion, and social ethics they are more often radical than happily married women. . . .

Happily married men show evidence of an even and stable emotional tone. Their most characteristic reaction to others is that of cooperation. This is reflected in their attitudes toward business superiors, with whom they work well; in their attitude toward women, which reflects equalitarian ideals; and in their benevolent attitudes toward inferiors and underprivileged. In a gathering of people they tend to be unself-conscious and somewhat extroverted. As compared with unhappy husbands, they show superior initiative, a greater tendency to take responsibility, and greater willingness to give close attention to detail in their daily work. They like methodical procedures and methodical people. In money matters they are saving and cautious. Conservative attitudes are strongly characteristic of them. They usually have a favorable attitude toward religion and strongly uphold the sex mores and other social conventions.

Unhappy husbands, on the other hand, are inclined to be moody and somewhat neurotic. They are prone to feelings of social inferiority, dislike being conspicuous in public, and are highly reactive to social opinion. This sense of social insecurity is often compensated by domineering attitudes in relationships where they feel superior. They take pleasure in the commanding roles over business dependents and women, but they withdraw from a situation which would require them to play an inferior role or to compete with superiors. They often compensate this withdrawal by daydreams and power fantasies. More often than happy husbands, they are sporadic and irregular in their habits of work, dislike detail and the methodical attitude, dislike saving money, and like to wager. They more often express irreligious attitudes and are more inclined to radicalism in sex morals and politics.

The emotionally mature person is the one who is adequate to meet normal adult situations, who is in control of, and responsible for, his actions. Emotional maturity has little to do with chronological age; the one requires learning and adjustment, while the other is entirely automatic, is independent of one's wishes or efforts. Though it is generally assumed that one "grows up" as he gets older, in the emotional sense this does not always happen; and being a certain age, therefore, is no guarantee that one is ready for marriage.

Biological Adequacy.—Maturing on the biological plane is not entirely automatic, though nearly so, and is highly correlated with chronological age. Heredity sets up the potentials within each individual and the general "time table" that will determine his development. The inevitable process of unfolding for these biological potentials, wherein they mature or find expression, is called "maturation." Experiments with animals have shown that changes in the physical environment can frequently slow down or speed up the maturational process. Also, it is known that such things as climate and diet can have some effect upon human maturation. But society and culture cannot. Puberty will come when it is ready, for example, and one's stature will develop but gradually, and only to the approximate height predetermined by the genes.

Adequacy with respect to one's body functions is the first step toward competence on other levels. Without good health and heredity, the personality is handicapped and marital success becomes more difficult. This, of course, is not to imply that all biological handicaps are insurmountable; where not extremely severe, emotionally mature persons are able to find happiness in spite of them.

Outstanding biological problems as they apply to personality and marriage include the following: (1) hereditary deficiencies or blights in the germ plasm; (2) acquired illnesses or physical incapacities which are serious enough to interfere with making

a living or caring for a home; (3) sexual inabilities or infer-
tilities, such as impotency, frigidity, and sterility; and (4) immaturities in the physical development which may either mean
that the person is too young for marriage or that there have
been abnormal obstructions to the natural maturational processes and that medical or surgical attention is needed. Some of
these handicaps have been discussed earlier; others will be taken
up in later chapters. In general, it can be said that where these
exist in serious proportions marriage should either be ruled out
or delayed until the difficulty is removed. The only exceptions
would be where the difficulty is not considered serious, or, as
in the case of sterility, the handicap would not affect other
people and the couple would decide that it wants marriage in
spite of the condition.

Social Normality.—Since man is a member of society, it
follows that he is not mature until he has become oriented to
the ways of society and to the roles he must play in the total
drama. He needs to learn how to fit in with the group, to accept the essential conventions of the culture, to find security
and satisfaction in association with others. Anything short of
this leaves him either subnormal or abnormal and unprepared
for marriage.

A child who has not yet learned to play cooperatively with
others is only unsocial, not antisocial. A youngster who inno-
cently offends an adult pattern of modesty cannot be said to
be immoral, only unmoral or amoral. Socialization takes time.
It also proceeds at varying rates among different individuals.
Sometimes a person will turn against society, though aware
of the conventions he is breaking. Abnormality, in the sense
of social adjustment, really takes two forms: a failure to assimilate what culture and society prescribe, and a rebellion or
turning against group patterns. This is not to ignore the role
of the reformer who seeks to change culture along desirable
lines.

Marriages are usually more successful when the mates have
had a fair degree of education, either formal or informal. To
be most successful in life one needs to be aware of the culture

around him, and to be most happy in marriage one needs to know and assimilate major principles upon which such happiness is based. It is particularly important that marriage partners be willing and able to play the roles expected of them, that the husband be prepared for earning a living and the wife for homemaking. There are instances of mates finding happiness in patterns other than the traditional—sometimes even when they are reversed, with the wife earning the money and the husband taking care of the home—but these are exceptions.

A very common inadequacy is the tendency to be overly shy and self-conscious in group situations. Shyness most generally comes from early psychogenic conditioning wherein the individual, during socialization, fails somewhat in his adjustment to the outside world; he draws within himself, becomes introvertive. The art of getting along with others, of mixing well in society, of making and holding friends, is of great significance in family relationships. Burgess and Cottrell not only found successful marriage correlated with high educational attainment, considerable church activity, and membership in a large number of organizations, but also found that those mates are most happy who have many friends.[20] Being at home with the social arts gives one a real advantage in courtship and marriage.

It has been found that marriage operates best when its participants are essentially conservative and conforming. Radical and rebellious individuals are likely to be emotionally unstable and to reflect this by getting into trouble with others. Chronic conflict with parents, with brothers and sisters, with acquaintances outside the home, or with the law or culture in general is likely to carry over into the marriage relationship of the spouses. Since marriage is surrounded by numerous conventions it is generally the conventional type of person who is best able to make it succeed.

Another phase of social and emotional maturing is learning how to be cooperative with others. This requires a certain amount of ego adjustment during the socialization process.

[20] Ernest W. Burgess and Leonard S. Cottrell, *Predicting Success or Failure in Marriage* (New York: Prentice-Hall, Inc., 1939), pp. 121-32.

Young children are naturally selfish, but normally they grow out of it. Some never do, and we call them "spoiled." Marriage is a "We" proposition; it requires its members to put self-interest secondary to group interest. Failure is made imminent by such traits as selfishness, egotism, stubbornness, and domination. Success is made possible, and more probable, by such traits as kindliness, thoughtfulness, willingness to share, a sense of fairness, and respect for others.

Acceptance of Responsibility.—Extreme dependency upon others is a mark of weakness. To say that maturity requires a certain amount of conformity and cooperation is not to say that these must be carried to the point of servility. Mature individuals are able to stand on their own feet, make their own decisions, and accept responsibility; they have poise and confidence, independence and initiative. Every child needs to be given increasing degrees of freedom as he matures and progressively proves himself capable of new responsibility. Without this he is likely to remain immature. The external controls and restraints necessarily imposed upon children by parents in the early years of life must be made to yield gradually to self-control.

In this connection, it is well to note the great importance of "emancipation from the home." Some individuals never cut loose from the strong family ties established during childhood, never become sufficiently "weaned" to be able to successfully establish a home of their own. Parents are frequently responsible for this condition in children by being overprotective and domineering.

Chronic indecision frequently shows itself in personalities that have been kept free of responsibility. It is one way of attempted escape, of trying to dodge problems that seem to be difficult. Before marriage everyone needs to be adult enough to have his goals and purposes pretty well defined, though remaining flexible and adaptable enough to meet new situations as they arise.

Capacity for Love.—Some marriages fail because of childish or undeveloped love interests on the part of the mates. It may be "romantic infantilism" that is blinding them to reality. Or it may be faulty sex education that has warped their perspective. If the latter, there is likely to be disharmony over sex in marriage because one or both mates is either cold and unresponsive or has been conditioned in the direction of excesses and perversions.

Occasionally young people fail to make a heterosexual transition (the transferring of their affectional interests to those of the opposite sex). Normally every person passes through three stages of love development: (1) the stage of self-love where his interests are largely in himself; (2) the stage represented by strong friendships or attachments to others of the same sex; and (3) the stage of attractions and involvements with the opposite sex. It is during adolescence that this last phase really begins. Where undue discouragements or obstacles come in to block this natural but new interest, the person may remain fixated on one of the earlier levels of love attachment, which is almost certain to handicap his marriage later on.

Peace of Mind.—It can be said that one has achieved emotional maturity when he has learned to be at ease with himself and others. He is in control of his emotions. He can take advice and criticism without getting ruffled. He can bear tension and strain without blowing up; but will direct his hostilities along socially accepted channels instead. He has a sense of humor. He has patience and is able to maintain suspended judgment. He is settled and adaptable, both at the same time.

Neurotic individuals are those who lack this calm and balance. They are filled with emotional anxieties which cause them to be nervous, rattled, irregular, irritable, moody, sulky, jealous, overpossessive, and inclined to worry. Behavior patterns are apt to be childish or adolescent—crying to get one's own way, holding grudges when offended, kicking the tire when it goes flat, throwing down the tennis racket when the game is lost.

To a large extent emotional maturity rests upon emotional security. Without peace of mind life becomes erratic and fretful. Culture imposes many of the emotional disturbances which handicap marriage. There are methods of therapy, though treatment is often difficult and expensive. Prevention is always the more profitable. Providing children with a happy home life is a first step in that direction.

The Happiness Habit.—For those who achieve it, happiness is both a contagion and a habit. It is a contagion in that one's temperament becomes affected or molded by the social climate within which he grows; children of happily married parents are more likely to be happy themselves; those happy in life are the ones most likely to be happy in their marriages, and vice versa. It is a habit in the sense that personality tendencies established early usually persist; patterns of optimism or pessimism picked up in the home environment tend to carry over and to either make or mar the relationships which follow; persons happy during childhood are the ones most likely to find later happiness in marriage.

Nothing, perhaps, is so crucial to the success of marriage as is the factor of personal maturity. Society provides the setting within which personalities develop and marriage operates; it wields an influence, therefore, makes marriage difficult or easy as the case may be. But society is sometimes used as a convenient target for blame when marriage fails. We hear such expressions as "The odds were against me" and "I didn't have a chance." In the final analysis it is the people who are responsible—for their own marriages, directly; but also for society.

Growing up involves many things, some of which are largely automatic and others which require learning and effort. Though a person may be mature chronologically and biologically, if he remains relatively undeveloped on any of the mental, social, or emotional levels he cannot be said to be adult and hence is not ready for marriage.

We have been writing of maturity and immaturity and of happiness and unhappiness almost as though there were distinct categories into which every person could be placed. This has seemed necessary for purposes of simplification. It must be remembered, however, that all these terms are relative. No individual is ever completely mature or happy, nor is the opposite likely to exist. Actually, every marriage experiences a certain amount of failure along with its success. What matters is the *degree* of maturity or happiness that is achieved.

Problems and Projects

1. Should anyone be denied the right to marry? If so, who? Why?

2. If acquired characteristics cannot be inherited, how have changes come about in man's physical nature since the days of the cave man?

3. What is inherited? Answer with reference to several sources recently consulted.

4. Check recent sources for current information on the Rh blood factor and its effects upon childbearing.

5. Discuss the effects upon society of the tendency of college graduates to fail to reproduce themselves.

6. Why are the early years of a child's life so vital in the development of his personality? Discuss and illustrate.

7. What are some of the serious mistakes that parents and families make which may result in a maladjusted child or later in a poorly adjusted adult?

8. Relate experiences from childhood which have affected your present attitudes toward marriage.

9. Consider the different ways in which you sometimes react to your failure to obtain some object or to achieve some goal you desire very much. Rate these reactions as to their relative degree of maturity.

10. How may the shy individual approach the problem of making a better social adjustment?

11. Apply each of W. I. Thomas's four wishes to some practical situation of personality development.

12. "Happiness is both a contagion and a habit." Present supporting evidence from things you have either experienced or observed.

Selected Readings

Becker, Howard, and Hill, Reuben (eds.). *Family, Marriage, and Parenthood*. Boston: D. C. Heath & Co., 1948. Chaps. vi, "Producing Marriageable Personalities"; xiv, "Heredity and the Family."

Bergler, Edmund. *Divorce Won't Help*. New York: Harper & Bros., 1948.

Bossard, James H. S. *The Sociology of Child Development*. New York: Harper & Bros., 1948.

Burgess, Ernest W., and Locke, Harvey J. *The Family: From Institution to Companionship*. New York: American Book Co., 1945. Part II, "The Family and Personality Development."

Duvall, Evelyn Millis, and Hill, Reuben. *When You Marry*. Boston: D. C. Heath & Co., 1945. Chap. i, "What You Bring to Marriage."

Nimkoff, Meyer F. *Marriage and the Family*. Boston: Houghton Mifflin Co., 1947. Chaps. x, "Heredity and Personality"; xi, "The Family as the Nursery of Human Nature."

Scheinfeld, Amram. *You and Heredity*. New York: Frederick A. Stokes Co., 1939.

Strecker, E. A. *Their Mother's Sons*. New York: J. B. Lippincott Co., 1946.

Truxal, Andrew G., and Merrill, Francis E. *The Family in American Culture*. New York: Prentice-Hall, Inc., 1947. Chap. xvii, "The Social Nature of Personality."

Waller, Willard. *The Family: A Dynamic Interpretation*. New York: The Dryden Press, Inc., 1938. Part I, "Formation of Personality in the Parental Family."

Young, Kimball. *Personality and Problems of Adjustment*. New York: Appleton-Century-Crofts, Inc., 1940. Part I, "The Foundations of Personality."

Chapter 4

MEN AND WOMEN

Every marriage involves at least two individuals. Its success, therefore, depends upon more than the situations which surround it or even the separate personalities which compose it. There is the matter of mate combination and personal interaction. Not only do men and women need to be personally prepared and socially oriented to be most happy in their marriages, they also need to be well matched and to understand themselves and the opposite sex, each in relation to the other.

Must there always be a "battle of the sexes"? We think not. Though different in some ways, men and women are nevertheless very much alike. They both belong to the same human species, perform the same body functions, are broadly motivated by the same sort of things, and live generally the same kind of lives. Though physiological differences may mean that complete understanding of the other will not be possible, better understanding is both possible and desirable. Males and females are complementary to each other; antagonisms, where they exist, are learned, not natural. There is need for some "unlearning" on the part of many, followed by a "relearning" in the direction of greater understanding and cooperation.

DIFFERENTIATION

It will aid our analysis to see first of all how men and women differ, and why.

The Sex Ratio.—Life begins with a preponderance of males. There are at least 120 males conceived to every 100 females (some believe this ratio to be as high as 150 or more males to every 100 females).[1] Reasons for such a large male surplus are not entirely known, though it is thought that sperms containing characteristics for maleness are a little lighter in weight or are otherwise more agile, so that they travel faster and more frequently reach the egg first, than do sperms with female determining characteristics. Credence is given to this theory in that Y chromosomes are known to be somewhat smaller in size, which should make the sperms containing them lighter in weight than are the sperms carrying heavier X chromosomes.

The sex ratio at birth, though also showing a surplus of males, is considerably lower than at the time of conception. It remains fairly constant at about 105 or 106 male live births to every 100 female.[2] Explanation for this lower ratio at birth, compared with conception, is found in a higher prenatal male death rate. The male stillbirth rate stays consistently above that for the female, which quite naturally reduces man's initial numerical advantage over woman.

Comparisons in live-birth sex ratios reveal both variation from group to group and fluctuation from time to time. But differences are usually small. The following facts seem significant: (1) The Negro ratio is below that of the white; (2) births from young parents show higher sex ratios than from parents who are older; (3) live-birth sex ratios go up during and following war; and (4) the long-time trend in this country is toward a higher sex ratio at birth. Since there has been little real research on the subject, we can only speculate as to why these differences exist. There is good reason for believing, however, that the major factor is variation in the stillbirth rate, which, as has been seen, affects males more than females. Negroes have more stillbirths per family than do whites, due to their lower economic and social levels, and this higher rate probably eliminates male embryos in greater proportion than it does female, thereby reducing the sex ratio of live births. So

[1] Amram Scheinfeld, *Women and Men* (New York: Harcourt, Brace & Co., 1944), p. 31 and *passim*.
[2] Hope T. Eldridge and Jacob S. Siegel, "The Changing Sex Ratio in the United States," *American Journal of Sociology*, 52:224-34, November, 1946. The live birth ratio of males to females is shown to average 105.9 for the white population and 103.0 for the Negro.

too, young parents, being usually the most healthy and fit, have fewer stillbirths and hence produce higher sex ratios in their children. Similarly, wartime means more marriages, younger parenthood, and therefore fewer stillbirths and higher sex ratios in the offspring. Finally, our decreasing of the stillbirth rate in recent years through better nutrition and better medical care has permitted proportionately more males to survive the prenatal period than formerly, which in turn has tended to increase the live-birth sex ratio.[3]

For the 1940 population of the United States taken as a whole, all ages considered, there were 100.7 males for every 100.0 females. This was a near balance between the sexes. Earlier counts had shown greater male surpluses due mainly to heavier immigration in earlier periods (it being well known that males migrate in greater numbers than do females). Present estimates indicate that there are now a few more females than males—for the first time in our national history.

As age increases there is a gradual diminishing of the male's initial numerical advantage. After age fifty females start to predominate numerically, and continue to do so throughout the rest of the life span. This observation is for a standardized population calculated from uniform birth and death rates; for the actual population as enumerated in the 1940 census there was shown a female surplus in ages 20 through 39 and then again from 60 on up. One reason for this discrepancy is the tendency of middle-aged women to report their ages as younger than they actually are.[4]

This shift from a male to a female surplus throughout the life span finds explanation in a consistently higher male death rate. From conception through until death males experience greater difficulty in surviving than do females. The median age at death is now about 63 for the male and nearly 67 for the female, a difference of practically four years. This is why women predominate numerically in the older ages and it is a major factor in producing the condition of almost three times

[3] *Ibid., passim.* Cf. also, Paul H. Landis, *Population Problems* (New York: American Book Co., 1943), pp. 251-76.
[4] Eldridge and Siegel, *op. cit.,* pp. 224-34.

as many widows as widowers in this country. Reasons for a higher male mortality probably lie in both nature and nurture. Higher prenatal and infant death rates in the male give evidence that he is biologically handicapped to start with. So also do the facts that he is more susceptible to most of the diseases and that he more frequently enters life with organic weaknesses and malformations. On the side of environment, man lives a less sheltered life—is more exposed to the hazards of occupation, warfare, and the like.

Considered ecologically, there is a male excess in the Western states compared with a female surplus on the East Coast, and males predominate in farming areas while females outnumber them in the city. Migration is the explanation here, there being relatively greater tendencies for women to move to the city and for men to migrate westward. Imbalance in the sex ratio tends to have certain effects upon the patterns of courtship and marriage. One of these is opportunity for marriage. To illustrate, the rural female living in the Western United States has some advantage so far as mate selection and marriage opportunity are concerned, as has also the urban male living in the East.

Thus there are both biological and sociological factors operating to determine how the sexes are balanced at any given time or place or with any given group. Nature gives man an initial advantage numerically, but puts him at a disadvantage from the standpoint of survival. Environmental factors—diet, medicine, working conditions, war or peace—act as selective agents in the survival process. Migration then shuffles the population, deciding finally on the composition of its various segments.

Control over the sex ratio is only partially in man's possession. He can improve living conditions and legislate certain behavior patterns that will alter the balance, but he cannot as yet determine the sex of the child at the time it is conceived. There have been claims to the contrary, most of which must be relegated to the area of superstition and quackery. Research continues on the problem and in time science may solve it, but until then parents will just about have to take what nature sends.

It is interesting to speculate as to what would happen if parents could establish the same control over the sex of a child as contraception has permitted them to have over the number of children, if they could have a boy when they wanted it and a girl when they wanted it. Particular families would likely show a more evenly balanced sex ratio than is now the case. But what about society as a whole? Would the male preference which has been characteristic of the past, and which is likely still present in this day,[5] continue? As women become more emancipated and the sex roles more nearly equalized, would the cultural definitions concerning sex values also undergo a change, would men lose preference and cease to be surplus as a result of their losing special privilege? What kind of sex ratios would warlike peoples try to establish? Though most questions of this kind must for the present remain largely unanswered, it seems likely that militarism would stimulate a higher sex ratio among those who were able to control it, while equality and democracy would lead in an opposite direction toward a nearer balance.

Birth control has made possible one type of sex ratio control not commonly recognized. By stopping the family with a child that represents the desired sex, parents, with luck, can increase the proportion of the kind preferred. For example, if males are preferred and a family of three or four children desired, parents will likely stop with the third child if it is a boy but try again if it is a girl. Winston first suggested this phenomenon when he found a disproportionately high sex ratio among the last children of completed families, indicating a male preference and the possible use of birth control as a selective device.[6] It doesn't determine what the sex of any particular child shall be, of course, but it does exert some control over the sex proportion in the family and in the population.

Some Biological Comparisons.—The usual classification of persons into two sex groups, male and female, where it is

---

[5] For one evidence for the persistence of a male preference see Harold T. Christensen, "Mormon Fertility: A Survey of Student Opinion," *American Journal of Sociology*, 53:270-75, January, 1948.

[6] Sanford Winston, "Birth Control and the Sex-Ratio at Birth," *American Journal of Sociology*, 38:225-31, September, 1932.

assumed that all within each group are pretty much alike, does not present a correct picture. Sex is more of a continuum than it is a dichotomy, with gradations running all the way from extreme maleness on the one side to extreme femaleness on the other. Some males are more male than others, so to speak, and the same goes for females.

Individuals at or near dead center on this continuum are known as hermaphrodites. True hermaphrodites, those with both ovaries and testes within their single bodies, are extremely rare. False or pseudo hermaphrodites, those with only ovaries or testes (not both) but also with some of the secondary sex characteristics of the opposite sex, are much more common. Hermaphrodites are sometimes referred to as "the third sex." They are not that, but are only unfortunate enough to have been born in a mid and somewhat neutral position, or condition, with their sexual capacities and tendencies all confused. Nature on occasion plays strange tricks.

Surgery and endocrinology have been used successfully in some of these cases, helping nature decide which line of sexual development such individuals shall take. In rare instances people have been known to change from one sex to the other quite naturally, without intent and without the aid of medical science.

But even the so-called "normal" individuals are never either all-male or all-female. There is a blending of sex within each person. Everyone is, in a sense, bisexual. Proof for this is found in two facts: (1) The reproductive organs of the male and the female are in many cases homologous to each other, with each sex having some rudimentary organs of the opposite sex along with the developed organs of its own sex. (2) Both male and female endocrine secretions (hormones) are common to both sexes; though male hormones predominate in the male, there are female hormones there as well; and though the female is served mainly by female secretions, her body produces and uses some of the male hormones also.

A word or two more about endocrinology and the hormones may prove useful. There are a number of ductless glands located throughout the body, each of which emits its own particular type of hormone for its own particular purposes. While all these purposes or functions are not yet known, many are, and it is known that the hormones are very powerful and necessary body regulators. Whenever one's delicate hormone balance is greatly disturbed, therefore, whether by the removal of a gland or its malfunctioning, serious abnormalities may develop. At least four of these glands have something to do with sex—the *gonads* (testes and ovaries), the *pituitary,* the *adrenal,* and the *thyroid.*

The gonads serve two important functions, only the second of which concerns us at the moment: (1) They produce the sperms and ova necessary to reproduction and (2) they secrete hormones (testosterone in the male and estrogen in the female) which profoundly affect the secondary sex characteristics of the body as well as the sexual behavior of the individual. Where the gonads are removed, individuals either do not develop the secondary characteristics peculiar to their sex (if removed early in life) or they revert to a more neutral position sexually and lose part or all of their sexual desire. Ailing or undersexed individuals can frequently be helped by hormone treatments taken under the direction of a physician.

The other glands mentioned affect one's sexuality less directly. The pituitary, a small gland located at the base of the brain, is exceedingly important to normal life and health. One of its functions is the control of general body growth. Another is the partial regulation of the reproductive processes—it stimulates the testes and the ovaries to function normally and it is related to the contraction of the uterus in childbirth. The adrenal glands, located in the proximity of the kidneys, emit their secretions during emotional excitement—as preparation for an emergency. Their malfunctioning is known to sometimes cause disturbances in the menstrual cycle and to influence masculinity in women. The thyroid gland, located in the neck, is the general regulator of body metabolism and influencer of body energy; deficiencies in the thyroid hormone result in slowed activity and underdevelopment, while oversecretion here produces an excess of activity leading to excitability, nervousness, and tension. The sex function is indirectly affected by the influence of the thyroid gland over the activity of the other sex-connected glands.[7]

Anatomical differences between the sexes are pretty generally understood and will need concern us here only briefly. The following is intended to present major comparisons in summary fashion: [8]

1. Genital structures differentiate the roles of men and women in reproduction. Man has testes, a penis, etc.; while woman is equipped more elaborately with ovaries, clitoris, vagina, uterus, etc.[9] Not only is woman's sexual nature more complex in organization, but woman, because of this fact, remains closer attached to the entire reproductive process. Man, for example, has never yet been made pregnant; nor has he been able to nurse a child.

2. Men, on the average, are larger and stronger (in the muscular sense) than women. They are taller; their bones are heavier; and their muscles represent a larger proportion of the total body weight. These facts, plus the additional one that man is freed of the child-bearing function, give him a real advantage over woman so far as physical strength is concerned.

3. In body contour, males show wider shoulders, narrower hips, and more angular features. Females, in contrast, have relatively narrow and slanting shoulders, broader hips because of a wider pelvic bone made necessary for childbirth, and more rounded or curved features in general. The breasts are well developed whereas with males they are only rudimentary. Part of the roundness and lack of angularity in females is due to a layer of fat found just under the skin, and found more with them than with males. As this acts as insulation, the female has less difficulty keeping warm.

4. As to hair distribution, males have more on the face, on the chest, and in general all over the body. At the pubic region it is more diffuse than with females, and takes more the shape of an upward-

---

[7] For a brief treatment of the influence of the endocrine glands upon the developing and functioning of sex, see August A. Werner, "Sex Behavior and Problems of the Climacteric," Part V, chap. v, in *Successful Marriage,* ed. Morris Fishbein and Ernest W. Burgess (New York: Doubleday & Co., 1947), pp. 472-73.

[8] Cf. Scheinfeld, *op. cit.,* pp. 148-49 and *passim.*

[9] Important as an understanding of sex anatomy is, that is not the task of this book. There is a growing list of reliable literature on this subject which can be found catalogued in any good library. Some of these titles are listed at the end of this chapter. For an excellent brief treatment see Robert L. Dickinson, "Anatomy and Physiology of the Sex Organs," Part II, chap. i, in *Successful Marriage,* ed. Morris Fishbein and Ernest W. Burgess (New York: Doubleday & Cc., 1947), pp. 69-91.

pointing triangle. Males also exhibit a greater tendency toward baldness.

5. Physical development comes faster for the female than for the male. This is true during the prenatal stage, and there is even some evidence that birth takes place a few days earlier where the pregnancy produces a girl. It is true after birth as well. Girls mature more rapidly in their skeletal structures and in their total body processes. Puberty comes to most girls at about twelve, whereas with boys it is not until a year or so later. Physical maturity is complete for the female somewhere around twenty, though not for the male until he is twenty-three or twenty-four.

Masculinity and Femininity.—Individuals are born male or female, but learn to become masculine or feminine.[10] It is the biological factors in sexual differentiation that have been our concern up to the present. We have seen that sex is determined almost entirely by nature; that man's control in this regard is extremely limited (though by birth control, death control, migration, and the like he can exercise some influence over the sex ratio). We have also seen that sex is a relative term, that everyone is to a small extent both male and female, and that people vary greatly in degree as well as in direction of their sexual development. What we have not fully recognized as yet is that sexuality is more than biology, that it takes more than the genes and the hormones to explain why men and women behave as they do. Masculinization and feminization are parts of the larger learning process called socialization, discussed in Chapter 3. Through exposure to society, individuals in varying degrees learn how to curb their natural impulses and to assume the roles of men and women that their culture prescribes.

Thus, little girls are encouraged to play with dolls and discouraged from being rough or aggressive. They imitate their mothers by playing house. In time they learn how to sit properly, and they learn that there are certain rules of conduct for being "ladylike." Boys, on the other hand, find themselves teased when they play with their sisters' things, but approved

---

10 Cf. Evelyn Millis Duvall and Reuben Hill, *When You Marry* (Boston: D. C. Heath & Co., 1945), p. 9.

by all when they act "like a man." They therefore tend to identify themselves with the father's role and to assume the attitudes and the mannerisms that go with it. In this way boys and girls become men and women according to the established patterns around them. A female infant isn't any more frightened by a mouse than is a male, for example, but she stands a better chance of learning this somewhat typical feminine response as time goes on. Imitation of that which is made to seem attractive or proper, together with pressure in the direction of social expectation, incline children to the masculine and feminine roles. Culture is changing, however, and today there is less difference between the roles expected of boys and girls than formerly.

A sexual division of labor is to be found in every society. Generally speaking, man has handled the governing function, warfare, and economic production outside the home, while woman has kept busy preparing meals, fixing clothing, taking care of children, and the like. Division of labor, in other words, has mainly followed the biological lines of cleavage between the sexes—man taking up those pursuits that are most compatible with his superior physical strength and woman keeping to those activities that are closely associated with her childbearing function. Though the basic roles of men and women are thus related to biological differences, they are nevertheless cultural in nature and are highly variable from society to society and from time to time. Women are expected to be rather submissive in most societies, for example; though in some they are aggressive, and this aggressiveness is accepted.[11] The modern American female is more open and less inhibited than was her grandmother. But whatever the culture, men and women will be molded to conform.

Conformity, though, is never perfect; there are always those who remain only partially socialized in this respect—remain as masculine women and feminine men. We told earlier of the anatomical abnormalities and hormone malfunctionings that occasionally cause men and women to be sexually off balance.

---

11 See Margaret Mead, *Sex and Temperament in Three Primitive Societies* (New York: William Morrow & Co., 1935), p. 335.

Later, in Chapter 5, we shall give brief treatment to the phenomenon of homosexuality. Here we can only emphasize the fact that virtually all problems of this nature have sociological and psychological roots, while it seems probable that only a few result directly or solely from the biological. Abnormal sexuality is usually the result of unfortunate conditioning, of distortion in the learning process.

We now present a partial list of personality contrasts between men and women as present in contemporary American culture. These are to be considered as tentative propositions only, based upon observations and researches that are as yet inadequate. They are to be understood as the products of both heredity and environment in interaction.[12]

1. Though there is nothing in science to prove that either sex has more intelligence than the other, men seem to do better in mechanical, mathematical, and abstract reasoning tests, while women usually excel in tests based upon memory, language ability, artistic taste, and social awareness. Sometimes it is said that men are interested more in impersonal things, in facts as facts; while women are primarily interested in personal things, in people, in human relationships. Men more often indulge in "shop talk," while women talk about people—only to be accused of gossiping. It is said, too, that women have greater difficulty keeping a conversation objective, are more inclined to become personal or to take offense from a statement not intended that way.

2. Men are more aggressive than women. This is shown in their greater tendency to be pugnacious, to get in trouble with the law, and to pursue the opposite sex rather than be pursued. Women, in contrast, are more submissive, docile, "domesticated." There is no question but that part of this difference is to be explained in biology, by the genes and the hormones. But it is also highly probable that culture has had a lot to do with it. Denied until recently any real opportunity for open or aggressive maneuvering, woman has developed an art of being pursued and of getting her way indirectly and by subtle devices. This fact may also explain why women seem to have more insight into men than men have regarding women—they have had to study men more in order to better control them and adapt to them.

3. The sex drive of the male, in comparison with that of the female, is more constant, more easily aroused, and more physical. That of the

---

[12] Cf. Amram Scheinfeld, *op. cit., passim.*

female, though just as real, is more complex, more involved with affection and emotion, and, one might even say, more spiritual. There are a number of facts which will bear out this generalization: It is the male who most often seeks premarital intimacy; female frigidity is many times more common than male impotence; husbands desire sexual intercourse more frequently on the average than do wives; male prostitution is an almost unheard of phenomenon. Here again, part of the explanation lies in the different biological natures of the two sexes and part in the divergent cultural patterns to which the two are exposed. These are points that will be referred to again in discussions which follow.

THE QUESTION OF EQUALITY

To say that men and women are different does not necessarily imply that they are unequal. Differentiation can be either horizontal or vertical, both of which mean, when applied to men and women, that the sexes are separate and apart from each other, but only the latter of which implies that one sex is above or superior to the other. What is the truth of the matter? Is sexual differentiation vertical or is it horizontal?

The "Weaker Sex."—There has been a great deal of bantering back and forth between the sexes, wild claiming, and selfish exploiting, all of which have only further clouded the issue. Masculine ethnocentrism has been responsible for much of the misunderstanding and injustice extant in this area, it being "admitted" on man's part that he is unquestionably the superior, that woman is by nature the weaker sex. This is an assumption that needs further examining.

There is nothing in science to show that either sex is innately superior to the other. Each is superior in some respects, and inferior in others; together they are complementary and equal.

As to sheer physical strength, man is superior, due partly to a larger and stronger bone and muscle structure by nature and partly to greater development through more exercise.[13]

---

[13] Woman in our culture ordinarily lives a much more sheltered and sedentary life than does man, which means that her muscles are used less and therefore remain relatively undeveloped. In some societies, primitive and otherwise, where women are called upon to do the heavy work, they are known to possess physical strength not much below that of man.

Then, too, being free of the childbearing function, he is left with other advantages which he has often exploited. It is this greater physical power that has made it possible for man to define and control things pretty much in his own way. Thus the saying, "It is a man's world."

But in other ways woman gives evidence of a superior physical nature. Her chances of survival are greater than man's, both before birth and after (woman outlives man on an average by three or four years, partly because man is exposed to greater hazards, it is true, but partly also because she has a tougher constitution.) She is more resistant to disease, can seemingly endure pain more easily, and is not as plagued with hereditary defects. Feeble-mindedness, insanity, tuberculosis, and many other afflictions of this sort are more frequent with the male than with the female.

Insofar as science can discover, the sexes are also equal in mental ability. Psychological tests show divergent lines of specialization in the mental processes, as noted earlier, but there is nothing that can be interpreted as placing either sex above the other in total ability. Though anthropological measurements indicate that the male brain is slightly larger than the female, the difference is almost infinitesimal. It must also be kept in mind that man can be expected to have a larger brain to go with his larger body, and that in the last analysis it is the quality not the quantity of the brain that really counts. (Witness the abnormally large heads of some feeble-minded individuals.)

Another claimed evidence of man's intellectual superiority is the fact that genius seems to manifest itself more in males. Judged by our standards of success (which in a man's world are largely man's standards) more men than women have achieved in one way or another. It is true that most of our great statesmen, philosophers, scientists, artists, and literary figures of the past have been men, and that among *Who's Who* listings today there is revealed the same imbalance between the sexes. But it must be remembered: first, that woman, because of childbearing and social discrimination, has not had the same opportunity to achieve as has man in a man's world;

and second, that her achievements have been along different
lines, in ways that bring little publicity or public recognition.
As Bowman puts it:

> . . . to say that women are inferior to men because there have been
> more male than female geniuses is absurd, because in fulfilling their
> traditional role women have had neither the need nor the opportunity
> for exhibiting the particular type of genius that men exhibit in science,
> invention, and the arts. It would be just as sensible to reverse the
> picture and say that men are inferior to women because throughout
> history men have been poorer mothers and homemakers.[14]

Man not only achieves eminence more regularly than woman,
but he also fails life more frequently. We have observed how
both mental deficiency and mental breakdown show higher
incidences among males. It should now be pointed out that
the male suicide rate is three or four times as high as the
female, and that in the area of vice and crime males outdo
females by an even greater margin. Regarding the follies of
the flesh, man can more accurately than woman be called "the
weaker sex."

It would seem, therefore, that man tends more toward the
extreme and woman toward the mean so far as ability and
social adjustment are concerned. Just how much of this is
natural and how much cultural no one knows, though it is
probable that each of these factors has played its part.

Nearly everywhere and at all times in society man has had
the dominant or controlling position. With few exceptions,
woman has had to submit to the wishes of her male counterpart and in some instances she has virtually been his slave.
Man, with his greater physical strength and his freeness from
childbearing, has been able to define the situation quite a bit to
his own advantage.

Can we say, then, that neither really is "the weaker sex";
that there are differences, specializations, but no general subor-
dinations and superordinations so far as nature is concerned?
While some males are superior to some females, the reverse

can also be said; and these two facts tend to balance each other.

When we come to the way society is organized, however, it can be observed that there *is* a stratification, a vertical differentiation between the sexes, and that man has probably been given most of the advantages. This, of course, in no sense means that he is innately superior.

The Emancipation of Woman.—There is little need to labor the fact that in most cultures woman's social status has been significantly and consistently lower than man's. Suffice it to remind the reader that in some groups the husband has had the right of life and death over her; in others she could be beaten or abused almost at his will; and practically never, until recently, has woman been privileged to hold office or otherwise to participate in public affairs alongside man. She has been discriminated against politically, economically, socially, and morally. We are not saying that woman's lot has always been an unfortunate or an unhappy one. There is a dignity about motherhood, a contentment to be found in home-making. Men have very frequently loved their women, furthermore, and have been kind and considerate toward them—though with the power to do otherwise. What we are saying is that society has generally placed woman at a disadvantage, left her pretty much at the mercy of man, treated her as an inferior. Even kindness, if it is paternalistic and condescending, can be no real substitute for the kind of justice that is born of equality.

The recent trend, particularly in the western world, has been toward an equalization of sex roles. Woman, in other words, is being emancipated, is becoming equal in the sense of having equal opportunity, free in the sense of having the prejudices and pressures that have been directed toward her gradually removed. She can now vote, has been able to in this country for approximately three decades. She can hold public office, though group opinion and childbearing responsibilities still work against it, and one seldom sees a woman mayor, congress member, or other prominent public official. There are a few outstanding examples of women in public office,

however, and the future is likely to bring increasingly more.[15]
Women have made great inroads in the field of economic production and can now hold down just about any job, whether it
be common labor, clerical, business, or professional. During
1947 women made up 28 per cent of the total labor force, and
approximately half of these were married women.[16] This was
a drop from the wartime peak; but it is still substantially
higher than the prewar level, and it reflects the general trend
and probably represents a permanent addition to the number
and proportion of women gainfully employed. Among other
evidences of a trend toward sex equality are these: the recent
removal of some of the discriminatory legal statutes; the large
and growing enrollment of women in college; and the increasing amount of freedom females express in such things
as dress, asking for dates, and proposing marriage.

It would be a mistake, nevertheless, to assume that social
equality between the sexes has now been achieved. Woman
has come a long way in the short span of one hundred years,
but if equality be her goal she is not yet there. Public opinion
keeps her out of some activities and handicaps her in others.
She is the last to be hired by some employers and the first to
be fired. Her rate of pay is frequently less than for man, even
when her work performance is the same. She cannot be as free
in asking for dates or in proposing marriage, and in cases
involving sexual indiscretion she receives the greater condemnation. Family laws, while improving in some states, continue in others to discriminate against woman regarding property rights, place of residence, and the like. All in all, it would
seem that this is still a man's world.

Margaret Mead has suggested that the full implications of
sex equality are not often realized. We have built glamour
around man's work and given priority to the considerations

<hr>

[15] Cf. Virginia Rishel, "More Women in Government?" *American Association of University Women Journal,* November, 1948, pp. 21-24. At the time
this article was written women composed only about "1.3 percent of the
representation in Congress, and from two to 27 percent of those in state legislatures," p. 21.

[16] *Business Week,* March 20, 1948, pp. 114-15. See also Paul C. Glick,
"Family Life and Full Employment," *American Journal of Sociology,* 54:520-
29, May, 1949, p. 527.

that pertain to it. At the same time we have robbed home-making of most of its public dignity; what is there to being "just a housewife"? Equal roles for men and women would suggest that men take an equal interest in the children and the home. How many men, when asked what they are going to do, would answer in this manner: "I am going to be a lawyer —unless I marry, of course," and would explain themselves by saying that if they married they would have to live on a farm because that would be best for the children, which would mean giving up law? Not many! Yet women are constantly placing personal ambitions secondary to family welfare.[17]

Over the last quarter of a century there has been before Congress a proposal for an Equal Rights Amendment. It reads: "Equality of rights under the law shall not be denied or abridged by the United States or by any state on account of sex." Supporters of this amendment point to the obvious discriminations against women that exist in many state statutes and common law practices at the present time—not permitting women to work in certain occupations, or at night, or if they are married; setting female wage and salary levels lower than for men; allowing only men to serve on juries; not letting the wife decide on her own domicile; giving the husband various discriminatory rights over the wife's earnings and property. They argue that legal equality established in this way would relieve woman of her present inferiority feelings and would give her a chance to develop and function in dignity and with justice. There are those who oppose the idea, too, as should be evident from the fact that the bill has not yet passed Congress. One reason for the proposal's not getting farther than it has may be that the majority of Congress members are men. Opponents consist of both women and men, however, and they reason that women need certain protection under the law and that such an amendment, if passed, might cause women to neglect home and family "all the more." Legislation must frequently wait upon shifts in ideology. Public opinion is changing in support of sex equality. Whether this will result in the

---

[17] Margaret Mead, "What Is Happening to the American Family?" *Journal of Social Casework*, 28:323-30, November, 1947.

passing of equal rights legislation at some future time remains to be seen.

Meaning of Sex Equality.—Equality does not require identity. People can be dissimilar and still be on the same level. Nature made men and women different as classes but did not make them unequal. Society then established divergent roles for the two sexes, corresponding roughly with the biological differentiations already established. But the social alignment between men and women somehow or other got tipped at the axis; it tended to become vertical in arrangement, with men having most of the advantage; sex assumed status.

Recent developments have been away from stratification within marriage, and in the direction of partnerships. The older patriarchal family is yielding to an emerging democratic or equalitarian type. The newer assumption is that of a love relationship based upon a horizontal division of labor; it is the application of democracy to marriage.

Sex equality, therefore, shall mean that neither men nor women will be discriminated against because of their sex. They will have somewhat different roles to play, both biological and cultural, but roles of equal dignity and opportunity. There will be individual differences in ability and achievement, but these will not be drawn along sex lines. It will be a differentiated equality where opportunity is the same for all but where men and women are given certain divided functions. The sexes will be equal, each within its own sphere.

PROBLEMS IN ROLE ADJUSTMENT

Attainment of the goal of differentiated equality, where men and women complement each other socially and culturally as well as biologically, is proving to be rather difficult. The task, as has been seen, is more than the establishment of equality; it is also one of reorganization, of role adjustment between the sexes. Even equals can be disorganized in their relationships to each other. Earlier cultures pretty well prescribed the separate roles that men and women were to play; their systems were well ordered, though usually on a vertical basis and with discrimination. In our reaching for equality we have disturbed the traditional divisions of labor between the sexes, and there hasn't yet been time to incorporate new ones into the culture.

To illustrate, the girl of yesterday usually knew what to expect when she accepted marriage; it was within the culture that she be submissive and subservient, and there was little that she could do about it. Not so today. The modern girl hopes for a partnership arrangement in marriage, though neither she nor her husband may have any clear understanding of what this means in terms of their respective family roles. Where formerly culture patterned these relationships and the mates generally conformed because society expected it, now marriage is more or less on its own, with relatively little that is prescribed in custom and with each couple forced to maneuver its own arrangements. In a transitional age, such as this, culture is less well integrated and more is left permissible with the individual.

While the long-time results of the movement toward sex equality will undoubtedly be beneficial (certainly it is compatible with the broader ideals of democracy and Christianity), the immediate effects are disorganizing. We are in a period of transitional turmoil where values are confused and roles are in conflict. In time, perhaps, society will find a way to have both equality and harmony at the same time. It is toward this goal that the following comments are directed.

Cultural Contradictions.—Not everyone is agreed on what the roles of men and women should be in this modern world. Some indication of how people feel on the problem may be found in a 1946 *Fortune* Survey. Here is a brief summary.[18]

1. Evidently this is still a man's world, even in the mind of women. While only 3.3 per cent of the males said they would rather be a woman if they could be born over again, 25.2 per cent of the females said they would rather be a man. In addition, a plurality of females

---

[18] "The Fortune Survey: Women in America," *Fortune,* 34:5-6 ff., August 1946; and 34:5-6 ff., September, 1946.

thought that it was the men who have both the easier and the more interesting time in contemporary America. Males agreed on this so far as an interesting time is concerned, but disagreed that their lives are any easier. It was the women who wished they were men who also placed highest in claiming that man's life is easier and more interesting.

2. Equality within the home seems now to be the aim of the majority of men and women. Half, or near half, of both sexes thought that the rights and privileges of husband and wife should be the same on such matters as deciding how the family money is to be spent, deciding when to have children, disciplining the children, and choosing a place to live. Approximately two thirds of both sexes indicated that they thought it equally bad for either husband or wife to be unfaithful in marriage. Traditional interpretations were still upheld to some extent, however. Relatively speaking, more of both sexes thought that the husband should have more to say in such matters as deciding where to live, while the wife should have more to do with deciding when to have children and managing child discipline, and should be blamed more in cases of infidelity. Males thought husbands should have more control over the family money than wives, while wives claimed just the reverse. In all these matters women claimed more privilege for themselves than men were willing to concede. It was significant that many more men than women thought that child discipline should fall largely to the wife, showing that men want women to play a bigger part here than the women are willing to assume.

3. Both men and women harbor attitudes that make for discrimination against women in the world outside the home. Large percentages from both sides feel that married women should not work except in cases of necessity. Over one fourth of the males and nearly one fifth of the females believed that there are times when employers are justified in paying women less than men for exactly the same jobs. Most of both sexes thought that women should take as much interest in public affairs as men do, though in groups such as the PTA and the Red Cross, not as mayors or members of Congress.

4. "While blocks among both men and women level fairly serious charges against each other, consistent man-haters or woman-haters are but a fringe. The battle of the sexes seems to be a series of skirmishes, not a mass action." [19]

It is encouraging to see that large portions of both sexes now accept the idea of equality within the home. But it be-

[19] *Ibid.*, September, 1946, p. 6.

comes evident, too, that agreement is far from general, and that woman's lot in comparison with man's is still much more narrowly prescribed.

Margaret Mead, in an exceptionally penetrating analysis following this *Fortune* Survey, shows how the modern woman, in spite of her advances toward equality, remains essentially and deeply discontented. She says:

American women are better fed and better sheltered than almost any other women in the world. By and large their husbands seldom beat them. They are free to go almost anywhere in public life; they walk with faces uncovered, yet unexposed to disapproving comment or molestation. They can go to school just as their brothers can, and in fact often have a chance at a more modern education because it has seemed safer on the whole to do our experimenting on our daughters rather than on our sons. They can hold jobs, join unions, own businesses, sign checks, run for office, wear pants in public places. In most states their property is their own, and the worst limitations on their freedom are a few laws designed to protect their potential or actual maternity. If we were to go back and look over the issues raised by earlier generations of feminists, it would look as if a very large part of the battle that they fought has been won.

And yet the persistent fact is that the most articulate, the best-educated, the most mobile group of American women is disturbed. Roughly, this disturbance takes two forms, discontent with the present conditions of homemaking for the woman with children, and confusion about how a woman is to look at herself: should she see herself as a person or primarily as a woman? [20]

To remove the dullness and loneliness that many married women experience in the home today, Mead suggests about three things: (1) that men assume a larger responsibility in child care and homemaking; (2) that certain drudgery tasks be taken out of the home; and (3) that women be given more opportunity for self-realization on the outside or in addition to their home and family functions. She believes that woman should be regarded first of all as a human being, and only secondly as a female. Failure to do this on the part of society has made woman restless and discontented. Given a chance to

---

[20] Margaret Mead, "What Women Want," *Fortune,* December, 1946, p. 173.

choose, most women would still take homemaking, Mead believes. But the point is that woman ought to be given that
chance so that her life can be guided by choice rather than
necessity. It is not a man's life that woman particularly wants,
Mead contends, but only the dignity accorded personality
when given the right to choose. Her final paragraph:

> . . . Once parenthood is regarded as a joint job for both parents
> and women are no longer regarded as persons to whom a certain
> amount of drudgery is biologically appropriate, we can make the in-
> ventions required to take a good part of the drudgery out of the home.
> Some of these will be technological: for example, precooked-food
> services and dishwasheries that launder the dishes the way laundries
> now do the linen. Some of them will be institutional; for example,
> residential emergency centers where children can be cared for when
> there is illness in the home. Some of them may even be new forms
> of housing and new neighborhood ways of living in which a group
> of women share in the care of the children. When we eliminated
> slavery we opened the way for a million labor-saving inventions in
> field and factory. Elimination of the semivoluntary slavery to house-
> keeping that we now impose on married women in the U. S. should
> open the way for an equally significant set of inventions in that key
> spot of our civilization, the home, where not "things" but human be-
> ings are produced and developed.[21]

Komarovsky, in a study at Barnard, shows how the typical
college woman is thrown into a whirl of cultural contradictions
regarding the sex roles she is to play. One set of roles is
characterized by "the glamour girl," "the good sport," and
"the domestic type," where she is expected to be less aggressive and more emotional and sympathetic and where her attitudes toward the male are more or less traditional. Another
role cluster is that of the "modern woman," which isn't really
a sex role for it assumes the same virtues, privileges, and
standards of success as for the male. "What are assets for one
become liabilities for the other and the full realization of one
role threatens defeat in the other." Forty per cent of those
studied indicated that they had occasionally "played dumb" on
dates—concealed an academic honor, pretended ignorance, al-

---

21 *Ibid.*, p. 224.

lowed the man the last word, etc.—in order to remain attractive. Typical comments were:

> I was glad to transfer to a women's college. The two years at the coed university produced a constant strain. I am a good student; my family expects me to get good marks. At the same time I am normal enough to want to be invited to the Saturday night dance. Well, everyone knew that on that campus a reputation of a "brain" killed a girl socially. I was always fearful lest I say too much in class or answer a question which the boys I dated couldn't answer.

> I am engaged to a southern boy who doesn't think too much of the woman's intellect. In spite of myself, I play up to his theories because the less one knows and does, the more he does for you and thinks you "cute" into the bargain. . . . I allow him to explain things to me in great detail and to treat me as a child in financial matters.

> I let my fiancé make most of the decisions when we are out. It annoys me, but he prefers it.

Komarovsky points out that the family frequently fails to smooth the passage from one role to another; in the younger years, for example, girls are often taught that it is all right to be capable and to compete equally, but then are told at the dating age "not to win all ping-pong games" but to slip at times to let the boy friend win some. "Society confronts the girl with powerful challenges and strong pressure to excel in certain competitive lines of endeavor and to develop certain techniques of adaptation very similar to those expected of her brothers. . . . Suddenly . . . the very success in meeting these challenges begins to cause anxiety. It is precisely those most successful in the earlier role who are now penalized." She concludes by saying that the girl who has the "middle of the road personality," who is flexible enough to play both roles, is the one who will be most happily adjusted in present culture.[22]

Dilemmas Women Face.—Until recently most discussion on problems of personal maladjustment has been concerned with the male. Yet in many ways the adjustment difficulties facing

---

[22] Mirra Komarovsky, "Cultural Contradictions and Sex Roles," *American Journal of Sociology*, 52:184-89, November, 1946.

girls and women are even greater today than those for boys and men. This is partly so because of the greater changes that are taking place in the roles women play; more women are adopting man's traditional mannerisms and activities, for example, than is true of the reverse. This is still a man's world, as defined by culture, and woman, to be equal, has had to do most of the changing. Change always involves a certain amount of confusion. Furthermore, though woman has invaded "man's world," his world has yielded only in part; prejudices against the fairer sex still hold her back. Woman, in other words, has been hit harder than man by the transition and at the same time she continues to suffer more by way of discrimination.

For this reason we have chosen to examine woman's problem's first, and at greater length. Much of what is discussed here will apply to man also, for the sexes are interacting and complementary. Man's part in the adjustment of sex roles is to be pointed out more specifically later in the chapter.

1. One of the dilemmas facing modern woman is the problem of knowing how to be cooperative without being either overly aggressive or unduly submissive. Stated another way, it is the question of how to deal with the masculine ego. Two mistakes, opposite in nature, are commonly made: first, accepting the traditional subservient role that has been woman's lot throughout most of history; and second, becoming too aggressive or independent. Neither is compatible with equality.

In attempting to overcome their servility, women have sometimes pushed so hard that they have ended up at the other extreme which is just as objectionable—they have assumed an independence so strong as to ignore responsibility and preclude cooperation; they have wanted to "have their cake and eat it too," to enjoy the privileges that come with equality without facing or accepting the responsibilities. This is not to say that all women have committed this error; only the minority. Neither is it to say that woman should necessarily be more dependent than man, but neither more independent. As woman finds her rightful place side by side with man, the masculine ego will need to adjust somewhat, and rightly so. But let the woman who is wise be neither too impatient nor too aggressive. Arguing, being obstinate, making demands, acting independently, fighting—these do not make one equal or free. Equality is more than the assertion of equality.

How can a capable woman protect herself against unreasonable masculine dominance? Since dominance by the male is rooted in both biology and culture, and abuses of it are as old as history, it may take some time before male-female relationships become established on an equalitarian basis. Nevertheless, the trend is in the right direction. Women who chafe under this seeming, and in some cases actual, injustice have but two alternatives. One is to assert their rights openly or to react against the injustice aggressively, in which case their chances for marriage become less, either by their own choice or because their challenge to the masculine ego frightens away possible suitors. If the rebellion against male dominance comes after marriage, the most likely results are either continual conflict in the home, with the possibility of divorce, or the acceptance by the husband of a "henpecked" status. Neither of these developments can be called ideal. The other alternative for the capable but discontented woman is to accept the fates and to play the game in the light of what is. In adjusting to man throughout the ages, woman has had to develop many subtle techniques for asserting herself, for getting her way without open conflict. These devices (known well to most women) are still available, and while they should never be abused, they can be used. Women can be equal with men, even superior, without letting men know it. While it may seem unjust to have to resort to such methods, the subservience is only surface deep, it should be remembered, and this is one way of solving the dilemma of "equality without equality" that some women face. Until men as a whole can recognize that women too have ability and are entitled to equal rights, it is probably the best way.

This does not mean that women are justified in tricking their lovers; only understanding them, and then adapting personally to make the relationship run more smoothly. This kind of self-sacrifice really requires love and bigness of character, but it is a way to harmony. The woman should be cooperative, as should the man also, but never be completely docile or servile. There is a difference. Marriage, to be successful, always requires a division of labor between husband and wife and a willingness of each to give in and sacrifice for the other. Never, however, does it require blind submission to an overlord. Woman should be man's partner, never his servant or slave. To make it so frequently requires scheming as well as love; but it can be done.

2. Another dilemma is the problem of how to assert one's rights in a man's world without becoming unwomanly in the process. Woman has sometimes made the mistake of confusing equality with identity, and in her desire for the former she has unwittingly struggled for the latter. Wanting to be equal with man she has striven to be like him, aping him in dress, speech, and mannerisms. This masculinization of woman has led to some confusion and unhappiness, for woman cannot go the full way because of biological conditions, and she very frequently feels misfitted and frustrated as a result.

The so-called *masculine protest,* where some women resent the fact that they are females, has already been observed. It is well known that many more women wish they were men than is true of the reverse. Reasons for this condition are probably both biological and cultural: biological, in that some women feel sorry for themselves over the necessity of menstruation and other inconveniences or disadvantages connected with the childbearing function; and cultural, in that social discriminations have often made them feel inferior and caused them to protest their lot. Feelings of this kind, if at all strong or persistent, lead inevitably to discontent and maladjustment. Extreme cases are women who became mannish in their ways or who turn into man-haters, adopting attitudes of ruthless competition and exploitation. Marriage is not made successful by any of this.

There is reason for believing that: "Men and women who are good specimens of their respective sexes are most likely to be sought in marriage and to be happy subsequently in marriage." [23] Certainly we know that homosexuals as a rule are

---

[23] Paul Popenoe, "Of Women and Men," *Family Life,* 8:8-9, April, 1948.

unhappy. So also are many misfits who have not reached this extreme condition. While research on the point is scanty, it seems likely that effeminate men and masculine women rate high in the ranks of both the permanently unmarried and the divorced but low among those who are happily married. Popenoe presents some evidence to show that women don't generally care for the effeminate type of male, and men very strongly dislike the mannish type of female, who is aggressive, sometimes neurotic, and "who tries to be the feminine equivalent of a 'man about town.'" He also shows, from a study of nearly three thousand married individuals, that happiness in marriage is correlated with masculinity in husbands and femininity in wives.[24] This conclusion needs further testing, we know. But it seems reasonable.

Lundberg and Farnham speak of modern woman as "The Lost Sex," blaming her for her struggle to become like man and attributing most of the world's ills to this unfortunate mixing of sex roles. They argue that she was cut out by nature for motherhood and homemaking, and that she is only becoming unnatural and frustrated in her effort to be something else. She should surrender her struggle for equality, should stop trying to compete in masculine fields, and should strive to make a genuine feminine contribution to society by aiding in the restrengthening of the home. The authors even contend against the emerging single standard of morality.[25]

Most students of the problem, including the present writer, tend toward a position somewhat less extreme than this. We concede the fact that modern woman is frequently confused and discontented, and that part of the explanation is her apparent attempt to be like man. We believe, however, that this can be corrected without any retrenchment into inequality, and that it will be in time. The trouble is not that woman has tried to be equal, but that the difference between equality and identity has not always been understood. Then too, woman can't do it alone.

---

[24] *Loc. cit.*
[25] Ferdinand Lundberg and Marynia F. Farnham, *Modern Woman: The Lost Sex* (New York: Harper & Bros., 1947), 497 pp.

Part of the problem is woman's desire to be attractive to men as well as equal with them. This would cause no difficulty provided that men saw it the same way. But to fight for equality women have seemingly had to assume mannerisms and resort to tactics that are masculine in nature, and in so doing certain of them have lost "sex appeal." Probably the majority of females would rather win a man's heart than to fight for wages equal to his. It has been this fear of being without man's love that has frequently stopped woman from fighting for his justice.

Until recently, sexual morality has most generally followed the "double standard"—one standard for men and a higher one for women. This has meant that more men than women have engaged in sexual relations outside of marriage. Undoubtedly more still do. But recently the trend has been toward a single standard of morality, with each sex being held equally responsible. Paralleling this change in standard is a convergence in practice; today there is less difference between the sex practices of men and women than formerly. Here again, however, it is woman who is making the greater change, and in the direction of masculine patterns; there is no proof that man is becoming more continent, but there are several indications that woman is becoming more promiscuous than before.

3. Finally, there is the question of career versus marriage. Most normal women desire marriage, in this day as in the generations gone by. But they are also coming to want careers, and these two drives are now in conflict. Woman's recent emancipation has opened up to her new interests and opportunities which make her restless and anxious to be productive along lines other than marriage and motherhood. College-trained girls, for example, often feel that their time and effort will have been largely wasted if they don't capitalize upon their training in terms of a job. Yet in the majority of cases they will also hope to marry, to have children, to establish a home. How is this conflict of interests to be resolved? There are only three major alternatives: a career without marriage, marriage without a career, and a career combined with marriage.

The "career girl" who remains permanently unmarried does so either out of circumstances or choice. There are undoubtedly a great many cases of women who would have liked most of all to marry, but didn't for one reason or another, and who then turned to other activity as sublimation for the desire that was denied them. There are numerous other cases of women who have put their career first, though wanting marriage too, and who have thereby lost out in love because of delaying too long or by becoming personally less attractive to the somewhat fickle male or by overchallenging the masculine ego. And there are still other cases of women who have deliberately decided against marriage, women who have either been soured on men or marriage or who have decided that all their energy should be devoted to the chosen career. It seems likely that the proportion in this latter class is on the increase, due to both the increasing incident of marriage failure and the increasing opportunities that are opening up for women outside the home. Certainly no one who believes in equality would deny woman that choice. As a person, she needs the right of free expression, just as do men. There are women of exceptional ability, just as there are men, and each should have the opportunity to develop and use her talents. Motherhood is not the only contribution that women can make to society.

Yet motherhood is very important. Only woman can perform this function; if she neglects it, it will be left undone. While some can be of distinct benefit to society by becoming "career girls," it is a fortunate thing that all don't want it that way —at the exclusion of childbearing and homemaking. One often hears it said that homemaking should be considered the career for most women. The saying is trite, but it is also true. Homemaking, of course, is much more than mere procreation; it is managing the intimate affairs of family members and maintaining an atmosphere favorable for the highest in personality development; it is being a good wife and a good mother. Homemaking is no easy job; it requires knowledge, skill, patience, and perseverance comparable to that for any career. The successful homemaker must be a good lover, a skilled cook, a neat housekeeper, an informed purchaser, a tactful

manager, and an able disciplinarian, all at the same time.
Neither is homemaking any less important than other careers;
quite the contrary, for upon its success depend the characters
and actions of men. This is the truth of the matter, even if
society hasn't seemed to recognize it as such and has given
more dignity to man's work. Women who remain discontented
over their lot can in one sense hardly be blamed for our culture has made man's life seem more glamorous; but in another
sense they err. All of this can be changed if we will but
dignify the roles of womanhood, motherhood, and homemaking.

In saying that marriage itself should be viewed as a career,
we do not imply that woman's full time should be spent in the
home. Many women find that they are more contented personally and more effective as homemakers when they maintain moderate outside interests of the recreational, cultural,
and service varieties. Also, studies seem to show that the
best wives are those who have had some work experience
before marriage.

Outside employment of the wife after marriage, however,
does frequently lead into difficulties of one sort or another,
such as child neglect, an unkept house, irregular meals, fatigue
and irritability of family members. There are some women
who can successfully carry out their family responsibilities
and hold down a job on the outside as well, but the strain is
usually great. The woman is exceptional that can do justice to
these two interests at the same time. Without laying down any
absolute rule we can say that employment and career activities
are justifiable only if they can be successfully fitted into a
happy home life; that for most normal women the home and
family should come first.

With proper planning it is entirely possible for the women
of ability to have marriage and a career. Some try to work the
career in before marriage, which, unless it is for just a year or
two, has the disadvantage of postponing family life too long
and even risking spinsterhood. Others seek a career along
with their marriage. This has the shortcomings listed above
which can come from divided interests and neglect. The third,

and usually most successful, method of harmonizing a career with marriage is having the career after the family has been reared. In addition to its avoidance of interference with the family, this scheme has the additional advantage of making vital the later years of life which are otherwise so often left empty.

Additional suggestions for helping woman combine a career with marriage include the following: making more part-time jobs available to her; providing more well-staffed day nurseries for young children; developing more community services, such as commercial kitchens which provide home-cooked meals on order; and encouraging husbands to help more with the housework and care of children.

But, whatever the arrangement, utopia is not to be expected; not yet anyway, for there is personal and cultural readjustment that must first be done. In trying for both marriage and a career, woman has found it necessary to fight on two fronts, so to speak; she has taken on a dual job and has just about doubled the difficulty of her task. Unless the husband can be encouraged to assume a larger and more nearly equal responsibility with her in the home, or unless she can come to give up most of her ambitions on the outside, she will remain at a distinct disadvantage and may fail in both her tasks.

In summary, we can say that the dilemmas women face in their fight for equality center primarily around difficulties found in avoiding excessive independence, partial masculinization, and double duty jobs that result in divided effort. Equality is the ideal, but the processes for attaining it seem often to prove frustrating. The better way is to aim for relationships between the sexes that are supplementary and complementary rather than duplicative, cooperative rather than competitive; and to strive for maturity and responsibility in the personalities of both males and females.

New Roles for Men.—The roles of men and women are so oriented to each other that when one alters the other cannot remain fixed. As the status of woman rises, therefore, and as she invades those fields of activity traditionally taboo to her, man must inevitably learn to move over. Adjustment, in other words, is two-sided. While woman's role is probably undergoing the greater change, as has been seen, and while it is woman who still must do the major part of the adjusting required of mates in courtship and marriage, man too has responsibility.

It is his partial neglect of this responsibility that is making woman's task doubly difficult. Many men tend to resist the cultural advances that women are experiencing, and to regard these changes as invasions into their own rightful domain. Such holding on to tradition for the sake of vested interest or special advantage only accentuates the contradictions of culture, thus contributing to the maladjustment of men as well as women. Many, if not most, of woman's problems concern her relationships with man, and unless man understands these sympathetically and tries to adjust them cooperatively woman will continue to flounder and will pull man down with her in the process. The new roles for men are those that will best aid woman in the solution of her dilemmas—to the mutual advantage of both.

1. Men need to understand that any "assumption of woman's inferiority is as outmoded as a belief in evil spirits." [26] They must not only concede verbally that women are equal, but permit them equal opportunities and assist them in climbing. Anything short of this forsakes both the findings of science and the principles of democracy. It will require fundamental ego adjustments on the part of the male. But is there any real reason why women should continue to have most of the disadvantages or to do most of the yielding when there are differences to settle?

2. Men need to assist women in finding and defining their new role patterns. Part of this would require an honest striving for a type of role differentiation that is both flexible and democratic. Women can be helped to see that to be feminine is not necessarily to be unequal. But this will come only if men define it that way, if they really come to respect woman's in-

[26] From *Marriage for Moderns,* by Henry A. Bowman. 1948. Courtesy of McGraw-Hill Book Co., p. 25.

tellect without forcing her to keep silent or to become overly aggressive in fighting to express herself equally. Woman too needs understanding and companionship. Man's function in marriage is not adequately performed by just procreating children and supporting and protecting family members.

3. Men need to assume an equal share of responsibility in moral conduct, actually to accept the single standard of morality. Women should be encouraged in the maintenance of standards so that as mothers and sweethearts they can continue in their somewhat unique position of influence. Men can further this by making the "good girl" popular. Too often men date the kind of girl who will give them the most thrill, only to look for a more stable "home type" when they get ready to settle down. This is hardly fair, for it encourages a looseness in morals and it keeps the female confused as to what the male really wants.

4. Men need to take a larger interest in homemaking. The tradition that leaves mother almost solely responsible for children and the household makes it difficult for many couples to adjust themselves sensibly and practically to the changing requirements of the family.[27] There are still many men who feel that child care and housework are beneath them, that this is woman's work. While it is true that there will be a division of labor within the family, and that ordinarily the housewife will spend more time than her husband on these one-time feminine tasks, it is also true that tradition is changing and that there are any number of satisfactory combinations for harmonious relationships within the home, depending upon the personalities involved and the various family jobs that must be done. There is little justification for fixed role patterns, sharply defined and arbitrarily assigned. Though there must be a differentiation of tasks, each mate needs to feel responsible to the other and work toward the common purposes of both; successful marriage is a partnership. Housewives commonly complain that their husbands leave everything about the home up to

---

[27] Cf. Sidonie M. Gruenberg, "Changing Conceptions of the Family," *Annals of the American Academy of Political and Social Science,* 251:128-36, May, 1947. Here is an excellent analysis of changes that are taking place in family patterns and principles that are needed for democratic family living.

them, and they don't even have enough interest to take enough time to talk things over. This condition, where true, needs correction. Many more girls than boys interest themselves in school courses dealing with child development and homemaking. There is some evidence that this is changing, though slowly. But if the ideals of companionship and democratic family life are ever to be reached, men will need to give much more thought to preparing for marriage and to sharing the responsibilities of homemaking.

MATCHING FOR MARRIAGE

Our concern throughout this chapter has been to analyze men and women: their likenesses and differences; their equalities and inequalities; their role combinations and adjustment problems. These interrelationships between the sexes may be regarded as factors in successful marriage; the most favorable situations being those in which men and women understand each other, are given equal opportunity to develop and function, and their various sex roles are adjusted to be complementary and to produce a minimum of friction. It would be a mistake to end the discussion without mention of the problem of personality matching, which is also important to marriage. Treatment here will be brief, however, owing to the fact that this subject is to receive a more elaborate analysis in Chapter 8 that deals with mate selection.

Since every marriage includes more than one person, its success quite naturally depends to some extent upon the combination of traits found in the pair relationship. It isn't only the qualities of the personalities entering marriage that is important, in other words, but how these personalities are matched. Mates who are both mature and of high quality individually may be quite incompatible considered together, and their marriage may fail because of it. And conversely, even those who are weak personally might, if well mated, gain real strength from the marriage combination.

Research findings, unfortunately, are extremely meager on this extremely important problem. We don't even know as much about personality matching as we do about blood grouping. Earlier it was explained how mates need to be compatible in Rh blood type and how, if they are not, the fetal and infant death rates are likely to be increased. It is regrettable that we can't do as much with personality types, that we can't tell ahead of time which traits will not mix well and in that way avoid catastrophes that are otherwise imminent. What is the "Rh factor" in personality? This should prove to be one of our most fruitful fields in family research.

But we are not totally in the dark. Experience and common sense tell something, and in addition there have been a few careful studies that have thrown light upon the problem. In general it can be said that marriages are more successful when the mates are similar—in backgrounds, in philosophy or values, in interests, and in temperament.[28] There may be exceptions to this, however, such as where both mates have neurotic temperaments, as evidenced by tendencies to extreme lonesomeness and touchiness; in such cases the marriage is handicapped, even though husband and wife are similar.[29]

PROBLEMS AND PROJECTS

1. Discuss the effects upon courtship and marriage of variations in the sex ratio of the population. How does the preponderance of women over fifty affect the lives of men and women?
2. Consider some of the social effects of the earlier physical maturity of girls than boys.
3. From reference material dealing with the anatomy of the sexes, show how the reproductive organs of males and females are in many instances homologous.
4. Can woman be equal with man without at the same time becoming masculine? Discuss.
5. What are the reasons for a "masculine protest"? Is woman's newer freedom making her more, or less, contented? Discuss.

[28] Cf. Ernest W. Burgess and Leonard S. Cottrell, *Predicting Success or Failure in Marriage* (New York: Prentice-Hall, Inc., 1939).
[29] Cf. Ernest W. Burgess and Harvey J. Locke, *The Family: From Institution to Companionship* (New York: American Book Co., 1945), pp. 464-66 and *passim*.

6. If the trend toward sex equality is making for more family conflict, wouldn't it be better to leave the culture undisturbed? By educating women, do we undermine happy marriage? Which would be better, equality without happiness or happiness without equality? Can we have both? Discuss.

7. Is there any way in which the capable woman can express her abilities openly without at the same time making herself less acceptable to the marriage-minded male? Discuss.

8. What connection do you see between man's superiority in mechanical, mathematical, and abstract reasoning tests and his superior position in society?

9. Are there important reasons why Congress should hesitate to pass the Equal Rights Amendment? Do you consider them sound?

10. In what ways can society help the married woman who has a real need of greater outlet for talents and abilities than is afforded by her home, without forcing her to sacrifice her desire for children?

11. Look up reference material on woman's fight for equality. Where does she still fall short of equality or opportunity with men?

12. Discuss society's evaluation of what is called "woman's work." What are the effects of this evaluation upon women today?

13. List the pros and cons of married women's working outside the home. Weigh each against the other and state whether, or under what conditions, you think married women should work.

14. Is it possible for a woman to have both a career and a family at the same time? What are some of the problems that would need to be met? Make suggestions.

SELECTED READINGS

BABER, RAY E. *Marriage and the Family*. New York: McGraw-Hill Book Co., Inc., 1939. Chaps. xii, "The New Status of Women"; xiii, "Some Social Implications of Women's New Activities."

BOWMAN, HENRY A. *Marriage for Moderns*. New York: McGraw-Hill Book Co., Inc., 1948. Chaps. i, "A Point of Departure"; iv, "Marriage Versus Careers."

BUCK, PEARL S. *Of Men and Women.* New York: The John Day Co., Inc., 1941.

FISHBEIN, MORRIS, and BURGESS, ERNEST W. (eds.). *Successful Marriage.* New York: Doubleday & Co., 1947. Part II, chap. i, "Anatomy and Physiology of the Sex Organs"; Part V, chap. vi, "How Women Adjust to Marriage."

FOLSOM, JOSEPH KIRK. *The Family and Democratic Society.* New York: John Wiley & Sons, Inc., 1943. Chap. xviii, "Men and Women in a Democracy."

HARPER, ROBERT A. *Marriage.* New York: Appleton-Century-Crofts, Inc., 1949. Chap. iv, "The Social Psychology of the Sexes."

LANDIS, JUDSON T., and LANDIS, MARY G. *Building a Successful Marriage.* New York: Prentice-Hall, Inc., 1948. Chap. ii, "Roles in Life."

LUNDBERG, FERDINAND, and FARNHAM, MARYNIA F. *Modern Women: The Lost Sex.* New York: Harper & Bros., 1947.

MEAD, MARGARET. *Male and Female.* New York: William Morrow & Co., 1949.

SCHEINFELD, AMRAM. *Women and Men.* New York: Harcourt, Brace & Co., Inc., 1943.

Chapter 5

SEXUAL PERSPECTIVE

Sex on the human level means more than the anatomical structures and physiological processes that have to do with mating and reproduction. It is all of that, but it is also a part of the emotions and the social processes. Sexual behavior is a very complex phenomenon relating to the whole of life; it is rooted in biology to be sure, but in psychology and sociology as well.

In filling out a campus questionnaire one college freshman is reported to have started as follows:

Age:_____18_____

Religion:_____None_____

Sex:_____Occasionally_____

Though he was probably trying to be facetious, his answer on sex does illustrate some of the confusion and distortion so prevalent in this field today.

There is need for understanding and perspective. How important is the sex factor? What is the over-all picture of sexual behavior? What relationships do the various behavior patterns bear to successful marriage? How should one be taught or trained to avoid misconceptions and to come to accept sex as a normal though controllable part of life? These are questions to be considered in the present chapter.

IMPORTANCE OF THE SEX FACTOR

To some persons sex is a mania; to others, a phobia. Some are obsessed with sex, finding little else to think about, or talk about, or participate in. Life for them becomes one continual process of erotic stimulation, of overindulgence and dissipation. Others are repulsed by sex, regarding it as evil, and living in constant fear or dread. For such, life usually means either celibacy or frigidity—and frustration. Both of these approaches are extremes and they result in something short of the happiness goal.

There is a middle way. Sex can be regarded as important, though not all-important; it can be put in its place, relegated to a lesser role than it sometimes plays, given perspective, but never ignored. This is the way we view it here. Sex is a part of life, and as such it should be accepted (though controlled) and used constructively. It is not the whole of life, however, and should not be made to seem so.

As applied to marriage, most authorities are agreed that, while sexual compatibility is important, it is the personality factors and how they are matched in the mates that really count. Where husband and wife are mature personally and are well mated psychologically and socially, they will tend to adjust better sexually and to overlook any minor maladjustments that may be experienced in the process. The opposite is also true; immature and poorly matched mates find greater difficulty in reaching sexual harmony and are less tolerant of each other in their difficulties. Conversely, sexual adjustment contributes to harmony in other segments of the marriage relationship, and incompatibility in sex only adds to incompatibility in other things. Sex, then, is both cause and effect. In substantiation of these points, several sources will be cited.

Two pioneer studies dealing with factors affecting success and failure in marriage were published about a decade ago, one by Terman [1] and the other by Burgess and Cottrell.[2] These studies were in essential agreement on most points, and later research has only added support to their findings. They will be referred to rather frequently throughout this text. Concerning the sex factor, we quote from Terman:[3]

---

[1] Lewis M. Terman, *Psychological Factors in Marital Happiness* (New York: McGraw-Hill Book Co., 1938).

[2] Ernest W. Burgess and Leonard S. Cottrell, *Predicting Success or Failure in Marriage* (New York: Prentice-Hall, Inc., 1939).

[3] From *Psychological Factors in Marital Happiness,* by Lewis M. Terman. 1938. Courtesy of McGraw-Hill Book Co., p. 376.

Our . . . data . . . indicate that the influence of the sexual factors
is at most no greater than that of the combined personality and background factors, and that it is probably less.

Somewhat typical of statements found in modern textbooks
dealing with marriage is the following:

The exact relative importance of the combined physical factors is
difficult to state, and varies in the opinions of various observers. It is
a matter of common observation, however, that marriage partnerships
which are based chiefly or exclusively upon physical attraction have a
poor chance of success. Indeed, most qualified students of the family
feel that the temperamental, intellectual, and spiritual elements are
perhaps of more fundamental importance than sexual attraction and
compatibility. It is probably wisest to consider the latter as only one
supplementary building block in the stability of the marriage partnership.[4]

The recent study made by Kinsey and associates is to be summarized in the next section of this book. Here, however, we
should like to report what the study records on the general
importance of the sex factor:

Sexual adjustments are not the only problems involved in marriage,
and often they are not even the most important factors in marital
adjustments. A preliminary examination of the six thousand marital
histories in the present study, and of nearly three thousand divorce
histories, suggests that there may be nothing more important in a
marriage than a determination that it shall persist. With such a determination, individuals force themselves to adjust and to accept situations which would seem sufficient grounds for a break-up if the continuation of the marriage were not the prime objective.

Nevertheless, sexual maladjustments contribute in perhaps three-
quarters of the upper level marriages that end in separation or divorce, and in some smaller percentage of the lower level marriages
that break up. Where the sexual adjustments are poor, marriages are
maintained with difficulty. It takes a considerable amount of idealism
and determination to keep a marriage together when the sexual ad-

Edgar S. Gordon, "Physical Aspects of Marriage," chap. xii in Howard
Becker and Reuben Hill: *Marriage and the Family*. Reprinted by special
permission of D. C. Heath and Company, Boston, Mass., 1942, p. 252. The
chapter from which this quotation is taken is an excellent treatment of the
sexual side of marriage.

justments are not right. Sexual factors are, in consequence, very important in a marriage.[5]

Patterns of Sexual Behavior

No realistic understanding of the role of sex in life, or of its relationship to marriage, can be obtained without first of all knowing what actually takes place. This section, therefore, is to give a general over-all picture of human sexual behavior—not as to techniques, which are incidental to our present purposes, but as to types, amounts, and trends.

A Classification of Types.—Considered broadly, human sexual activity falls logically into three categories: (1) autosexuality, (2) homosexuality, and (3) heterosexuality. While any given individual might be active in one, two, or three of these, each type is separate and distinct from each of the others. And there are subdivisions representing the many varied activities coming under these general types.

Autosexuality, sometimes called autoeroticism, refers to sexual behavior that is oriented toward oneself. On the psychological plane its most common form is narcissism, the narcissistic individual being one who loves himself and is more or less incapable of directing his love interests toward another person. On the physical plane, masturbation or self-stimulation, often to the point of orgasm, is its most usual type. Nocturnal emissions, which refer to the involuntary ejaculations normal with most adolescent males during sleep, should probably also be listed here. So too should intercourse with animals. Someone might object to classifying nocturnal emissions with autosexuality on the grounds that it is not willful, and animal contacts as autosexual behavior on the grounds that they are not carried out alone. Both are types of human sexual expression, nevertheless, and in neither case is another person involved. There would be other ways of listing these patterns, to be sure, but then any classificatory system must be arbitrary when it comes to borderline cases, and for present purposes it seems best to

---

[5] Alfred C. Kinsey and others, *Sexual Behavior in the Human Male* (Philadelphia: W. B. Saunders Co., 1948), p. 544.

consider all sexual activity involving no more persons than one as autosexual.

Homosexuality describes the condition of love fixation on the same-sex level, male with male and female with female. It runs the gamut all the way from ardent friendships to both crude and artful physical stimulations leading to orgasm. Variations are about as many and of the same kind as for heterosexual conduct, the chief difference being that in homosexuality the love object is of the same sex. Thus there is homosexual promiscuity, there are homosexual prostitutes, and there is homosexual incest.

Heterosexuality denotes love and sex responses between individuals of opposite sexes, males with females and females with males. By society at large this pattern is considered most normal. Not all heterosexual activity is within the mores, however. Nonmarital sexual intercourse includes the premarital which takes place before marriage, the extramarital which is during marriage but with someone other than the married mate, and the postmarital which is sexual intercourse after divorce has taken place or widowhood set in. Where sexual intercourse is for pay, the term used is "prostitution"; where it is with a close blood relative such as a son, daughter, brother, or sister, the act is "incest"; where it is forced by the male it is called "rape." Heterosexual stimulation short of intercourse is in this culture usually called "necking" when it involves just the lighter forms of kissing and embracing, and "petting" when there is some of the more intimate caressing and fondling. For before marriage, necking is about the only form that receives near universal approval. Marital intercourse is, of course, fully sanctioned by the group—except in cases of abuse.

The Kinsey Report.—One of the most provocative studies of this day, and certainly the most extensive and intensive piece of research on human sexual behavior ever attempted, is the work now in process by Alfred C. Kinsey and associates at Indiana University. Begun approximately a decade ago, it has now accumulated well over 12,000 records of detailed interviews. But even that isn't enough; the work is projected another twenty years into the future and the goal is set at 100,000 cases. The first release on this study came out early in 1948 and is known popularly as "The Kinsey Report." It is based upon the sex lives of 5,300 white males, with statistics adjusted by weighting to represent the entire population. Other volumes on special groups and special subjects will follow as the interviewing proceeds and as the sample in all of its parts becomes more adequate. The first volume is regarded as a progress report only and it is recognized by the authors that the percentages may need to be revised slightly after all the data are in. The general approach has been that of the scientist, not the moralist. Following is a summary of major findings.[6]

1. Human sexual activity includes a wide variety of experiences, some of which are largely emotional while others are definitely or predominantly physical. The natural culmination of physical stimulation is sexual climax, called orgasm. Since emotional situations short of this release do not permit much precision in measurement, the Kinsey analysis ignores them, in the main, and confines itself to those activities that result in orgasm. These are referred to as sexual outlets, and there are six chief types: Masturbation, nocturnal emissions, heterosexual petting to the point of climax, heterosexual intercourse, homosexual relations, and animal contacts.

2. While recognizing great individual variation in all these sources of sexual outlet, it is nevertheless possible to describe general or central tendencies. Most males resort to several of these outlets during a lifetime. In terms of frequency of total outlet, the average is two or three per week, with persons under thirty years of age experiencing nearly 3.3. These figures are for both married and single males taken together, but for the "under thirty" single males alone the average number of outlets is nearly three per week. Broken down by type, it was found that in the total population approximately 69.4 per cent of the total sexual outlet is from heterosexual activity (intercourse and petting), 24.0 per cent from solitary sources (mas-

---

6 *Ibid., passim.* This summary has been gleaned from the entire volume and is in the words of the present writer.

turbation and nocturnal emissions), 6.3 per cent from homosexual experiences, and only 0.3 per cent from animal contacts.

Of particular interest are the percentages of those who have ever had experience in each of the several outlet patterns. Most males have masturbated, according to this study (93.8 per cent by age 24). Nocturnal emissions involve 83.0 per cent at sometime during their adult lives. Eighty-eight per cent engage in some heterosexual petting prior to marriage, and 28.0 per cent of these to the extent of orgasm. Premarital intercourse has been experienced by 68.2 per cent of males eighteen years of age, 83.3 per cent of males twenty-five years of age, and 92.2 per cent of males still single at the age of thirty-eight. Extramarital intercourse is admitted by about one third of all married males, but Kinsey believes that there has been some cover-up in reporting, and that the real figure for intercourse with someone other than the wife, sometime during marriage, would be nearer fifty per cent. Ultimately, some 69.0 per cent of adult males (single, married, widowed, or divorced) have intercourse with prostitutes, though the frequency of contact is low, as is also the proportion of total outlet derived from this source. Marital intercourse provides only about 85.0 per cent of the orgasmic outlet of married individuals, the rest coming from other sources. Homosexual stimulation is at some time experienced by the majority of males, with 37.0 per cent carrying the practice to orgasm at least once during the lifetime, and with 4.0 per cent being exclusively homosexual from adolescence on through to old age. Only about 8.0 per cent of the male population ever experiences orgasm from animal contacts, and the average frequency of this outlet for those who participate is exceedingly low.

3. Age affects both the amount and the type of sexual activity. As to frequency of total outlet, age is the most important factor of all. Nearly all boys engage in some preadolescent sex play, and at least one fifth of them attempt intercourse. But with the onset of adolescence, which is at about 13 years and 7 months on the average, comes a great and sudden increase in sexual activity. The most sexually active period of a man's life comes in late adolescence (from ages 16 to 20), at which

time active single males average 3.4 outlets per week and married males 4.8. After this peak sexual activity gradually declines until old age, when with many it stops altogether. It is to be noted, however, that the outlet patterns established during one's teens tend to persist throughout the rest of his life.

Adolescence comes to boys at different ages, and one's age at its onset is related to the pattern of total sexual outlet. In general, those who mature earlier start their regular sex routines sooner and have higher frequencies of outlet all through their lives. This is true whether they are single or married. Also, they have higher incidences of premarital intercourse, homosexual contacts, and masturbation; and this latter is more likely to be their first source of orgasm.

4. Social level is likewise highly correlated with the amount and patterns of sexual outlet. Lower level males (those with little education and/or low socioeconomic status) are more active sexually, having higher average frequencies for total outlet, and showing larger percentages participating in homosexual practices and all types of heterosexual intercourse (marital, premarital, extramarital, and prostitution). Upper-level males, in contrast (those with some college education and/or high socioeconomic status), show a lower frequency in total outlet, but greater percentage participations in masturbation, nocturnal emissions, petting to climax, and animal contacts. Heterosexual intercourse is more likely to be the first source of ejaculation on the lower level, by way of comparison, and nocturnal emissions are on the upper level. Lower-level males tend to shun nudity and to regard masturbation and petting as unnatural. Upper-level males, on the other hand, are more concerned with convention and less with being natural; they give little objection to nudity and variety in coitus; and they are more likely to regard technical chastity as a virtue and to resort to such practices as petting and masturbation in order to protect it. Thus there is a difference in philosophies, a conflict in cultural values.

5. Rural-urban differences in sexual outlet are not great, though the city does show slightly higher frequencies in total activity and greater percentage participations in petting, pre-

marital and extramarital intercourse, prostitution, and homosexuality. Nocturnal emissions and masturbation are about the
same in both cultures. Regarding animal contacts, however, the
rural male, probably because of greater opportunity, participates in greater numbers and with greater frequency.

6. Comparisons among active and inactive groups of Protestants, Catholics, and Jews reveal that there is little difference
among the religions themselves but considerable difference between the active and inactive within each religion. In general,
active church members have lower frequencies and percentages
both as to total outlet and as to nearly every specific type of
outlet—most especially masturbation, nonmarital and marital
intercourse, and homosexuality. This would seem to show that
religion, when active in the individual, has power to control
conduct.

7. Marital status is another factor in sexual behavior. For
those married, most outlet, as might be expected, is from
marital intercourse (85.0 per cent is from this source). Also,
as might be expected, married individuals are more sexually
active than the single (3.4 outlets per week for single males
16-20 years of age as compared to 4.8 for the married). Postmarital rates are generally in between those of the premarital
and the marital, higher than the first but lower than the second.

8. Although data released up to now are for the male only,
it is possible, from statements in the book, to draw a number of
sex comparisons. Males, on the whole, are more sexually active
and aggressive. Boys engage in preadolescent and adolescent
sexual expression about five times as extensively as do girls,
reaching their peak in activity from ages 16 to 20, while females do not usually reach their peak until about the 30's or
40's. Sexual interest within the female is more gradual in development. Neither is it as great. Petting activity is most often
started by the male. It is generally the male who desires marital coitus more frequently. The female is less easily aroused
sexually and is more susceptible to the social restraints about
her. While the variation in total outlet is greater with females,
there is a larger proportion of them in the lower frequency
groups. Some 30.0 per cent of the females are more or less

sexually unresponsive, a condition that is especially high in the educated segment of the population. Women are much less interested in a variety of partners than are men, and if widowed or divorced are much more likely to do without sexual activity.

9. Contrary to popular opinion, and to the findings of earlier research, there seems here to have been no significant increase in sexual activity either in or out of marriage. The college group has become more active in petting, and it is more common for petting to take place in public places than formerly. The lower social group has become a little more active sexually in some of its outlets and has started this activity at younger ages. But these changes are slight and fragmentary, it is claimed; they do not substantially alter the total picture.

Some Criticisms and Additions.—So mammoth an undertaking is the Kinsey study, and so comprehensive is its coverage, that for the present most other research on this aspect of the subject seems to be outdated. Yet to regard this as the last word would be to err. While Kinsey is free with his criticisms of other studies, it is worth noting that in the minds of competent critics he has problems of his own.[7] The methodological aspects of his task will not concern us here, however. Suffice it to say that we regard the work as imposing, and most of the findings as significant, though we may not hold to all of the interpretations. It is fortunate that the study is to continue, and, with the enlarging and increasing representativeness of the sample and the possible further refining of techniques, we may come to have even greater confidence in the statistics.[8] It is fortunate also that a work so important as this is being exposed to the searchlight of criticism, and that other researchers will undoubtedly come to test their findings against those given here.

Whatever the final verdict regarding varieties, incidences, and frequencies in human sexual behavior, we can agree now

---

[7] See any number of book reviews appearing since the publication of the report.

[8] Kinsey recognizes that his present data are but fair approximations of the fact. Cf. Kinsey, *op. cit.*, p. 153 and *passim*.

upon a few things: (1) the sexual urge is rather strong in man, and somewhat constant, finding outlets of one sort or another from early childhood until old age. (2) Individuals differ rather widely, both as to the strength of the sex drive and the variety of its expressions. (3) Much of this difference is to be explained by biological factors—age, onset of puberty, hormones, and perhaps conditions in the parental genes not as yet too well understood. (4) But environment also makes its mark, and particularly the sociocultural environment, conditioning persons toward the patterns it prescribes. Behavior, therefore, varies by religious participation, place of residence, and social level. (5) Marital intercourse, judged by a greater relative frequency and a greater social acceptance, is the most "normal" mode of sexual expression. Saying this another way, heterosexual activity is more frequent and more sanctioned than either homosexual or autosexual behavior, and marital participation in sex is both more common and more acceptable than that which takes place outside of marriage.

More concerning this last point. Though Kinsey would likely agree that marital intercourse is the most usual and socially permissible form of sexual release, he objects to calling it the "normal" form, choosing instead to regard sex as largely biological and to consider any expression it may take as normal.[9] Such a nonsocial and nonmoral view of sex, if accepted, may succeed in lifting the social controls and thus inviting maximum indulgence within the limits of biological capacity. Indeed, some critics of this work fear that that is the very thing his report will lead to. Surely mankind is entitled to decide what is best for its own welfare, to go beyond biology. Our position is that society has also legitimately a hand in these matters, and that if a thing is preponderantly accepted and practiced by a group then it is "normal" for that group. Normal in this sense means modal, rather than either "natural" or "good" (in the absolute). Yet there must be reasons why our society holds up marital intercourse as the desirable mode, and attempts to curb most other patterns of sexual expression. We shall examine some of these in the next section of the discussion.

---

9 Kinsey, *op. cit.*, pp. 7, 199, and *passim*.

The question remains as to how effective social restraints are in the field of sex. That they are not completely effective should be evident from the relatively high proportions of the population that engage in nonheterosexual and nonmarital activities, as indicated above. But that they are at least partially effective cannot be denied. Many of those who are sexually antisocial (and therefore abnormal so far as the mores and the laws are concerned) indulge only once, or at best only a few times, in a lifetime. We have already seen how the average total outlet is less for the unmarried than for the married, how autosexual and homosexual activities are relatively low, and how religious participation and college education result in a less active and more conventional type of sex life.

Trends are not so easily determined. Mores and folkways do change, however, and it is only logical to expect that there have been and are to be corresponding changes in the sexual practices of man. Kinsey's comparisons, as we have seen, show that lower class males start their sex lives a little earlier than formerly, that college males engage in a little more petting and do it more openly, and that a few other minor variations are taking place in the total pattern. But they do not show any general or significant increases in the nonmarital sexual behavior of the male. In striking contrast are the findings of Terman made back in 1938. By comparing older and younger generations as to per cent virgin at marriage, he found that premarital intercourse was rapidly on the increase for both sexes, but especially for the female; this meant both a changing of standards and a narrowing of the gap between male and female practices.[10] Though the Terman study is older, and was based upon a smaller and probably less representative sample, it lines up with logic and is not to be dismissed lightly. Certain it is that contraception has removed some of the danger from premarital intercourse, that church and community controls over sexual conduct have lessened, and that two great wars have disturbed the moral equilibrium of this age. (See Chapter 2.)

Unless sexual outlet were already at a saturation point, a proposal that Kinsey himself claims is not true due to social

---

[10] Terman, *op. cit.*, pp. 320-23.

pressures, one would expect these fundamental currents of social change to alter sexuality in the direction of greater activity. Since the matter is not clear with respect to the male, however, we must await further research. But regarding the female
we can be fairly certain. Terman showed an increase in premarital intercourse for her, and at a more rapid rate than for
the male. Kinsey has not as yet reported on this aspect of the
problem, but he has stated that "The drives against prostitution have succeeded in diverting a third to a half of the intercourse that males used to have with prostitutes to premarital
activities with other girls." [11] If this means anything it means
that more girls are engaged in promiscuous, unpaid contacts
than formerly. We can assume, then, that so far as the female
is concerned, premarital intercourse is on the increase; that
male participation, which has always been the higher of the
two, is either remaining somewhat constant or increasing less
noticeably; and that there is, therefore, a convergence in sexual
practice.

IMPLICATIONS FOR MARRIAGE

Now, what has all this to do with happiness in marriage?
Do the sexual nonconformists endanger marital happiness by
their deviant behavior, or do they, as some claim, gain an experience that may aid in marital adjustment? We do not have
all the answers to these questions, but we have some, and our
analysis should be permitted to take us as far as it can.

Nocturnal Emissions and Menstruation.—Nocturnal emissions in the male and menstruation in the female are perfectly
natural biological phenomena. While only the first of these
gives sexual release, both are a part of the over-all process
having to do with sex and reproduction. They come automatically as expressions of physiological maturation at the time
of puberty. While normal biologically, they can be an inconvenience socially and, if not understood and accepted, can so color
one's notions of sex as to make it all seem obnoxious and vile.
Since these processes are inevitable for most males and fe-

---

11 Kinsey, *op. cit.*, p. 413. Cf. p. 603.

males, and the inconveniences they require are not usually great, it is time we stop looking at them as "sickness" or "curse" and start accepting them as necessary and natural. When preadolescents are left unwarned so that shock and worry accompany their first experiences, or where conversation regarding these acts of nature is of a hushed or unnatural sort, young people may be early conditioned for an unhappy marriage. (See the discussion on sex education, pages 159-67.)

Masturbation.—Next to heterosexual intercourse, masturbation is probably the most commonly used means of sexual release. Lester W. Dearborn, Director of the Boston Marriage Counseling Service, has this to say:

It may be safely assumed, therefore, from all the studies to date, that were we to take the histories of men and women who had reached the age of twenty-five we would find that masturbation has played a part in the lives of more than 90 per cent of all males and more than 70 per cent of all females, with the frequency running from once or twice a month up to several times a week, and that no evidence has been presented to prove that the greater frequency was any more productive of harm than the lesser.[12]

It was at one time claimed that masturbation led to insanity, weakened reproductive power, or other ailments of one sort or another. These claims are known now to be absolutely unfounded, the best medical opinion of the day being that, except in extreme or violent instances, masturbation results in no physical harm. Social and emotional disturbances may sometimes result, however, and these in turn reflect themselves on later life and marriage. When this happens it is usually because parents and others react neurotically rather than naturally to the early exploratory and erotic self-behavior of children, or, because those who masturbate experience worry or guilt feelings over the act, having been victims of misinformation and overmoralization. Here again it is matter of proper sex education. More will be said about this later. When one becomes

---

[12] Lester W. Dearborn, "Masturbation," chap. v in Part IV of Morris Fishbein and Ernest W. Burgess (eds.), *Successful Marriage* (New York: Doubleday & Co., 1947), p. 361.

conditioned or habituated to this autosexual level or response, he may later find difficulty in making a transference to the heterosexual. While not enough is known about the subtleties of these psychological processes, it seems safe to say that certain individuals do find it harder to attain a satisfactory marital sexual adjustment because of their masturbatory experiences. Reconditioning to the heterosexual level is not nearly so difficult here, however, as it is in the case of the homosexual.

Animal Contacts.—Animal contacts, as will be recalled from our summary of the Kinsey Report, are very rare in the population. This is almost exclusively a male phenomenon. In the sense of its being solitary so far as other human beings are concerned, it is like masturbation and its results are somewhat similar. But because of an extreme social disapproval, more extreme perhaps than for any other form of sexual outlet, participants in this activity are more likely to suffer the damaging guilt feelings and frustrations that accompany many types of nonconformity. To the extent that these are deep-seated and chronic, the personality becomes adversely affected and marriage is made to suffer.

Homosexual Practices.—We have already observed that from one third to one half of the adult male population has had some homosexual experience, according to the Kinsey Report, and that at least four per cent are confirmed homosexuals. Though we do not have comparable figures, it is felt from earlier studies that the female incidence is at least as high as for the male. It may be surprising, therefore, that social condemnation is as great as it is. But persons homosexually inclined need understanding rather than condemnation, help rather than punishment. This is illustrated by the following excerpts from a letter to the author:

I have traveled a great deal and have seen many homosexuals. In all cases it has been a very unhappy lot. I know, because I am one of them, and I can't remember when it first started. As long as I can remember I have found contentment with my own sex, and men mean nothing to me. I enjoy talking to them, as I would my brother. I have associated with them and at one time was going to marry. But I couldn't go through with it. I find much greater happiness being with my girl friend. I look toward a girl as a man would. I know I have no right to. . . .

I know people who have tried married life and because of their abnormality their marriage was a failure.

Doctor, I would like to study on this line and to have a knowledge of it. I know it's an unhappy life, but I feel it's no fault of the individual. Could you please give me some information??? I will appreciate it very much. Perhaps I can be some help to someone else.

Doctor, what will God do to this kind of people?

Causes of homosexuality are not well understood and cures are most difficult. While it is not known how much of this condition is to be explained by biological nature stemming from the genes and the prenatal environment, and how much by conditioning after birth, it is believed by the best authorities that both these factors enter in, though the second probably looms larger in total occurrence. Hermaphrodites (those rare individuals who have both ovaries and testes within their single bodies), and near hermaphrodites, may, by their original nature, be inclined toward abnormal love patterns. Then there are those whose hormone balance is off center, so to speak. As medical science has recently demonstrated, each of us is supplied with both male and female hormones, though with normal individuals it is predominantly one or the other according to his sex. The point we are now making is that where males have an overabundance of female hormones in their system, or where females are oversupplied with male hormones, there may be natural inclinations toward homosexual activities. In the above instances the "cure" would lie in the fields of surgery and endocrinology, though frequently at this stage of knowledge there isn't too much that can be done.

In the majority of cases, it is thought, homosexual inclinations develop from the early interactional patterns of infancy, childhood, and adolescence, and then are reinforced by later practicing. Though the specific conditioning processes are not well known, it is thought that the following patterns are involved: a parent being overaffectionate with a child of the same sex; treating a girl as a boy, or a boy as a girl, so that these opposite roles become defined for the child as normal; overwarning the child against the opposite sex or in other ways discouraging or blocking its heterosexual adjustment. Sometimes an adolescent becomes introduced to the practice by seduction from someone more experienced or (and this is more common) by simply turning to homosexual love interests as an out when early heterosexual reachings are for one reason or another denied fruition. In any event, what happens is that the individual's love interests become fixated on the same sex level; he fails to make the heterosexual transition and becomes homosexually habituated. While reconditioning in the direction of heterosexuality is the way out, psychiatrists recognize that the problem is a difficult one requiring long periods of counseling and often proving to be impossible. For that reason many therapists, rather than trying to remove the condition, simply attempt to remove the guilt feelings—to help the homosexual accept the fact and to adjust within that framework, though without getting into trouble with society and without recruiting others into the practice. How much better it would be if the causes were better understood and the problem could be prevented from developing in the first place. Though more research is needed, there is much by way of better education that could be done right now.

Homosexuality throws up serious handicaps for marriage. Experience has shown that when the homosexual marries he is usually not very satisfied nor is he able to make his mate completely happy. Consequently many such marriages break up. But the homosexual condition is, of course, simply a matter of degree, and all of those with inclinations along this line needn't feel that marriage for them cannot be successful. Some people are both homosexual and heterosexual at one and the same time, though in differing degrees. But where one is clearly and predominantly homosexual in his interests and drives, better that he remain single.

Heterosexual Petting.—One often hears the question, "How far can a good girl (or boy) go?" There is no easy answer.

While no one would object to young lovers holding hands, and only the prude would take exception to moderate kissing and embracing before marriage, there is a rather wide difference of opinion concerning the more intimate fondlings just short of sexual intercourse. Should these be reserved for marriage? Are they to be expected during the engagement? Ought they to be permissible on any date? How does petting before marriage affect adjustment afterward?

There is a school of thought which claims that premarital intimacy may actually be an aid to marital adjustment. The argument runs something like this: Frigidity and impotence are largely the products of sociocultural inhibitions. In order to control children and youth, we teach them that sex is wrong. Then, after twenty or more years of this kind of conditioning, we let marriage take place and expect them to be sexually adjustable—overnight. Kinsey's findings seem to support this contention for he reports a positive correlation between premarital petting and sexual adjustment in marriage.[13]

Counterarguments are about as follows: (1) Granted that some non-petters may also be cold in marriage, there is no proof that the relationship is a causal one. The likely thing is that non-petting and frigidity are both the result of negative sex education, rather than one being the cause of the other. If so, then the solution will need to be better sex education, of a positive and constructive sort, rather than the encouragement of petting. (2) Granted, also, that the transition into complete intimacy is more successful when it is gradual, there is nothing to show that *all* of the transition needs to come before the marriage ceremony. As a matter of fact, those who give themselves completely, or nearly so, before the wedding are without protection. (3) Instead of aiding marital adjustment, in some cases premarital petting actually serves as a hindrance. One reason is that it tends to encourage irresponsible experimentation and exploitation; people sometimes learn to take advantage of each other for the sake of personal thrills. Even where there is mutual responsibility the experience is intensely emo-

---

13 Kinsey, *op. cit.,* p. 546.

tional and can produce premature or unwise emotional involvements; these, in turn, may result in either a frustrated love, or an ill-mated marriage, or both. Then there is the possibility of habituation in response patterns, which means that when a person becomes accustomed to responding sexually and emotionally on the petting level he or she may remain satisfied with that and find difficulty transferring to complete sexual intercourse in marriage. In this way intimate and continued petting can be a factor in the development of frigidity.[14] Finally, there is the factor of guilt feelings imposed by the culture; these may contribute to personality instability, and that in turn to unhappy marriage.

The culture is changing. Petting before marriage is more widely accepted today than formerly and very likely more widely practiced. This is tending to remove some of the guilt feelings surrounding petting. Certain other hazards remain. There is nothing "wrong" with intimacy itself, only that it has consequences and needs to be protected by responsibility. Marriage has been society's way of accomplishing this. The degree to which a couple necks or pets prior to marriage should, perhaps, depend upon the nearness of the wedding prospect and the completeness of mutual responsibility surrounding the relationship. Engagement justifies greater intimacy than in early dating; but there needs to be propriety in necking and petting, even there.

Nonmarital Intercourse.—Though nonmarital intercourse includes several types, as we have seen, our discussion here will focus upon the premarital. Except for the fact that extramarital relations usually denote infidelity and are therefore particularly disrupting to the marriage union, these various patterns of nonmarital intercourse do not greatly differ as to their causes or their consequences anyway, and our analysis of the premarital should therefore give us a fair picture of the whole.

It has been shown that premarital intercourse is fairly extensive, with lower-level males especially, and that it is very

---

14 This appears to be especially true for the female. See, for example, Margaret Banning, "The Case for Chastity," *Reader's Digest,* 31:4-5, August, 1937.

likely on the increase. This increase, if it be admitted (Kinsey believes that there has been no significant increase among males), can be explained in large part by the following factors: (1) the perfecting of contraceptives, together with their increasing availability and acceptability, which makes intercourse seem safe; (2) the decline of certain social controls, particularly those of the home and the church, in this age of science, technology, and individualism; (3) the rise of liberal schools of thought regarding sex morals, which trend reflects itself in suggestive literature, movie eroticism, and other media to which people are more or less constantly exposed; (4) the emancipation of woman, which has meant greater sex freedom for the female; and (5) the impact within this last half century of two great wars and one great depression, the like of which this world has never before seen. So our older sex mores are breaking down, controls over sexual behavior are being greatly relaxed, and, since practice follows attitude, premarital intercourse is becoming more common.[15]

There is some evidence of a relationship between premarital intercourse and the success or failure of marriage. Davis, in her study of 1,000 married women, found that marriages were reported to be more happy where the wife had had no premarital petting or sexual intercourse.[16] Hamilton, from a smaller sample, found this same thing for sexual relations before marriage.[17] Terman, in a study of both husbands and wives, also reached this same general conclusion, although where relations with future spouses were considered alone, his correlations were not significant.[18] Though these findings are certainly worth considering, they are based upon inadequate sampling and there is need, therefore, for new and larger research. Kinsey promises something more on this problem for the future. Whatever the outcome, however—and at all times

---

[15] For evidence of our changing sex mores see Austin L. Porterfield and H. Ellison Salley, "Current Folkways of Sexual Behavior," *American Journal of Sociology,* 52:209-16, November, 1946.

[16] Katharine B. Davis, *Factors in the Sex Life of Twenty-two Hundred Women* (New York: Harper & Bros., 1929), p. 59.

[17] Gilbert V. Hamilton, *A Research in Marriage* (New York: Albert & Charles Boni Inc., 1929), pp. 393-95.

[18] Terman, *op. cit.,* pp. 324-25.

recognizing both the multiplicity of factors and the variability of individuals making up marriage—it seems reasonable to conclude from present evidence that for most persons pre-marital intercourse is risky. Following are some of the reasons why.

1. There is first of all the danger of infection, far greater than in marital relations. While there are five or more known types of venereal disease, the two most common are gonorrhea and syphilis. Largely because of the stigma attached to venereal ailments, many who are infected never go to a physician and some physicians are persuaded to falsify the records. For these reasons the exact numbers who have these diseases are never known. It is known that syphilis involves several million of this country's population at any given time (one measure is the 4 to 5 per cent of World War II military draftees who were found to have this disease) and that gonorrhea is at least twice as prevalent as is syphilis. Since many become cured, the incidence of persons ever infected would be considerably higher than for those infected at any one time. Contagion is largely by means of the sex act. Promiscuous contacts can soon spread these diseases over a wide area and involve many people. Prostitution is particularly troublesome in this regard, for contacts there are both random and frequent. Though some have recommended periodic medical examinations of prostitutes as a control against disease, and though this would undoubtedly help somewhat, it could never be very effective for the reason that simple examinations cannot prove the absence of disease and that infection can take place and be spread far and wide between examinations. Venereal disease in this country experienced an increase during and following World War II, for which there seems to be no other explanation than an increase in promiscuity and prostitution. Cures are possible in most cases if treatment is started early. Sulpha drugs and penicillin have in recent years proved to be extremely helpful against these diseases. But they are not always effective; there is no known "sure cure." In any event, prevention should prove to be the less expensive measure from whatever angle it is considered.

While prevention may be partially obtained through prophylaxis (the use of mechanical and chemical agents for the prevention of infection), this method is seldom certain and is effective only under conditions of utmost skill and care. Where sexual participants are uninformed, or are under the influence of alcohol, or are lazy or overconfident, they may fail to take the necessary precautions. Prophylaxis could be a reasonably successful means of control with the armed forces because of the rigid discipline there, but with the civilian population and in peacetime it is a different matter. Also, control was far from perfect even with the armed forces. It would seem, therefore, that the only really effective means would be the reduction of promiscuity and prostitution—through education and motivation primarily, but with legislation as a buttress. In this connection let it be noted that, though the wartime approach to venereal disease among service men was cold and hard (amoral), the military forces have since modified this position to include a recognition of social values and the need for reducing nonmarital sex contacts.

The consequences of venereal disease are many and far-reaching. Aside from physical sufferings and medical expenses are the guilt feelings and blame projections that so often handicap the personalities and interfere with marriage. Sterility is sometimes an outcome. Blindness occasionally results, though not nearly so frequently as before it became common practice to treat the eyes of each newborn infant as a protection against possible gonorrheal infection. Congenital syphilis (from prenatal contagion) can produce offspring that are diseased and deformed, though this need not happen; with more mothers following through with their doctors during pregnancy this condition is brought about much less frequently than formerly. Where disease is brought into marriage by one of the partners it usually results in infection for the other and causes resentments, conflict, or even divorce. Where both parties are free at the time of marriage, and then one becomes infected later, the logical deduction is infidelity and the natural and frequent result is maladjustment between the mates even to the point of separation.

2. Unwanted pregnancy is another real hazard connected with intercourse outside of marriage. While the perfecting of birth control has removed some of the risk from intercourse, it has certainly not removed all. Just as venereal infection is always a danger even when contraceptives are used, so is pregnancy a possibility. It is true that the better contraceptive techniques are between 95 and 100 per cent effective if practiced with intelligence and skill. But it is also true that certain birth control devices are less effective, and that many of those persons who resort to premarital practices are both uninformed and out of control. Where the practitioners are immature, ignorant, intoxicated, or otherwise unfit to apply all that science requires in the control of conception, they only act with a false sense of security and the risk becomes even greater.

When premarital pregnancy happens there are but three alternatives: marriage, illegitimacy, and abortion. Each of these will be examined in turn.

It is not known how many marriage ceremonies come after the advent of pregnancy, though the number is believed to be considerable. In an earlier study the writer estimated that 20 per cent of all first births within marriage were conceived before marriage.[19] Though this may not be representative of all first births in the nation, it gives some idea of the magnitude of the phenomenon.

Neither is it known how many of such cases are of persons who were engaged at the time of the incident as compared with those who were forced into marriage because of a reckless moment. Undoubtedly there would be some of each sort. Relatively speaking, the first-named type would be the less serious, for presumably the couple would be in love and in other ways ready for marriage. But even so there would usually be feelings of guilt, or blame, or worry lest the child would later know, and these would tend to affect the marriage relationship unfavorably. Where the marriage is forced because of pregnancy there will often be an absence of love, or the mates will

[19] Harold T. Christensen, "A Comparative Study of the Time Interval Between the Marriage of Parents and the Birth of their First Child, Based on 1670 couples in Utah County, Utah, 1905 to 1935" (Unpublished thesis, Brigham Young University, 1937), p. 85 and *passim*.

be poorly matched, in addition to these emotional disturbances and other psychological handicaps just mentioned. Then, too, society is likely to disapprove, and either gossip or the threat of gossip is likely to cause tension. In any event this gives marriage a poor start—or poorer at least than it would have otherwise. Though, of the three alternatives, forced marriage is sometimes (not always) the best; at best, it is none too good.

Illegitimacy refers to birth outside of marriage. In the prewar years approximately 3 per cent of all live births were of that kind. During and following the war, rates have been even higher, which is one more evidence of the breakdown in our sex mores. The problem is a serious one for both the unmarried mother and the illegitimate child. For the mother there is the dilemma as to whether to keep the child or offer it for adoption. If she keeps it, there are the problems of economic support and social stigma. She may be seriously handicapped so far as future marriage is concerned. For these reasons most unmarried mothers are inclined to give up their children. If this can be done early, as soon after birth as possible, there will be less of an emotional trauma, though for many the crisis is a serious one even then. It may be sufficient to disorganize the personality. If the illegitimate child is adopted into a good home, he is fortunate indeed, though even there it takes very wise handling to avoid disturbances over his lack of legitimacy. If he is kept by his mother, he must suffer the scorn of society and the handicap of a fatherless home. If neither adopted nor kept by the mother, his problems of normal personality development become greater yet, as most social workers can testify. While illegitimacy is not an insurmountable handicap, neither is it desirable.

Abortion is of two kinds, spontaneous and induced. Induced abortion is likewise of two kinds, therapeutic and criminal. Spontaneous abortion is involuntary and cannot therefore be counted on as a way out from unwanted pregnancy. Therapeutic abortion is permitted by the various states in cases where the health or life of the mother is endangered by the pregnancy, but it is surrounded by legal safeguards to insure against its misuse. Criminal abortion is so named because it violates state law. Yet there are a great many which take place, estimates ranging from a half million to well over a million annually in this country. It is thought that possibly 85 or 90 per cent of these are with married women, but even that number leaves many tens of thousands among the unmarried. Not only does one become a lawbreaker by submitting to an illegal abortion, and lose an exorbitant amount of money to the physician or quack who plays the racket, but both life and health are endangered. It is estimated that some ten thousand women in this country lose their lives each year through this practice.[20] Many others suffer long periods of illness or have their health permanently impaired. Then there is the psychic shock brought on by worry, pain, crude and unesthetic operative procedures, and the prick of conscience if one gives the act a moral interpretation. Often just the emotional upset surrounding this experience is sufficient to cause a nervous breakdown or to incline one toward frigidity.

3. The third large group of hazards involved in premarital intercourse has to do with the psychological aspects of one's personality. We have already shown how sex is more than physical release, how it is intricately interwoven with one's feelings and social behavior as well. It follows, therefore, that consequences of the sex act reach deeply into one's personality, affecting, among other things, his marriage.

We have seen how emotional tension over venereal disease, forced marriage, illegitimacy, and abortion can weaken or disorganize one's personality. Now we are saying that this same type of disorganization can come to one who engages in premarital intercourse, even if none of these aforementioned disasters takes place. Worry about the rightness or wrongness of what has been done, fear about being found out, offended sensitivities due to circumstances surrounding the act, all of these and more can produce worry, frustration, unhappiness, and instability.

As with petting, premarital intercourse can often mean a cheapening of love, a developing of premature involvement, or

---

20 Margaret Banning, *op. cit.,* p. 3.

a conditioning against marriage adjustment. Premarital inter-course is too often performed in the spirit of reckless experi-mentation or exploitative thrill-seeking; consequently it tends to overemphasize the physical and to distort the total love pic-ture. When love involvement becomes great, as it frequently does in intercourse for at least one of the partners, someone is likely to get hurt emotionally or a marriage might take place prematurely or between persons ill-matched or poorly prepared otherwise. Finally, the undercover, hurried, and unesthetic na-ture of so many of these clandestine unions, coupled with the fears and guilt feelings that our society imposes, mean that many sensitive youth become maladjusted from the start. Pre-marital intercourse, therefore, might be a very real factor in producing frigidity and marital maladjustment. Satisfactory sexual adjustments are not easy to attain, especially for the female, and the process from the start needs the protection in love and security that marriage provides.

4. Social stigma is our final reason for confining sexual intercourse to marriage. In no culture is sex left uncontrolled; always it has been deemed important enough to group welfare to require regulation from the outside. That is why all so-cieties prescribe marriage and usually frown upon relations not covered by this contract. Persons who claim that what they do is their own business are mistaken, for each is a part of the group and every act has its impact upon others. Society does care. The social stigma leveled against the offender in the field of sex often results in the loss of reputation, social position, and even employment.

There are those who argue that there is nothing intrinsically wrong with nonmarital intercourse, that our social conven-tions can be changed and should be to remove the guilt feel-ings of those who would follow their natural impulses. To this we would say that the mores, though they do differ some in both time and space, are fairly constant when it comes to prescribing marriage as a safeguard for intercourse. Both the antiquity and the ubiquity of the marriage institution, we believe, are to be explained by consequences inherent to the sex act—reproduction, emotional envolvement, possible disease. To tie responsibility with opportunity, to protect children and dependent mothers, and to reduce personal exploitation, societies everywhere and at all times have ruled that marriage is the proper, or at least preferable, place for sexual intercourse. This fact is significant for it shows that our standards are intrinsic in the culture of man, if not in his original nature, and that they are deemed important to group welfare.

There is, of course, another side of the picture. One claim which we have already presented is that premarital relations give experience and thus aid in preparing a person for marriage. They give experience all right, but there is a real question as to whether this is any help or is actually a hindrance. Future studies will undoubtedly throw more light on this problem but at present it seems probable that more are handicapped by premarital experience than are helped. Another claim is that the sexual urge is natural and that the satisfying of it by intercourse is important to both mental and physical health. Yes, it is natural, but so are other things, such as crying and bed-wetting, which human beings in time learn to control. As to continence being harmful to health, we can only say that some of the best medical authorities claim otherwise. The unmarried, sexually mature individual may need to consciously avoid erotic stimulation and to redirect this drive along other channels, but this can be done and without any apparent impairment of health. A third claim is that premarital intercourse can aid one in selecting his mate. This approach not only tends to put too much emphasis upon sex as a factor, but it forgets or ignores the many hazards that are present while this testing is taking place. Furthermore, premarital intercourse, because of the insecurities peculiar to it, is not a fair test of one's sexual responsiveness; a girl could be frigid there, for example, who would be responsive under the protection of marriage. Still again, most fears concerning anatomical abnormalities and other difficulties of this sort are not justified and do not need testing in the sex act; the organs of both sexes are extremely adaptable and where abnormalities

they can be detected by a physician's examination.
e claims are placed side by side with the many rea-
or not engaging in premarital sexual intercourse, they
make a pretty weak case. In the words of Duvall and Hill,
"morality makes sense." [21]

Treatment of the Offender.—Regardless of standards and goals, people do make mistakes. Though society prescribes the norms, there are always those who deviate. What then?

One reaction to these breakers of the mores is to treat them harshly so as to make them realize the magnitude of the "sin." Too often this has been the approach in the past, but it has accomplished no good. What chance for a comeback has a young son or daughter banished from the home and scorned by society, for example? Yet comebacks are important if men and women are to be happy, if marriage is to succeed, and if society is to progress.

Another approach, and a more promising one, is to consider the past as past and to regard the present and future as of first importance. It is to emphasize rehabilitation rather than punishment. There are too many who permit themselves to be held down by mistakes of the past, and there are too many of the self-righteous who sanctimoniously hold them down instead of extending a helping hand. Once a mistake has been made, regardless of how unfortunate or serious it may be regarded, it should be first rectified so far as is possible and then forgotten. There is no point in brooding over what has happened. The Christian principles of repentance and forgiveness apply here as in other segments of life; they provide a means by which one might become released from his former indiscretions. How one faces the future is even more important to the success of marriage than what he may have done in the past.

Society's approach to chastity should ever be that of teaching rather than preaching, understanding rather than scolding, helping rather than condemning.

---

[21] Evelyn Millis Duvall and Reuben Hill, *When You Marry* (Boston: D. C. Heath & Co., 1945), chap. viii, pp. 145-64.

SANE SEX EDUCATION

In any program of sexual control, prevention is to be regarded as even more important than rehabilitation, and self-control must be recognized as more effective than restraints superimposed from the outside. This means education.

General Principles.—Marital success is at least partially contingent upon the sexual attitudes and habit patterns established early in one's life. Terman found those married mates to be most happy who, as children, received their first sex information from parents, received it in a frank and open manner, and had not experienced any serious fright or shock over sexual matters.[22] These findings conform with those from other studies and they line up well with the opinions of sociologists, psychiatrists, and others working in this field. They demonstrate a need for the right kind of education.

Two mistakes, opposite in nature, have been made in our treatment of sex. The first is to regard it as something evil, to be hushed up and avoided. The other is to be too openly brazen and crude about something so delicate, flaunting it before the public at all times. The first of these has made for prudery; the second has encouraged immorality; both are unfortunate. A proper approach would be to avoid these extremes, recognizing sex for what it is and according it a rightful place in life. In this way there would be fewer indiscretions before marriage and less incompatibility after marriage. Sex itself is not immoral; it is only when perverted by the low-minded and the irresponsible that it is made to seem so.

Parents and teachers would do well to realize that young people will find out about sex in one way or another, and, in realizing this, help them to find out the best way. Too often are the natural curiosities of children left unsatisfied by their elders and in consequence these children too frequently turn to the smutty story or other erotic sex talk in the dark alley or back of the billboard. This, of course, usually means that

---

22 Terman, *op. cit.*, pp. 237-52.

they become filled with factual misinformation and emotional distortion.

Case studies collected by the writer make it clear that young people, even in this day, rather commonly experience periods of morbid curiosity and warped perspective regarding sex. A great many college students still complain that as children they found their parents unapproachable on such matters, that whenever sex was mentioned in the home it was colored as evil or sinful, and that instructions, when they were given, were too vague and full of mystery to do much good. Consequently many of these students relate experiences of surprise, or worry, or disgust at the first menstruation, or nocturnal emission, or in first learning of intercourse. More than occasionally a young and uninformed girl will think she is pregnant because she has been kissed by a boy, or a naïve young male will feel that he must have intercourse in order to maintain his health or prove his manhood. These are but examples of the many misconceptions and emotional conflicts still found with those whose sex education has been faulty. While the present generation is undoubtedly doing a better job in this respect than did its grandparents, status quo is nevertheless a long way from status perfect.

The following case histories, one by a college male and the other by a college female, illustrate some of the problems and principles involved.[23]

Male. It has been only within the past two years that I have felt the beginnings of a definite moral code take shape in my mental make-up. Prior to that time I had been torn between ideal and desire, as most adolescents probably are. I admit that, once, I admired those who were unafraid of illicit relations with the opposite sex. With the beginnings of maturity, however, I have come to realize that virginity really is its own reward.

The foundations of my consequent sex problems were laid in my early childhood. I do not recall the sensual pleasure a child is supposed to receive from parental caresses, etc., but it must have been there. I do recall, however, being seriously scolded and spanked for playing with my own bodily organs. It seemed instinctive to me then,

---

[23] From the author's files.

and perfectly natural, and I must have continued the practice until I started school. Here, I suppose my occupancy with other people and things brought to a stop this, then delightful, business.

When the family moved to a town I was about eight years old and my associates were almost entirely boys. We were definitely an anti-girl group. From these associations, where I heard the obscene talk of older boys, and jokes I did not quite understand, I misconceived my first picture of sex. Naturally, there were many questions in my mind, and when I made them verbal I was severely reproved by my parents. I became convinced that sex was essentially bad.

At this time, my father should have, I suppose, informed me frankly of the so-called facts of life, but I had to be content with the twisted facts I had gleaned from my group.

I continued puzzling over the problems of sex, and as my curiosity grew, so grew my awareness of an actual sex desire. I masturbated a number of times. The actual act had never been pointed out as being particularly bad, but each such act was followed by an extreme sense of guilt and revulsion. This feeling probably dated back to the time I was scolded for playing with my organs. It had obviously conditioned me to associate the sexual organs with social disapproval.

This did not stop the overt sex act. We moved back to the country where I became one of a group who practiced homosexuality. The effect on me was similar to that of masturbation but the reaction was more severe. I would suffer whole days of misery, feeling I had done some great wrong. The fact that practically all the boys of my acquaintance were slightly homosexual made the thing seem less serious.

When I was about fourteen years old I began reading erotic books and magazines. This seemed to compensate, on occasion, for the sex drive. I'm certain that all this extensive reading of lurid tales was a godsend, because it led to my reading the sociology books I could obtain concerning sex. I reasoned that—if people could write so freely about such a thing, surely one could speak of them freely. Out of the maze of conflicts accompanying my adolescence was a desire to rebuke my father. Fortunately, I had a sister, older than I, who wanted to understand and help me. It was she who corrected many of my views. I still cannot discuss sex with my parents. Between us, we seem to have created an unsurmountable barrier of misunderstanding.

By the time I was sixteen and a junior in high school, I began to look at sex frankly. I was still too adolescent to be able to state my moral code, but it was there subconsciously. I dropped my auto- and homosexual practices—not suddenly, but gradually, as my interest waned and heterosexuality set in.

I suppose this was a crucial moment in my life. I know that it was embarrassing at times. My sexual attention was focused on the opposite sex, but fortunately, the old conditioned response to contact with sexual organs remained. Had it not, I might easily have indulged in premarital sex relations as was customary with half my acquaintances.

When I was about seventeen I adopted what I considered a broadminded view concerning sex. Fear held back, but I conceded that premarital relations were all right for other people.

About this time I left home, for the first time, to attend business college. There I met two girls from my home town, also attending business school. It is strange how close one can get to a formerly slight acquaintance in a place where both are strangers. Through one of these girls I came to realize the full effects of premarital mating. She had had an abortion which had left her psychologically twisted. She was nervous, worried, and unable to concentrate for any length of time. The abortion had disillusioned her as to the value of love, and she took to smoking, drinking, and became morally loose. She pretended nonchalance, but it was evident that, underneath, she was under constant strain. Looking at her I became convinced that I would never want to be responsible for such a condition in anyone.

Perhaps this acquaintance, more than anything else, cleared up my conflicts on sex and set me on the road to more logical thinking. I took to books again, only this time it was to satisfy a desire for knowledge rather than to satisfy a sex urge.

Female. Since I have grown up enough to observe other people, I have been astounded many times by their ideas of sex and things that have to do with sex. This winter I met and became a good friend of a girl who was shocked at how I took this "sex-business" in my stride. She had always thought of it as something morbid and unpleasant. True, she liked boys and was very fond of "dates," but when we girls spoke of married life and children she thought we were vulgar.

After I had talked with her several times I began to realize what she was up against. In the first place her mother was a woman who could not talk to her children. She was shocked or embarrassed if they asked questions. All my friend knew about this she had picked up from other girls and a few not too good books and magazine articles. She told me, "I can't talk to my mother or dad. I just hate to be alone with them." I began to wonder where our lives had differed.

I knew of no one whom I'd rather be with than Mom, and Dad and I were always such pals. But let me tell you of a little of my life.

I remember Dad teaching me to pray, to read, and to tell time. I went every place with him and we continually talked. In these early days of my life we were living on a dairy farm—thirty-two cows, no less. Betty and I had the honor of herding the cows. One day we brought them in at noon; Dad met us, as usual, but instead of going to dinner we three sat down on the top rail of the fence and Dad told us where babies came from. He told it very simply and left out all the details which were not interesting or important to us. As I remember it, I had asked very few questions concerning this, but, as Dad told us later, it was best we knew, for on a farm births can occur almost anytime.

Betty was born less than two years after I was, but I was six before Ruth came. Thus I noticed things develop; I naturally asked questions. Every question was answered truthfully and with no embarrassment on the part of Mother, Dad, Betty, or me. If any new problem came up I asked Dad—or Mother if Dad wasn't around.

When I was in the seventh grade the kids were becoming "sex conscious." We spent hours talking about it. However, around school the talk was carried on in secret and we were embarrassed if anyone caught us at it. This embarrassment bothered me, so one evening I went to the barn where Mom was talking to Dad while he milked. I told them how we were acting at school and how ashamed we were if someone heard us. I wanted to know what was wrong. Now, I realize this was a perplexing problem, but then I could not understand why it took them so long to answer. After several minutes it was explained to me that even though sex was natural and that there was nothing bad about it, it was better if girls didn't talk about it too much. They said for me to spend more time playing and less time talking and everything would work out all right. I took their advice and everything did work out all right.

Faulty sex education, by being inadequate, or distorted, or overtoned emotionally, can result in at least two unfortunate situations for marriage. The first of these has to do with the erotic stimulation and the resulting higher antisocial participation in sex on the part of those who have been incorrectly informed. The second concerns conditioning, it being well known that such abnormalities as homosexuality and frigidity frequently find their roots in an unfortunate introduction, or later exposure, to the phenomenon of sex.

Sane sex education will include both the imparting of facts and the building of attitudes. No one ever made a mistake because of knowledge, though some have erred in spite of it and many have gone wrong without it. While ignorance leaves one vulnerable, knowledge and understanding make chastity easier. Yet this alone is not enough; to be effective facts must be accompanied by incentive. That education is most valuable which both helps people to know the facts and then makes them want to constructively apply what they know.

Procedures and Sources.—Sex, being so highly charged with emotion and so surrounded by social pressures, is sometimes considered difficult to teach. Probably that is the reason so many parents and teachers, though recognizing its importance, still shirk the task. Then, too, views on the subject remain highly controversial; not all are agreed concerning just what should be taught, or how, or when. Most authorities would accept the following, however:

1. Example is of prime importance here as in most other fields of learning. Not that the physical aspects require demonstration (they do not), but only that those who deal with this subject be mature and well balanced personally, and be in harmony socially so that children can see marriage in proper perspective.

2. The approach needs to be positive rather than negative. The venereal diseases should not be one's first introduction to the field of sex, and neither should scolding, nor punishing, nor threatening, nor overmoralizing. Explaining is the thing, so that the child comes to see sex as having a purpose and a place in life. Too many girls are overwarned with reference to men only later to become either homosexual or frigid. Too many of both sexes are either frightened or disgusted over what should be considered both beautiful and acceptable.

3. Closely related to this point, just made, is the principle that control should come to be internal rather than external, self-control rather than mere conformity to pressure. This

can never be brought about by preaching or forcing, only by informing and leading. A part of it is helping the child to understand the necessity for social regulation, building within him a respect for custom though without blinding him to the need for cultural change.

4. Sex education is most effective when it is gradual, starting in the early years and extending throughout most of life. The parent who avoids these matters when his child is young makes a great mistake, even though he may think to pick it up again at adolescence and at that time explain all the "facts of life" in one dose. If this be the procedure, the parent is likely to discover that his child already knows more than expected and that the interview is embarrassing for both. Better that each question be answered as it comes up and the curiosity satisfied then—answered in simple language and with just enough information to satisfy, but also enough to build up confidence and insure his coming back for more.

5. The child's questions need to be answered quite naturally and by either parent that happens to be present. This requires that there be no embarrassment or change of voice and that the child will be given no feeling that he has done wrong in asking. Though simple, answers must nevertheless be truthful and given with the use of correct names for the various body parts and the processes. This will help avoid the development of unnatural attitudes and practices. It may need to be explained to the child, however, that there are certain things people talk about only within their own families.

6. Instances of the child's exploring his own body need to be handled in much the same way. If the parent acts shocked or gives punishment for such behavior (which is normal for most children and is performed in innocence), he may thereby start the conditioning process in the wrong direction and at the same time establish a barrier that may in turn make later sex education more difficult.

7. Sex education need not be left exclusively to the parents. While parental responsibility in the matter is great, the facts are that personalities are the products of many agencies and that some families fail in carrying out even their most ele-

mentary duties, including this one. Schools and churches can fill a valuable niche, therefore, both in taking up the slack when families fail and in supplementing that which normal families regularly perform. But the educational principles would be the same whether applied in or out of the home— truthfulness, naturalness, neither over- nor underemphasis, maturity and training on the part of the teacher.

8. Good literature can be used to help supplement the work of parents and teachers. Though a great deal of what one is exposed to these days is trashy and harmful, there is much that is both wholesome and helpful. Leaders of the young need to be aware of what is available, and of its quality, so as to be discriminating in their recommendations. Following is a brief list of some of the most useful and widely tapped sources:

FOR CHILDREN

DE SCHWEINITZ, KARL. *Growing Up*. New York: The Macmillan Co., 1943, 95 pp.

LEVINE, MILTON I., and SELIGMAN, JEAN H. *The Wonder of Life*. New York: Simon and Schuster, Inc., 1940, 114 pp.

STRAIN, FRANCES BRUCE. *Being Born*. New York: Appleton-Century-Crofts, Inc., 1936, 144 pp.

FOR YOUTH

KELIHER, ALICE V. *Life and Growth*. New York: Appleton-Century-Crofts, Inc., 1938, 245 pp.

STRAIN, FRANCES BRUCE. *Teen Days*. New York: Appleton-Century-Crofts, Inc., 1946, 183 pp.

WELSHIMER, HELEN. *Questions Girls Ask*. New York: E. P. Dutton & Co., 1939, 128 pp.

FOR ENGAGED AND MARRIED

BUTTERFIELD, OLIVER M. *Sex Life in Marriage*. New York: Emerson Books, 1937, 192 pp.

STONE, HANNAH M., and STONE, ABRAHAM. *A Marriage Manual*. New York: Simon & Schuster, Inc., 1939, 255 pp.

VAN DE VELDE, T. H. *Ideal Marriage*. New York: Random House, 1943.

Conclusions.—Sex and marriage are not synonymous, but they are related and neither can be quite complete in our society without the other. Marriage is more than sex, most certainly, and sex is more than its physiological manifestations.

Patterns of human sexual behavior are many and varied. Marital intercourse is the pattern considered most normal, however, it being the most productive biologically, the most sanctioned sociologically, and the most common statistically. Certain deviant patterns, such as homosexuality and premarital intercourse, are believed to be unfavorable to marital happiness.

Though sexual "purity" is an ideal, prudery is no way of bringing such a condition about. Negative and arbitrary controls over sex have been used far too much in the past, with frigidity as one of the results. Is it possible to have chastity without at the same time producing frigidity? Yes, if the approach be positive and in the directions of intelligence and self-control.

With proper perspective, therefore, one can accept sex as an important fraction of life, rejecting its distortions, developing its potentials. Perspective here can help men and women know that there are many factors back of the great marriage adventure, only one of which is sex.

PROBLEMS AND PROJECTS

1. Some people take the position that there is too much open talk about sex in this day. They argue that by removing the mystery surrounding it we tend to make it less sacred and less easily controlled. Do you agree? Why or why not?
2. Does knowing "the facts of life" aid in the control of sex? Is knowledge alone enough? Discuss.
3. Is it possible to promote sex education without at the same time inciting erotic stimulation? How?
4. Some people feel that an important cause of sexual maladjustment in marriage is the lack of understanding by each sex of the psychological approach of the other to physical relations. How do males and females differ regarding sex drive and response?
5. It has been claimed that the Kinsey report, by revealing what goes on, will have the effect of encouraging greater sexual laxity. What is your opinion and why?
6. How much physical intimacy is advisable before marriage? Will petting during the engagement help or hinder adjustment? What about sexual intercourse? Give your reasons for

either agreeing or disagreeing with the point of view taken by the text.

7. Are there ways in which society can promote chastity without at the same time conditioning for frigidity? Name some common mistakes. Discuss.

8. Do you believe in a single or a double standard of morality? Give reasons.

9. When and where should sex education for children begin? How should it continue?

10. Consider methods by which a young couple, who plan to marry but are unable to do so for some time, may control sexual impulses in a satisfactory and constructive manner.

11. Discuss the pros and cons of legalizing abortion. Is there anything that can be learned from the Russian experience?

12. Why does our society take such a serious view of homosexuality? Are we handling the situation wisely?

13. What should be society's position regarding those who have offended the sex mores. Can it forgive and assist the offender without condoning and encouraging the offense? Discuss.

SELECTED READINGS

BABER, RAY E. *Marriage and the Family*. New York: McGraw-Hill Book Co., 1939. Chap. xvii, "Conflicting Sex Patterns."

BANNING, MARGARET C. "The Case for Chastity," *Reader's Digest*, 31 :1-10, August, 1937.

BECKER, HOWARD, and HILL, REUBEN (eds.). *Family, Marriage, and Parenthood*. Boston: D. C. Heath & Co., 1948. Chap. x, "Taking Physical Factors into Account."

DUVALL, EVELYN MILLIS, and HILL, REUBEN. *When You Marry*. Boston: D. C. Heath & Co., 1945. Chaps. vii, "Marriage and the Facts of Life"; viii, "Morality Makes Sense."

FISHBEIN, MORRIS, and BURGESS, ERNEST W. (eds.). *Successful Marriage*. New York: Doubleday & Co., 1947. Part IV, chap. vi, "Sex Education and the Child"; Part V, chap. i, "Sex and the Social Order."

FRANK, ROBERT. *Personal Counsel: A Supplement to Morals*. New York: Informative Books, 1946.

GRUENBERG, BENJAMIN C. *How Can We Teach About Sex?* New York: Public Affairs Committee, 1946.

HIMES, NORMAN E. *Your Marriage: A Guide to Happiness*. New York: Farrar & Rinehart, Inc., 1940. Chaps. i, "Our Point of View"; ii, "Sex Problems of Modern Youth"; iii, "Premarital Sex Relations."

HYMES, JAMES L., JR. *How To Tell Your Child About Sex*. New York: Public Affairs Committee, 1949.

JUNG, MOSES (ed.). *Modern Marriage*. New York: Appleton-Century-Crofts, Inc., 1940. Chap. xi, "Physical Aspects of Marriage."

LANDIS, JUDSON T., and LANDIS, MARY G. *Building a Successful Marriage*. New York: Prentice-Hall, Inc., 1948. Chaps. vi, "Premarital Sexual Relations"; xxii, "Sex Education."

LEUBA, CLARENCE. *Ethics in Sex Conduct*. New York: Association Press, 1948.

POPENOE, PAUL. *Building Sex into Your Life*. Los Angeles: American Institute of Family Relations.

SEWARD, GEORGENE H. *Sex and the Social Order*. New York: McGraw-Hill Book Co., 1946.

SHULTZ, GLADYS DENNY. *Letters to Jane*. Philadelphia: J. B. Lippincott Co., 1949.

Chapter 6

PREDICTING SUCCESS AND FAILURE

This is an age of science. For some time now childish super-stition and armchair speculation have been yielding to the penetrating searchlight of scientific investigation. In the solving of his problems, man has been turning more and more to a rigorous and objective reaching for the facts.

It is in the physical and biological fields, however, that the scientific method has received its widest application and greatest success. Within the social field, that having to do with interrelationships on the human level, scientific development has lagged. There are two reasons primarily: (1) Sociological data are more complex and less accessible, more difficult to measure and control for purposes of analysis. Better scholarship is the only answer to this. (2) The human element has crept in, making it difficult for man to look objectively at himself; man has too frequently been ignorant and superstitious, has too often been willing to let either the "cake of custom" or his present vested interest interfere with progress. This can be overcome, in time, and at least in part, by persistence in the use of the scientific method applied to social phenomena so that its value as a problem-solving tool can become better known.

Love in its various manifestations has for a long time been looked upon as instinctive and largely personal. To lay these intimate urges and behavior patterns upon the dissecting table, so to speak, and to analyze them as one would a piece of clay in the physics laboratory, has seemed to be just a little too indelicate or even indecent. So science has been slow in applying itself to marriage. But medicine met a similar resistance during an earlier period of its development as a science; the attendance of male physicians at childbirth was considered by some to be immoral, for example, and the use of cadavers for research and training purposes brought feelings of horror to many. Yet it was only by overcoming these and other obstacles that the science of medicine is where it is today. And other disciplines have had similar experiences. With regard to the family, it should be evident from the seriousness of the trouble it knows that instinct alone is insufficient. By isolating the factors responsible, seeing how they operate, and then applying what is learned, science can do much to untangle the marriage muddle.

The aim of science is a knowledge of truth as background for prediction and control. Its method is the objective analysis of facts, directed particularly toward cause and effect relationships. Social phenomena undergo cause and effect sequences, just as do those that are physical or biological in nature; and in every case a knowledge of the forces back of the action, or behavior, can enable one to predict what will happen in given situations and to control the outcome by changing some of the elements that are involved.

How is it with marriage and the family? Has science gone far enough there to permit prediction regarding marital adjustment and then control in the direction of greater success?

A Prediction Schedule

The following test, prepared by Ernest W. Burgess, Leonard S. Cottrell, and Paul Wallin, is designed to measure one's probability of success in marriage.[1] It is given here for two purposes: (1) to illustrate the marriage prediction technique and (2) to aid the reader in better understanding his own chances for successful marital adjustment.

---

[1] Reproduced by permission. From Ernest W. Burgess and Harvey J. Locke, *The Family: From Institution to Companionship* (New York: American Book Co., 1945), pp. 760-71; 785-87. Words requesting information not used in the scoring have been deleted; otherwise all instructions, listings, and interpretations are essentially as they appeared in the original.

There are other marriage prediction schedules that the reader may have seen or that can be found in any good library. Most of these have been based upon the findings of two important studies appearing a little over a decade ago: (1) Ernest W. Burgess and Leonard S. Cottrell, *Predicting Success or Failure in Marriage* (New York: Prentice-Hall, Inc., 1939); (2) Lewis M. Terman, *Psychological Factors in Marital Happiness* (New York: McGraw-Hill Book Co. 1938).

INSTRUCTIONS

This schedule is prepared for persons who are seriously considering marriage. Although designed for couples who are engaged or who have a private understanding to be married, it can also be filled out by other persons who would like to know their probability of success in marriage.

The value of the findings of the schedule depends upon your frankness in answering the questions.

The following points should be kept in mind in filling out the schedule:

1. Be sure to answer every question.
2. Do not leave a blank to mean a "no" answer.
3. The word "fiancé(e)" will be used to refer to the person to whom you are engaged.
4. Do not confer with your fiancé(e) on any of these questions.

	For scoring		
PART ONE	1	2	3
1. What is your present state of health? (check): poor health [(a) chronic____, (b) temporary____]; (c) average health____; (d) healthy ✗ ; (e) very healthy ✓			
2. How would you rate the physical appearance of your fiancé(e)? (check): (u) very good looking ✗ ; (v) good looking____; (x) fairly good looking ✓ ; (y) plain looking____; (z) very plain looking____			
3. Your present marital status (check): (u) single ✗ ; (v) widowed____; (x) separated____; (y) divorced____			
4. Check highest level of schooling completed at present time: (a) grades____; (b) high school____; (c) some college ✓ ; (d) graduate of college____; (e) postgraduate or professional training____			
5. Work record (check): (u) regularly employed____; (v) worked only during vacations or/and only part time while in school ✓ ; (w) none, because in school or at home____; (x) always employed but continually changing jobs____; (y) irregularly employed____; (t) other____			
6. Your activity in church (check): (a) never attend____; (b) attend less than once a month____; (c) once or twice per month____; (d) three times a month____; (e) four times a month ✓			
7. At what age did you stop attending Sunday School? (check): (a) never attended____; (b) before 10 years old____; (c) 11-18 years____; (d) 19 and over____; (e) still attending ✓			

For scoring

	1	2	3

8. How many organizations do you belong to or attend regularly such as church club, athletic club, social club, luncheon club (like the Rotary, Kiwanis, Lions), fraternal order, college fraternity, college sorority, civic organization, music society, patriotic organization, Y.W.C.A., Y.M.C.A., Y.M.H.A., C.Y.O.? (check): (a) none____; (b) one ✓; (c) two____; (d) three or more ✓

9. In leisure time activities (check): (u) we both prefer to stay at home ✓; (x) we both prefer to be "on the go" ✓; (y) I prefer to be on the go and my fiancé(e) to stay at home____; (z) I prefer to stay at home and my fiancé(e) to be on the go____

10. Check what you consider to have been the economic status of your parents during your adolescence: (u) well-to-do____; (v) wealthy ✓; (w) comfortable ✓; (x) meager____; (z) poor____

11. Check what you consider to be the social status of your parents in their own community: (j) one of the leading families ✓; (k) upper class____; (l) upper-middle class ✓ ✓ (m) middle class ✓; (n) lower middle class____; (o) lower class____

12. Marital status of your parents (check): (l) married (both living) ✓; (m) separated____; (n) divorced____; (t) other

13. Your appraisal of the happiness of your parents' marriage (check): (i) very happy ✓; (k) happy____; (l) average ✓; (m) unhappy____; (n) very unhappy____

14. Check your attitudes toward your parents on the following scales: (1) Your attitude toward your father when you were a child: (j) very strong attachment____; (k) considerable attachment ✓; (m) mild attachment ✓; (n) mild hostility ____; (o) considerable hostility____; (p) very strong hostility____

    (2) Your present attitude toward your father: (j) very strong attachment____; (k) considerable attachment ✓; (m) mild attachment ✓; (n) mild hostility____; (o) considerable hostility____; (p) very strong hostility____

    (3) Your present attitude toward your mother: (j) very strong attachment____; (k) considerable attachment ✓; (m) mild attachment ✓; (n) mild hostility____; (o) considerable hostility____; (p) very strong hostility____

    (4) Your attitude toward your mother when you were a child: (j) very strong attachment____; (k) considerable attachment ✓; (m) mild attachment ✓; (n) mild hostility (o) considerable hostility____; (p) very strong hostility____

For scoring

	1	2	3

15. Rate the marital happiness of your father (check): (*i*) extra-ordinarily happy____; (*k*) decidedly happy____; (*m*) happy ____; (*n*) somewhat happy____; (*o*) average____; (*p*) somewhat unhappy____; (*q*) unhappy____; (*r*) decidedly unhappy ____; (*s*) extremely unhappy____

    Rate the marital happiness of your mother (check): (*i*) extraordinarily happy____; (*k*) decidedly happy____; (*m*) happy ____; (*n*) somewhat happy____; (*o*) average____; (*p*) somewhat unhappy____; (*q*) unhappy____; (*r*) decidedly unhappy ____; (*s*) extremely unhappy____

16. Outside of your family and kin, how many separated and divorced people do you know personally? (check): (*j*) none ____; (*k*) one____; (*m*) two____; (*n*) three____; (*o*) four____; (*p*) five____; (*q*) six____; (*r*) seven or more____

17. With how many of the opposite sex, *other than your fiancé(e)*, have you gone steadily? (check): (*v*) none____; (*w*) one____; (*t*) two____; (*l*) three or more____

18. Defining friends as something more than mere acquaintances but not necessarily always boon companions, give an estimate of the number of your men friends before going steadily with your fiancé(e) (check): (*a*) none____; (*b*) few____; (*c*) several ____; (*d*) many____

19. Estimate the number of your women friends before going steadily with your fiancé(e) (check): (*a*) none____; (*b*) few ____; (*c*) several____; (*d*) many____

20. How many of your present men and women friends are also friends of your fiancé(e)? (check): (*u*) all____; (*v*) most of them____; (*x*) a few____; (*y*) none____

21. Have you ever been engaged before (or had any previous informal understanding that you were to be married)? (check): (*u*) never____; (*w*) once____; (*x*) twice____; (*y*) three or more times____

T

For scoring

	1	2	3

PART TWO

1. Do you plan to be married (check): (*u*) at church____; (*v*) at home____; (*x*) elsewhere____

2. By whom do you plan to be married? (check): (*v*) minister ____; (*x*) other person____

3. Where do you plan to live after marriage? (check); (*j*) private house____; (*k*) small apartment building____; (*l*) large apart-

	For scoring		
	1	2	3

ment building____; (*m*) apartment hotel____; (*n*) hotel____; (*o*) rooming house____

4. Check: (*j*) have you bought a home?____; (*k*) are you planning to buy a home?__✓__; (*m*) will you rent a home?____

5. Population of city or town where you plan to live (check): (*i*) open country____; (*j*) 2,500 and under____; (*k*) 2,500 to 10,000____; (*l*) 10,000 to 50,000__✓__; (*m*) 50,000 to 100,000 __✓__; (*n*) 100,000 to 500,000____; (*o*) over 500,000____; (*u*) suburb____

6. After marriage do you plan to live (check): (*j*) in own home __✓__; (*n*) with your parents____; (*o*) parents-in-law____; (*p*) relatives____; (*q*) relatives-in-law____; (*r*) other persons____

7. Check *your* attitude toward having children: (*v*) desire children very much__✓__; (*x*) mildly desire them____; (*y*) mild objection to them____; (*z*) object very much to having them ____

8. How many children would you like to have? (check): (*u*) four or more__✓__; (*v*) three____; (*w*) two____; (*x*) one____; (*y*) none____

9. Check what you think your fiancé(e)'s attitude is toward having children: (*v*) desires children very much__✓__; (*x*) mildly desires them____; (*y*) mild objection to them____; (*z*) objects very much to having them____

10. Do you think your fiancé(e) is spending a disproportionate amount of present income on? (check): (*a*) clothes (or other personal ornamentation)____; (*b*) recreation____; (*c*) food or rent____; (*d*) education____; (*e*) do not think so__✓__

11. What is the attitude of your closest friend or friends to your fiancé(e)? (check): (*v*) approve highly__✓__; (*w*) approve with qualification__✓__; (*x*) are resigned____; (*y*) disapprove mildly____; (*z*) disapprove seriously____

12. Do you smoke? (check): (*u*) not at all__✓__; (*w*) rarely____; (*x*) occasionally____; (*y*) often____

13. Do you drink? (check): (*u*) not at all__✓__; (*w*) rarely____; (*x*) occasionally____; (*y*) often____

14. Check: (*u*) do both your father and mother approve your marriage__✓__; (*y*) do both disapprove____; (*z*) does one disapprove____

15. What is your attitude toward your future father-in-law? (check): (*k*) like him very much__✓__; (*l*) like him considerably____; (*m*) like him mildly____; (*n*) mild dislike____; (*o*) considerable dislike____; (*p*) very strong dislike____

For scoring

	1	2	3

What is your attitude toward your future mother-in-law? (check): (k) like her very much____; (l) like her considerably____; (m) like her mildly____; (n) mild dislike____; (o) considerable dislike; (p) very strong dislike____

16. Was your first information about sex? (check): (v) wholesome____; (x) unwholesome____

Where did you get your first information about sex? (check): (j) from parent____; (k) from wholesome reading ____; (l) brother, sister, or other relative____; (m) teacher or other adult____; (n) other children____; (o) from pernicious reading____

Do you consider your present knowledge of sex adequate for marriage? (check): (v) yes____; (x) no or doubtful____

17. How long have you been keeping company with your fiancé(e)? (check): (a) less than 3 months____; (b) 3 to 5 months____; (c) 6 to 11 months____; (d) 12 to 17 months ____; (e) 18 to 23 months____; (f) 24 to 35 months____; (g) 36 months or more____

18. How many months will elapse between your engagement (or time at which you both had a definite understanding that you were to be married) and the date selected for your marriage? (check): (a) less than 3 months____; (b) 3 to 6 months ____; (c) 6 to 11 months____; (d) 12 to 17 months____; (e) 18 to 23 months____; (f) 24 to 35 months____; (g) 36 months or more____

| T | | | |

For scoring

	1	2	3

PART THREE

1. Do you and your fiancé(e) engage in interests and activities together? (check): (v) all of them____; (w) most of them____; (x) some of them____; (y) a few of them____; (z) none of them____

2. Is there any interest vital to you in which your fiancé(e) does not engage? (check): (v) no____; (z) yes____

3. Do you confide in your fiancé(e)? (check): (i) about everything____; (k) about most things____; (m) about some things____; (n) about a few things____; (o) about nothing ____

4. Does your fiancé(e) confide in you? (check): (i) about everything____; (k) about most things____; (m) about some things____; (n) about a few things____; (o) about nothing ____

For scoring

	1	2	3

5. Check the frequency of demonstrations of affection you show your fiancé(e) (kissing, embracing, etc.): (*i*) occupies practically all of the time you are alone together____; (*j*) very frequent____; (*m*) occasional____; (*n*) rare____; (*o*) almost never____

6. Who generally takes the initiative in the demonstration of affection? (check): (*u*) mutual____; (*m*) you____; (*x*) your fiancé(e)____

        I do

7. Are you satisfied with the amount of demonstration of affection? (check): (*j*) yes____; (*p*) desire less____; (*q*) desire more____

    Is your fiancé(e) satisfied with the amount of demonstration of affection? (check): (*j*) yes____; (*p*) desires less____; (*q*) desires more____

8. State the *present* approximate agreement or disagreement with your fiancé(e) on the following items: Please place a check in the proper column opposite every item.

Check one column for each item below	(*j*) Always agree	(*k*) Almost always agree	(*l*) Occasionally disagree	(*m*) Frequently disagree	(*n*) Almost always disagree	(*o*) Always disagree	(*t*) Never discussed			
Money matters										
Matters of recreation										
Religious matters										
Demonstrations of affection										
Friends										
Table manners										
Matters of conventionality										

For scoring

								1	2	3
Check one column for each item below	(j) Al-ways agree	(k) Al-most al-ways agree	(l) Occa-sion-ally dis-agree	(m) Fre-quently dis-agree	(n) Al-most al-ways dis-agree	(o) Al-ways dis-agree	(t) Never dis-cussed			
Philosophy of life										
Ways of dealing with your families										
Arrange-ments for your marriage										
Dates with one another										

9. When disagreements arise between you and your fiancé(e) they usually result in (check): (v) agreement by mutual give and take____; (y) you giving in____; (z) your fiancé(e) giving in____

10. Do you ever wish you had not become engaged? (check): (u) never____; (x) once____; (y) occasionally____; (z) frequently ____

11. Have you ever contemplated breaking your engagement? (check): (u) never____; (x) once____; (y) occasionally____; (z) frequently____

12. Has your steady relationship with your fiancé(e) ever been broken off temporarily? (check): (v) never____; (x) once____; (y) twice____; (z) three or more times____

13. How confident are you that your marriage will be a happy one? (check): (v) very confident____; (w) confident____; (x) a little uncertain____; (y) extremely uncertain____

T

PART FOUR

Rate yourself on each of the following personality traits:

Check *one* column for each item below	Very much so	Consid- 'erably	Some- what	A little	Not at all	For scoring 1	2	3
Takes responsi- bility willingly	u___	v___	w___	x___	z___			
Dominating.....	a___	b___	c___	d___	e___			
Irritable........	a___	b___	c___	d___	e___			
Punctual.......	u___	v___	w___	x___	z___			
Moody.........	a___	b___	c___	d___	e___			
Angers easily...	a___	b___	c___	d___	e___			
Ambitious......	a___	b___	c___	d___	e___			
Jealous.........	a___	b___	c___	d___	e___			
Sympathetic....	u___	v___	w___	x___	z___			
Easygoing......	u___	v___	w___	x___	z___			
Selfish.........	a___	b___	c___	d___	e___			
Stubborn.......	a___	b___	c___	d___	e___			
Sense of duty...	u___	v___	w___	x___	z___			
Sense of humor..	u___	v___	w___	x___	z___			
Easily hurt.....	a___	b___	c___	d___	e___			
Self-confident...	u___	v___	w___	x___	z___			
Nervous........	a___	b___	c___	d___	e___			
Likes belonging to organiza- tions.........	u___	v___	w___	x___	z___			
Impractical.....	a___	b___	c___	d___	e___			
Easily depressed	a___	b___	c___	d___	e___			
Easily excited...	a___	b___	c___	d___	e___			
						T		

Part I_4_, Part II_2_, Part III_5_, Part IV_4_, Total_6_

SCORING

The three narrow columns at the right-hand side of each page of the Marriage Prediction Schedule are reserved for scoring the replies to the questions. The score values assigned are arbitrary in the sense that usually each gradation in reply differs by one point. For example, the following question is scored as follows: Do you and your spouse engage in outside interests together? (check): (*j*) all of them, $+2$; (*k*) most of them, $+1$; (*l*) some of them, 0; (*m*) few of them, -1; (*n*) none of them, -2. Although arbitrary, the score values are in general conformity with the findings of the studies in this field, particularly those of E. W. Burgess and L. S. Cottrell, *Predicting Success or Failure in Marriage;* L. M. Terman, *Psychological Factors in Marital Happiness;* and E. W. Burgess and Paul Wallin, *A Study of 1000 Engaged Couples.*

The letters in italics before each subdivision of the question provide the code for scoring the replies. The code value of each letter is as follows:

a	-2	n	-2
b	-1	o	-3
c	0	p	-3
d	$+1$	q	-3
e	$+2$	r	-3
f	$+2$	s	-3
g	$+2$	t	0
h	$+2$	u	$+2$
i	$+3$	v	$+1$
j	$+2$	w	0
k	$+1$	x	-1
l	0	y	-2
m	-1	z	-2

The following is the procedure for scoring the replies to the questions:

1. For each question enter in column 1 at the right-hand side of each page the letter in italics which precedes the answer which is checked for the given item.

2. Enter in column 2 all the plus scores and in column 3 all the minus scores corresponding to the appropriate code value for each letter as indicated above.

3. Add the scores in columns 2 and 3, entering them for each part; then transfer them to the appropriate place, as indicated at the end of the schedule.

High scores, those above 60, are favorable for marital adjustment, as indicated by research findings that approximately 75 per cent of persons with these scores in the engagement period are well adjusted in their marriages. Low scores, or those below 20, are much less favorable for happiness in marriage, as shown by the probability that only 25 per cent of persons with these scores will be well adjusted in married life. Intermediate scores, those between 60 and 20, should be regarded at present as nonpredictive since the chances of persons with these scores for marital success may tentatively be considered as about even.

The prediction score of a person and his corresponding matrimonial risk group assignment should be interpreted with extreme caution. The following points should be kept in mind:

1. The prediction does not apply directly to the individual. It states the statistical probabilities of marital success for a group of persons of which the individual is one. If he belongs to the lower risk group, in which 75 per cent of the marriages turn out unhappily, there is no way of telling by this statistical prediction whether he falls in the 25 per cent of the marriages with varying degrees of happiness or in the 75 per cent of unhappy unions.

2. The prediction is an individual's general matrimonial risk, irrespective of the particular person to whom he is engaged. The individual's specific matrimonial risk for marriage to a given person is much more valuable but also more complicated and therefore not suited for self-scoring.

3. In the majority of cases the specific matrimonial risk of a couple may be roughly estimated from the two general matrimonial risk groups

to which the two persons are assigned. An average of the two scores will generally be close to what may be expected from a specific matrimonial risk group assignment worked out by combining the answers on each question given by the two members of the couple.

4. With the above reservations in mind, a low prediction score should not be taken as indicating lack of suitability for marriage. It should, however, be helpful to the person in stimulating him to secure adequate preparation for marriage, to be more careful in the selection of a marriage partner, and to give attention to the solving of any difficulties in the relation before rather than after marriage.

STUDIES IN PREDICTION

The essential idea or principle back of any such predictive skill is that one's personality characteristics and past performance records may be used as partial indices of his future adjustments, that conduct is contingent upon backgrounds and habit patterns. It is for this reason that human predictive studies have tried to correlate behavior patterns with background items associated with them, the assumption being that those items have the highest predictive values which show the greatest correlations with the pattern under consideration (i.e., happiness, adjustment, etc.).

Scientific prediction of human behavior began in fields other than marriage. It was found, for example, that one's performance in college could pretty well be predicted from his high school record and from scores based upon intelligence and achievement tests. It was also found that the probable success or failure of prison parolees could be determined ahead of time by analyzing the personalities and past behavior patterns of prisoners. In no instance, of course, could performance be predicted with certainty—though with a probability far above that of mere chance or guesswork.

It should be clear from this that any valid knowledge of probable happenings can prove extremely valuable to school principals, prison officials, and others in administrative positions; knowing the tendencies and the risks, they are more able to alter the situations and to control the outcomes. Equally obvious, and important, is the need for knowledge among those who plan to marry.

"Common-sense" predictions concerning marital adjustment can be made by just about anyone who has any understanding of the factors involved. The reliability of each prediction will depend, however, upon the extent of the understanding and the skill with which it is applied to the analysis of the case, and may range from zero where there is mere guesswork to near one hundred per cent where the insight is considerable. Predictions based upon dreams, hunches, superstitions, misinformation, or wishful thinking have absolutely no scientific value.

Better than all these "common-sense" traditions and impressions, handed out too freely by relatives and acquaintances, are the case-study analyses of trained specialists. By conducting interviews and analyzing letters and other human documents, clinicians and research workers can frequently gain sufficient insight into a courtship or marriage situation to be able to predict the outcome. One shortcoming of this method is its high degree of subjectivity; though an analyst may be proficient, there is no guarantee that he is right or that other analysts would arrive at the same prognostic conclusions.

Statistical prediction of marital success began about a decade ago with the works of Terman [2] and of Burgess and Cottrell.[3] Terman used the self-rated happiness scores of his subjects as his criterion for successful marriage, while Burgess and Cottrell used "marital adjustment," determined largely by measures of agreement and disagreement between the spouses. In both cases several hundred background items were compared with measures of successful marriage to determine which items showed the highest correlations and hence had the greatest predictive values. Both studies dealt largely with upper middle class, urban, educated, Americans who were married at the time they were contacted (Terman's 792 couples were from California, while Burgess and Cottrell's 526 were from Illinois). The two studies paralleled each other and conclusions are similar.

2 Terman, *op. cit.*, pp. 167-266.
3 Burgess and Cottrell, *op. cit.*, pp. 269-374.

Terman found that the ten background circumstances that are most predictive of marital happiness are: (1) superior happiness of parents, (2) childhood happiness, (3) lack of conflict with mother, (4) home discipline that was firm but not harsh, (5) strong attachment to mother, (6) strong attachment to father, (7) lack of conflict with father, (8) parental frankness about matters of sex, (9) infrequency and mildness of childhood punishment, and (10) premarital attitudes toward sex that were free from disgust or aversion. He concluded by saying: "The subject who 'passes' on all 10 of these items is a distinctly better-than-average marital risk." [4]

The Burgess and Cottrell study showed that the following correlate rather highly with adjustment in marriage: [5]

The marriage of the parents of both husband and wife reported as happy; approval of marriage by parents of the couple; superior family background of husband and wife; similarity of their family backgrounds; husband and wife not only children; husband closely attached to, and having little or no conflict with, his father and mother; wife's close attachment to mother; husband and wife reared in country; both attended Sunday School beyond 18 years of age; church attendance by husband two or more times a month; husband with graduate or professional education, and wife with college, graduate, or professional education; certain occupations for husband, and teaching for wife; wife employed at occupation the same as or similar to the one she prefers; income of wife $150 to $200 a month; husband had several or many men friends and several women friends; wife did not lack men friends and had many women friends; wife 15 or more pounds underweight; at time of marriage husband resided in suburbs; couple acquainted with each other two or more years; husband and wife kept company three years and were engaged three years and over; husband and wife 22 to 30 years old at time of marriage; couple married by minister, priest, or rabbi.

On the basis of these and other factors a prediction scale was constructed for use by the prospective husband and wife. [6]

[4] From *Psychological Factors in Marital Happiness,* by Lewis M. Terman. 1938. Courtesy of McGraw-Hill Book Co., p. 372.
[5] Burgess and Cottrell, *op. cit.,* pp. 354-55.
[6] *Ibid.,* pp. 275-84. The original schedule was built to be filled out by both the man and the woman, and was scored to predict probabilities for the combination. The schedule given earlier in this chapter is similar, except that it is designed to be used by just one person.

Limitations of this approach, as it has been developed up to the present, might be listed as follows: (1) The research samples are much too small and too skewed in the direction of urban and upper classes to be considered representative of the population as a whole. (2) Data on the predictive (pre-marriage) items were gathered after marriage had taken place, which means that answers could have been biased by conditions of the marriage relationships. (3) Correlations between predictive factors and marriage adjustment were found to be relatively low (from +.43 to +.56) and account for only about one fourth of the variations in marriage adjustment. (4) Statistical prediction must always be in terms of probability, never certainty; it can measure central tendencies but has no way of determining how any particular case might turn out.

Research on the problem of marriage prediction continues, however, and with new data piling up we can expect some of these shortcomings to be removed. Terman and Oden have recently completed an analysis of approximately 600 gifted persons and their spouses.[7] Burgess and Wallin are following several hundred engaged couples through a number of years of marriage in order to determine which of the premarital factors continue to exert an influence.[8] Kelly is doing a similar thing with another large group of engaged and newly married couples.[9] Locke is approaching the question through a comparison of a divorced and a married group.[10] Kinsey promises to throw additional light on the problem when he is farther along with his research.[11]

So far, all of the published data from these and other recent studies give general support to the earlier findings.

[7] Lewis M. Terman and M. Oden, *The Gifted Child Grows Up* (Stanford University, Calif.: Stanford University Press, 1947). For a convenient summary see Lewis M. Terman, "Marital Adjustment and its Prediction," chap. iv in Part II of Morris Fishbein and E. W. Burgess (eds.), *Successful Marriage* (New York: Doubleday & Co., 1947), pp. 117-31.

[8] Burgess and Locke, *op. cit.*, pp. 458, 472-75.

[9] E. L. Kelly, "Concerning the Validity of Terman's Weights for Predicting Marital Happiness," *Psychological Bulletin*, 36:202-3, March, 1939.

[10] Harvey J. Locke, "Predicting Marital Adjustment by Comparing a Divorced and a Happily Married Group," *American Sociological Review*, 12:187-91, April, 1947.

[11] Alfred C. Kinsey and others, *Sexual Behavior in the Human Male* (Philadelphia: W. B. Saunders Co., 1948), p. 7 and *passim*.

Kelly,[12] for example, in a preliminary report on fifty-two couples carried through two years of marriage, showed that predictive scores correlated with marital happiness at approximately .50—which is about the same correlation as was found by Terman and by Burgess and Cottrell in their studies of married couples. Locke reports that prediction scales based on such things as happiness of parents' marriages, length of acquaintance, conventionality, sociability, and church affiliation and participation are found to be highly correlated with marital adjustment.[13]

Though our powers of prediction will undoubtedly improve as we perfect the tools, precise prediction will likely never be possible. There are several reasons : (1) It seems highly improbable that all the factors which account for personality development and mental behavior can ever be sufficiently quantified. (2) Every person is unique in some respects, and to the extent that he is, he is statistically unpredictable. (3) Both people and circumstances are in continual flux—what is true for one time or place may not be for another.

But it has been demonstrated, nevertheless, that marriage prediction is feasible. Any improvement over superstition and guessing is to be regarded as a real improvement. Statistical measures must be adapted to the cultures they are designed to represent, and interpreted cautiously, but they do have their place.[14] When supplemented with common sense and careful case studies they can lead to the type of understanding necessary for prediction and control.

Control can come about through the realization on the part of individuals with high or low scores (which are the ones most predictive) that their chances for marital happiness are either good or poor as the case might be. High scores may

---

12 Kelly, *op. cit.*, pp. 202-3.

13 Locke, *op. cit.*, p. 191.

14 For a further examination of the problems and cautions involved in marriage prediction see : William L. Kolb, "Sociologically Established Family Norms and Democratic Values," *Social Forces*, 26 :451-56, May, 1948 ; Albert Ellis, "The Value of Marriage Prediction Tests," *American Sociological Review*, 13 :710-18, December, 1948 ; and Lewis M. Terman and Paul Wallin, "The Validity of Marriage Prediction and Marital Adjustment," *American Sociological Review*, 14 :497-504, August, 1949.

tend to crystallize and reinforce a decision to get married. Low scores would serve as a warning and would give lovers the option of either changing themselves or the situations surrounding the marriage (where that were possible), or of calling off the match.

Group control can be furthered by the application of research findings to such fields of action as education, legislation, and community programs.

Summary of Factors

Marriage is the product of a multiplicity of forces, interrelated and interacting. We have examined most of these in previous chapters. Some will receive further amplification in the discussions to follow. As Part Two draws to a close, we should like to pull all this material together into a kind of "overview" or composite picture.

Burgess of Chicago, who is pioneer and Dean in the field of family research, has this to say:

In modern society research is imperatively needed because the family is confronted with new conditions of life growing out of technological changes. These have transformed a rural culture into an urban civilization. They have introduced rapid means of transportation by railroad, automobile, and airplane. They have multiplied the ease of communication by telephone, moving picture, and radio. The family is no longer a self-sufficient, rural institution surrounded with the protection of the kinship group, the church, the school, and the neighborhood. It is now a unit of interacting members subject collectively and individually to the pressures and strains, stimulations and frustrations, protections and risks of life in the "Great Society."

. . . .

What research findings do we now have . . . which will provide a firm foundation for marriage and the family?

First of all research demonstrates that many of the problems of the family are those of a transition period from the older institutional type to the emerging companionship type of family. The solution, then, to the problems of family life is not to return to the institutional family with its emphasis upon the authority of the head, upon duty and obedience of its members, upon rigid discipline and upon community pressures, the mores, and the law. The task of the family and its friends is rather to realize the conditions which contribute to the development of the companionship family which inhere in such inter-personal relations of its members as mutual affection, sympathetic understanding, and comradeship.

Second, new findings are becoming available upon the factors which make for success in modern marriage. These may be briefly summed up: (1) the possession of personality traits such as an optimistic temperament, emotional balance, yielding disposition, sympathetic attitude, self-confidence, particularly on the part of the husband, and emotional dependence; (2) similarity of cultural backgrounds; (3) a harmonious and understanding family environment; (4) a socialized personality as evidenced by number of friends, participation in organizations, educational level; (5) the keeping of religious observances; (6) an occupation with moderate economic status, superior education, high degree of social control, reasonable security, and little or no mobility; (7) a love relationship growing out of companionship rather than infatuation; and (8) wholesome growth of attitudes toward sex and similarity in strength of sex desire of husband and wife.[15]

A Classification of Factors.—It should be evident by now that marriage is under the influence of forces that are both personal and social, that its destiny is determined by both the quality of people who enter it and the nature of the environment that surrounds it. Breaking this twofold classification down still farther, we have the following as factors affecting the marriage outcome:

I. *A 'Compatible Society*. This refers to the milieu or social setting within which marriage must operate. It involves such factors as:

    A. Economic level of living

    B. Condition of war or peace

    C. Degree of cultural integration

II. *Emotional Maturity*. This is a matter of personal development, and it depends upon such things as:

---

[15] Ernest W. Burgess, "Research," from a symposium called "New Foundations for Marriage and the Family," *Marriage and Family Living*, Summer, 1946, pp. 64-65.

A. State of one's heredity and general health
B. Presence or absence of neurotic traits
C. Degree to which the personality has been socialized

III. *Pair Unity*. This has to do with the pair relationship, and it refers to such items as:
A. Degree of similarity between mates
B. Patterns of differentiation and equalization
C. Type and amount of love solidarity built up

IV. *Marital Adaptability*. This is largely a matter of attitude and effort within marriage. It is contingent upon such factors as:
A. Amount of cooperation between spouses
B. Ways in which stability and flexibility find balance
C. Strength of determination to make marriage succeed

Let us summarize, in turn, points pertaining to each of these factors.

COMPATIBLE SOCIETY. There is enough known about the repercussions of society upon the family to warrant at least a few generalizations. Marriage has the best chance of succeeding:

1. When society is family-minded. A spirit of indifference to marital responsibility, an extreme individualism at the expense of family values, an easy acceptance of divorce, antiquated family laws, disrespect for law, materialism, sensualism —all of these, and more, make it difficult at times for the marriage institution even to survive. Research has shown that children of divorced parents are more likely to become divorced themselves later on, a fact which, coupled with the long-time increasing divorce rate, means that society might be moving in a vicious circle. Research also shows that marriages are more successful where the mates are not "only children" and where they desire and have several children of their own; yet, society seems to be moving the other way, toward a lower birth rate and an increase of childless and one-child families.

2. When society is reasonably well integrated. A large part of the family trouble of this day arises from the speed and

complexity of modern culture. Technology is ushering in a new world. Institutions are changing. Populations are on the move as never before. The family has lost many of its original functions and is now struggling to find some new ones. But it is experiencing what we have called "transitional turmoil," and it will continue to do so until society finds for itself a new level of integration. In this connection we should again note that while the trend is in the direction of urbanization, it is the person who is reared in the country or small town that is generally most successful in his marriage. This is undoubtedly because present rural culture shows more integration and reflects greater family-mindedness than does the urban.

3. When income is adequate and secure. Studies reveal marriage as more successful if the mates came from homes of average or above average socioeconomic status, had premarital work experiences that were regular and steady, are able to own and live in their own private home, have an occupation that does not keep them too mobile, and have a moderate and steady income together with some savings. Poverty, unemployment, and substandard housing all make for tension and conflict. Ogburn has shown correlations between marriage failure on the one hand and both low schooling and low income on the other. He says:

> Families, white nonfarm in United States in 1940, broken by separation and divorce were in percentages twice as numerous when husbands had not finished the elementary school as when husbands were college graduates. But this increased family unity may be owing to income rather than to education, since income is more highly correlated with family unity than is education.[16]

4. When there is peace in the world. War separates families, puts people under tension, undermines morals; war starves, kills, overstimulates, distorts. It is no wonder, then, that during and following war, delinquency increases, illegitimacy and venereal disease rates go up, and divorce reaches new peaks.

---

[16] William F. Ogburn, "Education, Income, and Family Unity," *American Journal of Sociology*, 53:474, May, 1948.

EMOTIONAL MATURITY. Mature individuals can make a success of marriage under the most discouraging conditions, while the immature usually fail even when circumstances are highly favorable. It is quality of personality, more perhaps than anything else, that decides how each marriage shall be. Research has pretty well demonstrated that marriages are most successful:

1. When the mates are biologically adequate. They need to be in good health and free of serious hereditary blights, physical or mental abnormalities, and sexual incapacities. They should also be old enough chronologically to have attained physiological maturity. Marriage is too responsible a job, and too freighted with consequences, to be encouraged for those who are greatly underdeveloped or are in other ways seriously handicapped. This, of course, is not to deny marriage to those with minor physical problems or to those who are mature enough in other ways to be able to make marital adjustment and contribute to the happiness of each other in spite of the handicap. (See Chapter 3.)

2. When both partners show rather high degrees of socialization. Here are some of the things found to be correlated with successful marriage: (a) gets along well with both parents, feels a genuine attachment for both, favoring them about equally, without being either hostile or overdependent toward either; (b) has a wide circle of friends, of both sexes, but not excessive numbers with the opposite sex; (c) has the approval of parents and friends for the marriage, does not elope; (d) participates in several community organizations; (e) attends Sunday School and church frequently, favors a religious wedding; (f) comes from a superior cultural level and attains an above-average education; (g) is essentially a conformist, avoids excesses, is moderate in views and in conduct. All of these give support to the view that marriage needs persons who are conservative and considerate, who can get along well with others, who participate frequently and successfully in social or public affairs.

3. When each of the pair has a balanced and mature personality. Very important in all this is a temperament that is

optimistic and cheerful; those mates are most happy who came
from happy home situations of their own (had happy childhoods and lived under parents who were happily married) and
who now choose their associates from among other happily
married people. Other favorable personality traits are found
to be a sympathetic attitude, a yielding and sharing disposition, a sense of humor, an emotional dependence, self-confidence (especially for the husband), emancipation from the
parental home, punctuality, and a sense of duty and responsibility. On the opposite side are the neurotic traits which cause
marriage to fail—dominating tendencies, inconsiderateness,
pessimism, irritability, touchiness, moodiness, jealousy, excitability, chronic feelings of loneliness.

4. When there is a well-proportioned sexual perspective.
This relates to other factors, of course, but it seems important
enough for a separate listing. Studies show marriages more
successful where the mates: (a) were given their first sex instruction in the home and school, their parents were frank and
adequate regarding these matters, no severe sex shocks had
entered into their experiences, and their present attitudes are
wholesome and free of shame, disgust, or aversion; (b) had
passed the heterosexual transition successfully, did not wish
to be of the opposite sex, but were satisfied with their own
sex roles; and (c) had avoided extreme sexual intimacy prior
to marriage.

PAIR UNITY. Since marriage always involves at least two
persons, its success quite naturally depends upon more than
the quality of each considered separately. There is the matter
of pair unity as determined by mate combination and personality interaction. Success is most likely:

1. When the mates are essentially similar. Research has
shown that there are fewer sources of conflict, and hence
greater chances for harmony, if husband and wife (a) are approximately equal in ability; (b) are not too much different in
age; (c) have similar social and cultural backgrounds—racial,
religious, educational, economic, family patterns, etc.; and (d)
are temperamentally compatible as shown by a tendency to

agree on most things, to show like interests and values. There are only about two exceptions to this rule on similarity—first, a marriage may be handicapped if mates are alike in their immaturities and neurotic tendencies; and second, it may be put to a disadvantage if the sex roles are insufficiently differentiated, if the wife is too masculine or the husband too feminine.

2. When the sexes are socially and culturally equal. This is true for democratic societies, though it may not be for other cultures. Unity through equality is not the only type of family unity possible, but it is the only kind that is compatible with our democratic ideals. As observed above, however, sex equality needs always to be of the differentiated variety. (See Chapter 4.)

3. When a love solidarity has become well established. Studies show marriage to be more happy where the mates: (a) have an affection for each other that is not one-sided and that is demonstrated mutually, and frequently; (b) have learned to take pride in each other and not to dig or criticize; (c) have worked out a system of resolving conflict, of accommodating their differences in a cooperative and constructive manner; (d) have built their love upon companionship rather than infatuation and romance; (e) have had only the one engagement, and not too many prior love affairs; and (f) have adjusted to each other's relatives and built up a circle of mutual friends. Adding to this last point, there is some evidence that it is better for the mates to be similar in personality to their respective parents-in-law of the same sex; wife to her husband's mother and husband to his wife's father.

4. When the courtship period has been sufficiently long. Love's first impulses need testing and strengthening before taking the important step of marriage. Pair unity can come only through interaction and mutual adjustment. All of this takes time. Consequently one will usually find disproportionately high failure rates among marriages that were hasty. Statistically speaking, marriage is more successful when the mates have had a relatively long period of acquaintance, courtship, and engagement—a total of several years.

MARITAL ADAPTABILITY. Life is dynamic; nothing holds still or remains exactly the same for any great length of time. To succeed one must be able to continually adjust. Being comfortable socially, mature personally, and well matched maritally would give any couple an excellent start for family happiness. But unless they carried through, unless they had the mind and the ability to adjust, unless they were adaptable, they would certainly fail. Conversely, some couples make marriage succeed who, at the start, had the statistical probabilities against them but who prove later to be highly adjustable. In a changing society, adaptability is the only sure road to family stability. As Burgess puts it: "The seeming instability of the family is largely a symptom of this transition which may be regarded as a vast social experiment in which adaptability becomes more significant for success in marriage and family living than a rigid stability." [17] To amplify, marriage is most likely to succeed:

1. When the mates are flexible and adaptable in their personalities. They must not only be able to adjust to each other, but to new and continuously changing circumstances. Rigidity only causes lags, tensions, maladjustments. With adaptability present, the pair unity, started in courtship, can become enlarged and strengthened throughout the period of marriage. Also, with adaptability, difficult family problems can be met and solved, head on. In discussing adaptability as a personal characteristic, Burgess listed the following three components: (a) "The degree of flexibility in the emotional reaction of a person to a shift from an accustomed to a different situation"; (b) "Tendency of the person as culturally or educationally determined to act in an appropriate way when entering a new situation"; and (c) "The possession of knowledge and skills which make for successful adjustments to a new condition." [18]

2. When both husband and wife are family-minded. Indices of family-mindedness found to be associated with successful marriage are as follows: (a) a desire for children; (b) a will-

---

[17] Ernest W. Burgess, "The Family in a Changing Society," *American Journal of Sociology*, 53:417, May, 1948.
[18] *Ibid.*, p. 420.

ingness to talk things over, to confide, and to share and co-operate at the expense of self-interest; (c) an absence of regret over the mate choice, or over having married, with there being no thought or consideration given to breaking up the marriage; and (d) a strong confidence that the marriage will succeed plus a determination to make it succeed. Boiled down, success is quite largely a matter of attitude or mental-set favoring the thing undertaken—which in this case, of course, is marriage.

PROBLEMS AND PROJECTS

1. What are the objections some people raise to a scientific inquiry concerning marriage? Are any of these sound?
2. How might educators use the findings of research in the teaching and counseling of students regarding marriage? What precautions need be used?
3. Suppose your score on the marriage prediction test contained in the chapter was a low one. Does this mean that you will inevitably fail in your marriage? What does it mean?
4. Does success in marriage come more from personality factors or from social circumstances—is it people or society that is mostly responsible? Discuss. Do you think marriage prediction schedules could be improved by taking the social and cultural factors more into account?
5. In your opinion, do divorces happen more because the mates are immature or because they are poorly matched? Defend your position.
6. Which do you think is the more important to successful marriage, the preparation preceding the ceremony or the effort following it? Give reasons for your answer.
7. Which of the criteria suggested for judging pair unity do you feel are most neglected by young people marrying at present? Discuss.
8. Pick out the most happily married couple you know, and then list the things about them and their relationship that you think are responsible for the success.

Selected Readings

Burgess, Ernest W., and Cottrell, L. S. *Predicting Success or Failure in Marriage.* New York: Prentice-Hall, Inc., 1939.

————, and Locke, Harvey J. *The Family: From Institution to Companionship.* New York: American Book Co., 1945. Chap. xv, "Predicting Marital Adjustment."

————, and Wallin, P. "Predicting Adjustment in Marriage from Adjustment in Engagement," *American Journal of Sociology,* 49:324-30, 1944.

Fishbein, Morris, and Burgess, Ernest W. (eds.). *Successful Marriage.* New York: Doubleday & Co., 1947. Part II, chap. iv, "Marital Adjustment and its Prediction."

Horst, P., and others. *The Prediction of Personal Adjustment.* New York: Social Science Research Council, 1941.

Locke, Harvey J. "Predicting Marital Adjustment by Comparing a Divorced and a Happily Married Group," *American Sociological Review,* 12:187-91, April, 1947.

Nimkoff, Meyer F. *Marriage and the Family.* Boston: Houghton Mifflin Co., 1947. Chap. xiv, "Prediction of Marital Happiness."

Terman, Lewis M., and associates. *Psychological Factors in Marital Happiness.* New York: McGraw-Hill Book Co., 1938.

————, and Oden, M. *The Gifted Child Grows Up.* Stanford University, Calif.: Stanford University Press, 1947.

PART III

PROCESSES

Chapter 7

LEARNING TO LOVE

There is no clear-cut line separating what we have called the "factors" and what we are now referring to as the "processes" of marriage. Our analysis of factors has emphasized the structural or organizational aspects of the phenomenon under study; it has let us examine the major elements of marriage, though without particular reference to dynamics or over-all processes. Our present concern, throughout Part III, is with the application of this knowledge to the developmental stages or sequence patterns in the family life cycle. We shall want to examine the period of premarriage, mate adjustment within marriage, parenthood as a fruit of marriage, widowhood and other aspects of postmarriage, and spinsterhood or nonmarriage.

Love seems to be the logical starting point. Though not synonymous, love and marriage are nevertheless very much interrelated and are generally thought of together. Marriage is the natural consummation of love interests. Love is the magnet that brings people together and the cement that holds them together; it is the most essential element in pair unity.

Yet there are perhaps few concepts so misunderstood and abused. In the name of love people sometimes flounder, when they could have intelligent direction; dissipate, when their energies could be spent constructively; exploit, when they could, and should, cooperate. Some people regard love as a blind force that can be neither understood nor controlled. Others see it as an excuse for indulgence or for the satisfying of narrow self-interest. Only a few, relatively speaking, learn the full meaning of the term and are able to use well the full power that love provides.

NATURE AND FUNCTION OF LOVE

Love might be simply defined as any sentiment of attachment that is centered upon any person or thing; it is a pleasurable feeling, in other words, and it is directed toward some object. The love object might be entirely nonmaterial, as when we say that one loves some standard, principle, or cause that he shows a strong devotion for; he can love democracy, for example, or peace, or the Christian Church. Similarly it can be said that one loves a certain type of activity such as swimming, reading, or listening to musical concerts. Again, the love object might be material though nonhuman, as when we say that one loves ice cream, or new hats, or horses. Finally, the love object might be a human personality. There are many varieties of this latter also: there is self-love; there are filial and parental loves; there are friendships everywhere, regardless of age, sex, or social relationships; and there is the sweetheart love of courtship and marriage. Broadly considered, love exists whenever and wherever people obtain satisfactions from the objects and the activities that attract them.

It is to the narrower usage of the term, to sweetheart love, that attention is now being turned. Though love is of many types, it is only that which relates to marriage that will concern us here.

Common Fallacies.—Someone facetiously defined sweetheart love as "an insane desire to squeeze orange juice out of a lemon." We can smile at this analogy because it comes so close to the beliefs and practices of so many. But it is incorrect. True love is neither insane nor is it based upon deceit.

A frequent fallacy is to regard love as an irrational force, mystically and mysteriously operating to shape man's destiny. It has been said, for example, that "love is blind." Though we would agree that some persons are blinded by what they think is love, we contend that real love comes from understanding, not ignorance; and from self-effort and adjustment rather than from any supposed manipulation by the fates.

It has also been claimed that everyone has a "one-and-only," a "soul-mate," who is waiting and searching for him, just as he is in return. Part of this belief is that people are "meant for each other," predestined to get together; and that unless one finds the right person, the one intended, he can be only partially happy. We say nonsense. (Given an equal start, there are very likely any number from the opposite sex that each person could be equally happy with—or if not, the reason would be in the matching combinations rather than in the fates.) Our position will be discussed more fully in the next chapter; here we would only say that in mature love there comes an intelligent *choosing* rather than any mysterious *searching* or intuitive *reaching* for "signs."

Another notion, which can hardly stand up under analysis, is that people "fall in love," suddenly and completely, whenever the right person comes along. We have heard some people talk about "love at first sight." We have listened to claims that "when love strikes, you will know it." To all of this we would say that there is a difference between the infatuations and "puppy loves" of romantic youngsters, and the tested loves of mature companions. There may be the *beginning of love* at first sight, but that is all. Whether that beginning will ever develop into "the real thing" it will take time and testing to determine. (Love is a process, not a static fact; we *grow in love, not fall.*) Many have thought, at first sight, that they were in love, only to change their minds after taking another and a closer look. On the other hand, many have thought that they didn't particularly care for the one they were going with, only to find themselves coming to love this person after time and close association.

Sometimes, too, people hold to the mistaken idea that "love is all that matters," that if man and woman are madly in love they should be willing to give up everything else in order to have each other; that if they are in love and marry, they cannot but be eternally happy regardless of everything else. All we can say to this is that other things are important too; things that the head must decide; things that, if favorable, will give love itself a better chance of maturing and enduring. Madness in love is dangerous, for with it people are irrational and impetuous in what they do. Emotional love needs to be tested, strengthened, and controlled by the intellect. Complete surrender to love leaves one open to exploitation by the unscrupulous, and it leads to decisions that may be regretted after the emotions have cooled. A large proportion of the heartaches men and women experience in courtship and marriage are attributable to this attitude of "all for love."

Students of marriage and family very commonly group all these mistaken notions concerning love under the term *Romantic Fallacy*. The fallacy lies not in the acceptance of romance as an element in love (for certainly every relationship needs some demonstration of affection to serve as a social lubricant, if nothing else), but rather in the belief that romantic love is just about everything that needs to be considered in choosing a mate or in making a happy union. Romance has overglamourized the love concept; it has discouraged rational action and has added mystery and superficiality to the whole thing.

This is particularly true, though not exclusively so, in American culture. It is no wonder that youth are so often swept off their feet by romantic infatuation, for almost everything they do in courtship tends to stimulate and reinforce the idea. The modern novel and the picture show usually depict the struggles and conflicts of courtship, highly flavored with romantic passion, and then end with marriage and the assumption that all conflict is over and that eternal bliss is certain. These modern fairy tales, although they do not say "they lived happily ever after," imply as much. Their harm lies in their overemphasis on romance and erotic stimulation and upon the unreal picture of life they paint in the minds of those who follow them. The popular song, which is given so much attention in the dance hall and on the radio, does very much the same thing; it stimulates the sentiments and builds up the idea that love is all that matters. This is the fallacy or the illusion that so many of our young people are living under. They are often "in love with love," and nothing more; they see their lover through colored glasses rather than with clear vision; they are blinded by romance.

Unless our culture can be made to change in this regard, unless the romantic infantilism which underlies so many of our marriages can be modified, the American family will continue to be in trouble.

Developmental Processes.—The kind of love needed for successful marriage is much more balanced and complete than all of this romantic tinsel referred to above. True love is no mystic entity that strikes without warning and that can be recognized at once every time it hits. Rather, it is a very natural sentiment that develops over time through association and mutual adjustment. Real love must be learned.

The learning process commences soon after birth and continues throughout all of life—this is as true of love as of other aspects of human growth. The infant first learns to love its mother, for it is she who makes him comfortable by taking care of his early body needs. Soon, however, father comes into the picture, then brothers and sisters, and family friends and numerous others outside the immediate family circle. All of this means a widening of one's love interests. People interact because of the needs they meet and pleasures they give to each other in the process. In supplying and responding to these needs and pleasures, they become interdependent, and in love.

We are attracted most, therefore, to those persons who offer the best promise of satisfying our basic personality needs. Generally speaking, we tend to like those who remind us of pleasurable experiences or who make us comfortable and happy in one way or another. Conversely, we tend to dislike or shun those who remind us of unpleasant happenings or who threaten to be disagreeable or incompatible with our present needs. W. I. Thomas's four wishes (see pages 80-82) are relevant at this point: (1) Since every personality has a desire for *recognition,* it follows that we are attracted to those who give us attention and status, who do not embarrass, belittle, or overchallenge our ego. (2) Affectional and sexual *response* is another need, which means that we are inevitably pulled in the direction of those who are sympathetic and warm toward us emotionally. (3) Then there is *security,* the pursuit of which makes us like those that are dependable and that we are used to. (4) Finally, our universal desire for *new experience* causes us to be interested in those who offer variety, adventure, or challenge. Other things being equal, we should come to love best those persons who best meet these various personality needs in combination. But since personalities differ in the ways their fundamental needs are proportioned, it follows that different people will seek different types of persons to love.

Habit is another of the factors underlying love development. Mature love is a matter of progressive involvement brought about through interaction and habituation. Proximity is a boon to love for it encourages association, which in turn makes for mutual adjustment and interdependence. There is a satisfying security that comes from sticking to what one has adjusted to and is accustomed to. In this fact lie both danger and hope: danger in that associates frequently become emotionally involved too early, or with someone the head could not sanction; and hope in that the comforts of love may expand, instead of contract, as time goes on.

Social pressure frequently adds reinforcement to these love foundations first established by need and habit. Once a boy and girl have started to date regularly, there is a tendency on the part of surrounding groups to treat them as a unit, inviting them out together, and more or less taking it for granted that they will marry. Thus public approval encourages the continuance of the love relationship. It is human nature to respond to the pressure of social expectancy; fear of disapproval almost always serves as a prod to the conscience.

It is possible for one's love development to become arrested somewhere short of the mature heterosexual level needed for marriage. Normally there are at least three important changes that take place in the love interests of the individual: (1) as he becomes socialized his early strong self-interests yield ground to an interest in others, usually those of his own sex at first; (2) starting at about the time of puberty there is a fundamental transition to an interest in the opposite sex; and (3) continuing throughout adolescence there is a gradual emancipation from the close parental ties which had characterized his childhood. If any one of these changes becomes blocked so that the love interests remain stuck on objects other than a potential mate, serious trouble may result.

In the first instance we have individuals whose love has turned inward on themselves, and who are therefore incapable of really loving others. Followers of Freud usually refer to these as narcissists (or narcists). Their chief problem is that their interests have become fixated on the self-love level. Duvall and Hill compare this type of love with the feeling one has when he loves oranges—in both cases he is concerned solely with personal satisfaction and is therefore really only loving himself. They compare this selfish kind of love with that which is socially oriented, which they call "outgoing love." [1]

Homosexual inclinations within the individual may come from either physiological abnormality or psychological conditioning, usually the latter. Where they exist one could hardly expect any full development of heterosexual love. For successful marriage a type of socialization is needed that will insure the arrival of adult heterosexuality. (See pages 145-47.)

Parental fixation is another condition that may interfere with normal married love. It comes from early "spoiling" within the home and from obstacles put in the way of the process of psychological weaning during adolescence. Husbands and wives who remain too emotionally tied to their parents are in no position to adjust completely to each other.

Love, then, is a matter of learning and development. It grows out of needs in the personality, of habits in association and adjustment, and of encouragements on the part of society. Also, it takes time. It progresses from self-love to the outgoing type; from autosexual and homosexual interests to attractions for the opposite sex; from parental fixations to sweetheart involvements based upon understanding, interdependence, and companionship.

Component Elements.—We have been examining love in its various dynamic or developmental aspects. Suppose we now

---

[1] Evelyn Millis Duvall and Reuben Hill, *When You Marry* (Boston: D. C Heath & Co., 1945), pp. 33-35.

take the cross-sectional approach to discover what are the elements that compose it.

Heterosexual love is a rather complex phenomenon made up of various images, ideas, drives, and emotional states, all grouped together and fixated upon some person through experience. It is a generalized response, broad enough to include the physiological, psychological, and sociological areas of attraction.

Folsom recognizes three main types of love feeling: (1) First there is what he calls *tenderness*. This is associated with light pressure and slow gentle movements upon the skin, particularly about the chest, face, and inner arms. It is largely nonsexual. Examples are the feelings involved in nursing, cuddling, and the noncrotic kiss. (2) Then there is *erotic feeling,* which is highly sexual in nature and is centered in the genital areas. It usually reaches a higher intensity than does tenderness. Stimulation comes from mental images, petting, and sexual intercourse. (3) Finally there is a rather broad category referred to as *joy* (sometimes called "cardiac-respiratory love"). It is characterized by muscular pleasure and by deep and rapid breathing; by feelings of rapture, ecstasy, exultation. This level of love comes from such experiences as pleasant surprises, ego inflations, senses of security, nostalgic remembrances, and gay and playful expressions. It is related to the habituations and need fulfillments which we discussed above (as are tender and erotic feelings also), and in Folsom's opinion is the keystone to the whole love complex.[2]

Burgess and Locke see love as coming mainly, though not exclusively, from man's fundamental wish for response, from his need for intimacy with other persons. They break the love sentiment down into four component parts, as follows: (1) There is *sexual intimacy,* which is made up of general physical attraction coming from beauty and charm, plus specific sexual desire coming from erotic stimulation. (2) There is *associational intimacy,* which is based upon affectional attachment to

---

[2] Joseph K. Folsom, "Steps in Love and Courtship," chap. vii in Howard Becker and Reuben Hill (eds.), *Family, Marriage, and Parenthood* (Boston: D. C. Heath & Co., 1948), pp. 210-12.

the other person and upon an emotional interdependence that grows up as mates come to satisfy the basic personality needs of each other. (3) There is *sublimated intimacy,* which grows out of an idealization of the desired mate and out of a sharing of interests and a companionable adjustment to each other. (4) Finally, there are the *nonresponse components,* which are not involved in intimacy itself but which are parts of the total love complex just the same. One of these is the stimulation or excitement that comes from the new experiences of courtship and marriage; another is the greater freedom of communication and action that is permitted under conditions of intimacy; still another is the emotional security or personal reassurance that the lover receives; and finally there is the recognition, ego support, or status value that is derived from possessing and from responding to another in line with social approval.[3]

These same authors go on to point out that there are many types of love relationships, differing with individuals and with circumstances. They say:

Certain of the components in the sentiment of love in any relationship may be absent, or slightly, or moderately, or strongly represented. For purposes of analyzing the different components of love, they may be thought of as a series ranging from physical attraction at one end with emphasis upon the physiological aspects of sex to mental interstimulation and response at the other end with the absence or at least the minimum of sexual feeling. This series may actually be conceived as a continuum from sexual craving at one extreme to the increasing sublimation of sex, with the progression through physical attraction, attachment, emotional response, idealization, and affectional and intellectual companionship.[4]

In line with this they proceed to list several very specific types of love patterns: *lust,* where sexual desire is paramount and other love elements are almost entirely absent; *infatuation,* where physical attraction is at the helm, but with sexual and emotional desires following in close order; *romantic love,* which stresses the sentimental, emotional, and sexual aspects

---

[3] Ernest W. Burgess and Harvey J. Locke, *The Family: From Institution to Companionship* (New York: American Book Co., 1945), pp. 372-76.
[4] *Ibid.,* pp. 376-77.

of the response pattern at the exclusion of nonresponse elements; *affection,* which is characterized by tender feelings and expressions and the development of emotional security; *comradely feeling,* which means that a close emotional friendship has been built up and mutual satisfactions are derived from joint activities; and *platonic love,* where the couple derives its sole satisfaction (for other elements are assumed to be absent) from its pattern of intellectual friendship.[5]

Thus the ingredients of love are many and are found to be patterned in a variety of ways. In whatever manner sweetheart love is defined, however, it will contain the following three general elements: (1) *bodily attraction,* including both sex and beauty; (2) *emotional involvement,* including sentiment and the affectional responses; and (3) *social adjustment,* meaning understanding and companionship. Bodily attraction alone is little more than lust. Accompanied by sentiment it may become romantic and tender. But only the understanding that comes from genuine adjustment can lift one to the full realization of love. Married love is built upon companionship, and, as it grows, both the physical and the emotional must come under control. Though submerged, these other elements must nevertheless be retained, for mature love cuts across all the important segments of life.

Recognition and Measurement.—An important question that nearly everyone faces at one time or another before marriage is this: "How can I know I am in love?" Sometimes the question is asked when there are several of the opposite sex that a person cares for and there is difficulty in making up one's mind. At other times it is asked when the choice has been narrowed down to one person, but there are doubts and contradictory emotions concerning that one.

The first prerequisite in recognizing love is to know its true meaning and nature. We have tried to explain love as the natural involvement of personalities, one with another. Instead of being a mysterious and uncontrollable force, as some believe, it is a normal unity based upon interdependence, and it grows

---

[5] *Ibid.,* pp. 376-81.

out of need fulfillment, habits of association, and achievements in adjustment. If this view is correct, then love does make sense; and can be understood and controlled. The title of this chapter is significant; successful loving is a matter of *learning*, which takes time and requires both study and effort.

The question, then, is not just, "Am I in love?", but "What *kind* of love?" and "How *much?*"

The kind of love one is able to give makes a great difference in the degree of happiness he is able to achieve in marriage. Narcissism, or self-love, won't get him very far. Homosexual love will only serve to block his adjustments to the opposite sex. Romantic love will leave him infantile and subject to serious disillusionment. And there are other kinds that can make for similar maladjustments. Duvall and Hill point out that "puppy love," when taken too seriously, may lead to a dog's life.[6] The only kind that can make for lasting marital happiness is the type that has been called *conjugal love*. This is the mature heterosexual love that we have been talking about. It is founded upon cooperation, and it is dynamic enough to change or grow with adjustment throughout marriage.

The amount of love one has for another will differ according to both time and circumstance. Normally, each of us loves a number of different persons but in different ways and in differing degrees. Presumably there will be one of the opposite sex that each will come to love best—not because of any supposed predestination but because of better matching and/or association and adjustment. Love, even with the one who is valued most, must not be presumed to remain static; it may go either up or down depending upon the direction of the couple's total adjustment; people can grow in love, and they can grow out of love.

It is possible, in fact quite normal, both to like and dislike the same person—liking him with respect to some things and disliking him with respect to others. This contradiction (and sometimes fluctuation) between love and hate of the same per-

---

6 Duvall and Hill, *op. cit.*, p. 30.

son is referred to technically as *ambivalence*. The problem presented is that of weighing the loves against the hates to determine which is predominant, of deciding if there is a sufficient "net love" on which to marry.

Although there is no formula by which one can be absolutely certain, there are ways in which love can be tested and most doubts removed. (It must be remembered, however, that doubting is normal and does not mean the absence of love.) So long as people are imperfect there will be doubts in their dealings with each other, and so long as adjustments are necessary there will be misunderstandings and conflicts in the process; but neither of these, if mild, need interfere with love. It is only with a few that feelings of absolute certainty precede marriage, and with many of them the reason is romantic illusion and the result post-marriage disillusionment. Better it is to be realistic, considering all angles before taking the plunge. If the following questions can be answered affirmatively, it is reasonably sure that one is on the right track:

Do you enjoy being together, talking together, working together?

Do you stimulate, but not antagonize, each other in conversation?

Are you interested in essentially the same things; do you have the same ideals and purposes?

Do you know each other well enough to be sure that your love is for the person and not the glamour?

Are you able to be agreeable most of the time and to settle your differences constructively; does each quarrel end with a better adjustment?

Do you think and plan in terms of we?

Do you try to make your partner happy; are you proud of him (or her) in public?

Have you made your growing relationship a matter of both study and effort?

If one is mature and reasonably sure, the choice should then be made. Frequently one or the other loses out by continually putting it off. Delaying the decision until one's judgment can mature is highly desirable, but needless indecision, related to exploitation, can never be justified.

Demonstrations of affection are not as important in the process of love involvement as is the reality of love itself. Superficialities in the art of lovemaking, such as are used by "wolves" to capture their prey, are not for real lovers. Better honesty than gloss. Nevertheless, love to be kept alive does require some demonstration. Preferable is that which is spontaneous, sincere, and not too much dictated by convention.

How important is love, in comparison with other factors? Our answer is that well-developed love is extremely important, for it can exist only when most of the other personal factors are favorable. Childish and poorly matched individuals can indulge in romantic infatuations, but it takes mature people, well mated, to lay out the conditions best suited for the development of successful conjugal love. Real love, therefore, is the product of a multiplicity of forces and experiences converging upon the relationships of sweethearts and making for unity in the pair.

COURTSHIP AS LOVE INVOLVEMENT

Love cannot develop in a vacuum. Since every love feeling must be oriented with reference to some object, it follows that sweetheart love requires interaction with other persons. The process by which the two sexes associate and adjust together as preparation for marriage we shall call "courtship."

Courtship is both the art of making love and process of love involvement; considered broadly, it extends all the way from when boys and girls are first attracted to each other to the time when married mates bid each other farewell at the sunset of life. There is a more narrow usage of the term, however, one that views courtship as being separate from both dating and marriage. According to this usage, dating refers to the early friendship activities of young people whereby they seek to have fun in pairs (emphasis upon friendship and enjoyment, not marriage); courtship connotes a more advanced stage in these boy-girl relationships, the stage just prior to marriage where the emphasis is upon choosing a mate and preparing for what lies ahead; and marriage is the consummation or end result of what has gone before. Dating evolves somewhat gradually into courtship as the marriage prospect becomes more real, and courtship gives way to marriage when the mates decide that the involvement process has gone far enough and has been successful enough to be made permanent. We are interested here in the dating and courting processes of the premarriage period.

Parents and teachers sometimes blunder, and young people flounder, for failure to understand adequately the customs and value systems of each other. As "time marches on," oldsters tend to lose track of the feelings and problems of the oncoming group. With males and females made differently, and trained somewhat separately, sex antagonisms are bound to develop. Consequently each generation is partially blind to the new one emerging, and each sex, to a degree at least, is ignorant of the other.

To come to any real understanding of how modern youth think and feel about the various patterns of courtship behavior, it is necessary to let them speak for themselves.

Preferences in Date Selection.—Six hundred and seventy-four unmarried and unengaged Purdue University students were asked to rate twenty-four items on a six-point scale according to what they most liked in a date.[7] (See Figure 2.) Greatest emphasis by both sexes was given to pleasant disposition, which was further described in the schedule as "cheerful, agreeable, optimistic, sense of humor, good sport." Next in importance was the quality of being well-groomed and mannered, meaning "clean, neat, wear clothes well, conventional, refined." Third preference was for sociability, where the date "meets people well, is able to mix well in most situations, is at home with the social arts." Other qualities regarded as extremely important for the date to possess are: emotional ma-

---

[7] This was part of a three-page survey on dating and mating preferences conducted during January and February, 1949. Completed schedules were returned from 933 students, 674 of whom (332 males and 342 females) were neither engaged nor married. Evelyn S. Wigent assisted the author in the preparation and administration of the schedule. A copy of the schedule may be found in the Appendix.

turity, physical attractiveness, considerateness, and fitting the traditional role of masculinity (if a man) or femininity (if a woman).

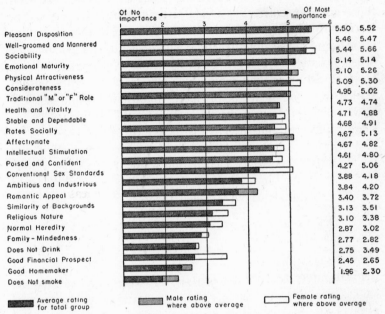

Pleasant Disposition	5.50	5.52
Well-groomed and Mannered	5.46	5.47
Sociability	5.44	5.66
Emotional Maturity	5.14	5.14
Physical Attractiveness	5.10	5.26
Considerateness	5.09	5.30
Traditional "M" or "F" Role	4.95	5.02
Health and Vitality	4.73	4.74
Stable and Dependable	4.71	4.88
Rates Socially	4.68	4.91
Affectionate	4.67	5.13
Intellectual Stimulation	4.67	4.82
Poised and Confident	4.61	4.80
Conventional Sex Standards	4.27	5.06
Ambitious and Industrious	3.88	4.18
Romantic Appeal	3.84	4.20
Similarity of Backgrounds	3.40	3.72
Religious Nature	3.13	3.51
Normal Heredity	3.10	3.38
Family-Mindedness	2.87	3.02
Does Not Drink	2.77	2.82
Good Financial Prospect	2.75	3.49
Good Homemaker	2.45	2.65
Does Not smoke	1.96	2.30

Average rating for total group   Male rating where above average   Female rating where above average

FIG. 2.—Preference patterns in date selection. When selecting a date, these college students want partners who are agreeable and socially acceptable. Male and female preference patterns are remarkably similar. Yet, males tend to stress more such things as being affectionate and having physical attraction, while females stress more such things as sex standards and financial promise. Based upon responses from 674 Purdue University students. For the complete schedule see the Appendix.

Some of the qualities which young people desire in a date they also want in a mate, but there is a difference in emphasis. In the next chapter we shall see how Purdue students rated these same twenty-four items from the standpoint of choosing a partner for marriage. In general, as will be seen, the two choices are strikingly similar, showing that most people tend to date with marriage in mind. But certain differences are also striking: in dating there is the tendency to play up appearances and the social arts, while in selecting a mate more attention is given to the considerations of family-mindedness and home-making ability.

It is to be noted that, though males and females agree with each other rather well concerning what they want in a date, there are some differences. Males tend more to want a date who is affectionate, romantic (in the sense of emotional infatuation), and physically attractive, who does not smoke, and who offers promise of being a good homemaker. Females, in contrast, stress more than males such things as conventional sex standards, good financial prospect, ambition and industriousness, religious nature, considerateness, and sociability. Thus there appear certain patterns distinctive of each sex.

An interesting question has to do with how well young people are able to satisfy their dating wants, or, in other words, to date with the kinds of persons they think are ideal. To test this, Purdue students were asked to go back over the list of items they had rated on importance in dating, and to check all of those that applied to their last date. An analysis of high-ranking items that were left unchecked revealed the following: (1) For each person, there were approximately two items which the last date did not possess, but which were considered above average in importance. This means that dating practice falls a little short of dating preference, that young people either compromise with their desires in making a date or become disillusioned to a degree after the date is in process—some of both, perhaps. (2) For both sexes the factors showing the greatest discrepancy between preference and practice were: being emotionally mature, giving intellectual stimulation, being considerate, being poised and confident, and being stable and dependable. (3) Males indicated greater discrepancies than females on such items as being affectionate, having romantic appeal, and possessing health and vitality; while females indicated greater discrepancies than did males on such items as conventional sex standards, similarity of background, and a religious nature. These, then, seem to be the major areas of frustration in dating.

Cross-Sex Criticisms Regarding Conduct.—On a number of occasions over the past several years the writer has asked groups of college students to prepare papers analyzing their own personality weaknesses, as they see them, and to criticize the opposite sex regarding traits and tendencies which seemed objectionable—both as applied to dating and courtship. Illustrations and summaries of some of the more common comments follow:

As the Man Sees It

There never seems to be any thought behind the actions of women, those of college age at least. They go blithely along, perfectly content as long as they have dates for everything. Anything that smacks of reality is avoided like the Black Plague. I perfectly agree that a girl should work a few years before marrying because I don't see how some of these coeds will ever be able to settle down long enough to manage a home.

Too many girls, especially of teen age, think that just because you go out with them once or twice they have a life lease on you. They should realize that we are dating for companionship and without wanting to get serious so soon.

Nothing irks me more than a girl that lets you kiss her as long and as often as you might desire, but manages to make it just about as interesting as kissing a cold stone wall.

A woman's constant griping about her delicate health is enough to drive a man to drink. His ire reaches its maximum when he notices that these frequent indispositions do not interfere in any way with the things she wants to do.

Girls seem to enjoy competition—competition of two boys over her, that is. The idea that these two fellows will finally get to the point where they could cheerfully strangle each other is, of course, no concern to her.

Girls worry too much about how they look. Every few minutes they have to powder their nose and apply more lipstick. The smell of the perfume and powder they apply is enough to bring on anyone's hay-fever. They worry too much about their clothes. They are afraid to engage in sports because they think they might snag a stocking.

Every man knows that he can't make a general remark about women, to a woman, without getting a personal comeback of some sort.

I can't understand why women seem to be always on the defensive. They act as if they were expecting a slight, or an attack, or an injustice.

I am of the opinion that it is woman's duty to society to be beautiful. If her only purpose on earth was to reproduce, I think God would have given her four legs, a glass door, a couple of internal racks, and in general designed her much on the same order as an incubator. Instead, he made her a work of art.

Even a physically beautiful woman can be ugly.

She displays her physical attractions in an obvious fashion, but pretends to be highly insulted that any man should think of her in such a "base" manner. She is adept in the ways of arousing the "animal" in man, yet she contrives to be quite hurt that he should "try to take advantage of her." Thus the man goes away bewildered and frustrated, while the woman retires confident and satisfied.

I dislike the necessity of making all of the first moves on a date. I do not mind asking for the date, financing it, and furnishing the transportation, but I would appreciate a little cooperation when it comes to determining what is to be the activity of the evening. If the girl refuses to make suggestions, but insists on doing "whatever you want to do," how can a boy know the kinds of things she likes to do or will do of her own volition after marriage.

I believe a girl should watch her actions so as not to become boisterous or disgustingly silly. If she is this way, the fellows will soon begin to avoid her.

No man wants to be reformed. But also no man who loves a woman will refuse to correct his own shortcomings when he realizes that they are objectionable. However, the smart woman will use the subtle approach and let the man think he is bringing about the improvement of his own free will.

What I want in a girl is easily put into words but not so easily found. She must be frank. She tells me the things she doesn't like about me and substitutes something for them that she does like. She must not flavor everything she says and does with premeditated femininity. Her habits and interests are on a level with mine. We get a kick out of being together. She feels that every date is important and makes a visible effort to prove it to me. We have fun. She is neat. Her appearance shows it. Her shoulders are straight. She stands as though she is proud of her figure. She is alive. She gives me a feeling of confidence that she will be able to adjust to taking care of a home, a family, and me, especially in cooking. She will remember that the seat of affection is the stomach, not the heart, and that many things other than food turn it sour. She honestly expects me to be courteous. She gives me every opportunity to be a gentleman. Not a manner-mad gentleman, but one that goes to the root of kindness, gentleness, and respect. She has succeeded in her family life. Her brothers and sisters love her. Her parents trust her. She is a good daughter and sister.

Here is a summary description of the girl that fellows dislike:

(1) She is inconsiderate, selfish, conceited, self-centered, snobbish, overly critical, and possessive. She talks all the time about herself, or brags about other dates, or flirts with other boys while she is out with me. She should be more sympathetic and helpful. (2) She is too forward in necking and petting, too free with kisses and caresses. She should make the fellow keep his place and shouldn't give in so readily in an attempt to hold him. (3) She is a "gold digger." She favors the boys who have money and cars, and she expects too many treats on the date. She should be more considerate of the fellow's pocketbook. (4) She lacks refinement, being too forward and loud around boys. She is boisterous, overtalkative, and flippant; she is sometimes slovenly and crude; she uses paint and perfume too freely and unskillfully; and she chews gum or puts on make-up or straightens her stockings in public. She should cultivate neatness in dress, graciousness in manner, and depth and interest in conversation. (5) She indulges in dishonest flattery, leads a fellow on, "strings him a line." She accepts dates when she doesn't care for the fellow or is dishonest or evasive in refusing. She tries to keep too many boys on the "string" at the same time, to have people fall for her, to be a woman of many loves. She should play the game fairly. (6) Miscellaneous criticisms are many, but these are among the most common: she drinks or smokes; she is overly dependent, and is too shy around boys; she is too emotional and romantic; and she pays too much attention to make-up.

As the Woman Sees It

The male attitude on sex has me completely baffled. Men say that they want to marry a virgin. However, most of them do everything to make this almost impossible, then pass it off by saying, "After all, I'm just a healthy American boy." It seems that it is the woman who must be firm and strong-willed these days.

Fellows are too abrupt in their love making, taking it for granted that the girl's feelings are emotionally on the same plane as their own.

There is one thing I'm definitely sure I don't like, and that's where the fellow expects the girl to feel obligated just because he has been footing the bill. Necking as payment for a date is like having to wash the dishes to pay for a meal; I don't like either.

Boys often call girls "gold diggers." This is, to some extent, their own fault. They should let the girl know how much money there is to be spent on the current date. It is as embarrassing to the girl to order beyond the fellow's means as it is for the boy to have her order. If he can only afford hamburgers why doesn't he say so? If the girl is the right sort at all, she will not hold it against him.

He wants you to be interested in the things he's interested in. He wants you to be good in any sport he's fond of, yet acts like a wounded puppy if you beat him at his own game. We can be liked as long as we allow the man to be certain that he's right on all debatable subjects. Prove him wrong and he'll pout the rest of the evening. Ask him what's the matter and he'll say, "Nothing."

Most men like to be babied. They'd never admit it, but they're all spoiled, overgrown boys.

Little courtesies on a date can almost make or break a girl's opinion of a fellow. Almost every boy I know could still stand a few pointers; little things such as taking off his hat when he comes into your house, being courteous and mannerly in front of your parents, helping you on with your wraps, and walking on the outside of the sidewalk. Men complain about the lack of femininity in modern women. Perhaps if these men treated women with more respect they would find that they more nearly lived up to their ideals.

You can talk to your folks and seem to act natural around them, then why don't you try to get along with my folks? They're human too. I want my friends to be their friends.

Of all the faults which I find in courtship, the attitude of many young men is the most aggravating. Some have a habit of calling a girl and giving her anywhere from two hours to fifteen minutes to get ready for an occasion, sport or formal, and expects to find her radiant and immaculate at the end of this time. They, of course, may appear in bag-kneed trousers, wrinkled shirt, or without a necktie. To top it all off, many act as if they are doing her a favor.

Men are too emotional. Biologically this is so, I suppose, and because of it we women are placed in a predicament. It isn't a pleasant thought that every time you go out with a boy you might be faced with a "battle royal."

Boys can't seem to help but brag about how many girls they have kissed in one week. They really gloat over their ability to vamp some little innocent freshman, feed her a well-worn line, get her all excited over a new love, and then without so much as an explanation or even a fond adieu they are gone, leaving a thoroughly perplexed and disillusioned man-hater. They keep their hearts in an iron case and yet think nothing of breaking yours.

It has been said many times that although boys like to date frivolous girls, when they decide to marry they almost always turn to the highly respected type. I think this is hardly fair.

The ideal man is nice looking, although not necessarily handsome. He is well groomed and very polite. In dating he states the time and the place definitely so as to leave no doubt in the mind of the girl. He is always on time. Above all, he does not pet until it is justified by their emotional relationship. He gladly meets the family, and he always complies with its restrictions. He can carry on an intelligent conversation without sounding like an encyclopedia.

In summary, here is a description of the fellow that girls dislike:

(1) He is egotistical and independent. He acts superior, often giving the impression that he thinks he is doing the girl a favor to go with her. He is boastful and argumentative. He shouldn't try to monopolize all the conversation or "try to explain the movies to us." He should be more thoughtful and attentive, and should show more consideration for our wishes and respect for our personalities. (2) He gives too much em-

phasis to necking and petting, making the girl feel indebted, and expecting intimacy as payment for the date. He is too abrupt and crude in his love-making, frequently making advances on the first date and occasionally in public. He should be more reserved and considerate in these things. (3) He is unfair in the way he asks for and carries out his dates. Sometimes he just drops in without even asking; often he doesn't tell her where they will be going so that she will know how to dress; and frequently he is late in calling. He should cultivate courage and poise and refinement in asking for dates, and should be more considerate of the girl's position. (4) He is often crude and ungentlemanly in both speech and action. He whistles or honks at girls; he swears, uses vulgar conversation, and tells dirty jokes; he is loud and boisterous in public, trying to show off and be the life of the party; he uses poor English and is awkward in social etiquette; he is unclean and untidy in public. He should try to be more cultured and refined. (5) Many of his compliments are insincere and even dishonest. He has a superficial politeness and engages in flattery and a "line" to make the girl feel good or to gain control. He plays with the girl's affections, pretending to be serious when he is not. In all fairness he should go with the kind of a girl he will want to marry, and should be honest with her. (6) Among miscellaneous criticisms are the following: he hangs around at all hours and stays too late on dates; he is unwilling to associate with the girl's folks and is unnatural around them; he lacks vigor and initiative; and he sometimes coaxes the girl to smoke or drink.

When engaging in self-criticisms of dating habits, college students were found to stress similar things as in their cross-sex criticisms—though with greater focus upon feelings of personal inadequacy. Here is a brief summary:

(1) I am too shy, bashful, and self-conscious. I am awkward in the art of conversation. (2) I am prone to worry excessively and to get moody. (3) I am overly serious, jealous, and possessive. (4) I am self-centered, acting egotistically, and flirting with or bragging about others while on a date. (5) I am

spoiled or have a bad disposition. My temper is quick. I make catty remarks.

Typical Male and Female Patterns.—From the above it becomes quite clear that there are patterns of likes and dislikes in courting behavior, and that these are structured differently as between males and females. To give the analysis greater precision, a list of thirty items was composed from the many statements found in the original papers, and this list was then arranged randomly and distributed to the Purdue group as a new study.[8] Students were asked to: (1) indicate which of the items they felt were more characteristic of males, and which of females, in dating; (2) check, in the spirit of honest self-criticism, all items that represented outstanding problems in their own dating practices; and (3) underline the traits that seemed most objectionable to them when present in dating.

The most striking discovery to come out of this approach was the very high degree of agreement between males and females on which traits are most characteristic of each sex. (See Figure 3.) The combined judgments of males agreed with those of females in assigning every item but three, and the correlation between the two sets of judgments on all items was found to be $.95 \pm .01$. By common consent, therefore, we can say that objectionable dating practices generally follow these typical sex patterns:[9]

Males, more than females, tend: (1) to tell off-color jokes and to use profanity or vulgarity; (2) to stay too late on a date, not knowing when to say "goodnight"; (3) to want too much necking or petting; (4) to be crude and unrefined in manners, lacking etiquette, and forgetting the common courtesies; (5) to use dishonest flattery, stringing the other a "line," and trying to be a person of many loves; (6) to be

---

8 This is another part of the same survey referred to above. Statistics reported here are for the 332 males and 342 females from the single and unengaged part of the sample.

A similar, though less refined, survey was made of 1,385 unmarried Mormon students at Brigham Young University during 1946-47. With the exceptions of smoking and drinking, which in Mormon culture are regarded as highly objectionable, there is a striking similarity between the findings of this and the Purdue study. See Harold T. Christensen, "Courtship Conduct as Viewed by Youth," *Journal of Home Economics,* 40 :187-88, April, 1948.

9 Statements are arranged here in the order of magnitude, as they differentiate one sex from the other (see Figure 3), and are amplified to more closely correspond with the original schedule (see the Appendix).

disrespectful of the opposite sex, making slurring remarks, and taking advantage; (7) to be weak in the social arts such as dancing, bridge, sports, and the like; (8) to be overtalkative and loud around others, a "show-off," full of "smart" slang; (9) to be careless in dress and mannerisms, sloppy appearance; (10) to be overly self-assured, egotistical, blind to own shortcomings, acting as if doing partner a favor; (11) to be unthinking in offering compliments or saying thanks, taking others for granted, inattentive, and inconsiderate; (12) to be overbearing, stubborn, impatient, bossy, always wanting own way, complaining, arguing; (13) to be too staid, conventional, and dull, lacking glamour or "sparkle."

Females, more than males, tend: (1) to be artificial in dress and manners, putting on airs, trying to be a fashion plate; (2) to ask stupid questions or make trite and silly remarks, showing shallow interests or excessive frivolity; (3) to be too cold emotionally, lacking warmth, or not being lovable; (4) to lack "life" and energy, complaining of being tired or sick; (5) to be a spendthrift, wanting always to do expensive things, or expecting expensive favors; (6) to be prudish regarding matters of sex and morals; (7) to be childish or a poor sport, lacking a sense of humor, being touchy and easily angered; (8) to show too much dependence upon others, with no mind of own, spineless; (9) to be indefinite and indecisive in dating, showing an indifference about planning or carrying out the date or a willingness to break it off for no legitimate reasons; (10) to be late for a date, keeping the other waiting; (11) to flirt with others or brag about other dates; (12) to be too serious, jealous, and possessive, overly sentimental, the "clinging vine" type; (13) to be too self-conscious and shy, awkward in groups, difficult to engage in conversation; (14) to be unwilling to share the spotlight with others, wanting to be entire center of attention.

In spite of general agreement on these matters, there are differences. It is interesting to note (Figure 3) the points at which each sex both accepts and projects blame. There was one item that each sex accepted as being more characteristic of itself than the other. This was described in the schedule as: "Acts nervous and rattled, isn't calm or at ease, lacks self-confidence and poise." Since each sex claims this shortcoming to itself, it is apparent that both sexes commonly feel rattled or ill-at-ease in the dating situation. In addition, males were more critical of their own sex than were females regarding such

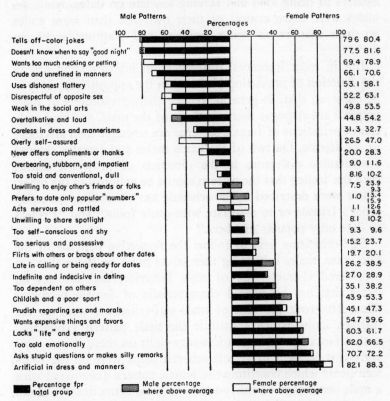

Male Patterns   **Female Patterns**

Percentages

100 80 60 40 20 0 20 40 60 80 100

	Male	Female
Tells off-color jokes	79.6	80.4
Doesn't know when to say "good night"	77.5	81.6
Wants too much necking or petting	69.4	78.9
Crude and unrefined in manners	66.1	70.6
Uses dishonest flattery	53.1	58.1
Disrespectful of opposite sex	52.2	63.1
Weak in the social arts	49.8	53.5
Overtalkative and loud	44.8	54.2
Careless in dress and mannerisms	31.3	32.7
Overly self-assured	26.5	47.0
Never offers compliments or thanks	20.0	28.3
Overbearing, stubborn, and impatient	9.0	11.6
Too staid and conventional, dull	8.16	10.2
Unwilling to enjoy other's friends or folks	7.5	23.9
Prefers to date only popular "numbers"	1.0	9.3
		13.4
		15.9
Acts nervous and rattled	1.1	12.6
		14.6
Unwilling to share spotlight	8.1	10.2
Too self-conscious and shy	9.3	9.6
Too serious and possessive	15.2	23.7
Flirts with others or brags about other dates	19.7	20.1
Late in calling or being ready for dates	26.2	38.5
Indefinite and indecisive in dating	27.0	28.9
Too dependent on others	35.1	38.2
Childish and a poor sport	43.9	53.3
Prudish regarding sex and morals	45.1	47.3
Wants expensive things and favors	54.7	59.6
Lacks "life" and energy	60.3	61.7
Too cold emotionally	62.0	66.5
Asks stupid questions or makes silly remarks	70.7	72.2
Artificial in dress and manners	82.1	88.3

■ Percentage fpr total group   ▨ Male percentage where above average   ☐ Female percentage where above average

(Calculated by subtracting from the largest number assigning an item to a particular sex, the number assigning it to the opposite sex, and expressing this net figure as a percentage of all answers.)

FIG. 3.—Comparison of male and female patterns of objectionable dating behavior. With the exception of three items, male and female students agree on which types of conduct are most prevalent with each sex. Males are characterized as being more offensive in regard to such things as manners and intimacy, while females are characterized by a tendency toward artificiality and shallowness. Though each sex is willing to partially accept the patterns ascribed to it, there is a tendency toward projecting blame upon the opposite sex. "Acts nervous and rattled" was the only pattern which was accepted more than projected by both males and females, suggesting that both sexes feel self-conscious in the dating situation. Based upon responses from 674 Purdue University students. For the complete schedule see the Appendix.

matters as being loud and staying too late on dates, while females were more critical of their own sex than were males on such matters as being artificial and wanting expensive favors.

But in most instances, differences in interpretation are in the direction of projecting blame upon the opposite sex. It is to be observed that, in general, female characterizations of male patterns are stronger than are those of the male, and that male characterizations of female patterns are stronger than are those of the female. On two of the items males and females showed considerable difference in the direction of projected blame, each sex feeling that the pattern should be assigned to the other. These were described in the schedule as: "Unwilling to enjoy other's friends or to associate with one's folks," and "Prefers to date only popular numbers."

Self-criticisms tend to follow the respective patterns of the two sexes, males criticizing themselves more on items that are considered characteristic of male behavior, and females on items that are considered characteristic of female behavior. Thus fifty-four per cent of male self-criticisms were on the thirteen items which constitute the male pattern (compared with a female percentage of twenty-eight on these items), and sixty-two per cent of female self-criticisms were on the fourteen items which constitute the female pattern (compared with a male percentage of thirty-seven on these same items). Males proved to be a little more self-critical than did females, and stressed such items as staying late on dates, being weak in the social arts, being self-conscious and shy, being late for a date, wanting too much intimacy, and being too serious and possessive. In contrast, females criticized themselves more on being self-conscious and shy, being late for a date, acting nervous and rattled, being too cold emotionally, being too dependent upon others, and being too staid and conventional. It is to be noted that being self-conscious and shy, and being late for a date, rated high in the self-criticisms of both sexes.

Ratings on objectionability were found to correlate negatively with both self-criticisms and the faults of one's own sex group. In other words, these students seemed to rationalize their own shortcomings and to project the more serious faults upon others, particularly others of the opposite sex. Females manifested this tendency more than did males. Both males and females regarded three traits as highly objectionable: being disrespectful of the opposite sex, being crude and unrefined in manners, and being careless in dress and mannerisms—and all three are within the male pattern. Three other traits highly objectionable to the female are these: wants too much necking or petting, tells off-color jokes, and is overly self-assured—which are also within the male pattern but are not regarded by the male as very objectionable. Traits highly objectionable to the male but not the female are these: flirts with others or brags about other dates, is childish and a poor sport, and is indefinite and indecisive in dating—all within the female pattern.

It goes almost without saying that all courtship is not of this kind. The things young people like in their dealings with each other are the reverses of the complaints given here—self-poise and confidence in place of being shy; courtesy and consideration in place of selfishness and egotism; respect and reserve in place of thrill-seeking intimacy; sincerity and honesty in place of superficial flattery; refinement to substitute for crudity and vulgarity; and cheerfulness and a sense of humor to substitute for touchiness and ill temper. Many relationships reach up to these high standards desired. But many also do not. Our only purpose in discussing the negative aspects of courtship behavior is to isolate the points of trouble so that these can be better attacked, eliminated, and positive constructive elements put in their places.

Some Miscellaneous Studies.—Another approach to this problem, of how young people today regard their courtship patterns, is to sample youth's opinions on specific questions. Rockwood and Ford have published a book, based upon a survey of 364 juniors and seniors at Cornell University, and comparing the results of this with those of other opinion studies throughout the country. One chapter of the book deals with attitudes toward premarital behavior; following is a brief summary:

General support was given to the conservative standard of pre-marital behavior. Approximately ninety per cent of the group considered petting unnecessary to a girl's popularity and about seventy-five per cent considered necking unnecessary. Around sixty-five per cent went on record as opposing premarital sexual intercourse for either sex. More would permit sex relations before marriage for men only than for women only. More men than women, and more urban than rural youth, accepted changes in the mores and approved of necking, petting, and premarital intercourse.[10]

During 1939 the writer made a careful survey of certain courtship opinions of 234 University of Wisconsin students. Among findings are the following:

"Mild necking or petting occurring as the rule or usual practice on dating occasions" was approved for the pre-engagement period by 53.6 per cent of the males and 14.5 per cent of the females, and for the engagement period by 90.9 per cent of the males and 83.9 per cent of the females.

"Heavy necking or petting (anything short of sexual intercourse) occurring as the rule or usual practice on dating occasions" was approved for the pre-engagement period by 7.3 per cent of males but none of the females, and for the engagement period by 30.0 per cent of the males and 12.1 per cent of the females.

"Sexual intercourse occurring as the rule or usual practice on dating occasions" was approved for the pre-engagement period by .9 per cent of the males but none of the females, and for the engagement period by 2.7 per cent of the males but none of the females.

Thus, the more intimate the behavior the less it was approved; on each type of behavior more freedom was approved for the engaged than for the unengaged; and males gave greater approval to all three of these intimate patterns of behavior than did females.[11]

Additional questions along this line were asked by the writer in a survey at Brigham Young University made during 1946-47. Thirteen hundred eighty-five unmarried Mormon students answered as follows:

To the question, "Do you believe that it would be a good thing if girls could feel as free as boys in asking for dates?", 42.6 per cent of

10 Lemo D. Rockwood and Mary E. N. Ford, *Youth, Marriage, and Parenthood* (New York: John Wiley & Sons, 1945), pp. 39-67.
11 Unpublished manuscript.

males answered yes, as did 19.2 per cent of the females. But when it came to, "Do you believe that it would be a good thing if girls paid about half the expense of college dates?", only 27.8 per cent of the males answered yes, as against 32.0 per cent of the females. Apparently most of this group favor the traditional patterns of dating, with females being especially reluctant to change over to date-making, and with males showing a disinclination to giving up their usual prerogative of footing the bill.

Only 5.9 per cent of the males and 7.5 per cent of the females thought that "one should save all his kisses for the one he marries"; and only .9 per cent of the males and 1.8 per cent of the females thought that "the first kiss should be delayed until the time of marriage." But to whether or not it is "all right for a couple to kiss on the first date," 35.1 per cent of the males agreed that it was, compared with 16.9 per cent of the females. By this standard the first kiss should come sometime between the first date and the marriage altar. On all of these points females were more conservative than were males.[12]

To summarize: Youth considers its chief problems in courtship to be those of both personal inadequacy and social irresponsibility. By introspection they become concerned mostly with their own tendencies to feel self-conscious, to act shy, to worry and get moody. In looking at the thing more broadly they tend to project blame upon the opposite sex and to see such major problems as irritable dispositions, unrefined mannerisms, egotistical dating, insincere love-making, and irresponsible intimacy. Males tend to define the courtship situation as involving naturalness and a considerable play upon sex; so females criticize them for being inconsiderate, crude, and "wolfish." Females, on the other hand, tend to see courtship as a sociable and sentimental adventure; and males complain of their being artificial, shallow, and poor sports. The traditional conservative standards of sexual morality are generally upheld (verbally at least), though with women more than with men. A higher degree of intimacy is agreed to for the engagement period than for early dating and courtship. Mild necking is approved more than heavy petting.

---

12 Unpublished manuscript.

Exploitation in Courtship.—Exploitive dating, where one deliberately keeps company with a type of person who differs from the one he will want to marry, or who selfishly encourages the kind of conduct he would not approve of for a permanent mate, is one of the major problems of courtship.

Exploitation exists because of the self-interests of people and the high variability of their bargaining powers. In courtship, as elsewhere, there is competition. In this competition some courters have certain advantages—money, physical attraction, family name, or a favorable sex ratio. All such advantages give one status which can be used as bargaining power in dating. Everyone knows that those with money, or sex appeal, or a good family name, can get dates easier than others not so fortunate. So, too, there is the principle of supply and demand, and when those of either sex find themselves very much in the minority they are also likely to discover that they are more popular. Sometimes bargaining power is built up by the mere fact that there has been an unequal love involvement. In all cases, those who either have the least, or care the most, are the ones most vulnerable to exploitation.

The chief bargaining agent of the male seems to be his money; that of the female, her sex appeal. These are power devices only because the opposite sex so strongly desires satisfaction from them. It would be a mistake, of course, to assume that men control women by means of money alone or that women control men by means of sex alone; there are other factors, and then, too, both men and women are normally interested in both sex and money. But man has more money and wants more sexual satisfaction, relatively speaking, while woman has more sex appeal and wants more of the things that money can buy. So, each sex uses what it has to bargain for what it wants.

"Gold digging" is woman's way of "working" man for all she can get. Not all women are gold diggers, of course, and it isn't confined to women. But it is a sufficiently definite female pattern of exploitation to warrant our attention. Common procedures are: going with only those males who have a car and pocketbook, and snubbing those who don't; encouraging fre-

quent treats, gifts, and other financial demonstrations of affection; and in some cases actually marrying for money. Sometimes the girl will be quite brazen about it, using sex appeal,
coquetry, and favors in intimacy as bait for her catch. In such
cases she actually sells herself, even though technical chastity
may be maintained. At other times, and let us think most frequently, gold digging is mere thoughtlessness, made easy by
masculine pride. While many girls need to be more considerate than they are of the fellow's pocketbook, it is also true
that many boys will need to adjust their thinking so as to permit female partners a larger role in the planning and financing
of dates. If sex equality is to become a reality, there is little
reason for thinking that "dutch dating" (the sharing of expenses) will not become the norm—for those going steady or
engaged, especially.

Sexual intimacy, though normal for marriage, frequently
causes trouble when engaged in during the courtship period.
This is particularly true if it is either extreme or lacks mutuality. Intimate fondling or intercourse, without the protection of marriage, may tend to cheapen sex, spoil love, and condition the participants against later adjustment. (See pages
147-58.) It isn't that intimacy itself is objectionable, only that
it has consequences, and that it ought, therefore, to be responsible and under control. (Sexual exploitation is the product of
the selfish appetites and irresponsible experimentations of some
of those who court.) There is too much of the thrill philosophy
in courtship today. Its fallacy lies in the illusions it creates.
When thrills are prematurely sought and excessively and irre-
sponsibly indulged in for their own sake, they soon lose their
force and leave the participants dissatisfied and restless for
something more. One thing leads to another, with disillusionment and frustration as almost inescapable results. To go out
on a date with the idea of "getting all I can" is to exploit a
personality for the sake of selfish and reckless indulgence. Fair
play calls for mutual respect and moderation. One of the primary purposes of the marriage institution is to protect mates
by making both responsible for their sexual acts.

Another and very common form of exploitation, for both

sexes, is what might be referred to as unequal or unfair monopoly. Often this takes the form of insincere flattery (sometimes called the "line"), along with deceptive actions designed to lead the person on or to get him to "fall." At other times (and this is usually the next step following the fall) it consists of using another person as a mere convenience—accepting his (or her) love but giving little in return, taking him for granted, not showing proper interest or consideration, flirting with others during the date. Still again, it is sometimes characterized by a tendency to be overjealous and possessive, to want complete monopoly without being willing to let the other one even function normally as a member of society (failing to realize that society is broader than any particular pair relationship). In all these instances there is exploitation, for self-interest is made paramount; in all there is a selfish attempt at ego inflation. Some courters, apparently, find comfort in adding broken hearts to their lives just as the early Indians used to like to add scalps to their belts; they take pride in being a man or woman "of many loves." Others seem to gain selfish satisfaction from being loved without reciprocating or from being able to push another around. The price of all such deceit, betrayal, and arrogance is human suffering for someone as deep as any ever known.

Love must not be treated as a plaything or as a power device for personal advantage. To do so is to exploit.

—**Traumatic Experiences.**—True love seldom runs smoothly. As early boy and girl friendships continue throughout and beyond courtship, free association between the sexes changes gradually into mate monopoly—first, going steady; then, engagement; and finally marriage. If there were some magic way of determining one's ideal mate so that his first love could be his only deep love, mankind could be spared many of the heartaches which it now endures. Though wishful thinking along this line has caused many to cling to the idea of a "one and only," there is nothing in our present store of knowledge that can enable us to avoid entirely the somewhat painful process of trial and error. Even if there were, it is reasonable to think that there would still exist difficulties and unpleasantries connected with the inevitability of ego adjustment in courtship, and the actuality of exploitation. In any event, courtship as we know it has its disappointments, its frustrations, its personal injuries.

One of these we would describe as mutual dissipation. There are those who, though reciprocal with each other, nevertheless carry out their courtships on relatively immature levels; they may not exploit, in the sense of taking advantage, but they dissipate, in the sense of overindulging. For example, alcohol and sex frequently lead to sorrow when used unwisely, even though experienced under conditions of mutuality.

Some people make the mistake of going steady too early, before they have had adequate time to look around, and without any definite marriage prospect. This frequently happens simply because it is the easiest thing to do—it saves the bother and risk involved in making new acquaintances and it gives the emotional security that comes from following established habit patterns. Then too, society is likely to encourage going steady by speaking of "his girl" or "her beau." Once started, participants may tend to continue the dating pattern out of sympathy or felt obligation. But, though easiest, it is not the most desirable. When the field is narrowed and monopoly established too early, like this, premature love involvement sets in and any of the following unfortunate situations are likely to develop: loss of chastity, heartaches following a possible breakup, marital incompatibility because of poor matching, or a too early wedding. The best plan is to explore the field early in courtship, even though this takes effort, and to leave monopoly for nearer the time of marriage.

Nimkoff and Wood have shown that the norm for social and emotional adjustment in college courtship is about as follows: started dating in junior high school, started going steady in college, has from one to three dates in two weeks, and has had some two or three "steadies." They found also that those who started dating late, who seldom or never date now, and who have never had more than one "steady," are socially retiring and slightly maladjusted emotionally. Finally, they found that those who started going steady in grade school or junior high school, who started against their parents' wishes, and who now had four or more steadies, tend to be aggressive socially and maladjusted emotionally. All of this is interpreted to mean that courtship patterns are influenced by personality types.[13]

Kirkpatrick and Caplow likewise measured a number of the significant aspects of courtship trauma among college students: (1) They found an average of slightly over two "serious affairs" among those of their sample, with nearly three fourths of these having been broken up prior to the time of study. (2) They found that a large proportion of the breakups resulted from a mutual loss of interest, and that in only about half of all cases was there any serious emotional or readjustment problem admitted. (3) But they also found that in nearly half of all responses there had been a differential loss of interest, which was the chief source of heartache.[14]

Though not usually as severe, the jilt in courtship is somewhat analogous to divorce in marriage; with both comes intense suffering due to the severing of social and emotional ties. "Falling out" is least painful where it is mutual, gradual, and where the love relationship was relatively superficial in the first place. The shock is most severe in case of one-sided feelings and for the party who is most deeply involved. Playing with another's love is, as has been observed, one of the most disastrous forms of courtship exploitation. But unequal love involvement may develop unintentionally. What then? It is well to recognize that marriage, to succeed, requires mutual love; sympathy alone is hardly enough. Fair play would require: first, that courters, insofar as possible, avoid leading each other on; and second, that they break off the relationship, or at least put their partner straight, just as soon as they can

[13] Meyer F. Nimkoff and Arthur L. Wood, "Courtship and Personality," *American Journal of Sociology*, V, 53:263-69, January, 1948.
[14] Clifford Kirkpatrick and Theodore Caplow, "Courtship in a Group of Minnesota Students," *American Journal of Sociology*, 51:114-25, September, 1945.

see that love is developing unequally, and do it tactfully but firmly, with as little hurt to the other as possible.

Lovers' quarrels are a normal part of courtship adjustment. Few sweethearts will get by without some misunderstanding and conflict; nor should they, for in this way comes the personality testing necessary for better understanding as time goes on. But though misunderstanding is normal, and to some extent desirable, quarreling can be carried too far. It can very easily sink to the level of petty bickering and personal insults. Furthermore, it can become habitual. To be constructive and worth while, misunderstandings must be sublimated into friendly discussion and then used merely as a means to an end —the end of adjustment. That couple is fortunate which early develops some satisfactory procedure for resolving its conflicts. Differences of opinion are inevitable in any group relationship; the only question is, "What is to be done with them?" If, in quarreling, lovers only become emotional about their differences, they solve nothing. But if, in the process, they are able not only to release tensions but to arrive at better understandings, they add strength to their love.

Jealousy is also an inevitable part of the love-developing process. Courtship normally sees self-love yield to a love of others, and indiscriminate dating gives way to monopoly and loyalty toward one. In all of this, jealousy exerts itself as a kind of ego-protest. But as adjustment takes place and true love develops, jealousy normally finds itself crowded out by confidence and trust. It is only when it is of the unreasonable or chronic variety that it can be considered as pathological; and this because mates are either immature or maladjusted. A moderate amount of jealousy is to be expected, though not accepted, for in time it must be brought under control.

Cultivating the Graces of Courtship.—Personal adequacy in matters of this kind requires both confidence and skill. One is not born to be the perfect lover, nor can he learn overnight, or in "ten easy lessons." Learning to love takes time and practice—though practice in self-control as well as in self-expression.

Some individuals remain crude and awkward in their dealings with the opposite sex all through life, which is unfortunate. Others learn early that to have friends one must be
friendly, that to be successful in dating one must make himself attractive personally.

There is a basic relationship between happiness in marriage
and the ability to make and hold friends. Research has demonstrated that those individuals who have a fair number of
friends, of both sexes, are the ones most likely to make a success of marriage.[15] Reasons for this should be obvious, for by
cultivating friendships and making them endure we demonstrate our ability to attract, to adapt, to mix socially, and to
make others happy in our presence. These same qualities are
important for marriage.

Shyness comes from a sense of personal insecurity in a social situation; lacking self-confidence, one quite naturally becomes self-conscious. Sometimes, as in instances of excessive
modesty, it takes the form of bashfulness. At other times,
though, it simply means that the person is shrinking from
social intercourse as such. Shyness is most frequently to be
explained in terms of either inexperience or early conditioning through ego injury or social frustration. It is a sign of
social and emotional immaturity. But it will yield, in part at
least, to social experience and self-effort. Too many with this
problem simply wait for someone else to take the lead in bringing them out of it, and then, failing to find friends because
they are not doing their part in being friendly, they start to
worry, get moody, complain, and feel sorry for themselves. If
the problem is to be solved it will be only by those who feel
shy taking the initiative, forcing themselves to do their part.
The following suggestions might help: get your mind off
yourself by becoming interested in other people and active in
other things; learn the art of conversation, which means both
being a good listener and knowing how to comment interestingly on current topics; learn a practical, but not too mechanical, social etiquette; acquire skills in sports, dancing, and

---

[15] See, for example, E. W. Burgess and L. S. Cottrell, *Predicting Success and
Failure in Marriage* (New York: Prentice-Hall, Inc., 1939), pp. 121-32.

other sociable activities; make opportunities to mix with people
—and then mix.

Personal charm is something that everyone can develop
through proper study and self-effort; no one needs remain
obnoxious or distasteful to others on account of his looks or
mannerisms. There are very few who are really, or greatly,
unattractive to others anyway. But then all can improve, and
in improving, become more likable and popular. Serious attention needs be given such matters as pleasantness in facial and
vocal expression, cleanliness and neatness in dress, attractive
posture and body carriage, and moderation and decorum in
social conduct. By self-analysis one can soon become acquainted
with both liabilities and assets and can learn to capitalize upon
the latter.[16]

But "self-appeal," of course, is more than skin deep; real
charm does not come from the veneer of surface mannerisms,
it emanates from within. If one is right on the inside, his
outward behavior will usually fall into line, and vice versa.
Grace and charm are important, not as a camouflage to deceive and gain advantage, but as the reflection of an inward
quality. We need constantly to strive to be courteous and
considerate of others; to use tact rather than attack in dealing
with them; to avoid the crude and the offensive; to be attractive
in dress, speech, and action. Nevertheless, popularity, if it is
to last, must be based upon character, and to try for it otherwise is to cheat.

Many, unfortunately, leave their personalities relatively undeveloped and by one substitute or another try to cheat or to
bluff their way through. A girl, for example, sometimes flaunts
her "sex appeal" as a substitute for charm, and a boy with
means may use his money as a bribe factor or a power device
in popularity. It is no compliment to have sex, everyone has
that; or to possess money, that may come by accident. The
real compliment is to possess character, ability, and charm
based upon genuine worth.

16 Cf. Dorothy C. Stratton and Helen B. Schleman, *Your Best Foot Forward*
(New York: Whittlesey House, 1940). This book discusses various aspects of
personal charm and social graciousness. For dating problems see chap. vi, pp.
119-50.

Dating etiquette, though undergoing change along with the rest of our culture, stays pretty close to the principle of mutual consideration without exploitation. The boy will usually do the asking, although in these days that doesn't seem to be so important as it once was, and certainly in all cases the girl should feel free to let him know if she would be agreeable to an invitation. Dates need to be arranged courteously and with poise on both sides. "Dropping in" for a date without first making arrangements is bad taste and is usually not appreciated. Sometimes, for one reason or another, the girl feels that she must decline an invitation; no date is best accepted through sympathy alone or because of coercion or lack of the courage to say "no." On the other hand, there is no harm in being socially gracious, in stretching a point or being a good sport so that others may have a better time. When refusals are made they can be done tactfully and respectfully, though clearly and firmly. When a date is agreed upon, it is best that both parties participate in the planning. If he wants her to go some place in particular he should let her know long enough ahead and should be specific enough so that she will know what to wear and how otherwise to plan. If he should ask her what she would like to do (and this is a proper courtesy) she can be ready to speak up with constructive suggestions. If the decision depends upon how much money is available, he can give an indication of what the limits are. Consideration for the desire and the welfare of the other needs be uppermost in the mind of each, all the way through the date. She can be considerate of his pocketbook, and he, in turn, is not to expect "favors" as payment for what he has spent. If he hangs on and doesn't know when to go home, it is then her place to take the initiative in saying "good night." Thus dating needs to be planned and carried out in a manner that is mutually beneficial. In this way it can be made constructive and can be kept from sinking to the level of mere intimacy for want of something better to do.

The graces of courtship include self-confidence without arrogance, charm without superficiality, and cooperation without surrender. Egotistical pride, affected mannerisms, and weak docility are all perversions of the thing we are talking about. Needed are people who feel secure, who act naturally though appropriately, and who are willing to give as well as to take.

Learning to Love Successfully.—In concluding this chapter let it be reemphasized that true sweetheart love is a process of reciprocal involvement, and that to be successful it must be learned. We quite naturally come to love those individuals who meet our personality needs and to whom we are most habituated or are best adjusted. Love matures, and endures, only when it is based upon a mutuality of interests and results in interdependence and companionship.

Courtship is the term used to designate the period or process of premarital love-involvement. Its major purpose is to allow for marriage preparation. It fails when participants are either personally inadequate or socially selfish, when they are either too immature or too exploitive.

A successful "date" has been defined as one that is mutually enjoyable and enriching. In a similar vein, successful love or courtship could be described as that which leads progressively in the direction of shared happiness through greater pair unity.

PROBLEMS AND PROJECTS

1. Describe what to you would be an "ideal date," telling why.
2. Make two lists: one of traits which you like most in the opposite sex, and the other of traits which you dislike most when present in the opposite sex. How do your last five dates rate on these standards?
3. In a spirit of honest self-evaluation, list the objectionable traits that you sometimes manifest in dating. How can these be improved?
4. Consider the courtship pairs and young married couples you know. What examples of "romantic infantilism" have you observed in their behavior or points of view?
5. Consider the last five movies you have seen or stories you have read which were concerned with married love. Which of these told of conjugal love? Tell why.

6. Can a person love two or more individuals equally well: (*a*) At different times, implying that love can hit more than once? (*b*) At the same time, implying that love does not necessarily center on one object? Discuss.

7. Discuss ways of recognizing love and of deciding whether it is of the kind and amount that would justify marriage. Should a couple get married if either member harbors any doubts about their love? Defend your point of view.

8. What are the advantages and the disadvantages of going steady? Should one go steady with a person that he has no intention of marrying? Discuss.

9. Sometimes a girl loses the one she cares for by wanting him so much, and showing it. Should she, then, "play hard to get"? Are there equal dangers in that position? Discuss.

10. It is frequently difficult for courting individuals to determine whether or not it is proper to give each other presents on birthdays, Christmas, at graduation, or similar occasions. Make practical suggestions for meeting this problem.

11. What should be the possibilities and limits of girls asking for dates? Of proposing marriage? Discuss.

12. What are the values and limitations of the "lines" which young people employ in association with the opposite sex?

13. Discuss techniques of quarreling with which you are familiar. Which do you feel are the more constructive and why?

Selected Readings

Becker, Howard, and Hill, Reuben (eds.). *Family, Marriage, and Parenthood.* Boston: D. C. Heath & Co., 1948. Chap. vii, "Steps in Love and Courtship."

Burgess, Ernest W., and Locke, Harvey J. *The Family: From Institution to Companionship.* New York: American Book Co., 1945. Chap. xii, "Love and Courtship."

Burkhart, Roy A. *From Friendship to Marriage.* New York: Harper & Bros., 1937. Chaps. i, "Friendship in Our World"; ii, "You As a Friend"; iii, 'Dates"; iv, "Intimacy."

Duvall, Evelyn Millis, and Hill, Reuben. *When You Marry.* Boston: D. C. Heath & Co., 1945. Chaps ii, "Love Enough to Marry On"; iii, "Dating: Practice Makes Perfect"; iv, "Becoming Involved: The Courtship Process."

DUVALL, SYLVANUS M. *Before You Marry*. New York: Association Press, 1949.

ELLIOTT, MABEL A., and MERRILL, FRANCIS E. *Social Disorganization*. New York: Harper & Bros., 1941. Chap. xxiii, "The Romantic Fallacy."

HARPER, ROBERT A. *Marriage*. New York: Appleton-Century-Crofts, Inc., 1949. Chaps. i, "Marriage in Modern Society: Romance and Realism"; v, "Dating and Courtship."

LANDIS, JUDSON T., and LANDIS, MARY G. *Building a Successful Marriage*. New York: Prentice-Hall, Inc., 1948. Chap. iv, "The Courtship Period."

NIMKOFF, MEYER. *Marriage and the Family*. Boston: Houghton Mifflin Co., 1947. Chap. xii, "Courtship."

ROCKWOOD, LEMO D., and FORD, MARY E. N. *Youth, Marriage, and Parenthood*. New York: John Wiley & Sons, 1945. Chap. vi, "Attitudes Toward Premarital Behavior."

STRATTON, DOROTHY C., and SCHLEMAN, HELEN B. *Your Best Foot Forward*. New York: Whittlesey House, 1940.

WALLER, WILLARD. *The Family: A Dynamic Interpretation*. New York: The Cordon Co., 1938. Part II, "Courtship Interaction."

Chapter 8

CHOOSING A MATE

Too many people are under the illusion that the key to marital happiness is wholly and simply that of selecting an appropriate mate. They are wrong. While marital happiness does depend partly upon the type of companion one has, it is also contingent upon the quality of one's own personality. Being a good mate is every bit as important as choosing the right mate, perhaps even more so. A common tendency, when marriage fails, is to rationalize one's position by projecting the blame upon the other. Frequently this takes the form of one's claiming that he was fooled during courtship and that he married the wrong person. This seems to be easier than acknowledging personal failure in marital adjustment. Actually, though, marital success is most likely when the mates are mature and adaptable as well as compatible. To stress any one factor at the expense of others is a mistake. It is true that mature personalities can often prove adjustable enough to overcome partially the handicap of an ill-matched marriage. But it is equally true that poor mating puts marriage at a disadvantage, that love has its best chance of developing and continuing when the traits of mates are compatible from the beginning.

Pair unity is dependent upon: (1) how well the mates are matched, and (2) how completely they have adjusted to each other. We have already examined this latter for the period of premarriage, calling it love involvement. Here we are to be concerned with the first named, with mate selection as a part of the process of successful marriage. There are few other problems that young people ask questions about so frequently or need help on so much.

Freedom of Choice

How much choice does one have in determini
marry? What are the conditions outside of onese
pressure or help shape the decision? Is marrying primarily a
matter of destiny or judgment?

The Soul-Mate Theory.—To answer the last question first,
we would say that marrying is more a matter of judgment
than it is of destiny. There are those who believe the opposite,
of course, thinking that each person has a soul mate who needs
only to be found. This is the mystical approach to love and
marriage. It fits with the "romantic fallacy" discussed in the
preceding chapter. If there were truth in such a position, one
would be caused to wonder why more people don't find their
intended mate—why, for example, marriage failure becomes
greater in this day of increasing intercommunication (which
ought to aid people in finding what they are looking for, and
reduce divorce if finding were all there is to it).

But we are talking about *choosing* a mate, which implies
intelligence and personal will. For many people this is the most
important of life's decisions. Since it is weighted with consequences and related to one's over-all level of happiness, there
are some who would dodge it. One way of attempting this is
to surrender to romance and wishful thinking. Many are those
who would leave the choice of their married partner to Divine
Providence if they could, though in trying they too often
simply leave it to chance.

From our point of view the only sense in which people are
ever meant for each other is that some matching combinations
are more workable than others, and all love involvements cause
participants to become progressively interdependent. Good
matching plus continued involvement makes for pair unity.
There is no question but that each person can be happier
with certain individuals than he can with others, but for natural
rather than mystical reasons. If people are ever meant for each
other, it is because of their own choosing and adjusting.

Successful matching, therefore, is not a process of romantic searching, as some would have it, but of intelligent choosing; it isn't a matter of destiny, but of decision.

Pressures from the Outside.—One's right to choose is never without qualification. Always there are forces and restrictions pushing in from the outside, swaying one's behavior. These pressures may emanate from other persons, from sociocultural definitions, or from attempts at legal control.

In many cultures, mates are selected by family heads, with the marrying individuals having little or nothing to say about it. Arrangements are frequently made while those to be married are still children, or, in some societies, even before they are born. Practical rather than romantic considerations are paramount, such as: "Will he be a good provider?"; "Will she be a good cook and housekeeper?"; "Will such a match be economically advantageous to the family?"; "Does the prospective mate come from a family with a good reputation, giving status value?" Sometimes a go-between or official matchmaker is employed to assist parents in the job of properly marrying off their children. This is the familistic way of doing things.

But contemporary American culture is highly individualistic. What then? It is in line with democratic principles, and the findings of research, to say that the influence of parents over the mate-choices of their children should be considerable, but that it ought never to be arbitrary or absolute. Both the Terman and the Burgess and Cottrell studies found marriage to be more successful where the mates had been rather closely attached to their parents and had not had serious or frequent conflict with them.[1] Burgess and Cottrell also found that marital adjustment is better accomplished in those cases that have had parental approval.[2] Popenoe found that elopement is associated with disproportionately high rates of marriage failure.[3]

---

[1] Ernest W. Burgess and Leonard S. Cottrell, *Predicting Success or Failure in Marriage* (New York: Prentice-Hall, Inc., 1939). See summary chart, pp. 357-59.

[2] Burgess and Cottrell, *op. cit.*, pp. 168-71.

[3] Paul Popenoe, *Modern Marriage* (New York: The Macmillan Co., 1943), pp. 222-25.

Because of their experience and their perspective, many parents are able to give valuable counsel to children. Fortunate are those families that have established harmonious relationships among members so that parents can approach their children on matters of counsel and children will come to their parents for discussion and advice.

When parents object it is generally for one or more of three reasons: (1) they think their child is too young or is not ready for marriage; (2) they don't care for the person chosen; or (3) they either consciously or unconsciously react against the whole idea of marriage, regardless of the time element or the person being selected. Parents are often right in wanting a child to wait until he is a little older, or until he has finished school, or accomplished some other goal, or made adequate preparation before getting married. Certain it is that child marriages more frequently fail, and because of both immaturity on the part of mates and insufficient testing and preparation before the ceremony. Parents are also very frequently right, though not always, of course, in talking against their child's marrying a particular individual. They are in a position to see things that the courting child may not see because of inexperience and possible romantic infatuation. But parents are never right in holding a child back because of failure in their own marriage, or because of strong emotional attachment to the child, or because they want to be taken care of in their old age. To force a child into permanent celibacy, out of either disillusionment or selfishness on the part of parents, is totally unfair.

There will be instances where the children will need to take a stand against their parents in matters of this kind. It is right that the final decision be made by the person marrying, for this is the one who must bear the consequences; if one is mature enough to marry he or she is also mature enough to make an adult choice. Strong and arbitrary parental objections sometimes have the opposite effect than the one intended; they may invite rebellion, causing the child to court or marry the forbidden one out of spite. The wiser procedure is to counsel and advise, but without too much pressure, and certainly without dictation. Children, on the other hand, will do well to seek help, to consider seriously what is said, and to take a stand against their elders only when they are sufficiently mature and have given the matter an extended testing. The twin errors are arbitrary dictation on the one side and impetuous rebellion on the other.

It is known also that marriage is more successful when given the sanction of friends and associates. Social approval gives the marriage a harmonious setting, making adjustment easier. Disapproval handicaps adjustment by putting the mates under tension, giving them extra hurdles to get over. One reason for the difficulties involved in interracial marriages (to be discussed below) is the burden of social prejudice coming in from the outside. Mate seekers do best when they actively invite opinions from others and when they steer their courses not too far from the conventional and the acceptable. Though it is undoubtedly true that some conventions need to be broken, or changed, breaking them puts one at a disadvantage.

Bates, from his study of parental roles in courtship, concluded that the majority of parents do attempt to influence the mating patterns of their children, though usually in a manner that is moderate and indirect. Mothers try to influence more than do fathers, and daughters are the objects of this pressure more than are sons. Nearly all of the secret marriages come from families where parents are severe or despotic in their control. Parental roles in courtship are far from standardized by our society; the particular role each parent takes depends more upon the adequacy or inadequacy of his own personality adjustments than it does upon "stereotyped cultural demands." Parents are most likely to interfere when their own marriages have been unsuccessful; it is then that they try to substitute for their own thwarted impulses the phantasy of success through their children.[4]

From early childhood until the time of marriage most persons formulate their idea of what an ideal mate should be like. The concept emerges somewhat gradually as one interacts with his parents, his brothers and sisters, and then others of

---

[4] Alan Bates, "Parental Roles in Courtship," *Social Forces*, 20:483-86, May 1942.

the great society. It is defined in terms of habit patterns, of personality needs, and of cultural prescriptions imposed by such agencies as the school, the church, the picture show, and the printed page. Once formed, this ideal mate concept acts in some degree as a cultural compulsive, influencing the mate choices of those who hold it. In a study of 373 engaged or recently married persons, Strauss found that nearly all held some idea of an ideal mate and that there was a marked resemblance between the ideal and the actual mate, both as to physical features and personality traits. Fifty-nine per cent of his sample judged the actual mate to be close to the physical ideal, and 73.3 per cent close to the personality ideal.[5] It is significant, too, that the ideal is not always realized in mate selection, that sometimes there must be a compromise. Apparently people are more willing to compromise in the area of physical appearance than they are with respect to other desired personality traits.

There is the Freudian claim that mates tend to be selected according to how well they match the parent of the opposite sex. According to this theory, a girl will have a "father image" which will act as her guide in selecting a mate, while a boy will choose his partner under the influence of a "mother image"; each will be after some kind of opposite-sex parent substitute. The assumption needs further testing; to date there has been no objective or statistical investigation of sufficient magnitude to give any dependable answer. What seems to be true is that a person will tend either to replace or reject the situation he has grown up under, that he will choose a mate who either fills the same needs in his personality that were previously filled by a parent, or who fills those needs that one of the parents left unsatisfied. Strauss found that it is the kinds of images that are important, more than any simple assumption of opposite-sex parent influence. For example, a boy would try to find a mate either like his mother, or opposite, depending upon the nature of his affectional relationships with that parent; but he could be similarly influenced

5 Anselm Strauss, "The Ideal and the Chosen Mate," *American Journal of Sociology*, 52:204-8, November, 1946.

by strong images built around his father, or a brother, or a sister. Strauss also found that physical resemblances between the mate and a parent are not as frequent or as marked as are resemblances in attitude and temperament.[6]

Legal restrictions upon marriage vary considerably from state to state. Common prohibitions are those against: (1) bigamy, where either of the parties is already married; (2) immaturity, where either is under legal age, usually 18 for the male and 16 for the female; (3) incest, where the prospective mate is a first cousin or closer by blood; (4) miscegenation, where the proposed marriage is to cross racial lines; (5) mental defects, where there is evidence of insanity or feeble-mindedness; and (6) infection, where there is a communicable disease, especially syphilis or gonorrhea. These will be discussed again in the next chapter; here we simply note that they exist and that they restrict one's freedom of choice.

The Question of Propinquity.—Not everyone in the world has an equal chance of being chosen. Nor would he, even if there were no cultural compulsives to set up lines of demarcation and selection. There is the matter of ecological opportunity. People come to love and marry only those that they have had the chance to contact and to mingle with in association. As Waller puts it, "One does not select a wife from the whole group of possible wives, but only from the group of women he knows."[7] Isolation and segregation tend to limit or narrow the range of one's choice.

From a study of five thousand Philadelphia marriages taking place in 1931, Bossard found that in over one third of the cases (33.58 per cent) couples had lived within five blocks of each other, and in over half of the cases (51.94 per cent) they had resided not more than twenty blocks apart.[8] Kennedy found essentially the same thing for New Haven, though

---

[6] See Anselm Strauss, "The Influence of Parent-Images upon Marital Choice," *American Sociological Review*, 11:554-59, October, 1946. See also his article, "Personality Needs and Marital Choice," *Social Forces*, 25:332-35, March, 1947.

[7] Willard Waller, *The Family: A Dynamic Interpretation* (New York: The Dryden Press, Inc., 1938), p. 291.

[8] James H. S. Bossard, "Residential Propinquity as a Factor in Marriage Selection," *American Journal of Sociology*, 38:219-24, September, 1932.

with slightly higher figures—for 1940 marriages, 35.79 per cent of the mates had lived within five blocks of each other and 76.31 per cent within twenty blocks. By comparing 1931 with 1940 she discovered a slight tendency toward an increase of propinquous marriages. She also found that rates of close residence marriages are higher in areas of distinctive racial and nationality groupings, showing that it is not only physical proximity that is important but that cultural factors likewise play a part.[9] The writer, in a study of 1,670 Utah County marriages, found that over half (55.2 per cent) were between persons who resided in the same neighborhood, village, or small city. From the years 1905-7 to the years 1929-31, the percentage of persons marrying someone of the same locality decreased from 69.1 to 43.5; while the percentages marrying someone from another part of the country, or of the state, or from out of the state, all increased.[10] These findings are fundamentally the same as those of Bossard and of Kennedy. The apparent discrepancy regarding the direction of the trend can probably be explained by differences in the populations of New Haven, Connecticut, and Utah County, Utah. In any event there seems to be no question but that the majority of people still marry from among those who reside close by.

Residential propinquity loses some of its influence in mate selection when other factors come into play. One of these is what we might call social or functional propinquity. When work or leisure-time activities bring people together, some of these people are likely to become acquainted and to marry. As locality groupings give way to special interest and functional organizations, in this day of rapid communication and transportation, it can be expected that people will more and more select their mates from among their social and occupational associates, regardless of how far apart the residences may happen to be. Marvin, in an early study of Philadelphia mar-

---

9 Ruby Jo Reeves Kennedy, "Premarital Residential Propinquity and Ethnic Endogamy," *American Journal of Sociology,* 48:580-84, March, 1943.

10 Harold T. Christensen, "A Comparative Study of the Time Interval Between the Marriage of Parents and the Birth of their First Child, Based on 1670 Couples in Utah County, Utah, 1905 to 1935" (Unpublished thesis, Provo, Utah: Brigham Young University Library, 1937), see pp. 46-51. For a partial report, see article in *American Journal of Sociology,* 44:518-25, January, 1939.

riages, found that men and women intermarried within the same occupation at a rate almost three times as high as could be expected from mere chance.[11] Harris followed with a study of Allentown, Pennsylvania, and found that the older people are when they select a mate, and the higher they are on the socioeconomic scale, the less they are influenced by the factor of residential proximity. The chief reason for this seems to be that the older and higher-leveled individuals have more time and money to travel and to meet people from other areas.[12]

An important part of both residential and functional propinquity is the sex ratio. From the standpoint of marriage opportunity it does little good to be associated with a large group of people if they are all of one's own sex. Women have the advantage in groups showing a surplus of men, and men the advantage in groups where women are abundant, both because there are more to select from and hence competition is less. The marriage rate is low whenever the sex ratio gets too far out of balance either way. Groves and Ogburn have shown that women are more dependent upon a favorable sex ratio than are men (both money and custom give men the greater bargaining power), and that a ratio of about 120 men to 100 women favors a maximum marriage rate.[13]

There are several types of imbalances in the sex ratio which affect the marriage rate. Regionally considered, the western states show a large surplus of males and the northeastern states a surplus of females. This would mean that females have a better chance of finding a mate in the West and males in the East. Rural-urban comparisons show the highest male surplus to be on the farm and the only female surplus to be in the city, which gives marrying advantages to the rural female and the urban male. Socioeconomic comparisons show

[11] D. M. Marvin, "Occupational Propinquity as a Factor in Marriage Selection," *American Statistical Association,* 16:131-50, September, 1918.

[12] Daniel Harris, "Age and Occupational Factors in the Residential Propinquity of Marriage Partners," *Journal of Social Psychology,* 6:257-61, May, 1935. See also T. C. Hunt, "Occupational Status and Marriage Selection," *American Sociological Review,* 5:495-504; and Richard Centers, "Marital Selection and Occupational Strata," *American Journal of Sociology,* 54:530-35, May, 1949.

[13] Ernest R. Groves and William F. Ogburn, *American Marriage and Family Relationships* (New York: Henry Holt & Co., 1928), chap. xiii, pp. 193-219.

an excess of females in the upper classes and of males in the lower classes, a fact that makes it difficult for many capable females to marry without marrying down—so, many of them remain single. In practice, certain of the occupations are reserved almost exclusively for the male and others almost exclusively for the female. While this puts both sexes to some disadvantage, it is the female who is handicapped most.

Opportunities for mate selection are best when the individuals concerned live close to and associate frequently with adequate numbers from the opposite sex. Residential propinquity encourages love involvement, though it is neither a prerequisite nor is it a guarantee. Functional propinquity is even more important; it is, in fact, essential to marriage, for how can love develop or mates be chosen without contact of some sort? Functional propinquity may come about through nearness of residence or from interaction away from home in one or more of the various socioeconomic activities. Though it is a prerequisite of marriage, it too is no guarantee that marriage will take place. Propinquity, then, is not the only factor involved in mate selection; there are the matters of culturally determined opportunities and of personal preferences and assortive tendencies.

Culturally Determined Opportunities.—People often live side by side without ever becoming acquainted, or they associate together in a perfunctory manner throughout the workaday world without ever becoming friendly. Being neighbors does not insure neighborliness, nor does interaction necessarily mean intimacy. One might have marriage opportunity from the standpoint of sheer physical proximity and yet lack any real opportunity because of culturally imposed restrictions.

' One of these restrictions is the disapproval put upon mixed marriages. American society generally frowns upon interracial marriage, less frequently interreligious marriage, and occasionally upon other mixings such as those involving two widely different social or economic classes. In addition to all such direct pressures from the source of public opinion are the inward controls which cause people to be suspicious or afraid of those who have very different backgrounds, interests, or ideals from those of their own. But even these inward tendencies and preferences reflect the culture, for they were organized and developed within definite cultural settings. It is not only important to be able to associate with adequate numbers of the opposite sex, therefore, but to be able to associate with a kind that is both socially and personally acceptable—either that or change the cultural definitions.

Then there are the rules of etiquette and other social customs and conventions which tend to make people reserved or backward in getting acquainted. Females, for instance, are usually at a disadvantage in seeking dates; they can't just go up and ask a fellow for fear of being branded as too forward.

Kirkpatrick and Caplow, in a study of a group of University of Minnesota students, found that even in this coeducational institution a surprising proportion of young people lack opportunity properly to meet persons of the opposite sex. At least one third of these students claimed that their opportunities to meet members of the other sex were inadequate. But when put to the question of whether or not they would patronize a respectable date bureau, 79.4 per cent of the men and 84.4 per cent of the women said "no." "Perhaps it is not just dates that students want but also success in competition for dates." [14]

Punke, in his analysis of white women teachers in a southern city, found that the marriage rate for teachers twenty to twenty-nine years of age was only from one half to five eighths as high as for the general population. The differential became less as teachers grew older, though it was not until they had passed the age of forty that the marriage rate among them became higher than for the corresponding age group in the general population. The significantly lower marriage rate for the younger teachers probably reflects a combination of factors such as relative isolation from masculine contacts, a school board's rule discouraging resignation, and personal ambitions. [15]

---

[14] Clifford Kirkpatrick and Theodore Caplow, "Courtship in a Group of Minnesota Students," *American Journal of Sociology,* 51:114-25, September, 1945. Data and quotation from p. 117.

[15] Harold H. Punke, "Marriage Rate Among Women Teachers," *American Sociological Review,* 5:505-11, August, 1940.

The so-called "White-Collar Girl" of urban areas has several special problems connected with getting married: (1) She has a disadvantage so far as the sex ratio is concerned; where she is, men are relatively scarce. (2) She usually enters the type of work that tends to segregate the sexes all the more, leaving her too few contacts with the opposite sex. (3) Being unusually capable and ambitious, she is frequently more career-minded than marriage-minded or, when the opposite is true, she finds that the number of available men is greatly cut down by her high standards of acceptability. (4) The business-like formality of the city leaves her somewhat isolated and alone; her chief contacts are professional and impersonal; she is often without opportunity for meeting, except superficially, or for becoming friendly with the type of man she would marry.

The best conditions for mate selection are filled when young people have abundant opportunity for meeting a large variety of those of the opposite sex and are able to meet them under conditions that encourage dating. In singling out the "White-Collar Girl" above we did not imply that the problem of marriage opportunity is peculiar to her nor that it is insurmountable. Many people find difficulty in getting acquainted in the right way. What are the possibilities for aiding the situation?

Meeting the Problem.—One possibility is self-help, where overshy and unsocialized individuals, through study and effort, learn how to take the initiative, to capitalize upon opportunities, and to be socially gracious. (See Chapters 3 and 7.) Another approach would be to work for a gradual reorganization of society, reorganization to the extent of giving the sexes equal opportunity in social intercourse (see Chapter 4), and of providing more and better facilities for the informal mingling of the unmarried. Various church and civic groups are striving to meet this latter need now—organizing youth centers, promoting recreational and cultural programs, and, in some cases, setting up files and guidance facilities to aid in matchmaking.

A third type of program, therefore, would be this last-named, direct aid in matchmaking. Professional matchmaking is an old institution, but one that may seem strange in present American culture where emphasis is upon romance and freedom of choice. We still have a few marriage brokers, individuals who make it their business to help people find mates and who charge fees for their professional services. This system is strong in some Jewish communities but is not general elsewhere. Advertising for a mate in the personal columns of newspapers or in magazines is occasionally done, though the practice is not nearly so common here as in some other countries of the world. There are a number of commercial agencies, popularly known as Lonely Hearts Clubs, that supply members with lists of marriage prospects. Such lists are usually distributed for a fee, and they contain the name, address, and a brief description of the physical features and financial circumstances of each client. Interesting prospects then are usually contacted by a letter from the suitor containing a request for a photograph, though in some cases contact is by a personal call. Date Bureaus have been organized periodically on college campuses and elsewhere, but with only moderate success. Their purpose is to provide a central clearing house for those who want dates; they supply information designed to increase opportunity for dating and to insure more agreeable social occasions through better matching. A similar practice, but one that offers more promise than any of the above-named, consists of the so-called Introduction Services. Here the aim is not so much that of providing dates or arranging marriages, but of introducing congenially typed people to each other (dates and marriages may follow, of course). Clients are registered, in some cases tested, background information is filed, and introductions are then arranged on the basis of matched characteristics.

Public acceptance of these various devices for getting marriage eligibles together has been only partial and for these reasons: (1) They have seemed too cold and calculating, too artificial, too lacking in romance. (2) Their approach has sometimes been cheap, superficial, and too highly flavored with commercialism. (3) They have attracted disproportionate numbers from among the socially inept, becoming so stigmatized that the more capable individuals in society hesitate to participate. One reason for this latter is that the more advantaged don't need these services as much, and tend, therefore, to regard participation in them as a mark of failure. Related to this, and serving as an additional handicap, is the fact that the sex ratio of participants is usually out of balance. Because there is such a surplus of widows in society, and because courtship patterns hold women to a condition of less opportunity on the open market, females turn to these services much more than do males.

The idea of helping marriage prospects get together has merit and should be further explored. While marriage brokerages, personal newspaper columns, Lonely Hearts Clubs, and Date Bureaus undoubtedly accomplish some good, they are frequently charlatan and they fail to reach many of those who want assistance. The need is for both opportunity in meeting and guidance in matching. Introduction Services have been designed to function in this twofold capacity, and, as professional organizations, bringing science to bear upon this important problem of human behavior. Several have failed. Society, it would seem, is not yet quite ready.

Factors in the Choice

As has been seen, no one is entirely free to choose his mate. There are parental, societal, and legal controls pushing in from the outside. There is the matter of residential and functional propinquity, which puts a person in contact with some individuals and out of contact with others. Then there are culturally imposed barriers and pressures which either limit or increase dating and marrying opportunities. Yet in this culture one does choose. Below are some of the factors involved in the process.

Head Versus Heart.—Each of us is attracted to certain members of the opposite sex on the basis of admiration and respect, but to certain others because of sentiment and emotion. If we were to draw a diagram of two circles, letting one represent those of our acquaintances that appeal to us by way of the head, and the other represent those that the heart would choose, from which circle should we select our mate? Young people in courtship are very frequently up against this specific problem.

Realistic mating leaves room for both the head and the heart, properly balanced and mutually reinforcing. In the previous chapter we saw how romantic love alone is not enough, how true conjugal love goes farther than either physical attraction or romantic infatuation—it involves also the deep-seated companionship that comes from intelligent adjusting over time. But, on the other hand, neither is cool calculation enough. It is only when reason becomes tempered and sweetened by emotion, and emotion strengthened and controlled by reason, that genuine love has a chance to develop and endure. If the circles posed in the illustration below were properly conceived they would overlap, for there is an area of acquaintanceship that is attractive to both the head and the heart. It is from this common area that one should choose his mate.

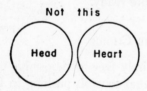

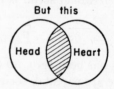

Someone has pointed out a need for using the head a little more before marriage and the heart a little more afterward. It is true that courtship is too frequently overweighted with emotion, as it is true also that marriage sometimes sinks to the humdrum level, void of affection. By balancing the head with the heart, both courtship and marriage could be improved.

With reference to choosing a mate, it should be emphasized that if the head is to accomplish much it must come into play rather early. Since emotional involvement develops gradually but progressively as young people associate together in courtship, it is extremely important that they associate with the right kind. Friendships started lightly may, if continued, change into emotional ties strong enough to leave little room for reason. (It is wiser, therefore, for one to decide early not to date or court the type of person that would be unsuitable for marriage. When there is a possibility of falling in love, it is a good idea to choose carefully where to fall.)

Heavy romanticism is an illusion that blinds many girls, and some boys, to the realities of life. If the romantic bubble were not blown so high it would not so frequently burst, leaving serious disillusionment and sorrow in its wake. On the other hand, marriage without affection and emotional warmth runs the danger of becoming drab and intolerable. Marriage is more than a business relationship for the sake of personal gratification; it is a human relationship based upon tenderness and mutual consideration.

Personal Qualifications.—Since personalities differ, it follows logically that each will look for slightly different qualities in the mate. The needs and value concepts of no two individuals are ever exactly the same, which is fortunate, for otherwise all might want to marry the same person. But people are enough alike to have many things in common. There are uniformities as well as diversities in the preferences of mate seekers.

In Figure 4 are presented ratings of 674 Purdue University students on factors they thought most desirable from the standpoint of selecting a marriage partner.[16] It will be noted that both sexes regard stability and dependability as of first importance; this was further described in the schedule as "sincere, honest, reliable, responsible, steady, can be trusted." A close second is family-mindedness, defined as "desire for homelife and children." Considerateness comes third, where the mate is "thoughtful, patient, understanding, kind, attentive" and where there is a sense of fairness and respect. Other qualities regarded as extremely important in the mate to be selected are:

---

16 This is from another part of the Purdue survey referred to in the previous chapter. A copy of the schedule may be found in the Appendix.

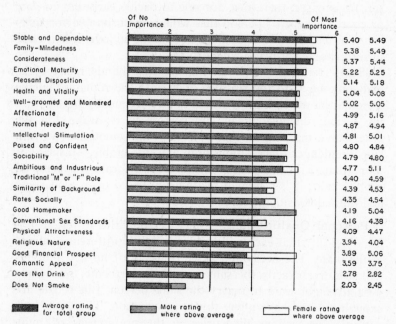

Of No   Of Most
Importance ◄———————————————————————► Importance

	Total	Male	Female
Stable and Dependable		5.40	5.49
Family-Mindedness		5.38	5.49
Considerateness		5.37	5.44
Emotional Maturity		5.22	5.25
Pleasant Disposition		5.14	5.18
Health and Vitality		5.04	5.08
Well-groomed and Mannered		5.02	5.05
Affectionate		4.99	5.16
Normal Heredity		4.87	4.94
Intellectual Stimulation		4.81	5.01
Poised and Confident		4.80	4.84
Sociability		4.79	4.80
Ambitious and Industrious		4.77	5.11
Traditional "M" or "F" Role		4.40	4.59
Similarity of Background		4.39	4.53
Rates Socially		4.35	4.54
Good Homemaker		4.19	5.04
Conventional Sex Standards		4.16	4.38
Physical Attractiveness		4.09	4.47
Religious Nature		3.94	4.04
Good Financial Prospect		3.89	5.06
Romantic Appeal		3.59	3.75
Does Not Drink		2.78	2.82
Does Not Smoke		2.03	2.45

■ Average rating for total group   ▨ Male rating where above average   ☐ Female rating where above average

Fig. 4.—Preference patterns in mate selection. When selecting a mate these college students seek partners who are dependable and family-minded. Though on most items males and females agree, there are some things, such as good homemaker, that males stress more than females, and others, such as good financial prospect, that females stress more than males. Based upon responses from 674 Purdue University students. For the complete schedule see the Appendix.

emotional maturity, pleasant disposition, health and vitality, and well-groomed and -mannered.[17]

It is interesting to see how male and female ratings compare: (1) The first thing to be observed is that the two sexes regard mate choice pretty much in the same light; there are some differences between them but these are mainly over the lesser items. Concerning what is most important, men and women are in essential agreement. (2) Where there are differences, men tend more to want a good homemaker, someone who is physically attractive, is affectionate, and who does not smoke. (3) In contrast, women tend more to want a good financial prospect, someone who is ambitious and industrious, who rates socially, conforms to conventional sex standards, and provides intellectual stimulation. (4) Women, on the whole, give evidence of being a little more particular or "choosy" than men, as evidenced by their higher average rating of all factors.[18]

There were 259 engaged and married students who filled out the Purdue schedule, in addition to the single and unengaged sample just mentioned. Since these were cases of individuals who had already chosen a mate, they formed the basis for a special kind of analysis. It was desired to know how well the actual or chosen mate conforms to the ideal. To answer this, engaged and married students were asked to go back over the list they had just rated on importance and to check those items that applied to their mate already chosen. When this was done it was found that: (1) The chosen mate fell somewhat short of the ideal; typically, more than two of the items which had been rated above average in importance were left unchecked. (2) This discrepancy between ideal and actual mate was nearly twice as great for males as for females. (3) The most frequently named gaps between preference and actuality as given

---

[17] Earlier research on this subject brought similar results. See Harold T. Christensen, "Student Views on Mate Selection," *Marriage and Family Living,* 9 :85-88. Cf. Reuben Hill, "Campus Values in Mate Selection," *Journal of Home Economics,* 37 :554-58.

[18] When ratings on all factors were averaged together, 4.52 was the figure for females and 4.43 for males. For dating, the average ratings were 4.24 and 4.02 respectively. Though the differences are not great, this tendency for females to stress nearly all factors more than do males has been observed in earlier research by the author; see Harold T. Christensen, *op. cit.,* p. 87.

by males were emotional maturity, poised and confident, considerateness, intellectual stimulation, and good homemaker. (4) The most frequently named gaps between the ideal and the actual mate as given by females were conventional sex standards, poised and confident, emotional maturity, considerateness, and intellectual stimulation.

It has been claimed that a good date does not necessarily mean a good mate. Do young people look for different things in a partner when they are thinking of dating as compared with when they are thinking of getting married? Or do they look for the same personal qualities in both instances, do they date with marriage in mind? Undoubtedly there is some of both, with great individual variation and with the identification between dating and marriage becoming more close as the individuals mature and the wedding date approaches.

A comparison of Figure 4 with Figure 2 (in Chapter 7) would reveal that students tend to stress many of the same things in choosing a date as they do in choosing a mate. In both instances the following factors rank high: considerateness, emotional maturity, pleasant disposition, and well-groomed and -mannered. In both dating and mate selection appear the same general patterns of differentiation between the sexes which have been outlined above. Correlation coefficients between date and mate selection in the Purdue sample are .55 ± .15 for males and .66 ± .12 for females. This suggests not only that college students tend to date with marriage in mind but also that females are inclined this way more than are males.

Figure 5 has been designed to show differences in the patterns of date and mate selection. On the left-hand side are traits that are stressed more during dating than in mate choice, while on the right-hand side are traits given the opposite emphasis. The following observations seem important: (1) Only about a third of the factors are stressed as being more important in selecting a date than in selecting a mate, probably indicating that people are more particular when marriage is the goal. (2) As contrasted with mate choice, a "good date" is defined as someone who is physically attractive, personally pleasant, and

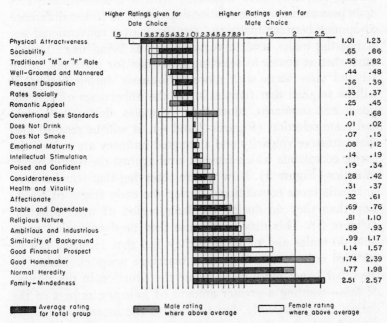

FIG. 5.—Comparison of preference patterns between choosing a date and choosing a mate. Two thirds of these items are considered more important in choosing a mate than in choosing a date. By way of comparison, mate choice gives more stress to such things as family-mindedness, normal heredity, and homemaking ability, while date choice gives greater emphasis to physical attractiveness, sociability, and the like. "Conventional sex standards" is regarded as more important in choosing a mate by the males, but in choosing a date by the females.

socially capable—emphasis is upon having a good time. (3) As contrasted with date choice, a "good mate" is defined as someone who is family-minded and capable of carrying out normal responsibilities connected with a home—emphasis is upon permanence of the relationship. (4) The widest difference of opinion between males and females is over conventional sex standards; males tend to regard these as being more significant when it comes to selecting a partner for marriage, while females view them with more seriousness during dating. It will be recalled that females stress the importance of conventional sex standards, more than do males, during both date and mate selection (Figures 2 and 4). It will be recalled also that excessive vulgarity and attempted intimacy are two of the major complaints which females level against the dating habits of males (Figure 3). Now we are observing that females want to remain more conventional during the early stages of courtship than they do during the later period of mate selection (Figure 5). This may be because they need protection more than do males and/or because they feel that intimacy can be justified only by marriage or a marriage prospect. Males, on the other hand, more often define the situation in the reverse of this—wanting a greater amount of intimacy as part of the dating fun, apparently, but turning to the more conventional type of girl when they get ready to marry.

Strauss approached the problem a little differently, attempting to discover what are the basic personality needs of each sex that can best be met by a mate. He found that males and females both recognize such needs as: being loved, having someone to confide in, being understood and appreciated, and having someone to turn to when making decisions. There were certain needs that males recognized more than did females: someone who respects my ideals, appreciates what I want to achieve, understands my moods, stimulates my ambition, and gives me self-confidence in my relations with people. Then there were other needs that females emphasized in their self-evaluations more than did males: someone who loves me, shows a lot of affection, helps me in making important decisions, and someone that I can look up to very much.[19] According to this, males tend to prefer women who will give them support and stimulation, while females tend to prefer men who will give them love and protection.

There are certain types of people that one would probably never want to consider marrying, and others that would be weighed very carefully and accepted only after desirable changes had been brought about. In the first class go all those with hereditary defects serious enough to impair life or seriously blight the offspring; one, for example would not marry an idiot. In the second class go those with less serious, or else temporary, health or personality defects. Here one will need to use careful judgment, letting the decision rest upon a number of things, such as probability of improvement and personal willingness to sacrifice for the sake of love. Usually it is best to wait for improvement before going ahead; ordinarily one would not want to marry a criminal until he had turned from the life of crime, for example, or a tubercular patient until there had been time for recovery. It is folly to marry either a potential penitentiary or a potential hospital, for before life is over the load might prove too great. But, on the other hand, if love is deep enough and the persons involved are mature enough for the sacrifices required, who is there to say that they should not marry?

Two common mistakes related to this problem are: (1) marrying out of sympathy and (2) marrying someone objectionable with the idea of reforming this person after the ceremony. With regard to the first of these, we can say that while sympathy is a valuable sentiment, it is not love; and to pretend to be in love when you are only sorry is to deceive and to do a disfavor to the one that was to be helped. As to marrying with the intention of reforming, we can only say that it is safer to see the change take place before the ceremony is performed; often personality traits are lifelong habits that do not change overnight. Furthermore, promises are often forgotten once the security of marriage has become established. It is

---

[19] Anselm Strauss, "Personality Needs and Marital Choice," *Social Forces* 25:332-35, March, 1947.

wiser to select the right one before marriage than to try to make one right afterwards.

Matching Combinations.—It isn't only quality of personality that is significant in one's selection, but the way in which the personal traits of the two individuals are combined. There is little doubt that marital compatibility depends first of all upon the maturity of mates. But it must also be remembered that adjustment is made easier, or more difficult, according to how well matched husband and wife are at the beginning.

The tendency is for likes to marry likes. A tall person is more likely to marry someone else who is tall, a heavy person someone who is heavy, an intelligent person someone who is intelligent, a neurotic person someone who is neurotic. In social and cultural matters, too, people tend to marry others of their own kind; a Catholic will more than likely choose another Catholic, a well-educated person will marry someone else with college training, a millionaire will pick from a family having wealth, and so on. It is well known that most people marry someone not too different from themselves in age. There have been studies which show a tendency for defectives to marry others in a similar condition, such as the deaf marrying the deaf. All in all, it can be considered as established that mate-seekers tend to sort themselves into groupings that are homogeneous according to a number of factors, such as: age, physical features, temperament, interests and values, intelligence and education, race and nationality, socioeconomic status, religion, and occupation. This tendency is described technically as *assortive mating* or *homogamy*.

Reasons for likes marrying likes are several. In the first place, social types are usually segregated, both geographically and culturally, which means that similar individuals are more frequently thrown into each other's company. Then there are the pressures of social approval and of one's mental images or ideals organized out of group definitions. Finally, it is to be noted that adjustment comes easier between persons who are quite a bit alike, for the simple reason that they don't have as much to adjust to. Because of this, people generally feel more comfortable in the company of persons who possess habits and tastes that are similar to those of their own.

The notion that opposites should marry in order to remain interesting and stimulating to each other has been exposed as false; for if differences are fundamental, that which seemed interesting at first may prove to be only irritating as time goes on. Men and women are different enough as it is, by nature, to provide all the stimulation that is necessary for marriage. In addition to these sex differences, there are always sufficient other personality variables present to liven the relationship. Real, enduring love is contingent upon how well the mates adjust to each other; and adjustment is always easier and surer when there are not too many differences that have to be settled. A poorly matched marriage may not always fail, but it is more likely to fail because of the additional problems it faces. Perfect matching is seldom possible, and all marriages present some problems. Still it is wiser to chart the course that has the fewest risks; which means marrying someone with backgrounds, interests, goals, and value interpretations similar to those of one's own.

So far as research has revealed there are only two exceptions to this rule on similarity: (1) In most instances marriage works best when the mates are dissimilar with reference to masculinity and femininity, with each mate filling the role that is more or less traditional. There needs to be a sexually oriented differentiation, in other words, with the mates functioning as a complementary unit. (See Chapter 4.) (2) Usually marriage operates best when both the mates do not possess similar personality weaknesses, such as bad tempers or other neurotic tendencies. Here, too, the principle is one of complementation. People differ greatly in their emotional tendencies and reaction patterns, and the best matching is one that permits each mate to supply what the other needs. Neurotic similarities often make this impossible. As Burgess puts it:

Certain personality characteristics may be listed in pairs as making for and against happiness in marriage. A person with an optimistic temperament is more likely to be happy than one with a pessimistic temperament. Emotional stability makes for, and emotional unstability against, marital adjustment. Submissive tendencies are favorable, while dominating and domineering behavior is unfavorable to success in marriage. A considerate and sympathetic person is a better matrimonial risk than the critical and inconsiderate person. Self-confidence, especially on the part of the husband, is a more desirable characteristic than lack of self-assurance. A person who is emotionally dependent has a better chance for marital happiness than the self-sufficient person who tends to face trouble alone and to avoid asking advice from others. Evidently *it is most desirable in mate selection for both the young man and the young woman to possess the favorable trait of any of the pairs listed, and least desirable for both to have the unfavorable one.* The person with the unfavorable trait may raise his chances of marital happiness by selecting a partner with the desirable characteristic. For example, two sympathetic persons are happier in marriage than two critical people; but the union of a critical and a sympathetic person has, on the average, an intermediate state of happiness.[20]

We propose now to list and briefly analyze some of the major problem areas of *mixed marriage*—where the mates are dissimilar in one or more of the factors involved.

1. Marrying someone of another race or nationality has its hazards. There will usually be cultural differences to hurdle and social prejudices to fight. Marriages involving different nationality groups may or may not be a mistake, depending upon how wide the gap is between the two cultures, how completely each mate has assimilated the culture of the other, and whether the resident society chooses to accept or reject the situation. Interracial marriages present a more serious problem. Though biologically unobjectionable, they are usually inadvisable on social and cultural grounds. This is especially true if racial prejudice is strong, for the newlyweds not only have to adjust their own differences growing out of separate backgrounds but they also need to buck the currents of public opinion and social stigma. Then there are the children to consider and the social handicaps they will be under. The problem in both of these types of marriages is that of prejudice

---

[20] Ernest W. Burgess, "The Wise Choice of a Mate," Part 1, chap. ii of Morris Fishbein and Ernest W. Burgess, eds., *Successful Marriage* (New York: Doubleday & Co., 1947), p. 24. Italics were not in the original.

plus cultural differences. Where these are nonexistent or only slight there isn't much of a problem, but where they are considerable the problem is correspondingly great.

2. Interfaith marriages lead to similar problems, though in some ways different, and sometimes even more intense. Religion strikes so close to the fundamental values and life interpretations of people that if persons differ greatly in regard to this they will likely be in disagreement over many of the things that matter. Furthermore, when children come and the question arises as to which faith they shall espouse, there is added cause for conflict.

Several studies give evidence of separation and divorce being significantly higher with couples whose church affiliation is either mixed or nonexistent. Landis compares his findings, from a study of 4,108 Michigan families, with those of Ashley Weeks based upon 6,548 families in the state of Washington, and with those of Howard Bell who analyzed 13,528 families in Maryland. The three studies tend to support each other; in each, the percentages of marriages ending in divorce or separation were approximately 5 for the Catholics and Jews, 8 for the Protestants, 15 for the mixed, and 18 for those with no church affiliation.[21]

Landis also reports the following: (1) Half of his student sample said that they would be willing to marry into another faith providing other conditions were favorable. One third of these would be willing to change to the faith of the partner. Protestants expressed a greater willingness to change than did Catholics. (2) The chief source of friction in mixed marriages seems to be over the religious training of children. The mother is regarded as largely responsible for this training and it is her faith that children most usually follow, especially the daughter. (3) Most handicapped are those marriages involving a Catholic father and a Protestant mother.[22]

Macrory and McCormick, in a study of 259 undergraduate women at the University of Wisconsin, found the following:

---

21 Judson T. Landis, "Marriages of Mixed and Non-mixed Religious Faith," *American Sociological Review,* 14:401-7, June, 1949.
22 *Loc. cit.*

Catholics dislike marrying Jews most, Protestants next; Jews dislike marrying Catholics most, Protestants next; Protestants dislike marrying Jews most, Catholics next. All groups preferred marrying within their own faith, although with Protestants the denomination made little difference.[23]

In appraising these findings it is well to keep in mind that the Catholic Church is highly authoritarian, and that both Catholics and Jews are set off by greater differences than are to be found among Protestant denominations. Generally speaking, interfaith marriage is least likely to succeed when differences between the two churches involved are greatest, when religious and social pressure against such a match is also greatest, and when the individuals concerned are both fervent and unyielding in their respective faiths.

3. Marrying someone from a vastly different social or economic class often presents more difficulties than is realized. Cinderella marriages are the subject of interesting fiction aimed at the minds of children and adolescents, but experience tells us that in a great many cases the mates of such unions do not "live happily ever after." Mercenary marriages, where one of the mates has deliberately married for money, fare no better—if as well. The problem is that of working out a money arrangement that will avoid both humiliation and dissipation on the part of either spouse, and of adjusting to widely different tastes and manners of living. An additional handicap is present when the families or relatives of either mate decline to accept the situation fully. Adjustment is usually easier if it is the man who is the wealthier or has the higher status, for that pattern is closer to the traditional one.

4. Additional adjustment problems are sometimes presented when the mates are greatly different with reference to intelligence and education. Where inequalities in ability or training are extensive, there is little basis for mutual understanding, respect, or companionship. In such cases husband and wife are frequently compelled to live in mental isolation, and as a result they grow apart. Exceptions to this are cases in which one of

---

[23] Boyd E. Macrory and Thomas C. McCormick, "Group Values in Mate Selection in a Sample of College Girls," *Social Forces*, 22:315-17, March, 1944

the mates has a dependent personality and enjoys being subservient and protected. (Research has suggested that marriages
generally succeed best if the mates are either approximately
equal or else the husband is slightly superior.[24] Where the wife
is superior, and shows it, the husband's ego may be injured
and conflict ensue.)

5. Marrying someone widely different in age or level of maturity may likewise cause trouble. There will frequently be dis-
parities in interests, energies, choice of friends, and patterns
of behavior. The older person is likely to be more rigid in
habits, finding it harder to adjust. In some cases the older one
will have had a previous marriage, which will have conditioned
him or her to certain habits and expectations. Emotional maturity is more important in the choosing of a mate than is
chronological age; yet the two are correlated. Generally speaking, marriages are more successful where the mates are not
more than a few years different in age. Though the usual practice is for the husband to be older than the wife, it has not been
conclusively demonstrated that this bears any relationship to
successful marriage.[25] Matching for age depends upon the
needs and the levels of development of both the individuals
involved. It is largely a matter of mutual maturity and of seeing to it that differences in this regard are not great.

6. Differences in family background are frequently reflected
in value conflicts and personality clashes of one sort or another.
For example, a girl raised in a home where females were encouraged to think for themselves, and to act on a basis of
equality, may run into difficulty if she marries a boy who
was brought up under the traditional patriarchal pattern. Ingersoll has found that the authority patterns of parental families tend to be perpetuated in the families of children, and that
when children from opposite patterns marry, the tendency is
toward conflict and compromise.[26] Since temperament and character are in large part products of the home, it follows that

[24] Cf. G. V. Hamilton, *A Research in Marriage* (New York: Albert &
Charles Boni, Inc., 1929), p. 513.
[25] Cf. Landis, *op. cit.*, p. 401.
[26] Hazel L. Ingersoll, "A Study of the Transmission of Authority Patterns
in the Family," *Genetic Psychological Monographs*, 38:225-99, November, 1948.

the backgrounds of those who marry need to be pretty much the same.

7. It is dangerous to marry someone possessing interests and values that differ widely from one's own. This has been implied in most of the categories discussed above. Studies show that men and women get along better in marriage where they like to spend their leisure time in about the same way, agree with each other concerning friends and associates, have similar desires about children, and do not conflict to any great extent over political matters.

8. Matching for physical features, while likely not so important as some of these others, cannot be ignored. As to physical size, it is sometimes embarrassing and disorganizing to a couple if the girl is larger than the young man. Opinion studies show that most girls want husbands who are taller than themselves. Small men married to large women often become either meek and submissive or domineering and aggressive, as compensation for the handicap. Genital abnormalities can make for poor matching in some instances, though cases like this are rare and may often be corrected. Genetic matching is important from the standpoint of offspring, which means that every careful mate-seeker will want to examine the ancestral lines of his prospects. Close marriages, such as those of first cousins, tend to bring out hidden recessive characteristics. (See page 70.)

Conclusions.—We have seen that successful mate-seeking in this culture requires a large amount of weighing and choosing on the part of those who marry. It is neither automatic nor blind. There are conditions and influences which favor one selection above another, yet in the last analysis the choice is that of the individual. There are emotional pulls that must be recognized, yet for best results it is the intellect that must finally be consulted. This means that there will be pros and cons preceding every decision, that one can be "sure" in the relative sense only, never the absolute. But if the things that favor a selection far outweigh those that disfavor it, the chance is a good one to take and love involvement will likely proceed upward.

Intelligent choosing will be based upon a consideration of two things: (1) the personal qualifications of the other, and (2) the manner in which the two personalities are matched. The first of these has to do with standards of personal maturity which are important to any marriage, such as dependability, stability, agreeability, consideration, affection. The second has to do with the particular needs of each individual and how these are met by the other. It will vary from case to case. Most matching, to be effective in the building of compatibility, must be on the basis of similarity—similar racial and cultural groups, similar social and educational levels, similar backgrounds of experience. But some matching, such as that having to do with sex roles and neurotic tendencies, is best when it is complementary rather than competitive. In both cases, that matching is best which best meets the needs of the two persons concerned. The determination of those specific personality combinations which will work best must wait upon further research.

PROBLEMS AND PROJECTS

1. It has been pointed out in previous chapters that a certain amount of "subtlety" or deception is sometimes expected of woman in order to protect the male ego. How might this practice create difficulties when it comes to choosing a mate?
2. Are there ways in which parents can help or guide their children in the selection of a mate without building up resentments or inviting conflict? Discuss.
3. Is elopement ever justified? Discuss pro and con.
4. Why do you suppose a population ratio as high as 120 men to 100 women is necessary for a maximum marriage rate? Is a maximum marriage rate desirable? Discuss.
5. Would you be willing to patronize a college dating bureau? An introduction service? Why or why not?
6. Is love the only justification for marriage? Are there instances in which you would justify marriage for money? For

convenience or position? For any reason other than love? Defend your answer.

7. Is it likely that a marriage between two people having little in common but "love" would work out successfully? Why or why not?

8. Would it be wise to marry someone who had proved himself to have a suspicious and jealous nature? Discuss.

9. What should one do when he finds himself in love with someone of another church? Defend your answer.

10. Consider marriages with which you are familiar which might be classified as "mixed" in some respect. What adjustments have been made and how successful have they been?

11. Be honest with yourself: outside what cultural limits would you be unwilling to go in selecting a mate? Give reasons.

12. In choosing a mate, young people are often advised to consider the parents of the loved one, for that is how he or she will someday be. How important do you think this is? Give reasons.

13. If the tendency is toward assortive mating, why are there so many ill-matched marriages? Or are there? To what extent does marital success depend upon mate choice? Make suggestions in the light of your answer.

Selected Readings

Adams, Clifford R., and Packard, Vance O. *How to Pick a Mate.* New York: E. P. Dutton & Co., 1946.

Baber, Ray E. *Marriage and the Family.* New York: McGraw-Hill Book Co., 1939. Chaps. vi, vii, "Mate Selection and Courtship."

Becker, Howard, and Hill, Reuben (eds.). *Family, Marriage, and Parenthood.* Boston: D. C. Heath & Co., 1948. Chap. viii, "How Mates Are Sorted."

Bowman, Henry A. *Marriage for Moderns.* New York: McGraw-Hill Book Co., 1948. Chaps. vi, vii, "Choosing a Mate."

Burgess, Ernest W., and Locke, Harvey J. *The Family: From Institution to Companionship.* New York: American Book Co., 1945. Chap. xiii, "Mate Selection."

Harper, Robert A. *Marriage.* New York: Appleton-Century-Crofts, Inc., 1949. Chap. iii, "Mate Selection: Causes and Effects."

Landis, Judson T., and Landis, Mary G. *Building a Successful Marriage.* New York: Prentice-Hall, Inc., 1948. Chaps. v, "Before You Choose a Mate"; vii, "Mixed Marriages."

NIMKOFF, MEYER. *Marriage and the Family*. Boston: Houghton Mifflin Co., 1947. Chap. xiii, "The Choice of a Mate."

TRUXAL, ANDREW G., and MERRILL, FRANCIS E. *The Family in American Culture*. New York: Prentice-Hall, Inc., 1947. Chap. xx, "Courtship and Marital Choice."

WALLER, WILLARD. "The Rating and Dating Complex," *American Sociological Review*, 2:727-34, October, 1937.

Chapter 9

THE TRANSITION INTO MARRIAGE

Transition means a change or passage from one state of affairs into another. Adolescence, for example, is the transition from childhood into adulthood. (Transition into marriage refers to the series of rapid events immediately surrounding one's entrance into this new way of life; it consists of the engagement, the wedding, and the honeymoon.)

Change requires adjustment. Where it is slow and in easy stages, man's adaptation does not usually prove to be hard. But where change is sudden, or of great magnitude, adjustment becomes proportionately more difficult. In our culture, adolescence is a problem period mainly because of the tempo and complexity of the changes it represents. There are similar problems, or adjustment difficulties, peculiar to one's shift into marriage. These are made even greater by the fact that they parallel adolescence, and by the fact that in this day society itself is in a state of rapid transition. (See Chapter 2.) Thus there is a piling up of tensions and pressures within the individual which require adjustment, and the cumulative effects are sometimes bewildering. (The transition into marriage will be most successful where the mates are mature enough and the change is gradual enough to permit adjustment.)

THE ENGAGEMENT

An engagement, or betrothal, is a pledge between a man and a woman who are presumably in love and are intending to marry. It is a step in the direction of mate monopoly, a phase of the ever-continuing family phenomenon. It follows the love-evolving and mate-selecting processes of earlier courtship, and it precedes the more or less complete monopolies and love expressions of marriage. Being interstitial and transitional with reference to courtship and marriage, it provides an opportunity to bridge a gap that might otherwise prove too great.

Two things are known regarding the relationship of engagement to marriage: (1) Marriage is usually more successful when it has been preceded by a definite engagement period. Without such, preparation is incomplete, which means that the transition will be more sudden and the risks greater. (2) Marriage has the best chance of succeeding when the engagement itself has been successful. It is not the mere fact of an engagement that makes for future happiness, in other words, but how well the couple has adjusted and prepared for what lies ahead. Engagements that are particularly stormy and that show increasing amounts of jealousy and quarreling spell ill omens for marriage. If the mates are basically immature or ill-matched, the engagement period is a good time to find it out; no mere ceremony can alter the facts.

Becoming Engaged.—The process of becoming engaged is not nearly so important as that which takes place afterward. Yet to avoid blundering it needs to be understood.

There is no single right way of initiating the engagement. Techniques will vary with the culture and with the times. In contemporary America, practices range all the way from a gradual understanding between mates, without any formal proposal, to an elaborate and definite ceremony including a request for the girl's hand. Generally speaking, the trend is away from this latter and toward the former; it is coming to be recognized that an informal spontaneity in the proposal is more sensible than speech that is awkward, artificial, or flowery. Being natural is more important than is being impressive or technically "correct." The actual proposal will usually be made by the man, though even this pattern is undergoing change. Where the courtship has been long enough, and reciprocal, each party will pretty well know where it stands and will have the assurance or confidence needed. It will then be of little consequence as to who makes the proposal or whether or not it is ever formally made. The important considerations are that there be naturalness, mutual sincerity and responsibility, and enough definiteness in understanding to let each one know how to plan.

An additional requirement is that engagements be made with the knowledge and consent of society. Secret engagements run into some of the same difficulties as do secret marriages. In both cases there is an attempt to ignore the social situation, to pretend that "what we do is our own business." Such reasoning creates an illusion, with inevitable disillusionment to follow. Each of us is a part of his society, and each affects and is affected by what goes on around him—even when in love. Adjustments during the engagement are of two kinds: those that have to do directly with the loved one, and those that pertain to the couple's new roles in society. Engagement involves new roles, just as does marriage, and to ignore this fact is to invite trouble.

Adjustment comes easier when the parents of both parties approve. Family opposition to an engagement tends to set up emotional tensions and to invite open conflict. Under such conditions one is likely to be irritable, rebellious, and harder to get along with. Furthermore, if the relationship to one's parents is kept cordial, there is much that they can do in a positive or constructive way to help. Whether or not the young man should ask formally for the girl's hand in marriage will depend upon the tastes and the circumstances involved. If she were under legal age, or if her parents would feel better were it done, there is every good reason for following this procedure. But there are other instances, and increasingly so in this day, where such a formality would seem artificial and unnecessary. The important thing is for each child to keep the avenues of discussion with parents continually open so that advice can be both sought and offered without strain or misunderstanding on either side. There are cases where the unreasonableness of parents makes it advisable for the mature child to become engaged or married against the parents' wishes (see pages 242-46). With the proper attitude, however, such cases will be rare.

Once the engagement has taken place, there needs to be some sort of public indication of the fact. This has the effect not only of reinforcing responsibility between engaged persons but also of helping those on the outside to reorganize their behavior with reference to the newly formed relationship. When people are pledged to each other they are presumably taken out of the marriage market. They will act differently toward others and others will act differently toward them, all of which will tend to further strengthen pair solidarity. Some couples choose to have a public announcement staged at a special social occasion or handled through the use of the newspaper or printed cards. Others prefer to let their friends know more or less informally. Most couples follow the age-old custom of an engagement ring for the girl. In some places, however, and on high school and college campuses particularly, the ring has been giving way to a practice known as "hanging the pin"; the boy lets the girl wear his fraternity pin or something similar. While with many couples this means an engagement, with many others it simply means going steady or is merely a declaration of friendship. Lack of any standardized meaning, such as there is with the ring, makes pin-wearing more open to misunderstanding and exploitation.[1]

(The only justification for ever becoming engaged is a serious intention to marry.) Sometimes young people take the pledge too lightly, being motivated by the glamour involved, the sense of security it brings, or by a desire for greater intimacy. It seems likely that girls are attracted more by such things as the thrill of a public announcement, the social recognition connected with a ring, or the comfort of being secure, while boys, when insincere, are looking more for excuses or opportunities in intimacy. All such reasons are spurious. Engagement serves a real or useful purpose only when it provides for a testing of the earlier choice and a preparing for the later union.

Personality Testing and Planning.—Engagement serves as a kind of proving field or testing ground for the marriage rela-

---

[1] Cf. Henry A. Bowman, *Marriage for Moderns* (2d ed.; New York: McGraw-Hill Book Co., 1948), pp. 255-56.

tionship that is being planned. In it, privacy and intimacy will be a little greater than formerly and monopoly a little more complete. In it also will come important premarital adjustments for the couple, both between themselves and with society.

In the process of mutual accommodation that takes place during an engagement, jealousies and misunderstandings sometimes arise. A moderate amount of this is natural, for to adjust closely and somewhat completely with another much different from oneself is not easy. But, though difficult, it needs doing. Sometimes one demonstrates lack of maturity by expecting the other person to do all of the adjusting; sometimes, too, by being overjealous and demanding.

Lovers' quarrels during the engagement are not serious if conducted by mature individuals honestly searching for a way out of their difficulties. Every couple can count on having some differences in taste and opinion and can expect to clash over them. Fortunate is the couple that discovers early a way to resolve its conflicts. Verbal disagreement frequently serves to bring the issue out in the open, leading to better understanding and adjustment. It is only when people become highly emotional in their differing, and resort to personal "digs," that quarreling becomes really destructive. In such cases marriage may be considered as inadvisable unless there is good prospect of a change.

There are rare circumstances that would seem to justify engaged individuals dating with someone else. Otherwise, during long periods of separation, they would need to remain alone and without normal social intercourse. Such dating when it does take place, however, needs to be with the full knowledge and approval of the engaged partner. It also needs to be infrequent, public, and without even the lighter forms of intimacy. In this way the engaged, though apart, can remain true.

Ordinarily, individuals will be together during engagement, and then, of course, there is no excuse for either dating or flirting with others. Sometimes persons become engaged, however, who are not yet mature enough to play the game; wanting the glamour and the security that come with monopoly, they are nevertheless not ready to accept the responsibilities or to settle down. It would have been wiser for these never to have become engaged in the first place for they were not yet ready.

On the other hand it must be remembered that no contract, not even marriage, establishes complete monopoly. During the engagement, as in marriage, a certain amount of personality privacy and individuality need to be expected in the other. Engagement cannot be permitted to shut one off from the normal social world. He who becomes jealous or offended every time his loved one seems to be enjoying himself or herself at a dance or in the presence of others (unless, of course, the person is actually flirtatious), only demonstrates how immature he really is. Families and friends cannot be shut out, and to try to do so during the engagement is to interfere with the adjustment necessary for marriage.

Another type of testing has to do with conduct and self-control. In the frequent and close association provided by engagement there is temptation, and in the knowledge that they will one day have each other anyway comes the tendency on the part of some to move too rapidly in the direction of complete intimacy—rationalizing, "if eventually why not now?" Sometimes, as we have seen, engagement is used simply as a means of sexual exploitation. It is true that ideally the engagement will permit a gradual but increasing intimacy between the mates so that there will be no sudden shocks along the way. But if extreme intimacy, including sexual intercourse, be participated in before the wedding, as a privilege of the engagement period, then the engagement becomes in effect a consummation rather than a transition, though without the protection of marriage. Engaged couples need gradually to learn how to respond to each other, but also how to control their emotional and sexual drives. Self-control is important even in marriage.

There are a great many things that engaged persons need to discuss and plan together. Some of these will have to do with the immediate details of the wedding: When shall we get married? Who shall we have perform the ceremony? Do we want a reception? Other questions or discussion topics will pertain more to long-range planning: Where shall we live after marriage and what shall we do for a living? Shall we plan to have the wife work for a few years until we get started or long enough to help put the husband through school? How large a family do we want and when shall we plan to start it? How well do we agree on religion, recreation, friends, the equality of the sexes, birth control, the discipline of children? The airing of all such matters is an essential first step in the reaching of consensus, compromise, or any other type of adjustment. It is important that those who are to marry first learn how to talk seriously together; to come to agree where possible, but to be agreeable even when in disagreement.

But, someone asks, should talking things over in this frank and realistic manner involve digging up the past; if there are weaknesses, or if there have been indiscretions, ought these to be revealed before marriage? Certainly, if they are serious enough to count for anything. There is no point in turning morbid or in causing the other to worry by recounting small things of little consequence. But neither is it right to deceive, nor is it safe to run the risk of detection and a consequently greater crisis later on. How much one needs to tell will depend upon the nature of the personality he is dealing with; some may not want to know anything, while others will feel better knowing all. Most people would want to know regarding the following: previous marriage, present financial obligations, prison record, hereditary defects, physical disabilities, and sexual abnormalities of a serious nature. Many would want to know if there had been instances of premarital sexual intercourse. In any event it seems better to start marriage with a clean slate, in complete honesty, and without the possibility of suspicion entering in to mar the relationship.

Engagement, then, is a kind of dress rehearsal for marriage. It permits a testing of the chosen mate to see if one's earlier impressions were well founded. It permits a testing of oneself to see if one is ready for the mature type of loyalty and fidelity required by marriage. It permits an exploring and adjusting in the direction of greater pair unity. Society comes to regard the couple as a pair, to invite them out places together, to treat them as one. In addition, the couple learns how to function as a unit; each member comes to understand the other, to consider him in his plans, and together they come to feel and express themselves as a "we group." Furthermore, intentions are given a chance to develop into tentative plans—as preparation for marriage ahead.

Learning the Law.—There are certain legal regulations pertaining to marriage. Some of these put restrictions upon the act of getting married; others specify as to the respective rights of husbands and wives; while still others deal with requirements and procedures for dissolving the union. Though there is some uniformity, there is also a great diversity in the legal provisions of the various states. As part of preparation for marriage, every engaged person needs to become familiar with the major features of marriage and family laws in general, and with those of his own state in particular. Following is a brief ten-point summary,[2] with special attention given to the laws of Indiana. This latter is for purposes of illustration only; any other state would do just as well.

1. All states provide that marriage shall be preceded by a license, performed by an authorized officiant, and that it shall be duly reported and recorded. Marriage, in other words, is regarded as a civil contract to be handled by definite legal machinery. Minor exceptions to this are found in nearly half the states, where recognition is given to common-law marriage. Such a marriage is one in which there has been no license or wedding, but in which the man and woman have been living together as husband and wife and have been accepted as such by the community. Recognition of such a union as a legal marriage is usually established only after the matter is brought into court. Common-law marriage is said to be justified as a means of protecting the children from illegitimacy and the heir or heirs from loss of property rights. Most students of marriage think the practice should be abandoned.

Indiana provides that a marriage license can be issued only

2 This is to be a general summary only; in cases of doubtful meaning, or for help regarding particular applications, the reader will need to consult an attorney.

after there has been a written application giving relevant information about both of the parties to determine if there are any legal impediments. The license is good for sixty days after the date of its issuance. The ceremony may be performed by a duly recognized religious officiant, or by a justice of the peace, a judge of the court, or a mayor of a city. A certificate of marriage is to be made out by the one who performs the ceremony. The application, the license, and the certificate of marriage are all recorded with the clerk of the circuit court within the appropriate county and so become public records. Marriages are void when performed in another state for the express purpose of evading provisions of Indiana law. But when entered into in good faith, with either of the parties believing it to be legal at the time, no marriage shall be void on account of legal technicalities. Indiana is one of the states that recognize common-law marriage.

2. All states forbid bigamy, or the marriage of persons who are already married. The Indiana law reads that marriages are void "when either party had a wife or husband living at the time of such marriage."

3. All states prohibit marriages of close blood relatives: brother and sister, parent and child, grandparent and grandchild, aunt and nephew, and uncle and niece. Such matings are branded as incestuous. Many of the states carry these prohibitions even farther than those listed above; over half, for example, rule out marriages between first cousins. Indiana is in this last-named group; her law reads that the mates must be "not nearer of kin than second cousin."

4. Many states rule against miscegenetic marriages, which are between white people and members of other races. Approximately two thirds of the states, including practically all in the South, have laws against the marriage of whites with Negroes. Approximately one third of the states, including most in the West, have laws which prohibit the marriage of whites with Orientals and in some cases with Indians. States without legal restrictions on interracial marriages lie mostly in the central and northeastern sections of the country. The Indiana law reads that the marriage is void if "one of the parties is a white

person and the other possessed of one eighth or more of Negro blood."

5. Minimum age specifications are universal among the states, though the standards are so low in some that it is occasionally still legal for girls to marry as young as 12 or 13 and boys as young as 14 or 15. The legislative trend is toward a raising of these standards. The most common present requirements are that the male must be 18 and the female 16, provided that they have the consent of parents or guardians, or 21 and 18, respectively, if they do not have consent. Indiana law conforms to the mode in both these respects.

6. There are a variety of provisions intended to insure accountability and capability on the part of those who marry. Most states prohibit the marriage of persons who are either feeble-minded or insane, and about a third extend the restriction to those that are epileptic. Undoubtedly there are eugenic reasons back of such laws, as well as the attempt to see that those who contract for marriage are able to understand the situation and to give intelligent consent. In addition, many states specify that there must be mutual consent, with both parties being in a normal state of mind and with neither acting under threat or duress. Some states require that the husband must be capable of rendering support.

Indiana provides that the marriage is void whenever "either is insane or idiotic at the time of such marriage." It further provides that a license shall be refused whenever either of the contracting parties is an imbecile, an epileptic, or of unsound mind, or is under the guardianship of someone with an unsound mind; or whenever the prospective husband gives evidence of being incapable of rendering support; or whenever either of the parties is under the influence of intoxicating liquor or narcotic drugs at the time of the application.

7. Marriage is frequently forbidden in cases where either party is afflicted with a communicable disease. Only a few states, however, have clauses general enough to cover all transmissible diseases. In some states tuberculosis is named as a disqualifying factor. But it is with respect to the venereal diseases that most of the health legislation pertaining to marriage

is written, and that has developed only in the last ten or fifteen years. At the present time approximately two thirds of all states have laws requiring premarital blood tests for the venereal diseases, although many of these apply to syphilis only, and in a few states only the male is required to be examined. In most instances it is provided that a marriage license will be denied where the disease is found to be present in an infectious or transmissible stage.

Indiana forbids the issuing of a license in cases where either of the parties "is afflicted with a transmissible disease." It also has a blood test law passed in 1939. According to this, both parties must submit to a standard serological test for syphilis (though not gonorrhea). Specimens are to be taken by a duly licensed physician and transmitted to an approved laboratory through the United States mails. After receiving his report, the physician is to certify in writing his opinion concerning whether or not there is infection and whether or not it is in a communicable stage. If the latter, a marriage license will in most cases be denied. If it is the opinion of the physician that syphilis is either not present or not in a communicable stage, the couple is free to obtain a marriage license any time within thirty days from the date of the test.

8. About half of the states require a waiting period between the time the couple applies for a license and the time the ceremony can be performed. In most cases the wait is between the application and the issuance of the license, though in some states it comes after the license but before the marriage. The most common length of waiting required is five days; the next most common, three days. The purpose of these laws is to stop hasty, ill-considered, and, in some cases, illegal, marriages— by giving advance notice in case anyone wants to object and by allowing the couple a little more time to think it over. Popenoe found that in one year's time in the city of Los Angeles, more than a thousand couples who applied for marriage never came back three days later to secure their licenses.[3] Sometimes these laws are referred to as "gin marriage laws," for they tend to

3 Paul Popenoe and R. H. Johnson, *Applied Eugenics* (Rev. ed.; New York: The Macmillan Co., 1933), p. 183.

prevent impetuous marriages that are being motivated by gin, or the moon, or such.

There is no waiting period provided for in Indiana law. But it so happens that the blood test law accomplishes about the same thing. It takes time for the specimens to be sent in to the laboratory, for the tests to be made, and for the results to be returned. This time lapse permits a rechecking of plans; in some cases a sobering up and a changing of mind.

9. States differ rather widely in their provisions regarding the legal rights of husbands and wives. In general, wives are still at a disadvantage, though the trend is definitely in the direction of greater equality. Some states give the husband almost complete control over the family purse, including what the wife earns. Sometimes, too, the husband is privileged with certain discriminatory rights over the wife's property. In many states it is the husband's prerogative to decide on the place of residence.

Indiana law reflects the newer trend. It provides that the wife may hold property separately, as if unmarried; she may carry on her own business, the income from which is to be her sole and separate holding; she may sell or make contracts with reference to her personal property without interference from her husband. Real estate property, however, may be sold or mortgaged only when the husband joins in the contract. Both husband and wife may either sue or be sued; neither is responsible for the debts, or the contracts, or the civil injuries of the other.

10. All states provide for the dissolution of marriage through one means or another. This may be done legally by annulment, separation, or divorce. Annulment is the court's declaration that the marriage was never legal in the first place, that it didn't actually exist, due to some misrepresentation or circumvention of the law. All states make provisions for annulment. Separation, legally sanctioned, is in operation in only about half the states. It permits (indeed requires) the mates to live apart, but while remaining married—that is, without the right of marrying anyone else. Divorce gives final dissolution to the marriage contract, though in many states not until after

a waiting period of usually one year. This waiting-period provision, whereby the divorce does not become final and remarriage is not possible until after a certain length of time, is
spoken of as the "interlocutory decree." All states grant divorces. Legal grounds are based upon the assumption of guilt
in one of the mates, and are for such occurrences as cruelty,
adultery, and desertion. There are certain requirements which
must be met in order to establish bona fide residence within
the state and county granting the divorce; in most states the
period required is one year; in Nevada, Florida, and some
others it is only six weeks.

In Indiana, marriage can be dissolved by any of the three
means discussed. Annulment may be brought about if it can
be shown that any of the legal provisions for marriage were
not met in the first place. "Separation from bed and board"
can be granted by the courts following a similar procedure as
for divorce and based upon similar grounds. If husband and
wife decide to cohabit while they are legally separated, they
are both guilty of a misdemeanor, and if either of them com-
mits adultery during separation he forfeits all rights under the
court decree. Divorce may be granted on any of the following
grounds: adultery (except when both parties are guilty, or
have voluntarily cohabited after knowledge of the fact, or have
connived together in order to get the divorce), impotence at
the time of marriage, abandonment for two years, cruel and
inhuman treatment, habitual drunkenness, failure to provide
during a period of two years, conviction of an infamous crime
subsequent to the marriage, and incurable insanity (where
there has been commitment to a mental hospital for a period of
five years next preceding the action, and where, in the opinion
of the court, the condition is incurable). With certain exceptions for members of the armed forces, the person asking for
the divorce must have resided within the state for one year,
and within the county for six months immediately preceding
the action. A summons is issued to the defendant, and the trial
must wait for at least sixty days after that. In case the defendant does not appear to contest, the petition is to be resisted by
the prosecuting attorney. Alimony is provided "as the circum-

stances of the case should render just and proper." Arrangements over the custody of minor children are made at the discretion of the court.

The Premarital Physical Examination.—Most authorities recommend that both the man and the woman submit to a rather thorough physical check-up and consultation with a physician prior to the marriage ceremony. This is for the dual purpose of determining the possible presence of biological abnormalities which might interfere with marriage, and of gaining additional instructions and understandings for the specific adjustments of marriage.

The examination will serve its purpose best if it is fairly complete. It needs to be more than a blood test for venereal disease, important as that is. It needs to be broad enough to throw light upon all the biological conditions relevant to marriage. There are questions pertaining to one's general health and heredity, and to the capacities and understandings relating to sex adjustment and reproduction. To be most useful, the premarital examination will include the following: (1) routine physicals of the entire body systems to determine the presence of diseases or other abnormal conditions; (2) detailed inspections of the reproductive systems to determine probabilities for a normal sex life and childbearing; (3) an inquiry into the hereditary backgrounds of the two individuals to determine chances for normal offspring; and (4) interpretations and instructions pertaining to it all, as background for marital adjustment.

While there are those willing to marry a potential invalid, or to take a chance on someone who is not expected to live long, everyone should know what he is getting as well as giving. The routine physical examination is for the purpose of discovering both functional and organic disturbances. It should involve tests of the nervous system and of such internal organs as the heart, lungs, and kidneys. The serological test for venereal disease could be considered as a part of it. So also could sputum tests and chest X rays for the detection of tuberculosis. Normally it would include such things as a urine analysis and a blood count. Special cases may require additional or more specialized techniques. In rare instances, of extreme and disappointing discovery, the couple may even want to give up the idea of marriage. In any event the examination will give them a better picture of their physical assets and liabilities so that their choices and preparations can be made more intelligently.

There are certain tests that have special significance from the standpoint of sexual adjustment and childbearing. Both sexes will be examined for genital normality and for the possibility of sterility. Most persons are entirely normal in these regards, but an examination is reassuring. Those who need correction can frequently obtain it by means of medicine or surgery. Where the female hymen is particularly thick, so that it is likely to cause difficulty in the first marriage union, there is good reason for it to be either mechanically stretched or surgically cut by the physician. In rare instances, adhesions about the clitoris may also need to be released. Pelvic measurements of the female will reveal her capabilities for normal childbearing, will indicate the probabilities of her having to submit to a Caesarian delivery in case of pregnancy. In a few cases the physician may see fit to advise against pregnancy because of a weak heart or some other unfavorable health condition in the female. In many cases the couple will want to know its chances of later miscarriage trouble due to possible incompatibility in Rh blood types. If the tests show the male to be Rh positive and the female to be rh negative, there may be trouble, though it is by no means certain. (See pages 69-70.)

Generally speaking, the least dependable part of the entire examination will be that pertaining to hereditary backgrounds and eugenic probabilities. This is largely because the physician has no way of definitely determining from his examination what kinds of characteristics are being carried in the genes of the germ cells. He can observe the outward characteristics, some of which he will know to be hereditary, but he cannot see what is being carried recessively or know with any certainty what will be produced in the offspring of any particular couple. If it is a family physician of long acquaintance, he will know whether there have been instances of feeble-mindedness, certain types of psychosis, or other inheritable defects. In any event he can inquire concerning the incidence of all such traits among close blood relatives. There will be cases in which it will become quite obvious that reproduction is eugenically risky. Other cases will seem certain the other way. But until our knowledge and controls are more highly developed, we will need to be satisfied with taking some chance. This does not excuse marrying individuals from learning all they can about their hereditary potentials and then applying what they learn.

The premarital examination affords the couple an opportunity to learn more about themselves and their impending sexual relationships. By consultation with the physician a great deal of valuable and additional information can be picked up concerning personal hygiene, sexual intercourse, birth control, and similar subjects. While some are better informed than others on such matters, no person knows it all. In many cases there will be items of misinformation that need to be cleared up, or fears and inhibitions that need to be released. The male might be worrying over nocturnal emissions or masturbation; the female might be apprehensive over the necessity of coitus or fearful concerning the pain of childbirth. The physician is in an excellent position to counsel with the young couple to help remove any ignorance or inhibition that may be there to interfere. In return, it is wise for the couple to take full advantage of the opportunity by asking their questions quite freely and frankly.

Though only the blood test is required by law, and that only of some people, more and more of those contemplating marriage are voluntarily asking for complete physicals and special counseling at the hands of their physicians. It is advisable that this take place some month or two prior to the date set for the wedding so as to allow time for follow-up visits or special treatments when these are needed. Whether the boy and the girl go to the same physician or to separate ones is optional. Similarly, it is optional as to whether or not they both go at the same time in order to have a joint consultation (the examinations will be separate, of course). These matters can be decided according to the tastes of the couple. The physician chosen needs to be well trained and have a modern appreciation of marriage and its problems. If the family physician is of that kind, he may be the one that should be consulted. If specialists are sought, it is better to have a urologist for the male and a gynecologist for the female. In cases having serious or special problems, the physician consulted may deem it wise to refer the client to another specialist, such as a geneticist or a psychiatrist.

(Conducted in this way, the premarital physical examination can serve three useful purposes: (1) It can be diagnostic of difficulties as a basis for decision—for a reconsidering or replanning of the marriage, when necessary. (2) It can include certain therapeutic measures, both physical and psychical, designed to correct the problems discovered. (3) It can be educational in the sense that it provides new information and helps to reshape some of the attitudes known to be basic in the marriage relationships.)

In addition to an examination of the couple's physical assets, should come a stocktaking of all factors involved in the two personalities and in the new and emerging relationship between them. Marriage clinics have been organized in some cities for this very purpose. (See pages 471-73.) A great deal of self-testing can be done along lines already suggested, and especially helpful are the prediction schedules based upon the findings of research. (See pages 171-81.)

Age and Time Considerations.—United States census reports on median age at first marriage reveal the following: [4]

Year	Males	Females
1890	26.1	22.0
1900	25.9	21.9
1910	25.1	21.6
1920	24.6	21.2
1930	24.3	21.3
1940	24.3	21.6

---

[4] U. S. Bureau of the Census, *Age at First Marriage* (Population; Special Reports, Series P-45, No. 7), May 28, 1945.

This means that over half of all males who marry do so before their twenty-fifth birthday, and over half of all females do so before their twenty-second birthday. Contrary to popular opinion, the average age at first marriage has been going down for at least half a century. This trend is especially strong for the male. The years 1930 and 1940 saw a slight check in the downward trend, due probably to the depression and the postponement of marriages out of economic necessity. If figures were available for the war and postwar years, they would very likely show another dip in the direction of young marriages. (See pages 45-48.) Legislative changes have been in the direction of raising the minimum ages at which marriage can legally take place, as we have seen. These changes, however, have been in only a few of the states and have not been sufficient to alter the direction of the national average. In 1940 there were still over sixteen thousand marriages in which the bride was under sixteen years of age.

In attempting to decide what are the best ages for marriage, it is well to keep in mind that chronological age is a much less important consideration than are emotional maturity and socioeconomic opportunity. Some persons are adult and ready for marriage at twenty, while others are still childish and ill-prepared at forty. Yet there is a relationship, and if exceptions are permitted, it is not entirely fruitless to try to tie the thing down in terms of chronological age. When this is done, most authorities come out with the recommendation that marriage take place during the early or middle twenties—somewhat in line with the actual practice as shown by census figures.

There have been statistical analyses which show that teenage marriages do not usually work out as well, that they have greater problems of adjustment and show higher divorce rates than others. Both the Terman and the Burgess and Cottrell studies reveal that marriage is less successful when the mates are in the younger age groups. Differences noted were not great, however, which impresses us that the last word on the subject has not as yet been said. But it seems safe to conclude that early marriage does carry some additional risk, and for the reason that the mates are more likely to be immature, impetuous in their choices, and unprepared to assume the social and economic responsibilities that marriage normally requires.

Late marriage may likewise carry with it certain risks or hazards. In the first place, the longer an adult individual waits before marrying, the fewer he has to choose from and the smaller are his chances of either getting married or of finding the right mate. This fact is especially true for the female, for she is culturally less free to seek a mate than is the male; and too, there is a tendency for the older male, when he marries, to reach down into the younger ages, skipping those females nearer his own age and leaving them stranded. In the second place, older persons are likely to be more rigid or set in their ways, more choosy and less adaptable in their attitudes and habit patterns. Finally, it can be noted that childbearing sometimes proves more difficult when not started until the age of thirty or forty, that the girl usually has the easiest time of it when she is in her late teens or early or middle twenties.

To a large extent the time of marriage must depend upon social and economic circumstances surrounding the couple. One of these has to do with work opportunity and financial readiness. In this day of specialization and keen competition it is frequently necessary to delay marriage beyond the time of biological maturity and personal desire. This fact makes for tension and contributes to the problem of premarital intimacy. It would be helpful if society were organized to subsidize the start of marriage through the extension of economic assistance at this crucial point, either by the parents or by the state. Government grants to veterans attending college represent a step in this direction.

Due mainly to the large enrollment of veteran students, and the special government grants they receive, college marriages are much more common than they have ever been before. This has established a new norm for the campus which many feel will continue. Though there are special problems connected with college marriage, these need not be insurmountable. Each case must be decided upon its own merits. There are the questions of having adequate income and of finding a place to live.

There may be the problem of the wife's having to give up her ambition for an education, or the problem of worry over an unplanned pregnancy even when she can afford to attend college. In some cases there may be objections on the part of parents or school authorities. If the couple is ready otherwise, though, and if the risks do not seem too great, marriage while in college may be the wisest thing.

From a study of 544 couples at Michigan State College, Landis reports the following: About one G. I. college student in four is married. One third of these married students were parents at the time of the survey, and one half could expect to be by the time of graduation. Of the wives, about one in ten was also a student and nearly one half worked outside the home. Three fourths of these men and women were sufficiently satisfied to say that, if they had it to do over, they would again marry before finishing college. Almost all men thought that the wife was an asset in their work for a degree, and the wives were almost unanimous in believing that their sacrifices were worth while and would pay off in the future. (A University of Wisconsin study was cited to show that married students average higher grades than single students.) Living costs averaged from $130 to $150 per month. One fourth of the couples were having to borrow or draw upon savings. Recognized disadvantages were: inadequate finance, unsatisfactory housing, and lack of recreation. More advantages than disadvantages were listed, however, chief of which was emotional security. For the majority, "shared experience during college years is making a worth-while contribution toward building a successful marriage." [5]

Though it is well to have something saved and to have the assurance of some sort of income before getting married, it should not be necessary, for example, to have the house bought and furnished with all of the luxuries that can be desired. Some couples make the mistake of being too self-demanding in their economic preparation and of waiting too long. There is value in married mates' sacrificing and building together so as

---

[5] Judson Landis, "Education for marriage: On the Campus," *Survey Mid-Monthly,* 84:17-19, January, 1948. Quotation on page 19.

to better understand one another and to better appreciate what they may come to own.

How long should the engagement last? This cannot be answered in any uniform or precise manner applying to all cases, for so much depends upon the personalities involved and the situations that surround them. In general, short courtships require longer engagements and vice versa. It all depends upon how long it takes the couple to do the job, already started, of preparing for marriage. If the engagement is too short, it will not permit the testing, adjusting, and preparing found to be so necessary; and if too long, it may lead to emotional tensions, excesses in intimacy, and the risk of spinsterhood in case of a breakup. Both the Terman and the Burgess and Cottrell studies found marital success to be associated with relatively long engagements—two years or more in the latter study. This finding is surprising and may be partly explained on the basis of unrepresentative samples. Duvall and Hill argue the pros and cons, then conclude:

Engagements need to be long enough to act as a screening device to alienate and separate incompatible couples who would otherwise marry, only to separate more painfully after some years of marriage. The answer to the question of length of engagement is given best, not as a definite number of months or years, but in terms of the indefinite "long enough." The engagement, then, should be *long enough* to perform the many functions of testing, discussing, learning, fighting, and loving which underlie successful marriage. If the student requires a more specific figure, it is probably safe to state that the engagement should rarely be shorter than six months and rarely longer than two years, depending on the length of previous acquaintance and the extent to which the engagement functions have already been started in the courtship period.[6]

It is usually not advisable to become either engaged or married prior to a lengthy separation. Absence does not make the heart grow fonder, except, as has been said, "for somebody else." It is true, of course, that short separations will often add to the relationship by giving perspective and greater ap-

---

[6] Evelyn Millis Duvall and Reuben Hill: *When You Marry*. Reprinted by special permission of D. C. Heath and Company, Boston, Mass., 1945, pp. 89-90.

preciation. It is also true that some of the adjusting can be done through correspondence. But it is likewise true that in time memories fade, letters become misunderstood, and under absence and contrasting experiences loved ones grow apart. Wartime separations and their resulting high divorce rates bear out this fact. (See Chapter 2.) When a long period of separation seems likely, better it is that the couple wait until it is over and see then if they are still of the same mind.

In conclusion may we say that the time to become engaged is when one is reasonably mature in his personality, reasonably certain in his choice of a partner, and when the chances are reasonably good that the couple can associate together and that the marriage can take place sometime in the not-too-distant future. The engagement should be just long enough to accomplish its purposes, no longer. One of its purposes is to permit the determination of its own termination—by setting the marriage date or by breaking up the relationship.

Breaking the Engagement.—Since betrothal is the testing ground for marriage, it goes almost without saying that if the test doesn't prove successful the project ought to be abandoned. This need not be taken as an excuse for irresponsibility, however; too many play lightly with love and become engaged only to exploit. But there are others of more serious intent who discover quite honestly that they made a mistake. It is better, then, to turn back—gently but firmly—so as to avoid a greater crisis in the years ahead. No marriage should be allowed to take place out of sheer duty or mere sympathy.

Only about half of those who marry have never had a previously broken engagement. From a study of one thousand engaged couples, Burgess and Locke report that "23.8 per cent of the men and 35.8 per cent of the women had broken one or more previous engagements, and 14.9 per cent later broke their current engagements." [7]

Breach of promise suits are becoming a rarity owing to recent court decisions and legislative revisions. This is probably

---

[7] Ernest W. Burgess and Harvey J. Locke, *The Family: From Institution to Companionship* (New York: American Book Co., 1945), p. 390.

a good thing for they were frequently used as a racket. Yet
there is considerable sorrow and bitterness connected with
broken engagements. Much of this could be avoided if the
pledge were taken a little more seriously by offenders in the
first place.

Marriage is known to be more happy where the mates have
not had large numbers of love affairs or engagements. Successful marriage requires the willingness and ability of its
members to "play monopoly" with only one, and the testing
and preparing for this apparently starts long before the ceremony.

The Wedding

Normally, engagement is followed by a wedding, and that,
in turn, by a honeymoon. Together, these constitute the transition into marriage. The wedding is central in it all, marking
the end of one way of life and the beginning of another.

The custom of requiring some sort of ceremony to designate entrance into marriage has been almost universal; details
have differed, but the essence of the practice has been, and is,
quite general. Except for common-law marriage, still recognized in some sections, this same generalization holds for the
contemporary United States. All marriage laws in this country
set up requirements for a license, for a ceremony, and for a
public recording of the act.

Reasons for this universality are not difficult to find. In the
first place, a public ceremony lets society know what is taking
place so that required social adjustments can be made and
appropriate personal responsibility can be fixed. It gives society
a means of controlling sex in the interests of those who need
protection; mothers and children, for example, are not so
easily left at the mercy of selfish and unscrupulous men. It
clarifies the situation, lets people know where the couple stands,
gives public support and establishes social control over the
relationship. In the second place, an appropriate ceremony tends
to impress participants with the importance of the thing they
are undertaking, helping them to try harder and to assume
more responsibility regarding it. Thus the wedding gives im-

petus to both self-effort and social control; without it, people would be more exploitative and society would be more chaotic.

Type of Ceremony.—One of the first essentials of an effective wedding, therefore, is that it be public. Just as the engagement needs to be announced in order that the couple can become accepted by society, so wedding plans need to be made known and to become approved by parents and friends. Secret weddings are escape devices, usually, and are resorted to for the purpose of dodging social control. But society has a stake in the marriages of its members, and to shut one's eyes to this fact is to invite trouble.

There are two kinds of secret weddings. One is the elopement or runaway type, which is particularly hazardous for the reason that it is usually impetuous, reckless, defiant, and without adequate preparation. Elopers are often under age, under the "spell of the moon," or under the influence of alcohol; they act on a dare, or for the sake of a thrill, and without either the knowledge or the consent of their parents; they are unadjusted to each other, for in most cases they will have by-passed the engagement experience. The other type of secret wedding differs from this first largely in degree; it is where a couple marries secretly in order to avoid the fuss and bother of a public wedding, or the expense involved, or they don't want to wait. In cases like this there will usually have been more careful consideration and preparation than in the former; there will have been an engagement, and parents and others will have approved of the match. The act here is simply that of the couple taking the matter of the wedding into its own hands and of "jumping the gun"; it defies parents and friends, not in the fact of getting married but in the manner by which this is done. By "taking over" the wedding arrangements and trying to make of them an elaborate social affair, parents sometimes invite this kind of rebellion. For this reason secret marriages, in some instances, seem to be justified. But they should be avoided whenever possible for they tend to hurt or anger those on the outside and to make for strained relationships which may work against the development of pair unity.

Popenoe made a study of 738 secret marriages and elopements. He found that the major motivations were: getting
around parental objection; desire either for, or to avoid, publicity; concern over the expense or elaborateness of what was
being planned; and felt necessity as presented by premarital
pregnancy. In all these categories the percentage of failure was
greater than for couples married in the traditional manner.[8]

Marriage may be regarded both as a civil contract and as a
religious sacrament. Legally considered it is a contract authorized and controlled by the state. Yet millions consider it as a
sacrament, sanctioned and supervised by the church. In this
country marriage may be solemnized by either a civil or a religious officiant—not just anyone, of course, but those authorized
according to state law.

Approximately three fourths of all marriages in the United
States are initiated by religious ceremony and, statistically
speaking, these are the ones more likely to succeed.[9] There are
probably two reasons why religious weddings show better results than do the civil. First, religion may tend to attract, and
hence select, the more cooperative and adjustable individuals;
that is, those who by personality are the ones most likely to
succeed in marriage are the ones who are also most likely to
seek religious weddings. Second, the religious ceremony is usually made more impressive, which may give added incentive
and result in a greater striving for success.

Though civil weddings can also be made impressive, so often
they are not. The civil officiant will most usually be a justice
of the peace, with his compensation arranged on a fee basis.
This means that he will be primarily interested in getting over
as many marriages as he can, for profit, and only incidentally
concerned with how the bride and the groom are impressed.
As a consequence he will frequently attempt to drum up business, will carry on in an unkempt basement office or the like,
will strip the ceremony of its beauty and to its bare essentials,

[8] Paul Popenoe, *Modern Marriage* (2d ed.; New York: The Macmillan Co., 1940), pp. 222-27.
[9] *Ibid.*, pp. 216-17. See also Ernest W. Burgess and Leonard S. Cottrell, *Predicting Success or Failure in Marriage* (New York: Prentice-Hall, Inc., 1939), p. 358.

and will be so abrupt and mercenary as to offend the sensitive and hopeful youngsters that come to him. All of this is reviewed in a popular magazine article appearing several years ago. Here is a sample:

At their best, the clerks are indifferent. I'd hear them mumble: "Sign here. Three bucks. Move on. Next." Many times I saw couples come in with radiant faces and go away chilled and downcast.[10]

Church weddings sometimes err on the other side. Though usually they are more beautiful and impressive, they frequently take on the nature of elaborate and expensive pageantry for the sake of show. Families often try to make a great social event out of the marriage of their daughter, hoping thereby to gain status. When this is done the affair may possibly become an ordeal for participants rather than a restful and impressive occasion. Extensive preparation is usually necessary, which means paying attention to every little detail of formal wedding etiquette and which may even require the holding of rehearsals. The cost is often considerable—in terms of strain and fatigue as well as dollars.

Timmons studied the prewar economic costs of weddings for 154 middle-class, mid-western couples. He found that there are "cultural compulsives" operating in our society which surround the wedding with considerable expense. Major expenditures are for such items as the following: engagement and wedding rings, clothes for the bride and groom, telegrams and printed announcements, receptions, fees for the license and the officiant, gifts to the bride and groom and certain of the attendants, the wedding trip, decorations, and special help. The average cost of these weddings was just under $400. But the postmarital utility of expenditures, plus gifts received, was slightly over $500, showing that these couples gained by the process. In most cases the groom took care of such expenditures as for the rings, for fees, and for the wedding trip; while the bride's parents financed the reception, announcements, special help, and the like. Elopements were less expensive than

---

10 Dorothy Walworth, "Just Married—and How!" *Reader's Digest,* October, 1942, pp. 31-34.

public ceremonies; weddings of couples with college training, but no degree, were less expensive than those in which both of the mates had graduated from college; and weddings performed by a justice of the peace were less expensive than where a clergyman had officiated.[11]

Writing more recently, Arlitt also itemizes the various expenses connected with an average wedding. Her figures are considerably higher than those from the study just cited. She claims that a simple home wedding will cost in the neighborhood of eight or nine hundred dollars, a simple church wedding more than two thousand dollars, and a large home or church wedding so much that she considers it beyond interest for the reader. She favors the simple home wedding for the reason that it requires relatively light expenditures and leaves the couple more relaxed and less worried at the start of marriage.[12]

Wedding Etiquette.—There has been a general loosening of social conventions surrounding the wedding so that it is now possible to adopt or adapt practices more according to the couple's desire.

June, representing the culmination of spring romance and academic commencement, is the most chosen month for the marriage ceremony to be performed. As in other things, the engaged couple will want to make broad plans together, setting the general date for the wedding at a time that will be convenient and acceptable to both. (The specific date, however, will usually be set by the girl, and for two reasons: (1) she can arrange it to miss the menstrual period; and (2) she, with her parents, is usually more responsible for the detailed arrangements and expenses surrounding the marriage.)

From the social point of view it makes little difference what is actually said or done in the ceremony just so long as it is sufficiently impressive to accomplish its purposes of setting up necessary controls and incentives. Usually both bride and

---

[11] B. F. Timmons, "The Cost of Weddings," *American Sociological Review,* 4:224-33, April, 1939.

[12] Ada Hart Arlitt, "The Wedding, the Honeymoon, and the First Marital Adjustments," chap. v in Part II of Morris Fishbein and Ernest W. Burgess, eds. (New York: Doubleday & Co., 1947), pp. 132-41.

groom will be asked to pledge loyalty to the other "until death do you part." The groom promises to "love, honor, and cherish," while the bride—until recently and in some ceremonies even now—promises to "love, honor, and obey." Many modern weddings are omitting the word "obey" so as to be more in harmony with the newer assumption of sex equality.

Following are some practices that have been common but are variable and entirely optional at the present time: having attendants at the ceremony, the bride's father giving her away, promiscuous kissing of the bride and groom after the ceremony, throwing rice or confetti at the couple as they leave the hall, tieing old shoes to the car that is to take them away, carrying the bride over the threshold of her new home.

Friends of the couple will do well to remember that while a little fun is always in order the "horseplay" referred to as "shivareeing" or "belling" can sometimes be carried too far. There are instances where enthusiasm and excitement carry crowd behavior beyond the point of good judgment and into the area of indecency or actual cruelty. When this happens the new marriage is put under a handicap because of the fatigue, embarrassment, anger, and sometimes physical harm that ensue. Childish pranks should be reserved for children or at least held down by good judgment and to the level of moderation.

There is no way of laying down general rules that will fit all cases. What is ideal for the marriage ceremony will vary according to the persons and the circumstances involved. Some individuals crave formality and social display, while others detest it. Many a girl has her mind set on having a glamorous wedding, and to deny her the experience may mean that she will always feel disappointed or cheated. Some families can afford a heavy expense, though many, because of convention or social ambition, spend far beyond their means. How some men feel about the fuss of an elaborate wedding is illustrated in the following:

I can't understand why every girl wants to have a big wedding, and why all the rest of the women want to go to it. The bridegroom loathes it. The men who attend are dragged there by their wives. And the crowd out front is as feminine as a ladies' sewing circle.[13]

Can we say that the wedding will generally serve its purpose best when it is public, though unpretentious; simple, though impressive; inexpensive, though adequate; and when it is compatible with the tastes and capacities of those involved.

THE HONEYMOON

Nominally considered, we know that a couple is married just as soon as the wedding is over. Actually, though, marriage solidarity may take years to build up. There is no magic in a ceremony as such; couples never shift from a state of disunity to one of unity overnight or by the saying of a few words. The wedding will have made them one so far as the law is concerned, but only time and mutual adjustment can make them one in terms of personal and social functioning. Part of this will have taken place prior to the wedding ceremony. Afterwards comes the honeymoon.

The purpose of the honeymoon is to provide a favorable setting for the first crucial adjustments of marriage. It is important that the couple's introduction into this new way of life take place under the best possible circumstances, for blunders then may cause misunderstandings and injuries that will later prove difficult to erase. There may be exhaustion, resulting from the exertion and excitement of the wedding. There is often a self-consciousness or shyness connected with sexual intercourse, especially for the bride. There will most certainly be new discoveries to be made and new understandings to be reached, now that the relationship has been placed upon a more intimate and monopolistic basis. All of these can be worked out best under conditions of rest, quietude, and privacy.

Honeymoon Evaluation.—Not every couple takes a honeymoon. Some claim that they don't have time; others that they can't afford it; and still others that they don't think it neces-

---

[13] Case study from the author's files.

sary. Sometimes it is only the husband who is against it; and the wife, though not wanting to say anything, carries secret longings or ego scars.

(Authorities generally agree that a honeymoon, in most cases, is advisable.) This need not require a large expenditure or a lot of time; and though most honeymoons involve travel of some sort, even that is not necessary. It should permit the couple to be alone and without worry for a little while, however, so that they can start their course unfettered and away from the prying eyes of all who might interfere.

Though research is scanty, some light has been thrown upon the effectiveness of honeymoons by a recent study of fifty married women in a small southern community. Three fourths of these women described their honeymoon as a complete success, while less than half of them claimed to have achieved complete sexual harmony during it, showing that many did not regard sexual harmony as the last word in honeymoon success. Approximately one fifth asserted that their honeymoon was far from ideal, and over one half remembered specific difficulties. Of the difficulties mentioned, sexual adjustment came first by all odds. Others were as follows: brevity of honeymoon, poor selection of place, financial matters, relatives, and clash of temperament.[14]

Common Errors.—It may aid our analysis to list some of the more frequent mistakes that are made in connection with the honeymoon and to suggest corrections.

1. In the first place it is a mistake for the couple to postpone the honeymoon with the idea of having it some months or years later when they will be better acquainted or when conditions will be more favorable. Becoming acquainted more easily is the very reason for having a honeymoon, and there is no better time for that than at the beginning. Postponing the honeymoon is just about as much of a mistake as not having one at all; in fact, that is what postponement often turns out to be. Married mates will want to plan occasional vacations or trips

---

14 Stanley R. Brav, "Note on Honeymoons," *Marriage and Family Living,* 9:60, 65, Summer, 1947.

together throughout the years, to be sure, but since these do not serve the purposes of a honeymoon they cannot be considered as substitutes. Too, if the husband wants to postpone, and for practical reasons, the wife is apt to become hurt and to feel that he is willing to put other things ahead of her.

2. Thoughtlessness and lack of planning may result in the type of honeymoon that is unsuited to one or both of the participants. Two weeks in the mountains, for example, while appropriate for some, might be monotonous and distasteful for the tenderfoot. It is well to plan the place and general activities of the honeymoon ahead of time, and to plan them mutually and according to the tastes and wishes of both.

3. Some couples quite foolishly take an acquaintance along with them on the trip or use their honeymoon to visit relatives and friends. This deprives them of the privacy so much needed during intimate adjustment. It may tend to make one or the other feel that he is being inspected, weighed, and judged by a critical audience, which in turn may produce fears and resentments at the very start.

4. Equally disastrous is the practice of turning the honeymoon into a recreational splurge of one kind or another. Traveling long distances, rushing here and there in sightseeing frenzies, dissipating by excesses in entertainment—these things are hardly conducive to rest and intimate adjustment. What the couple needs is not excitement and exhaustion but quietude and leisurely living. With fatigue comes irritability and with that come tension and conflict.

5. Overspending on the honeymoon may lead to worry, disagreement, and later deprivation. Sometimes it is a sensitive husband who is to blame, going far beyond his means out of fear of being considered "cheap." Sometimes it is a golddigging wife. Sometimes both. There is no good reason why lovers should not be at least moderately practical, even on a honeymoon. To do otherwise is to invite trouble, for there is danger in exhausting a "nest egg" needed for something else or in setting a pace that cannot be continued.

6. A honeymoon may be either too long or too short. It is too long if it results in either boredom or restlessness, and it is

too short if it leaves the couple unsatisfied and wanting more. Though a period of one to two weeks is frequently suggested, there is no attempt to imply that that length is ideal for every couple. What is best will depend upon such things as the finances of the couple, when either of them needs to get back to work, how rapidly and well adjustment takes place, and the respective tastes or desires of each. There is some virtue in planning flexibly so that the honeymoon can be either terminated or extended as the need or preference develops.

7. There is a lot of needless blundering over the early sex experiences of married mates. (The most usual error is for the husband to press for his "rights" before the bride is ready, or to be too crude or even brutal in it all.) Certain writers, in referring to this, speak of the groom's "raping" his bride—and in some cases it undoubtedly amounts to virtually that. The bride may submit, considering it her duty, but at the same time becoming hurt, frightened, or resentful over her lover's lack of consideration. Thus a divorce may have its inception on the wedding night. Not all brides are unready at this time, of course. But some are, and when this happens there is every good reason for the husband to wait, using patience, tact, and love to win his way.

Conclusions.—The engagement, the wedding, and the honeymoon all serve useful functions in the family process. Together they constitute a three-step transition from courtship into marriage. First there is the preparation, in terms of engagement. Next there is the legalizing and solemnizing, in terms of the wedding. Finally there is the initiation, in terms of the honeymoon. After that couples commence to feel and act like married individuals.

There are no absolute or uniform rules regarding these processes. In general we can say that they serve their purposes best when they result in the best possible transition—one that is gradual, and free from serious strains or shocks; natural, or without undue expense or show; effective, in the sense that there is progressive adaptation rather than either frustration or exploitation.

Problems and Projects

1. Do you consider it advisable for the man, when becoming engaged, to ask the girl's father for consent? Why or why not?

2. Name several motives back of becoming engaged which you think are not justified.

3. Suggest reasons why it is unwise for engaged couples to shut out families and friends. To what extent should they let others in on their problems and plans? Discuss.

4. Are there any serious incidents in your past which you would not care to tell your fiancé(e)? What type of incidents do you feel he or she would be justified in withholding from you?

5. How much intimacy is to be expected during engagement? How much do you think is desirable from the standpoint of long-time adjustment? What are the dangers?

6. How sociable should an engaged person be able to be with other members of the opposite sex without inviting jealousy from the fiancé(e)? Is there ever any justification for an engaged person's dating with someone other than the fiancé(e)? Discuss.

7. What would you do if engaged to someone who seemed disinterested in planning for marriage, who deemed it neither necessary nor desirable to talk over serious questions pertaining to the future?

8. List the pros and cons of getting married while still going to school. Compare your thinking with that of several married couples on the campus whom you know.

9. It has been argued that there is no reason for engagements' being as long today as formerly, due to youth's greater freedom which permits them to get better acquainted in a shorter period of time. Do you agree? How long do you think an average modern engagement ought to be? Discuss.

10. Do you have any suggestions as to the "best" age for young people to start dating? To start going steady? To get married? Qualify your answers with statements concerning personal and social factors that are involved.

11. Look up the laws of your state governing marriage; governing divorce; concerning the legal rights of husband and wife. How do these compare with those of other states?

12. Why do so few young people have complete medical examinations before marriage? What might be done to persuade more to do so?

13. Take a poll among your married friends concerning the type of marriage ceremony and honeymoon they had, and asking for opinions as to possible effects upon their marital adjustment.

Selected Readings

BABER, RAY E. *Marriage and the Family.* New York: McGraw-Hill Book Co., 1939. Chap. v, "A Medley of Marriage Laws."

BECKER, HOWARD, and HILL, REUBEN (eds.). *Family, Marriage, and Parenthood.* Boston: D. C. Heath & Co., 1948. Chaps. ix, "The Engagement: Thinking about Marriage"; xix, "What Family Members Should Know about Law."

BOWMAN, HENRY A. *Marriage for Moderns.* New York: McGraw-Hill Book Co., 1948. Chap. ix, "Wedding and Honeymoon."

DUVALL, EVELYN MILLIS, and HILL, REUBEN. *When You Marry.* Boston: D. C. Heath & Co., 1945. Chaps. v, "The Meaning of an Engagement"; ix, "Just Married."

FISHBEIN, MORRIS, and BURGESS, ERNEST W. (eds.). *Successful Marriage.* New York: Doubleday & Co., 1947. Part I, chaps. iii, "Courtship and Engagement"; iv, "Premarital Sex Relationships"; v, "Premarital Physical Examination"; Part II, chap. v, "The Wedding, the Honeymoon, and the First Marital Adjustments."

GROVES, ERNEST R. *Preparation for Marriage.* New York: Emerson Books, 1939.

HARPER, ROBERT A. *Marriage.* New York: Appleton-Century-Crofts, Inc., 1949. Chap. vi, "Functions of the Engagement Period."

HIMES, NORMAN E. *Your Marriage: A Guide to Happiness.* New York: Farrar & Rinehart, Inc., 1940. Chaps. vii, "Engagement: Personality Testing"; x, "The Premarital Examination"; xi, "The Wedding and Honeymoon."

LANDIS, JUDSON T., and LANDIS, MARY G. *Building a Successful Marriage.* New York: Prentice-Hall, Inc., 1948. Chaps. viii, "Engagement"; ix, "Legal Control of Marriage."

MAGOUN, F. ALEXANDER. *Love and Marriage.* New York: Harper & Bros., 1948. Chaps. vii, "The Period of Engagement"; viii, "The Honeymoon."

POPENOE, PAUL. *Modern Marriage.* New York: The Macmillan Co., 1940.

STOKES, WALTER R. *Modern Pattern for Marriage.* New York: Rinehart & Co., 1948.

Chapter 10

MATE ADJUSTMENT

Upon entering marriage, nearly everyone expects to be happy. Many succeed in this. Others fail. What is it that accounts for the difference?

Four factors are recognized throughout this analysis: (1) a harmonious society, (2) personal maturity, (3) pair solidarity, and (4) marital adaptability. There isn't much that an individual person or couple can do to improve its marriage by way of changing society; it can choose its place of residence, to be sure, and can even help to alter the social conditions which affect it, but at best such an approach to successful marriage is indirect and slow-moving. More significant are the personal qualities of those who marry, and the ways in which these are combined and forged into a working unity. Growing up, becoming involved, choosing a mate, and entering matrimony have been analyzed in earlier chapters. We are ready now to examine processes peculiar to the marriage itself.

Of first importance is a realization that the need for adjustment never ends. Successful marriage requires more than the right kind of preparation beforehand, as necessary as that is; it also demands that the mates ever continue to understand each other better and to adapt to new situations, as these are bound to arise. Becoming married cannot be taken to mean that one has "arrived" at a state of eternal happiness. Learning how to *stay married* is every bit as worth while as knowing how to get married, though the two are related.

Defining the Problem

We are not regarding marriage itself as a problem. Marriage permits a type and degree of happiness that can be known in perhaps no other way. Yet, through human error, the efforts of men and women are sometimes aborted, and suffering comes to substitute for satisfaction. There are difficulties within marriage which must be examined if we are to entertain any hope of their ever being solved. The problem is to discover wherein married mates fail and how they can better adjust.

One approach is to consider the legal grounds used in securing divorce. Today most divorces are granted on the claim of cruelty; but with desertion, adultery, neglect, drunkenness, and others also coming in for a share. Actually, though, this tells almost nothing about the real reasons back of divorce. It is relatively easy for incompatible mates to get around the law by agreeing on the grounds ahead of time and then letting the divorce go through without a contest.

Terman attempted to define the problem by asking husbands and wives to indicate the various criticisms each had concerning his mate and marriage. Out of the fifty-seven grievances that were given, the ten greatest for both mates are as follows, listed in the order of their seriousness: [1]

Grievances of Husbands	Grievances of Wives
W. nags me	H. selfish and inconsiderate
W. not affectionate	H. unsuccessful in business
W. selfish and inconsiderate	H. untruthful
W. complains too much	H. complains too much
W. interferes with hobbies	H. does not show his affection
W. slovenly in appearance	H. does not talk things over
W. quick-tempered	H. harsh with children
W. interferes with my discipline	H. touchy
W. conceited	H. no interest in children
W. insincere	H. not interested in home

Other complaints also high with both sexes are these: criticizes me, nervous and impatient, argumentative, not faithful to me, has annoying habits, and is either a poor housekeeper or a poor manager of income. Some of the grievances are more

---

[1] From *Psychological Factors in Marital Happiness,* by Lewis M. Terman. 1938. Courtesy of McGraw-Hill Book Co., Table 25, pp. 99-100.

closely identified with one sex than the other, though the vast
majority are common to both. In general, men complain more
of their wives' nagging, interfering, being conceited, and showing a quick temper, while women complain more of their husbands' being argumentative, impatient, unfaithful, and unsuccessful in business. Terman shows that all of the highest-rank-
ing grievances are those pertaining to personality faults in the
mates. He comments: [2]

> A majority of the faults are of the kind commonly thought to be
> indicative of emotional instability, neurotic tendency, or marked intro-
> version, as these terms are used in the current literature of personality
> psychology. Their position here lends support to the theory that one of
> the greatest dangers to marriage is the all-around unhappy tempera-
> ment of one or both of the spouses.

But there were some complaints uncovered by Terman that
had to do with the external circumstances or conditions of the
marriage, without any implication of personal blame. Among
these were: discontent over income and over the restrictions of
marriage; trouble concerning in-laws; and differences relating
to such things as intellectual interests, religious beliefs, choice
of friends, and recreation. Though frequently mentioned, these
did not rank as high in terms of seriousness as did the personality inadequacies mentioned above.

A similar procedure was followed by the Gallup Poll a few
years ago. Husbands and wives were asked to name the chief
faults or shortcomings of their mates and to indicate what it
was that they argued about most frequently. The ten greatest
complaints leveled against wives were as follows: nagging,
extravagance, poor homemaker, too much night-clubbing and
drinking, gossiping, selfishness, too many outside interests, too
bossy, careless and untidy personally, and interested in other
men. In contrast, husbands were criticized for the following:
drinking, lack of consideration, selfishness, too domineering,
interested in other women, stinginess, lack of interest in the
home, taking wife for granted, complaining too much, and

---

[2] From *Psychological Factors in Marital Happiness,* by Lewis M. Terman.
1938. Courtesy of McGraw-Hill Book Co., p. 101.

gambling and smoking.[3] Things argued about were, in order: economic matters, personal mannerisms, bringing up the children, being on time, deciding how to spend leisure, beliefs concerning religion and politics, household chores, the husband's job, and relatives.[4]

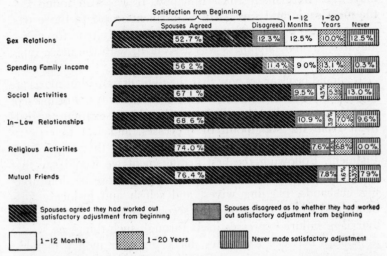

Fig. 6.—Length of time required for adjustment in six areas after marriage. More time was required for sexual and financial adjustment than for any other area. In each of the areas more than half claimed adjustment from the beginning. Adjustment improved over time. (Adapted from Judson T. Landis, "Length of Time Required to Achieve Adjustment in Marriage," *American Sociological Review*, 11:666-77, December, 1946.)

Landis approached the problem from the standpoint of areas of needed adjustment between husband and wife. He named six: sex relations, spending the family income, social activities and recreation, in-law relationships, religious activities, and mutual friends. His study at Michigan State College revealed that it takes longer for the spouses to work out satisfactory sexual adjustments than any other, with money matters coming next, and the others following in the sequence listed above. Within each of these areas, however, over half of the couples

3 William A. Lydgate, "Ten Faults of Wives and Husbands," *Reader's Digest*, July, 1946, pp. 88-90.
4 George Gallup, as reported in his syndicated newspaper column.

studied were agreed or adjusted at the beginning of their marriage. Most of the remainder found at least partial adjustment later. It was found that the greatest happiness was associated with adjustment in the largest number of areas, and that where couples failed to agree in at least two of these, their marriages were likely to be unhappy. It was also found that the most rapid and successful adjustments came to those who were married at age twenty or over (especially true for men), and that greater happiness was associated with the more rapid adjustments.[5]

It should be clear by now that the difficulties within marriage may be classified in a number of different ways. For present purposes, two schemes will be used: (1) to examine adjustment from the standpoint of processes, and (2) to concern ourselves with the special areas of marriage that require adjustment. Following the first arrangement we would say that the problem manifestations are essentially those of domineering husbands, nagging wives, and selfish and insincere husbands and wives. Following the second we would contend that marriage failure expresses itself through such things as sexual difficulties between the mates, bickering over money matters, disagreements concerning recreation, and the like.

Of course one does not get at the real causes of marital disharmony by simply asking people what they fight about or what they dislike in their mates. Even if they tell the truth, there is the question of which is cause and which effect. Such patterns as criticizing, quarreling, drinking, showing no affection, and going out with others may be as much the result of maladjusted relationships as the cause. Marriage fails when the mates either grow selfish through continued immaturity or become incompatible through neglected adjustment. Immaturity can forestall adjustment. Nonadjustment in marriage makes for maladjustment. But the symptoms of marriage breakdown must never be confused with the causes—which in their final analysis might be summarized, or epitomized, as *failure to adjust*.

---

[5] Judson T. Landis, "Length of Time Required to Achieve Adjustment in Marriage," *American Sociological Review*, 11:666-77, December, 1946.

Mental Hygiene in Marriage

If adjustment is at the crux of the problem, as we assume, then our central task ought to be that of trying to understand how men and women can best get along with each other and with society. Wholesome mate adjustment is blocked by neurotic traits in husbands and wives, more, perhaps, than by anything else. Mental hygiene, when practiced, makes for mature and well-balanced personalities; it tends to prevent undue tension and conflict in the social situation; it is the only way around marital difficulties, the only road leading to genuine adjustment.

Getting Off to a Good Start.—The start of any event is important to its outcome, and marriage is no exception. The intricacies and difficulties of modern living are many, and the person who gets off on the wrong foot or makes a poor start in any of life's episodes may find himself handicapped all the way through. Just as the first attitudes and habits acquired by the child are the ones that do most to shape his personality, so the earliest adjustments in marriage are the ones that set the stage and add color to the relationships that follow.

A large part of the start depends upon the nature of the premarital preparation that has gone before—how maturely each of the mates has developed, how well they are matched, how far their love involvement has progressed, how successful was the transition and the launching of their marriage. All of this is background and cannot be changed. Neither can the mates always alter or improve the immediate circumstances and environments that are to influence them. What they can do is to start marriage with the idea of improving upon their past and of rising above their present circumstances. It isn't enough to have made a good preparation. Successful marriage requires a "carry-over," or continuation, in terms of both attitude and effort.

Importance of the Right Attitude.—Attitude is the driving force back of action. Of all the factors influencing marital adjustment, the one that is probably of greatest significance is the attitude of participants—the spirit of fair play, the willingness to do one's part, the determination to make it go.) Where attitude is right, husband and wife can usually succeed in spite of personal weaknesses, or of being ill-matched, or of living under trying circumstances. But where wrong, even though other factors be favorable, attitude will drag men and women down, will result in conflict and failure. It is attitude, primarily, that makes one adaptable or unadaptable in marriage, that determines whether mates will adjust and cooperate or fight and separate.

One common mistake is to think and talk in terms of failure. The successful attitude is the one that expects success and is determined that there will be no failure. Once the marriage has taken place, there should be little thought of turning back, not, at least, until enough time for a fair trial has elapsed. There are many, just the same, who take marriage too lightly, entering it in a spirit of reckless excitement, or irresponsible self-interest, and leaving it whenever the going gets tough. "So what," they are sometimes inclined to say, "if it doesn't work out, we can get a divorce." It is better that the mates never even consider a breakup or admit that such is possible. Light talk, in the form of threats and defiances, often widens the gap and leads to deep sorrow. The first mention of one's leaving the other, the first suggestion of separation, may well be all that it takes to start the ball rolling in the direction of a breakup. For those who think and talk of divorce, divorce is imminent; but for others, because of a different mind-set, because of a hope and a determination, it need never come. It is the defeatist attitude that encourages failure. (Married mates must learn—in the words of a once popular song—to "accentuate the positive.")

Another error in attitude follows an extreme that is opposite to the one just discussed; instead of being sour and pessimistic, this one is simply naïve and overoptimistic. The successful attitude comes somewhere in between—it is hopeful yet realistic. Marriage is a job that needs to be approached earnestly and with eyes open; it is not without rewards, but

it is a task requiring sacrifice and effort just the same. To those
who have come into marriage somewhat unprepared and heavily freighted with romantic ideas unsupported by stern reality,
the time immediately following the honeymoon is usually one
of painful disillusionment. Their mistake has been the so-
called "romantic fallacy" discussed in an earlier chapter. Marriage isn't entirely a "bed of roses," even for the successful.
Bride and groom need to expect imperfections in each other
and problems in their marriage. No individual is perfect, nor
no situation absolutely and unchangingly ideal. There will be
discoveries, some disappointments, a few crises, all requiring
adjustment. Some tension and conflict between the mates is
only normal to the adjustment process and should be expected
and accepted. Each of the mates needs to have an attitude of
accepting the other for what he or she is, shortcomings and
all, though with both striving for improvement as they move
along. Each mate needs to be flexible enough to meet new problems as they arise, and philosophical enough to stand catastrophe should it come.

A third attitudinal handicap to marriage is that of selfishness. Authorities are agreed that whenever exploitation crowds
out cooperation, the relationships of love and marriage become
seriously impaired. This is just another way of saying that,
in the associations of the sexes, self-interest must yield to
group-interest. There are people who haven't become mature
enough for the responsibility that adult love implies; they have
failed to grow up emotionally and, like spoiled children, they
expect the favors that come from being loved while lacking the
capacity to really love others. For them the only hope is re-
education and re-motivation.

Marriage is a cooperative adventure that fails when family
members become self-centered rather than group-centered,
when they look toward "rights" and "privileges" rather than
"obligations" and "contributions." Whether one looks at husband-wife relationships or those between parents and children,
he will see that failure is almost invariably tied up with the
selfishness of someone. There is too much individualism in
family relationships today, too much emphasis on "I" and

"Me" rather than "We" and "Us." Successful marriage is a process of give and take, but there are too many today who try to do all of the taking and none of the giving. In courtship this kind of people put all of their attention on finding a mate who fits their fancy and who will do all the adjusting in the contemplated marriage rather than developing traits of congeniality within themselves. In marriage and family life they are quick to blame and to complain, but slow to cooperate or admit faults within themselves. Sometimes they cry or sulk in order to injure the other person or to get their own way. Sometimes they nag. Sometimes they quarrel. There is an urgent need today for more self-analysis and self-criticism which lead to greater cooperation in the marriage relationship. If people could only be made to face responsibilities a little more and expect favors a little less, if they could enter marriage with the spirit of making contributions rather than demanding rights, many of the heartaches now associated with family life could be avoided.

In short, married mates prove most adjustable when they have a spirit of mutually accepted responsibility and cooperation, when they are realistic about the task before them, and when they are determined that they shall not fail. Success here does not spring from romanticizing alone, nor from temporizing, nor from exploiting; rather, it comes first and foremost from the attitude of regarding marriage as a challenging job and accepting it as a partnership.

The Art of Settling Down.—Marriage ushers in a way of life that, in some respects, is entirely new. The unstable and highly emotionalized testings of courtship yield now to a more practical and exclusive pair arrangement. There will be startling discoveries, some pleasant and others disturbing, as the mates come to realize that marriage isn't entirely what they expected it to be. There will be new realities that need to be faced and routines that must be established. The glamourized excitements of the premarriage period cannot be expected to continue for ever. Marriage brings with it certain additional responsibilities; growing up requires settling down.

Settling down need not mean serious disillusionment. The fact that it does for some is evidence of their immaturity and lack of preparation. It is also reflective of our highly romanticized culture which blinds some to the realities of the situation. No amount of premarital preparation can avoid some discrepancy between anticipation and realization, but it can certainly narrow the gap and make the transition easier. There is no need for disappointment, provided that the approach has been realistic. Though there will inevitably be surprises, there is no reason why the majority of these cannot be in the direction of extended satisfaction so that the couple can come to find an even greater happiness than had been expected.

We have already defined love as something more than either physical attraction or emotional involvement. True and enduring love includes the physical and the emotional, to be sure, but it is something more—it is the ever-growing companionship that comes from working and sacrificing together. Marriage will usually bring a changing emphasis in love, a shift from sentimental excitement to solid companionship. But to only the immature and the blind will this be interpreted as a loss of love; the intelligent and the realistic will regard it as an inevitable part of love's growth.

As time goes on there will come a gradual and continual re-evaluation of one's mate as well as of the total marriage situation. No one is perfect, although the romantic colorings of courtship may have caused some to think so. With marriage, because of its greater intimacy and need for practicality, there will usually appear certain imperfections and blind spots not before realized. These can, unless accepted, prove to be extremely irritating. Coming to know the mate and to accept him for what he is, is an important part of settling down. In this process, self-analysis and criticism can and should serve as a healthy check against excessive de-evaluation of the other.

It must be recognized that marriage does not, in any fundamental way, alter or change the personalities involved. Men and women are essentially the same after their weddings as before, though, let us hope, with a certain amount of added incentive. Cooperative living within wedlock can mean the gradual improvement of both mates, of course. But it is too much to expect any revolutionary change or to attempt it by nagging and blaming. Improvement starts with understanding and acceptance.

Settling down also includes a certain amount of role-defining between husband and wife. A satisfactory division of labor will need to be agreed upon; working relationships will need to be established with reference to such details as earning and spending the family income, controlling or disciplining the children, managing and performing the various tasks about the home. Some of these will be discussed more specifically later in the chapter, the important point here being that some sort of role adjustment will need to be worked out or trouble will ensue.

Role conflicts are usually greatest in the early stages of the marriage before there has been a settling down. It seems likely that most marriages, past and present, would run into some of this kind of difficulty. The problem is particularly prominent today, however, and for the reason that social changes have disturbed the traditional roles which men and women formerly played in the marriage relationship and new ones are not yet well established. It used to be that the prospective mates knew fairly well what society expected of them and therefore what their roles were to be with respect to each other—the husband was to be at the head and was to provide, while the wife was to be submissive and was to busy herself with the children and household chores. Not so today; the emancipation of woman has tended to change this and, as a result the early part of modern marriage is usually a period in which husband and wife maneuver and struggle for positions of advantage and control—trying to define roles which were previously pre-scribed by the culture. This maneuvering, although a necessary part of adjustment, is bound to lead into conflicts of one sort or another.

By saying that marriage requires a settling down we do not mean that lovers must come to take each other for granted or let their relationship sink to the commonplace. There is too

much of that as it is. Some couples make the mistake of settling too far down.

Wives very frequently complain of their husbands' taking
them for granted, and occasionally a husband will level a
similar accusation against his wife. Men seem to be a little
more matter of fact in their marital relationships. Women, in
contrast, tend to give more importance to demonstrations of
affection; they want to be constantly reminded that they are
desirable and appreciated. It is easy to become complacent in
the security of marriage, taking the other for granted, forgetting the need for affectional expression, but to do so is to
settle too far down. Research has demonstrated that marriage
is most happy where these affectional patterns are maintained.

But this does not mean that love's survival requires the constant demonstration of affection on a level of the same intensity and sentimentality as existed during courtship. Love
expression is most meaningful when it is sincere and natural
rather than custom dictated. The modes of expressing sentiment have become so commercialized and standardized around
various special occasions that it is really difficult at times to
distinguish true love from its symbol. Anniversaries are worth
observing, but the wife or husband who becomes personally
insulted when forgotten and who makes it a matter of marital
conflict, is not the wife or husband who is mature in love. In
determining love, actions should be permitted to speak louder
than either words or costly gifts. Sentimental expressions and
demonstrations most certainly have their place; marriage would
be pretty drab without them. But by overemphasizing the material element and by building up patterns of expectation we
have made them altogether too artificial. Husband and wife
will do well to remember each other occasionally when it isn't
expected, and in ways that are spontaneous and heartfelt.

To make marriage succeed each mate will need to keep
alert so that every day can bring something fresh, interesting,
and full of challenge between them. When expressed artificially or not at all, love dies.

Another error, frequently committed, is the failure to keep
up. Some people slip into careless personal habits, ceasing to

care or else justifying themselves on the ground that it is better to be natural. This last is simply an excuse. Personality
development is always a process of "denaturalization." Character requires self-control rather than yielding to elementary
or natural urges. Untidiness in dress, sloppy housekeeping, disagreeable disposition, crudity in speech and manner, all tend
to cheapen the marriage relationship. Thoughtlessness and carelessness about the house result in the "tremendous trifles"
(e.g., rough table manners, not hanging up clothes, leaving a
ring around the bathtub) that sometimes irritate beyond endurance. Any mate who fails to keep up with the other, or to
remain interesting and attractive in the other's company, has
himself to blame when attentions stop and affections grow
cold.

The phenomenon of a married man's falling in love with
his secretary is of sufficient occurrence to warrant special attention. Writing anonymously, one of these secretaries some
time ago issued a "Warning to Wives." [6] It was her claim
that the wives are usually at fault. Too many of them, she
pointed out, become careless in their dress and mannerisms,
nagging and cross in temperament, and lazy or commonplace
as to intellectual interests. Failing to keep up, they cease to be
interesting or challenging to their husbands. The husbands, in
turn, grow lonely and restless. It is then that they turn elsewhere, seeking a love and attraction that are denied them at
home.

The all-too-frequent tendency of mates to nag and quarrel
can cause irritations that make home life a constant state of
dissatisfaction. While every marriage will experience differences of opinion, there is little excuse for the bickering and belittling that goes on within so many. Love without respect is
impossible. The tendency of some mates to intimidate the
other, to throw out slurs and insinuations, to make disparaging
remarks in public, can only destroy love by undermining the
mutual respect upon which it is based.

[6] Anonymous, "Warning to Wives," *Reader's Digest*, November, 1936, pp.
13-16.

Learning to Resolve Conflict.—It isn't that some couples experience conflict and others do not. Some learn how to resolve their differences, while others become increasingly involved in disagreement and maladjustment. Conflict is a normal and inevitable part of learning to live together. Personalities are too different from each other, and marriage is too intimate and emotionalized, for anyone to expect that all will be harmony and love. No couple agrees on everything all the time, but many learn how to be agreeable in their disagreements and to use these little tugs and pulls as steppingstones to better adjustment. Dead-level uniformity is too much to ask. Neither is it to be desired. With a little opposition comes the challenge and stimulation needed for improvement. (Understanding is more important than complete agreement, and unity than uniformity.)

Duvall and Hill distinguish between covert or "undercover" conflict, on the one hand, and overt or "in the open" conflict on the other. Covert conflict includes the resentments and antagonistic feelings that are sometimes suppressed within the individual. From the standpoint of mental hygiene these are extremely dangerous. They tend to accumulate into tensions which, in turn, may upset personality balance and result in emotional outbursts destructive to pair unity. In contrast, overt conflict is regarded as the natural and desirable method for releasing pent-up emotions and working out needed adjustments. This method is direct and aboveboard; it keeps the personalities well aired; and it exposes the problems that need to be tackled. "There is more to the art of getting along in marriage than the mere avoidance of quarrels." [7]

Continuing with this same thought, they say:

The modern couple will expect that in marriage they have a place of security and intimacy where they are free to behave like human beings with the normal variety of emotions. The workaday world, organized as it is, does not permit the frank expression of resentment,

[7] Evelyn Millis Duvall and Reuben Hill: *When You Marry*. Reprinted by special permission of D. C. Heath and Company, Boston, Mass., 1945, pp. 183-85.

vanity, jealousy, and selfish ambition along with tenderness and love, all of which exist in the normal person. The individual must control his annoyances and his affections, he must often act like something more than human to get along in our complex industrial society. If he flies off the handle at his boss he may lose his job. There needs to be some place, however, where the individual can give vent to his annoyances and be himself, and that place seems to be in marriage. If there is that kind of cantankerousness in a marriage, the couple should chalk it down as proof that their marriage is performing one of its main functions—providing a place to let off steam and re-establish emotional balance. If a marriage is so fragile that it must be maintained by the same kind of artificial manners that keeps an office force functioning, it is pretty precariously based. One insightful authority has stated in positive terms, "One of the functions of marriage is to weave a rope of relationships strong enough to hold each person at his worst." [8]

But Duvall and Hill, while regarding overt conflict within marriage as both normal and desirable, certainly do not advocate that the mates live at their worst. They are careful to draw an important distinction between productive and destructive quarreling. Productive quarreling is that which settles upon the issue or point of difference between the mates. It is constructive (or productive) because it releases the tensions, brings about better understanding, lays bare those factors that are causing the conflict, redefines the situation upwards, and ends in problem-solving or better adjustment. (Some might prefer to speak of this as discussion rather than quarreling.) Destructive quarreling, on the other hand, is that which is ego-involving and personal; the sparring partners become all wrought up, shifting attention away from the problem to be solved and toward each other. It is destructive because it bruises the love object, alienates affection, and at the same time solves or settles nothing. [9]

What happens when the mates are neurotic or lack the maturity and stability required for productive discussion and adjustment? Should they then be encouraged to use their marriage as an emotional dumping ground, for the sake of mental health? It is the writer's opinion that they should not. As al-

---

[8] *Ibid.*, pp. 187-88.   [9] *Ibid.*, pp. 188-99.

ready stated, some husbands and wives make the mistake of settling too far down, of glorifying their weaknesses on the pretext of being natural. While we agree that mental health requires a certain naturalness and releasing of tensions, and that the home can serve an extremely useful function along this line, we also believe that marital success depends in large part upon how much the mates are able to put into it, how "high" they are willing to live. If it is a choice between mental illness through suppression and marital bickering through expression, the individual will have to choose. It must be remembered, however, that mental health is also dependent upon marital harmony, and that failure in this relationship often proves to be a boomerang, pulling its victims further downward in a sort of a vicious circle. The ideal, of course, is where mates are mature enough to be natural without being petty, where they can argue objectively and constructively in the solution of their common problems.

But there needs to be a constant attempt to do one's best. A large part of this is simply maintaining the cooperative attitude—being willing to make up, for example, even when this involves giving in. Another part is having a sense of humor, being able to "laugh it off." However, care must be exercised to laugh *with* the other person, never *at* him or her. Too many people take themselves too seriously. A very common mistake in marriage is to become disturbed over every little occurrence or difference of opinion, taking things personally when they were not intended that way, and returning with a dig or threat that has no relevance to the problem. This only serves to block the discussion and aggravate the difficulty. The following opposite reaction shows how a husband found humor in a situation that could have proved troublesome:

Jean (my wife) has the habit of leaving her slippers and shoes on the floor right where she takes them off, which is usually next to the bed. If I forget to watch when I come into the room in the dark, I invariably stumble over them. Oftentimes I stumble, even though I am aware that they are there somewhere. If she were to leave them in the same place every night, I would be very happy. But no, she pulls a fast one and takes them off in a different place every time.

Some nights, not only do I have to watch for slippers but also for shoes. When she adds the shoes I am lost. I stumble twice and nearly fall flat on my face and think, "Well, that's that for the night"; then I run across another pair and all hell breaks loose in my mind. By this time I am so utterly confused that I am not sure I want to proceed any farther. I have tried diving for the bed from the door, but I found out this method wasn't very satisfactory. Not only is it hard on the bed, but it also scares the devil out of my wife.[10]

It cannot be hoped that any marriage will be entirely free of conflict. (The task which every couple faces is not that of learning how to dodge conflict, but how to handle it when it comes, how to use it constructively as a way to better understanding and adjustment.)Techniques by which conflict is resolved are by no means standardized; they will vary with the needs and habits of the couples involved. Every couple must find its own way, its system of settling differences; and the sooner it finds it, the better will be its over-all adjustment. Some seem to get along best when they explode and get it over with, then quickly make up. Others are happier by holding their tongue until they have cooled off. But sulking, nagging, bickering, belittling, and the like usually serve to block adjustment.

Monopoly Without Monotony.—By definition, marriage is a system of mate monopoly. As couples move from their early friendships through courtship and engagement and into marriage, their associations together become not only more intimate but more exclusive. Two dangers are imminent: one, that the monopolistic process isn't carried far enough, or later reverses itself, so that the mates are untrue; and the other, that it is carried too far, or is unaccompanied by other effort, so that the relationship sinks to the level of monotony.

Nothing, perhaps, will undermine love so definitely or destroy marriage so completely as dishonesty and cheating between the mates. Just as dependability is one of the most important considerations in choosing a mate (see pages 255-57), so fidelity is paramount in marriage. Lying to each other, flirting with or making love to someone else, stepping out behind the

---

[10] Case study from the author's files.

other's back, adultery; all lead to marriage failure. Sometimes these practices come because of an unwillingness to give up the acquaintances and good times of the courtship period. Sometimes they are encouraged by the development of conflict and monotony within marriage. Always, however, they are associated with some degree of personality immaturity, with a lack of responsibility in the social situation.

Marriage is a contractual arrangement between two persons, designed for the benefit of both, but requiring obligations. Whenever self-interest causes either to cheat on the other, the very basis for mutuality is thereby destroyed. This is true of any partnership arrangement, marital or otherwise. Until one has prepared himself for social responsibility and is ready to play the role of a partner, he is still too immature to be trusted in adult relationships.

But there is the other extreme. While monopoly must be accepted and adjusted to if marriage is to be successful, it is possible for the mates to become altogether too demanding of each other in time and interest. This can result in both jealousy and monotony.

Monopoly in marriage generally brings with it a feeling of security. Yet no marriage monopoly can be complete, for husbands and wives are also members of the broader society and must associate in one way or another with others in that society. If the mates are mature and their love genuine, there will be a willingness on the part of each to let the other cultivate separate friends and interests on the outside and to function normally in his or her own right as a member of society; security is maintained by trust coming in where monopoly leaves off. Of course all mates are not sufficiently mature for this, and where they are not the tendency is to try for security by extending the limits of monopoly; suspicion then crowds out confidence and jealousy eats away at love. Jealousy is one of the attributes of human nature which needs to be overcome during courtship and early marriage if marriage is to be successful.

Monotony comes to marriage whenever the mates cease to be challenging to each other, or let their relationships become too much of a routine, or their family tasks too much of a drudgery. It is possible for husband and wife to come to know each other too well and to become too matter of fact and drab in their mode of life. If there is to be a sustained interest in each other, and in the marriage, there will need to be retained a little variety and a few surprises.

It has been commonly observed that husband and wife frequently grow to look alike. Insofar as this is true, the explanation is twofold: first, the tendency toward homogamy, or likes marrying likes; and second, the necessity of mutual adaptation within marriage whereby the mates come to see alike, more or less, and to copy each other in various mannerisms and modes of expression.

Sometimes, though, a married mate makes the mistake of surrendering his individuality too completely. In doing this he not only lays himself open to greater exploitation but also runs the danger of becoming rather commonplace and uninteresting to the other.

Baber discusses this need for self-defense in marriage under the term "personality protection." [11] Here are several types: (1) There is a seeming need for some protection in regard to physical privacy. Though greater intimacy is to be expected of marriage, there are certain things that are better kept private, at least for a time. It has been said that "familiarity breeds contempt." Some persons, because of a sheltered or prudish upbringing, are more sensitive to a display of body functions than are others. Personal carelessness or aggressiveness in these matters frequently produces feelings of disgust, especially during the early days of marriage. Duvall and Hill, in talking about "Niceties Worth Preserving," claim that "A minimum of privacy will need to be maintained indefinitely, just because Americans react to bodily functions of urination and excretion the way they do." [12] Yet, even in this culture, variations in reactions to matters of this kind must be recognized. (2) There is need for mental privacy, where each of the mates is privi-

---

[11] Ray E. Baber, *Marriage and the Family* (New York: McGraw-Hill Book Co., 1939), pp. 234-37.
[12] Evelyn Millis Duvall and Reuben Hill: *When You Marry.* Reprinted by special permission of D. C. Heath and Company Boston, Mass., 1945, p. 177.

leged and encouraged to think, follow hobbies, and develop interests that are largely peculiar to himself. There is no good reason why either mate should feel compelled to "tell all" to the other or should permit the personality to become so merged with the other as to be stunted in its own development. Neither should a mate become so ordinary in thinking or predictable in behaving that it leaves nothing undiscovered, putting itself in the position of not being able to stimulate the other—except sexually, perhaps. None of this is to deny that, for good adjustment, most of the interests and interpretations of the mates must be held in common. (3) There is need for protection in the sense of having a certain amount of social freedom, of being able to associate with and enjoy others. This is essentially the same point as was made a few paragraphs above where we talked about jealousy. Here we would add that some couples even find occasional short separations beneficial, in that these give a build-up or rejuvenation to the personalities and a new perspective to the relationship, including a better appreciation of each other.

For best results no monopoly can be made complete, no privacy of the personality entirely violated, no intimacy so extended as to make further discovery impossible. There needs to be a segment in the life of everyone that remains free, private, and unmolested. In this way husbands and wives can stay interesting and challenging to each other.

Another reason for monotony in marriage is that the mates sometimes neglect to keep the relationship growing. Over and above the necessity for personality protection is the need for spontaneity, variety, and constructive effort. Too many let their marriages slip into either a dull routine or a drab duty.

Putting Something into Marriage.—If the mates are to remain happy, they must be able and willing to put something into their relationship that is over and above the ordinary. This, of course, has been implied all the way through our discussion. It is implicit in premarital preparation, getting off to a good start, maintaining a point of view that is both coopera-

tive and determined, settling down realistically, resolving conflict constructively, and in establishing monopoly without permitting the marriage to become monotonous. All these processes are interrelated. Together they constitute good mental
hygiene—first, there is *preparation,* which is given direction by
attitude, which carries over into *effort,* and ends with *adjustment.* The chief reason for "Holy Wedlock's" sometimes evolv-
ing into a kind of "deadlock" is that some mates fail to follow
through with their job.

There are husbands and wives who are essentially parasitic,
showing themselves willing to live off the virtues and efforts
of others but unwilling to make any substantial contribution
of their own. The parasitic wife is the one who sleeps until
noon, neglects her housekeeping, fails to prepare meals, shirks
her responsibility in motherhood, spends most of her time pur-
suing her own pleasure, or in other ways demonstrates her
willingness to sponge upon others. Many such give no more
to marriage than sex. Perhaps it could be said, therefore, that
these have not really married but only sold. The parasitic husband is the one who fails to provide adequately or in line with
his ability, takes little interest in the home, neglects his responsibility for the children, or in other ways shows that he is
thinking only of himself. Many like this give no more to marriage than money, and even that begrudgingly and stintingly.
In line with our analogy, these could be regarded as having not
wed but only bought. Whenever sex or money are used as control devices over the other in substitute for genuine compensation; whenever selfish demands are made, or selfish favors
sought; whenever either member thinks primarily of rights
rather than responsibilities or personal advantage rather than
mutual benefit; whenever these things are done, failure cannot
be far away.

Since marriage is for adults, mates can be considered as
parasitic whenever they lack the maturity needed for doing
their part on a high level of sportsmanship. Childishness in
marriage is demonstrated by such patterns as the following:
sulking, refusing to give in or to admit mistakes, making unreasonable demands of the other, showing excessive or unrea-

soning jealousy, going into temper tantrums, crying just to get one's own way, and feigning illness to obtain sympathy.

Instead of permitting oneself to become a drag upon marriage and to play the role of a parasite, every mate needs to aim at making a constructive contribution. Remaining neutral or indifferent isn't enough; though the negative must be avoided, the positive and active approach to marriage is also necessary if the job is really to be done.

A prime essential is for husband and wife to study each other and then supply the basic personality needs that each finds exposed in the other. According to W. I. Thomas, every person wants or needs four things: recognition, response, security, and new experience. (See discussion in Chapter 3.) Though these are proportioned differently in different people, everyone has all four to some degree, and love's survival depends upon how well each is met in marriage. (1) Married mates like to know that they have the attention and respect of the other; they don't like to feel that they are slighted, taken for granted, or belittled by their mate. Many a wife has made the mistake of not giving sufficient ego support to her husband, only to find him growing frustrated and resentful. Sometimes, too, it happens the other way round or is reciprocal. If there is to be poise and calm within either mate, it must be kept fed by a kind and considerate recognition from the other. (2) Related to this is the universal desire for response in the area of love and sex. Marriage, of all institutions, is best arranged to meet this need. When either of the mates fails to supply his part, the other is left unsatisfied. The most usual errors here are for the husband to be neglectful in the matter of affectional expressions and for the wife to be noncooperative when it comes to sex relations. (3) Feelings of security depend upon a number of factors. Basically, these feelings come from monopoly's being properly established, making for fidelity and mutual trust. This will quite naturally be reinforced if the needs of recognition and response have been adequately met. Husbands and wives also help each other to feel secure by making allowances for special needs of the other—such as the wife's "understanding" when her mate comes home from the office all tired and cross, or the husband's being patient and helpful when his partner is experiencing her "menstrual blues." (4) The need for new experience is best met in marriage when mates maintain a certain amount of "personality protection" and when they keep alive and alert so that there can be something new and challenging before them each day. Life is most interesting (even married life) when it is characterized by a moderate amount of variety and spontaneity. The husbands and wives who are successful in keeping their marriages full of variety and excitement on the inside are the ones who have least to fear from their mates' seeking variety and excitement on the outside.

AREAS FOR SPECIAL CONSIDERATION

We have been dealing with mental hygiene as applied to general processes in marriage adjustment. It has been our position that it is more important to understand why couples quarrel than to know what they quarrel about; that in-law troubles, money squabbles, sexual incompatibilities, and the like are usually only symptoms of deeper difficulty.

Nevertheless the picture would be quite incomplete if it were to be left here. Married mates not only need to adjust but they also need to adjust *to* certain things or *within* specific areas. One of these has to do with the problem of organization and control as between the mates; another pertains to the intimacies of sexual and affectional expression; still another to the couple's interactions with those on the outside, its relations and friends; again there is the matter of spending the family income; also the matter of leisure-time interests and activities; and finally the problem of adjusting to emergencies.

There could be chapters written on each of these. The somewhat brief treatment to be afforded them here is to be explained, not on an assumption of unimportance, but on the realization that we have actually been dealing with marriage adjustment—indirectly, if not directly—all the way through this book. The fact is that little trouble, sexual or otherwise, can develop in marriages that are between mature, well-matched, and mentally hygienic individuals.

But it is also a fact that many mates lack the preparation and specific understandings necessary for best adjustment in the marriage complex.

The Power Structure.—"Who's in charge around here?" This is a question familiar to all, for in dealing with people it is necessary to know how they are organized and where the authority lies. When the statement is made in a spirit of challenge or defiance, it represents an unfortunate struggle for power. When asked humbly, however, it may serve a useful purpose, leading to a clarification of issues and an understanding of the order of things.

Order in marriage requires that the mates come to agree upon their respective roles and interpersonal controls. In an earlier day society pretty well prescribed how husband and wife should behave. This prescription was usually in line with the patriarchal family pattern where the husband was in charge and obedience was a wifely duty. Today the ideal is based more upon equalitarian and democratic lines. This shift has produced a disturbance in traditional marriage roles. Modern mates, being less bound by cultural definitions, are forced more than formerly to define their own roles—which means more maneuvering and potential conflict.

Marital conflict is least likely where husband and wife are able to fit into the roles they have come to expect. Putting this another way, it is deviation from general expectation that so often causes disappointment, resentment, and even open fighting; having anticipated something else, mates tend to rebel against roles that are seemingly forced upon them. This is not to deny the need for spontaneity or little surprises coming within these broad role-expected patterns. (See above.) Modern youth expects marriage to be a partnership arrangement, a fifty-fifty proposition. It is understandable, therefore, that marriages based upon this assumption are the ones that seem to be most successful. Two studies, one by Popenoe [13] and the

---

13 Paul Popenoe, "Can the Family Have Two Heads?", *Sociology and Social Research,* 18:12-17, September, 1933.

other by Burgess and Cottrell,[14] show marital happiness to be associated most highly with the equalitarian pattern, with the husband-dominant type coming next, and the wife-dominant last. While we have no proof, it seems likely that present-day preferences regarding these patterns are in this same sequence (the equalitarian most preferred, the patriarchal next, and the matriarchal least), and that the happiness differentials just noted are to be explained on the basis of deviation from preferred pattern. Here is a hypothesis that needs further testing.

We are not assuming that all persons want the equalitarian arrangement nor that all marriages can be most happy within that framework. There are people who, because of training or need, prefer, and seemingly adapt best to, one of the other patterns. Though in the Western world the patriarchal family has been on the way out, it has not entirely passed; there are a number of people of both sexes who still accept this way and expect to function under it. Furthermore, people differ in their personality needs, some women needing the security and lift given them by a dominant husband. And the same can be said for certain men, men who have been brought up under a dominating mother or who for some other reason may now be in need of a mother substitute whom they can lean upon for strength. For some wives, therefore, the submissive role is the most agreeable, and for some husbands the wife-dominant arrangement is most productive. Trouble comes when either mate is pressured into assuming a role that he does not want or is not prepared to take, such as an emancipated woman married to an overly aggressive or domineering man, or an independent man married to the mothering type of female who may insist on "wearing the pants."

But let us suppose that both mates are emancipated and have come to accept the idea of equality in marriage: is adjustment then assured? No, for there is still the task of making family democracy work. Democracy is based upon some system of organization, never upon anarchy. There will be discussions to

---

[14] Ernest E. Burgess and Leonard S. Cottrell, *Predicting Success or Failure in Marriage* (New York: Prentice-Hall, Inc., 1939).

clarify the issues, and power maneuvers to establish working relationships. There must needs be a division of labor within the marriage, with someone "in charge" of each function; husband and wife need to know where they are and who is responsible for what.

Unity does not require uniformity even in wedlock. The democratic marriage accepts diversity between the mates, then seeks to find a way for forestalling conflict and for reinforcing the complementary relationship. This will include a facility for talking things over, plus a cooperative spirit. Given that much, there will be little reason for the spouses fighting over who is to be boss.

Sex and Affection.—As we have said before, sex can neither be ignored nor given the central role in marriage; it is an important factor, though not all-important. While sexual maladjustment usually accompanies other marital difficulties, and precedes divorce, it is as much an effect of these other troubles as it is a cause. Marriage is composed of a number of factors, all interrelated, so that harmony or disharmony in one segment of the whole tends to induce harmony or disharmony in the others.

Both the Terman and the Burgess and Cottrell studies show the sex factor to be secondary to personality factors, which serve as background for all marital behavior—the sexual included.

Though sexual activity in marriage is perfectly normal and to be expected, there are abnormalities that develop over it which lead to varying degrees of dissatisfaction and which need, therefore, to be corrected. Some mates err by their overemphasis upon the physical side of sex, or their lack of self-discipline and their readiness to exploit. Others err through an ignorance of "the facts of life" or a reluctance to accept them. Mistakes lie along the lines of both overemphasis and underemphasis, and maladjustment ensues whenever the mates fail to agree on what is done.

Sexual intercourse in marriage most usually takes place at the rate of two or three times weekly. There is considerable variation, however, ranging all the way from no marital intercourse to three or four times a day. Generally speaking, frequencies decrease with age, with religious participation, and with education and professionalization.[15]

There are some persons who, because of either nature or conditioning, are much more highly sexed than others. Those who regularly indulge in intercourse several times a day are referred to as *sexual athletes*. Though ordinarily it is the husband who desires sex more frequently than the wife, there are rare cases of women having a desire so great that it can hardly be satisfied; such persons are known as *nymphomaniacs*. Fortunately there are not many of either sex who deviate very far in the direction of extreme desire. Fortunately, also, human beings can be highly adaptable with respect to each other. Mates that can adjust within a normal range of variation, however, may have difficulty making their marriage survive a difference that is too great. The sciences of psychiatry and medicine can give some help to the sexually abnormal person but are still a long way from having "all the answers."

On the opposite end from these excesses is the lack of adequate sexual desire, capacity, or response. In the female, this condition is known as *frigidity;* in the male, as *impotence*. Frigidity precludes neither ovulation (which takes place automatically about midway in the menstrual cycle) nor intercourse (which, with the female, does not require sexual excitement); but it does preclude orgasm. Impotence is the inability of the male to maintain sufficient erection for the carrying out of his part of the sex act, and it precludes intercourse, ejaculation, and orgasm (since, in the male, these three processes are somewhat simultaneous). In both instances, someone is inadequate sexually; which may lead to frustrated desire, plus a strained relationship, due to an inability to completely satisfy the other.

The causes of sexual inadequacy are many. Generally speaking, it can be said that the condition results more from social and psychological factors than from physical or organic disturbances. There are instances of this latter, however, where

---

[15] Alfred C. Kinsey and others, *Sexual Behavior in the Human Male* (Philadelphia: W. B. Saunders Co., 1948), pp. 569-71 and *passim*.

surgery, hormone treatment, and the like have helped to remove the trouble. But in the majority of cases, it is simply that sex education has been faulty or that the conditions of marriage are not the best; sex is psychological as much—perhaps even more—than it is physiological.

Among the sociopsychological factors back of frigidity and impotence are the following: (1) Training and experience that have conditioned one to the feeling that sex is something evil, nasty, and to be feared. This harks back to childhood and courtship experiences, but it may also result from, or be accentuated by, a faulty procedure in marriage. Much depends upon how one is first introduced to sex and first initiated into the act of intercourse. Much also depends on how the marriage is carried through, for such things as uncleanliness, and inconsiderate or offensive actions, can bring disgust and ruin the relationship later on. (2) Fixation on another level of response, such as with the autoerotic person, the homosexual, and the girl who has become so habituated to necking or petting that she is satisfied with that only and has difficulty shifting her response to the act of intercourse when she marries. The inhibitions that society sets up to insure premarital chastity are sometimes so strong (as well as negative) and continue so long that they "jell" in the personality, interfering with later adjustment. (3) Poor health, lack of vitality, or actual physical discomfort experienced during intercourse. Malnutrition is known to diminish sexual vigor. Worry and fatigue often do the same thing. Pain occasionally accompanies intercourse (especially where there is ill health or has been a lack of emotional preparation) and can make the experience distasteful. Sexual activity diminishes with age. (4) Fear over one or more of the possible consequences, such as being discovered (especially significant in premarital intercourse), getting pregnant, contracting disease, or experiencing pain. (5) Disagreements in other fields of interaction (such as over money or in-laws) which create tensions and make for noncooperation in sexual matters. (6) Letting the relationship become commonplace or monotonous, without love, and void of variety. (7) Harboring thoughts of inferiority or defeat. Impotence, especially, is frequently but a reflection of feelings of general personality inadequacy.

Kinsey estimates that around 30 per cent of all females are "more or less sexually unresponsive." [16] Terman's study revealed essentially the same thing for wives, there being about one third who replied that they either "never" or only "sometimes" experienced orgasm in intercourse.[17] Masculine impotence does not represent nearly so large a percentage,[18] but it is likely that it is just as great a problem when it does exist.

Interestingly enough, Terman found significantly higher happiness scores among wives who said they "usually" or "always" experienced orgasm, and in marriages where the sexual desires of husband and wife were pretty much alike.[19] Apparently, frigidity and dissimilarity of desire work against marital harmony.

Though the roots of frigidity and impotence frequently reach back into the experiences of premarriage, there is much that husband and wife can do to forestall or overcome the problem. If there is already an inadequacy, they can strive for a reconditioning, using professional help when necessary, and engaging in mutual assistance. They can be careful to see that conditions surrounding the act are kept harmonious, aesthetic, and restful. They can study the needs and reactions of each other and adapt to them. Husbands can be more considerate and romantic, for example, and wives can come to be more interested and active than they sometimes are in the physical act. Gone are the days when it was thought normal for husbands to satisfy themselves selfishly and at will, and for wives to be merely dutiful though devoid of desire. Sex is a mutual experience and to make it most meaningful there must be mutual participation and responsibility.

Mutuality in sex is more a matter of attitude than it is technique. While we would not belittle the value of knowledge and skill as applied to intercourse, it seems clear that these alone are not enough. It is true that the spouses need to understand

[16] *Ibid.*, p. 209.
[17] Terman, *op. cit.*, pp. 300-1.
[18] Kinsey, *op. cit.*, pp. 209, 236-38, and *passim.*
[19] Terman, *loc. cit.*

themselves and each other sexually, and to know "the score," so to speak, with reference to precoitus preparation, mutual stimulation, and the like. But to apply the "art of love" when love is absent is to dissipate and exploit.

Affection and sex are so much a part of each other in a happy marriage that to speak of them as separate entities does not make sense. Not all marriages are happy, of course, one reason being that they fail to let these two love components reinforce each other. A very common mistake, as we have said, is to "settle too far down," letting the marriage relationship become monotonous, self-centered, and without an adequate or continual demonstration of affection. Adjustment requires that the mates not only learn how to enjoy each other sexually but that they also find a way to keep love alive—and growing.

Of Kith and Kin.—People who marry face the immediate task of reorganizing certain group relationships. Up until this time each of the mates has had his own circle of friends and set of relatives. Now each, of necessity, neglects some of the older acquaintances, takes on others, jointly chosen, and inherits a whole new list of in-laws. In addition to living within its own dimensions, therefore, or to bringing about an internal adjustment, every married pair has the job of getting along with the world on the outside.

It has been argued earlier that marriage is likely to fail whenever either mate shows an unwillingness to accept the monopoly pattern. While certain rights are acquired through marriage, others must be relinquished. One to be given up is the freedom of close and somewhat constant association with others—among both sexes but with members of the opposite sex especially. It stands to reason that if pair unity is to increase, mate association will need to become more or less exclusive. There are two reasons for this. In the first place disloyalty produces ego injury, suspicion, and conflict within the marital situation. In the second place, love needs to be fed in order to survive, which, for one thing, means spending time together, hence less time with others.

This must not be taken as an argument for complete exclusiveness and a consequent lack of sociability. There is danger in that extreme as well as in the other. Most people have observed, and been annoyed by, couples who were so wrapped up in themselves that they become ridiculous in conduct and oblivious to everything around them. Such behavior, over a period of time, can lose the couple friends and isolate it from society.

Nor should our monopoly argument be taken to mean that all contact with the outside world be on a joint basis. If the personalities are to keep growing, and the marriage kept from becoming monotonous, there will need be reserved for each mate a certain personal or private area of interests, friendships, and activities. (See pages 324-25.)

But since solidarity in marriage depends upon association, it is well that the mates very early build up a new circle of friends common to both. There will be occasions, naturally, when the husband will want to be "out with the boys" or the wife will want to spend time at her club. Unless excessive or deceptive, such occasions need cause no difficulty; by giving one a "lift" they can even add to the relationship. In addition, though, there need be a number of mutual friends and joint activities.

In-law troubles are a rather common source of marital tension, especially during the early years following the wedding. Marriage means a reshuffling of family patterns which takes time and requires a certain amount of intelligence and effort on the part of both parents and children. Parents have the problem of letting the child go after years of care and supervision over it. Married children have the problem of establishing a new family relationship without completely severing the old one. All face the task of getting acquainted with the in-laws and of learning how to enjoy each other in a constructive manner.

Conflict over in-laws usually means that one of the mates feels slighted, feels that he or she must compete for the respect and love of the partner. Landis reports criticisms of the following type as being common: "She takes her mother's advice, no matter how bad it is"; "He embarrasses me in front of them";

"—doesn't show any affection when the in-laws are around." [20]
Koos substantiates the point with the following case picture:

I think we'd get along better if it wasn't for her family. But they
don't want to let her get away from them, and she's always running
home to them instead of coming to me. Why, they even knew she was
with child before I did. Then she thinks I am unfair when I get mad
about it. I think she should have gotten rid of them when she married
me—I mean, she should have become part of our family, not stayed
with her own.[21]

In-law friction is more typically a feminine than a masculine
pattern.[22] It is the mothers who have had most to do with the
rearing of children and who therefore feel the greatest loss at
their departure; having cared for these children from infancy
in a close and intimate way, they now find it more difficult to
let go. Fathers, in contrast, are less closely concerned with
child-rearing in the first place, and are usually more busy with
other things after the children are married; hence their lesser
tendency to interfere. Furthermore, there is still the patriarchal
inclination to view a daughter-in-law as an addition to the
family, while a son-in-law remains with another family of his
own. The wife, therefore, frequently comes into direct competition with her mother-in-law over the care of her husband.
Sometimes trouble is started by the mother's feeling that her
son is being neglected or of wanting to retain more of his love
and attention than the wife is willing to share. Sometimes it is
the wife who is selfish. Occasionally the husband will aggravate the situation by making an unfavorable comparison between the way his wife does something and how his mother
used to do it. Though there are many patterns of in-law conflict, the one involving a wife and her mother-in-law is probably the most common.

There are several ways in which parents may add to the
marital maladjustments of their children. (1) One of these
is to reject the child-in-law, feeling that he or she isn't good

20 Judson T. Landis and Mary G. Landis, *Building a Successful Marriage*
(New York: Prentice-Hall, Inc., 1948), pp. 296-97.
21 Earl L. Koos, *Families in Trouble* (New York: King's Crown Press,
1946), p. 44.
22 Landis, *op. cit.,* pp. 288-89.

enough for their child and that the marriage should never have occurred in the first place. This leads to fault-finding and interference. As a result, the mate who is being picked on becomes annoyed and resentful, while the other one experiences split loyalties between long-time affection for the family and the new-found love for the marriage partner. (2) Another, but closely related pattern, is where parents remain overattached and emotionally dependent upon the married child, refusing to let go; they don't exactly reject the new child-in-law, but they hold on to their own child so strongly that it amounts to about the same thing. Feeling this way, parents sometimes give advice when it isn't wanted or in other ways try to claim a large share in the new relationship. Marital unity is made difficult whenever in-laws attempt to compete for the attention or affection of the mates. (3) Sometimes the trouble comes more from neglect and favoritism than from interference. Parents who treat their married children unequally invite rivalry and bickering among these children. This, in turn, tends to create tensions and conflicts within the homes. There frequently comes a disruption of family harmony over inheritance and property settlement following the death of a parent. Much of this could be avoided if parents would make out their wills in time and would exert every effort to have them just and equable.

But in-law difficulties are seldom one-sided; children, too, have a responsibility. (1) A common error is for married persons to remain too closely attached to their parents, turning to them more than to the mate, running "home" whenever anything goes wrong. This is one mark of emotional immaturity. Marital solidarity cannot proceed very far until husband and wife have first weaned themselves, psychologically, from old home ties. (2) Sometimes married children seem quite selfish and ungrateful in their behavior toward parents and in-laws. After all, parents have made an investment in their children and have a right to be concerned over how this investment is turning out. It doesn't hurt children to sacrifice a little, if necessary, as repayment for some of the parental sacrifices made in their behalf. (3) Occasionally married children exploit their parents in one way or another—draining them of resources, overusing them for family services, such as baby-tending.

In-law friction is accentuated by the necessity, which some couples face, of living with the parents of one or the other. This breaks down needed privacy and brings into focus, at close range, the differing systems and points of view of the two generations. The result is frequently a condition of misunderstanding, irritation, tension, and even open conflict.

It is well to remember, however, that all in-laws are not meddlers and that genuine interest on the part of parents is not interference. There are many parents whose experience and wisdom can contribute much to the marriage of their children if given a chance. Many family groups are successful in establishing enjoyable and mutually beneficial relationships between the generations. But this takes tact rather than attack, and it requires good judgment and emotional maturity on both sides.

Money Matters.—It isn't the amount of money coming in that determines how happy a family shall be, so much as the attitudes and arrangements over this income—regardless of the amount. Some of the wealthiest of families fail, while some of the poorest succeed.

It would be a mistake, nevertheless, to assume that level of living has nothing to do with marital adjustment. (See pages 48-52.) Love may partially compensate for poverty, but despite any effect love may have in alleviating the strain there is evidence that long-continued worry over money matters is not conducive to happiness in the home. Slum housing, ill health, and other unfortunate products of economic deprivation usually operate to undermine family stability. Insufficient income, along with feelings of insecurity which often accompany a low economic status, set up psychological tensions in the minds of family members—tensions which make them irritable and quick tempered, tensions which result in conflict. To be favorable for family adjustment, income needs to be: steady and secure; reasonably adequate from the standpoint of elementary human needs; and not too far below the expectations or desires of the couple. Unless or until society finds a way of providing the minimum essentials to all, many marriages will remain handicapped from their beginning.

There are ways in which the family income can be stretched to good advantage. One approach is through consumer education. Unwise spending means that the money will not go as far as it could. By studying quality connected with different brand names, patronizing only reliable dealers, comparing prices, watching for sales, avoiding the overuse of credit, staying within one's means, and economizing in other ways, a husband or a wife can in effect increase the family income.

Home production is another approach to the problem of economic inadequacy. Though society has been moving away from family self-sufficiency and toward a money economy, there are many things family members still can do to save expenses—gardens can be grown, fruits and vegetables can be canned, clothing can be made and repaired, the kitchen can be painted, the plumbing can sometimes be fixed. Generally speaking, the larger the family the more profitable is production within the home.

Family income is often increased by reason of the wife's working. Where the mates can agree on this arrangement, and where it can be carried on without the neglect of children, this method has merit—as a temporary expedient especially. But the preconditions which were named are not always met; then there is likely to be trouble. Sometimes, too, the expenses incident to the wife's job are so high (housekeeper, baby-tender, carfare, more clothes, meals out, etc.) that the added income she brings to the family turns out to be negligible. From the standpoint of successful marriage there is some evidence that husbands are made more happy by the fact of the wife's working.[23]

Disagreements over control of the family purse are among the most common. There are many methods used for handling money within the family, chief of which are the following: (1) The older, patriarchal system of a "dole" still hangs on. Under it, the husband handles all of the money and gives it out to

---

[23] Cf. Harvey J. Locke and Muriel Mackeprang, "Marital Adjustment and the Employed Wife," *American Journal of Sociology*, 54:536-38, May, 1949.

family members as he sees fit. The assumption is that the income is the husband's, since he earns it. Such a claim is at variance with the facts, however, for the wife who takes care of the home makes an economic contribution to the marriage in this way which is just as real as that of the husband, though she receives no salary. With marriage, personal income becomes family income. Failure to recognize this does injustice to the wife, and unless she has been brought up to expect and accept such a system there will be resentments and possible conflict over it. (2) The wife-allowance system, where she receives a certain fixed amount each month for her personal needs, has more to be said in its favor. It recognizes the wife's contribution to the home and allows her the dignity of a little freedom and responsibility in money matters. Nevertheless it sometimes leads to misunderstanding and conflict; the wife may scrimp on the food she buys in order to have more in her personal share, for example, or the husband may be too stingy in the allowance, or watch the wife too closely in the spending, or accuse her of poor management. (3) There is the opposite but less common system of husband-allowances which works rather well in some marriages. There are instances of where the wife is the superior manager of the two and where the husband prefers to turn the check over to her for supervision. In cases of this kind, such an arrangement is frequently the most satisfactory. (4) The system of a joint bank account, where husband and wife have equal access to the income, is becoming more popular among the young people of today. Of all arrangements, this one is the most democratic, the most compatible with the idea of equality. But it requires mature and responsible individuals to make it work—individuals who know how to buy wisely, who will not cheat on each other, and who take time together to plan how their money shall be spent. We are not suggesting that a joint bank account is preferable in all cases. More important than the particular system followed is agreement between husband and wife on that system, whatever it is.

Budgeting and record-keeping are essential to good home management. Properly used, they can help stretch the family income and bring greater unity between the mates. Many marital tensions derive from a lack of planning of the family finances and the misunderstandings and deprivations which result. Financial planning is as important in marital relationships as in the business world, though it may not require the same detail and precision. Some couples prefer a rather informal type of budgeting procedure, where the plan is laid out in broad categories and no attempt is made at accurate accounting. If the income is fairly stable and the persons responsible, this may be enough. Others desire or need a much more detailed procedure, where budget plans are made long in advance and accurate records are kept of expenditures. The particular method used and degree of precision sought may well vary from couple to couple, that system being regarded as best which works best. Nevertheless all couples need to plan their finances and to do it cooperatively and systematically, though with enough flexibility to allow for emergencies and consequent replanning when necessary. Long-range family planning requires that emergencies will be anticipated and prepared for insofar as possible by means of savings, insurance, and annuities.

Leisure-Time Activities.—Time budgeting is about as important in modern marriage as is financial planning. Not always have family members enjoyed the leisure that they know today. There was a time, not so long ago, when recreational activities were largely reserved for the privileged upper classes and the common man was required to toil from dawn until dusk. Now every class is a leisure class, in a sense. Since leisure-time activities occupy a larger proportion of the married couple's time today than formerly, there is need to know how these relate to family adjustment.

Without planning, time is often dissipated. The fact of leisure does not insure that it will be used to good advantage. Couples with too much time on their hands sometimes get bored with each other and become irritable. Sometimes, too, they turn to decreative activities of one type or another—gambling, intoxication, sexual infidelity, and the like—which can lead to further tensions or trouble between them. Leisure time is a potential asset, but unless utilized constructively it may become a liability.

Research has demonstrated that happily married mates share numerous outside interests and activities together, whereas those who are unhappy do not. Whether certain husbands and wives are unhappy because they do not go out together, or they do not go out together because they are unhappy, one cannot be too sure—possibly some of both, it being a vicious circle. In any event there is little question but that marital adjustment requires a large amount of joint participation.

It frequently happens that husband and wife are not together in their recreational and cultural interests, that they have different tastes, want to do different things. A little of this can be expected, for no couple is ever perfectly matched. If the differences are great, however, and chronic, they can be a source of constant friction. Sometimes the trouble comes from a difference in training and temperament. While this could have been discovered during the testings of courtship, there is much that married individuals can do to adjust to the situation once it is recognized; they can each learn new tastes and they can show themselves mature enough to compromise. At other times disagreements over leisure-time activities develop more from circumstances than from basic differences in personality. An example of this would be the husband who comes home tired from work and wants to curl up by the fireside with a book, while his wife, who has been at home and alone all day, wants to go out for the evening and participate in some social affair. Adjustment is a matter of coming to understand each other's needs and of being willing to give in or cooperate for the sake of harmony. Yielding must not remain one-sided, however, and it needs to be in the spirit of good sportsmanship rather than the grumbling attitude that goes with a feeling of martyrdom.

In an earlier chapter we observed how the family has been losing many of its original functions, including the recreational. Seemingly, many people have come to feel that to have a good time they must go out of the home and spend money.

There is need for a return to the idea of inexpensive family fun. Husband and wife can read to each other; sing songs together; play games; hold contests; take care of a garden; keep pets; develop handicraft or hobby interests. When the children are old enough they too can enter into the fun. Though technology has taken some things out of the home, it has put others in. The radio, home movies, and now television make it possible for family members to enjoy the best in entertainment and cultural development right within their own home. People who play together adjust more easily. Home recreation contributes to family solidarity.

"In Sickness and in Health."—Wedding ceremonies frequently contain such phrases as "for better or for worse," and "in sickness and in health." These are to impress the couple with the seriousness of what they are undertaking, with the fact that marriage may bring certain disappointments and crises which they must be willing to meet. One of these is ill-health.

Sickness may be viewed either as a cause or as a result of family trouble. Considered as a cause, we can note the incapacities to perform one's work and the mental frustrations and strains that frequently develop because of it. Continued illness on the part of a breadwinner may mean economic insecurity or even poverty, accompanied by worry, humiliation, and actual physical suffering. On the side of the housewife it may mean an unkept house, unprepared meals, and other unavoidable neglects that put extra burdens upon remaining members of the family. Lingering illness is often difficult even when there is no problem of income or housekeeping, for there will be worries and nervous tensions. In circumstances like this, love sometimes gives way and sympathy degenerates into irritability.

Chronic illness quite naturally requires some rather fundamental adjustments on the part of other family members. They must become accustomed to seeing their loved one suffer. They must change their habit patterns in the home, being more quiet perhaps, waiting on the loved one, and performing tasks that were formerly his or hers. They must learn to show sympathy without overdoing it or without offending, for some individuals resent an overshow of affection and care when they are powerless to reciprocate. And, too, they must avoid spoiling the ailing one, making him dependent, demanding, and expectant of favors. Above all, they must be patient and cheerful; yielding to irritation does not make for happiness in the home.

Considered as a result or symptom of family disorganization, we can note that illness sometimes develops when the affairs of the family become unstable and disturbed. Mental health requires a settled mind, which is dependent upon compatible group relationships. Since marriage involves men and women in the most intimate of interactional patterns, disharmony there can make for disorganization within the personalities involved. Furthermore, many physical ailments are mental in origin. Regrets over the past; worries, fears, and frustrations within the marriage; open quarreling and conflict; these things clog up the emotions and result in an inefficient functioning of the mental and physical systems.

In short, individual health and family harmony are interrelated; where right, these tend to reinforce each other, but where greatly wrong they are likely to pull each other downward in the pattern of a vicious circle.

Problems and Projects

1. Which do you think is the more important to successful marriage, similarity or adaptability? Why?
2. Is it normal for a mate to start wondering whether or not he has married the right person? If and when this happens, what should he or she do? Discuss.
3. Does the necessity for settling down in marriage mean that the couple necessarily becomes less in love? Or less happy? Discuss.
4. Why does marriage mean disillusionment for some? Discuss ways in which this can be avoided.
5. How can married couples best keep their love alive and avoid "settling too far down"? Make some practical suggestions.

6. What do you think of married mates who belittle each other in public? How would you react if this were done to you? Give reasons.

7. Which is preferable: to use the home as a place to "let off steam" for the sake of mental health or to keep one's conflict to oneself for the sake of marital harmony? Give your reasons.

8. Do you agree with the Duvall and Hill distinction between productive and destructive quarreling? Why or why not? Cite examples known to you of how married persons have found ways of constructively adjusting their differences.

9. What line of action would you suggest for the wife who discovers that her husband is in love with his secretary?

10. How much importance should married couples place upon the remembrance of anniversaries? Upon the daily kiss before separating for work? Upon other traditional demonstrations of affection? Make suggestions.

11. How friendly or intimate do you think a married person should be permitted to be with others of the opposite sex without his (or her) mate's objecting or becoming jealous? List things that you consider permissible. Objectionable. Discuss.

12. To those given in the text, add other behavior patterns of the parasitic wife and the parasitic husband which you may have observed.

13. Would you prefer that your marriage be patriarchal, matriarchal, or equalitarian? Give your reasons.

14. Make a list of major tasks involved in managing a home and family. Which of these do you think should be the responsibility of the wife and which of the husband? Discuss.

15. Research has been cited to show that the sex factor in marriage is secondary in importance to personality factors of husband and wife. Why do you think this is so? Discuss ways in which mature mates might prevent conflicts growing out of differences in sexual desire.

16. From the families you know, consider those in which in-law relationships are most harmonious. List the factors that you think are responsible.

17. Discuss ways of avoiding property squabbles among relatives after the death of a parent or other loved one.

18. If both husband and wife are working, should they then be expected to share household tasks equally? Make suggestions for a "division of labor" that would fit circumstances such as this.

19. Read other sources dealing with the family budget and make some practical suggestions.

20. From families you know, describe patterns of home recreation. What effects, if any, have these activities had upon family unity? Discuss.

SELECTED READINGS

BABER, RAY E. *Marriage and the Family*. New York: McGraw-Hill Book Co., 1939. Chaps. viii, ix, "The Husband-Wife Relationships."

BACAL, JACQUES W., and SLOANE, LOUISE. *ABC of Divorce*. New York: E. P. Dutton & Co., 1947.

BECKER, HOWARD, and HILL, REUBEN (eds.). *Family, Marriage, and Parenthood*. Boston: D. C. Heath & Co., 1948. Part III, "Marriage Interaction"; Part V, "Family Crises and Ways of Meeting Them."

BIGELOW, HOWARD. *Family Finance*. Philadelphia: J. B. Lippincott & Co., 1936.

BUTTERFIELD, OLIVER M. *Sex Life in Marriage*. New York: Emerson Books, Inc., 1937.

DUVALL, EVELYN MILLIS. *Building Your Marriage*. New York: Public Affairs Committee, 1946.

———, and HILL, REUBEN. *When You Marry*. Boston: D. C. Heath & Co., 1945. Part II, "What It Means to be Married."

EXNER, M. J. *The Sexual Side of Marriage*. New York: W. W. Norton Co., 1932.

FISHBEIN, MORRIS, and BURGESS, ERNEST W. (eds.). *Successful Marriage*. New York: Doubleday & Co., 1947. Part II, "The Marriage."

GROVES, ERNEST R., and others. *Sex Fulfillment in Marriage*. New York: Emerson Books, Inc., 1943.

HARPER, ROBERT A. *Marriage*. New York: Appleton-Century-Crofts, Inc., 1949. Part III, "Marital Adjustment."

HIMES, NORMAN E. *Your Marriage: A Guide to Happiness*. New York: Farrar & Rinehart, Inc., 1940. Part B, "Now That You're Married."

LANDIS, JUDSON T., and LANDIS, MARY G. *Building a Successful Marriage*. New York: Prentice-Hall, Inc., 1948. Chaps. x, "Achieving Adjustment in Marriage"; xi, "Sex Adjustment in Marriage"; xii, "In-laws and Marriage Adjustment"; xiii, "Religious Attitudes and Family Life"; xiv, "Finances and Adjustment in Marriage"; xv, "Getting Your Money's Worth"; xvi, "Buying Life Insurance."

LEVY, JOHN, and MUNROE, RUTH. *The Happy Family*. New York: Alfred A. Knopf, Inc., 1938.

MAGOUN, F. ALEXANDER. *Love and Marriage*. New York: Harper & Bros., 1948. Chaps. ix, "The Sex Relation"; x, "Emotional Adjustment."

MARIANO, JOHN H. *Shall I Get a Divorce—And How?* New York: Council of Marriage Relations, 1946.

STONE, HANNAH M., and STONE, ABRAHAM. *A Marriage Manual.* New York: Simon & Schuster, Inc., 1935.

VAN DE VELDE, T. H. *Ideal Marriage: Its Physiology and Technique.* New York: Random House, 1943.

WALLER, WILLARD. *The Family: A Dynamic Interpretation.* New York: Dryden Press, 1938. Part III, "Marriage Interaction."

Chapter 11

PARENTHOOD

Normally, every family runs through a cycle—commencing with marriage, continuing through various stages of parenthood, and ending with the death of the mates. Families have both beginnings and ends, and within that range, periods of both expansion and contraction. The 1948 National Conference on Family Life considered seven stages: early marriage and the expectant family; the child-bearing family; the preschool family; the school-age family; the family with teen-agers; the family as a launching center; and the family in later years.[1] This scheme, though recognizing prechild and postchild periods within the cycle, gives major attention to parenthood.

Glick, with the use of census data, makes some interesting comparisons between the family cycle of today and that of a half century ago. Here is his table.[2]

MEDIAN AGE OF HUSBAND AND WIFE AT EACH STAGE OF THE FAMILY CYCLE, FOR THE UNITED STATES: 1940 AND 1890

Stage of the Family Cycle	Median Age of Husband		Median Age of Wife	
	1940	1890	1940	1890
A. First marriage....................	24.3	26.1	21.6	22.0
B. Birth of first child...............	25.3	27.1	22.6	23.0
C. Birth of last child................	29.9	36.0	27.2	31.9
D. Marriage of first child............	48.3	51.1	45.6	47.0
E. Marriage of last child............	52.8	59.4	50.1	55.3
F. Death of husband or wife.........	63.6	57.4	60.9	53.3
G. { Death of husband if last........	69.7	66.4	....	....
{ Death of wife if last............	....	....	73.5	67.7

[1] Drawn from the working papers of the Conference.
[2] Paul C. Glick, "The Family Cycle," *American Sociological Review*, 12:164-74, April, 1947. Table taken from p. 165.

At least two significant observations can be made: (1) Families have longer life spans now than formerly, due both to a lowering of age at marriage and a lengthening expectation of life. At the present time both husband and wife can expect to stay alive for a married period of approximately 39 years, after which, if the husband survives, it will be for another period of 6 years, and if the wife survives, it will be for an added period of 13 years. The average duration of the cycle is some five or ten years longer than it was a half century ago. (2) There has been a shift in time allotments within the cycle, away from the child-centered and toward the "empty nest." The prechild period, which is of relatively short duration anyway (one year), has remained about the same. It is the period of parenthood, the time from the birth of the first child to the marriage of the last one, which has taken the drop. In 1890 the average mother was given her first child at the age of 23, continued bearing children for another 9 years (5.4 children in all), and had children living within the home for a little more than 32 years of her married span. In that day at least one of the parents was known to die in over half the families before the last child left home. But in 1940 the average mother gave birth to her first child when she was approximately 22½, continued in her childbearing for only another 4½ years (3.1 children in all), and had children still at home for only 27½ years of her married span. It will be noted that parenthood still claims the major portion of the family cycle, but less than formerly. Mates now survive jointly for nearly 11 years after their last child has married, or about one fourth of their total time together.

Family Size

Students of population differentiate between fecundity, which is the potential or possible number of children a couple may have, and fertility, which is the actual birth rate. In all but rare instances fecundity is greater than fertility or in other words most people can have more children than they actually have. Biologists estimate that human fecundity may be as high as fifteen or twenty children per average woman, not counting multiple births.[3] That very few modern families are this large should be obvious to all. Why the discrepancy?

Reasons are several, chief of which are these: (1) the delaying of marriage beyond the time of reproductive maturity; (2) the conscious birth control within marriage; and (3) the dissolving of marriage, by separation, divorce, or death, before the reproductive period has passed.

Trends and Comparisons.—Fertility was formerly closer to fecundity than it is now. Wilfully, people are having smaller families. The number of childless marriages has been increasing. So also has the number of one- and two-child families. Large families, on the other hand, are becoming more rare. There are still a few families of a dozen or more children, but the proportion of such has greatly declined. They are such a curiosity today that stories concerning them are frequently written up in the newspapers.

Statistics on declining fertility are rather convincing. The crude birth rate (number of births per 1,000 population) for the United States was 37.0 in 1875, 29.8 in 1900, 23.7 in 1920, and 17.9 in 1940. In a little over a half century it was cut in half. The 1930 census, for the first time in our national history, found fewer children under five than in the age group five through nine. The 1940 picture was the same.

But there has been a recent reversal of this long-time downward trend in the birth rate. With World War II came a new impetus to marry and reproduce. From record lows in the middle thirties, the birth rate started upward again; by 1943 it had reached a peak higher than anything since the late twenties; slipping a little for a couple of years, it again started to climb, and by 1947 had reached a point higher than it had been at any other time in the last quarter of a century. There have been slight drops since then, but nothing to take it back anywhere near the prewar levels. If the prewar trends in birth rate had continued, there would be several million fewer children in the nation than there are now and the population would have

---

[3] Paul H. Landis, *Population Problems* (New York: American Book Co., 1948), p. 52.

reached a stationary point and started to decrease somewhere about 1980. As it is, we shall probably have an increasing population for some time—it is hazardous to predict for just how long. There is considerable speculation as to whether the birth rate will remain high or return to its previous level, once the effects of the war have been dissipated. Does this recent increase in reproductive activity mean that motherhood is back in style, or does it merely reflect different social and economic conditions incident to the war? It is too early to tell. A disproportionately high percentage of first births among the total in recent years would seem to indicate that the phenomenon might be temporary (the high rate being explained largely by the fact that more families are being started, rather than by the claim that families are getting larger). On the other hand, families completed during the forties were a little larger than in the decade earlier, and there is some evidence that the present wartime generation tends to want more children per family than did their immediate predecessors.[4]

Population replacement requires that married couples, who can, must average between two and three children each. Prewar fertility (as measured by net reproduction rates) was not sufficient to replace the population in the generation to come. Though the postwar situation is somewhat different, there are still groups whose birth rates remain too low for self-replacement.

Certain group differentials in fertility are revealed through a study of Indianapolis marriages made a few years ago. Of the 6,551 native-white couples who had completed their families (were through with childbearing), 18.8 per cent were found to be childless, 23.2 per cent had one child, 23.6 per cent two children, 14.7 per cent three children, 8.1 per cent four children, and only 11.6 per cent five or more children. Thus nearly two thirds fell below average requirements for replacement in the population. In general, Catholics had the largest families and the smallest proportion of childlessness, with Jewish and

---

[4] Cf. T. J. Woofter, "Factors Sustaining the Birth Rate," *American Sociological Review,* 14:357-66, June, 1949. Various factors which sustain the birth rate are analyzed against those which tend to depress it, with the conclusion that the sustaining factors are at least temporarily in power.

mixed unions at the other extreme. In general also, fertility was highest among the poor and the uneducated, with Catholic differentials along these lines being less pronounced than in other groups.[5]

In a study of selected Wisconsin farmers the writer found that nearly two thirds of the parents would plan for smaller families if they could start over again today, and that the families would be smaller by about one third (an average of 5.9 children born to present families as compared with 4.1 desired by the parents if they could start over again). Group comparisons gave indication of larger families among the poor than among the more well-to-do, among the Catholics than the Lutherans, and among those of German descent than of Scandinavian descent. Differences by religion and nationality were greater on the low-income levels; with advancement in economic status came a lowering in the number of children desired and a lessening in the influence of other factors. In general, the larger the family the greater was the percentage by which the desired family would be smaller and the greater the percentage of parents who desired smaller families. Parents with a disproportionately large number of children still wanted families that would be larger than average, but larger by a smaller margin than was then true. Thus there is evidence of a convergence in desire regarding family size.[6]

Yearly comparisons of fertility according to level of education are made by the Population Reference Bureau. It finds that college graduates, as a group, are not having enough children to replace themselves. Figures for the 1924 graduating class are typical of recent reports. By 1949 members of this class would presumably have completed their families. At that

[5] P. K. Whelpton and Clyde V. Kiser, *Social and Psychological Factors Affecting Fertility* (New York: Milbank Memorial Fund, 1946), Vol. 1, pp. 63-64, 92-94, and *passim*.

[6] George W. Hill and Harold T. Christensen, "Some Factors in Family Fertility Among Selected Wisconsin Farmers," *American Sociological Review*, 7:498-504, August, 1942.

Cf. also, Harold T. Christensen, "Mormon Fertility: A Survey of Student Opinion," *American Journal of Sociology*, 53:270-75, January, 1948. Among other things, this study shows children wanting slightly smaller families than the families they came from, with the difference increasing in direct proportion to the size of the parental family.

time, male members of the class averaged 1.77 and female members only 1.26 children. The latter figure is to be compared with an average of 2.45 children for noncollege women of the same age group, and 4.33 children for women of the same age group who had had no more than four years of schooling. Though war and postwar percentage increases in the birth rate have been higher among college graduates than with the rest of the population, fertility within this group is still substantially lower than among groups having less education and is still below replacement requirements. The Bureau warns that the future generation is coming chiefly from those most likely to have both hereditary and environmental handicaps.

Major fertility differentials are as follows: (1) The rich have significantly smaller families than do the poor; those who can most afford children have the fewest, and vice versa. Relief families are generally larger than others and they continue to reproduce at more rapid rates. (2) There exists an inverse relationship between educational attainment and fertility, or, in other words, the higher the schooling the smaller the family. College graduates are not reproducing at a fast enough rate to replace themselves. (3) Catholics and Mormons [7] show highest birth rates among the religious groups. (4) Colored families are generally larger than the white, and foreign-born than native-born. (5) Occupational comparisons usually show farm laborers with the highest birth rate, followed by farm renters, farm owners, unskilled laborers, skilled workers, business and clerical classes, and professional people, in that order. (6) Rural-urban comparisons demonstrate that the country is the seedbed of America. As a matter of fact, urban fertility is so low that most of our large cities would decline in population and eventually die out were they not fed by migration from the rural areas. (7) Regionally considered, the Southern States stand out with the highest fertility, and the Far West with the lowest.

Defining the "Ideal."—The question of optimum reproduction may be considered broadly from the standpoint of society,

---

[7] For a picture of Mormon fertility, cf. Christensen, *loc. cit.*

and then more narrowly from the standpoint of family inter-action and personality needs. In the first, our concern is with social welfare as affected by the size and growth of population; in the second, it is with the relationship between number of children and amount of family satisfaction.

There is no general agreement as to what is an optimum size for any given population. So much depends upon the cri-teria used, which in turn depend upon the culture and objectives of the particular society in question. If the goal is war and conquest, for example, as it was recently with Germany and Japan, then a rapidly expanding population is needed to pro-vide the manpower. From the military point of view, any na-tion with a low birth rate is weak, either actually or poten-tially. If, on the other hand, the goal is a maximum utilization of economic resources for the benefit of all in a peacetime economy, then the highest birth rate may not necessarily mean the greatest good.

One thing that students of this problem do agree on is that population growth cannot be left uncontrolled. Under ideal conditions it is possible for a population to double itself in about twenty-five years. This would mean that if resources were adequate, the United States *could have* three hundred million people living within its borders by 1975, six hundred million by the year 2000, one billion two hundred million by 2025, and two billion four hundred million (as many as are in the entire world at the present time) by 2050, just a century away—and all of this without immigration. It is unrealistic to believe that any such growth will happen, or even could happen, because of limitations in food and other resources.

Man's welfare is to a considerable extent dependent upon the relationship between his numbers and the resources avail-able. It is this 'man-land ratio" which frequently spells the difference between poverty, malnutrition, and a high death rate on the one hand, and a respectable level of living on the other. When there are too many people for the resources available, hu-man suffering is inevitable. We call this "population pressure." One way of relieving pressure is through a better utilization of resources; recent technological advances are a demonstration of what can be done in this manner to raise levels of living and make room for more people. Even so, resources are not inexhaustible; eventually the question must come down to that of population control.

Another side of the problem is presented by Carl Zimmerman, whom we referred to earlier in the book.[8] He has advanced the theory that low fertility is one of the chief causes of family breakdown and that family failure is a major threat to modern civilization. He has even suggested that we consider abridging the citizenship rights of those who fail to marry and raise a family, by denying them public office. Zimmerman wants less childlessness and larger families. It is doubtful, however, that he would want married couples to bear all the children that nature permits.

Just as optimum population is that which is best from the standpoint of general social welfare, so optimum family size is one that brings the largest amount of satisfaction and development to family members. It, too, is difficult to settle upon. Furthermore, it will vary from time to time and from marriage to marriage. A family that was considered ideal in the day of our great grandparents would probably be too large for these times; circumstances have changed. People differ from each other in many ways—with respect to genetic potentials, health, financial ability, education, love of children, personal maturity —and it would be unreasonable to expect the same rate of reproduction from all, regardless of desire or capability.

Is there a relationship between family size and marital adjustment? Research on this problem has been rather limited and inconclusive. Popenoe reports a positive relationship between number of children and happiness in marriage. In a study of several thousand completed families selected from the educated part of the population, he found that the happy couples averaged 2.04 children each as against 1.67 for the unhappy, and that only 59 per cent of the childless couples were happy in marriage as compared with 71 per cent for

---

[8] See pages 42-43; also, Carl C. Zimmerman, *Family and Civilization* (New York: Harper & Bros., 1947).

couples having three or more children.[9] But the Indianapolis study, already cited, came up with a different conclusion; there the relationship between family size and marital adjustment was found to be an inverse one—the better adjusted couples had the fewest children, and vice versa.[10] It is likely that this difference in conclusions derives from the widely different samples studied. In any event there seems to be no general relationship which holds in all cases.

Only about one third of all divorces involve couples with children. Sometimes this fact is cited in support of the contention that children help to hold the marriage together. Though undoubtedly the claim is true for some cases, for others it is not. One reason for the above-average proportion of childlessness among divorcees is that many divorces take place in the early years of marriage before the family has been started. Another is that, in some instances, childlessness and divorce are both the result of incompatibility. Some couples seem to be "allergic" to children, are able to adjust better without them. Furthermore, when the marriage relationship is going badly, children can be an added source of worry and contention; sometimes a parent will use a child as a weapon against the mate. Not everyone loves children or has patience to deal with them within the framework of intimate family relationships. On the other hand, with a great many couples the situation is just the reverse of this. Very often children serve as a common core for love, as a cement for the marriage relationship, as a nucleus around which successful family life can be built.

Perhaps it isn't so much the presence or number of children which is important in marital happiness as it is the attitudes of couples regarding them. From the Indianapolis data Reed found "an increase in marital adjustment with increasing success in controlling fertility according to the desires of the couple."[11] Though Terman found no correlations between

9 Paul Popenoe, *Modern Marriage* (New York: The Macmillan Co., 1940), p. 268.
10 Robert B. Reed, *Social and Psychological Factors Affecting Fertility;* VIII, "The Interrelationship of Marital Adjustment, Fertility Control, and Size of Family" (New York: Milbank Memorial Fund, 1948), p. 392 and *passim*.
11 *Ibid.*, p. 423.

presence of children and happiness in marriage, he suggested that this may be because opposing influences tend to balance each other out and that the presence of children may actually affect any given marriage either way.[12] Burgess and Cottrell found happiness in marriage to be associated with desire for children, whether couples had any at the time of the study or not. These authors also found that poorest marital adjustment was with couples who had children which they did not desire.[13] Landis and Landis found that the happy and unhappy groups of their sample both tended to get larger as size of family decreased, and that childless couples fell at the two extremes of the happiness scale.[14]

In deciding on family size, consideration also needs to be given to the welfare of the offspring. It is generally agreed that children have the best chance of normal development in a home environment composed of brothers and sisters. An "only child" frequently starts out with a disadvantage;[15] he may be overindulged or denied an early training in sharing and getting along with others. Wise parents will foresee the dangers and devise means for overcoming the handicap—letting a nursery school help provide needed socializing experiences, for example. Yet, where possible, it seems better for the child's sake to let him have playmates near his own age right within the family.

The size of family considered as ideal will vary with the personalities of the couple and the circumstances surrounding them. There is no good reason for thinking that all families should be of the same size. It is conceivable, however, that a reversal in some of the fertility differentials would be of benefit to society. From the standpoint of economic welfare it would be better if those who could most afford it would have more children, and those who could least afford it, fewer chil-

---

[12] Lewis M. Terman, *Psychological Factors in Marital Happiness* (New York: McGraw-Hill Book Co., 1938), pp. 171-73.

[13] Ernest W. Burgess and Leonard S. Cottrell, *Predicting Success and Failure in Marriage* (New York: Prentice-Hall, Inc., 1939), p. 260.

[14] Judson T. Landis and Mary G. Landis, *Building a Successful Marriage* (New York: Prentice-Hall, Inc., 1948), p. 434.

[15] Research on this point is inconclusive. Cautiously, Terman says that his data "mildly suggest that only children find successful marital adjustment slightly more difficult"; see Terman, *op. cit.*, p. 211.

dren. From the standpoint of cultural opportunity it would be better if the well educated would play a larger role in reproduction, and the uneducated a smaller role. Since economic success and higher education are at least partially selective, it follows that a reversal of present birth-rate differentials in these areas would be eugenically beneficial. There is need for some kind of public policy and educational program directed toward these ends.

Between the limits of childlessness and complete disregard for family size, every normal married couple will want to set its goal. In modern times, fifteen or twenty children may be too many; such a number will usually mean a violation of both health and economics. Consequently there is need for planning and control. It is common for modern couples to define the ideal in terms of about three children or enough to replace the population.

Planned Parenthood.—By planned parenthood we mean the elimination, so far as possible, of unwanted pregnancies on the one hand and unwelcomed sterilities on the other; we mean helping some people to have children and helping others not to have children, or to have fewer, or to have them better spaced.

Why the widespread and long-continuing decline in fertility? It is not because of any great decrease in man's capacity to reproduce. While some authorities claim that the tensions and indulgences of modern life do contribute to sterility, the question is still in doubt. Virtually all agree that the increase in sterility is but slight if at all. Furthermore, modern medicine is successful in removing many of the conditions responsible for sterility.

Neither are Americans delaying their marriages more than before. Contrary to popular opinion, the facts are that the average age at first marriage has been getting younger over the past half century, and the percentage of the total population that is married has been increasing. Both of these facts would encourage a higher birth rate. Since the long-time fertility trend is downward, its explanation must be found elsewhere.

Since divorce terminates marriage, the increasing divorce rate would tend indirectly to reduce the birth rate. But in view of the magnitude of the decline in family size, the retarding influence of divorce may be regarded as only slight and incidental.

The major explanation for smaller families today is voluntary birth control. Under this heading would come all practices which are intended to prevent conception among potentially fertile couples. The term would not include sterilization, since that is a method for making the person permanently infertile. Neither would it include abortion, since that is a frustration of pregnancy after conception has already taken place. But it would include abstinence from the sex act, the limiting of intercourse to the least fertile days of the menstrual cycle ("safe period" method), and withdrawal by the male prior to ejaculation (coitus interruptus). It would also include the many chemical and mechanical devices which are designed either to kill the sperms or to prevent them from reaching the ova. Whenever such means are employed, the practice is known as contraception. Reliability in the various methods of birth control is highly variable. Also, protection depends upon the degree of understanding and skill present. Couples wanting help, therefore, need to consult a reliable physician or birth-control clinic.

Acceptance of contraception as a means of family limitation and child spacing has become rather general. This was not true a few decades back. Around the beginning of the century there was considerable resistance to the movement. Margaret Sanger, an early proponent, was forced to spend several terms in jail because of her advocacy of contraception. But the case has been largely won. At the present time there are some seven hundred birth-control clinics scattered throughout the country. Physicians regularly extend their services to those wanting help along this line. Surveys reveal that contraception is accepted and practiced by the majority of married couples today.

The legal status of contraception is still a little confused. The Federal Comstock Act, passed during the latter part of the last century, is still on the statute books. Originally this law prohibited interstate traffic in birth-control literature and materials. Recent court decisions, however, have interpreted it as not applying to medical practice; furthermore, public opinion has taken over and the law goes unenforced. In only two of the states, Massachusetts and Connecticut, is contraception expressly illegal. The laws of these two states have been interpreted to prohibit physicians from advising patients on contraception for any reason whatsoever—even for married women whose health would be gravely endangered by pregnancy. There have been a dozen or more unsuccessful attempts to repeal these laws, the latest of which was in Massachusetts during the general election of 1948. In all other states there are either no laws covering the prevention of conception or the medical profession is exempted from the controls established.[16]

Contraception is still officially condemned by the Catholic Church; under certain conditions this organization sanctions family limitation through self-control, but never by means of "artificial" methods or devices. A large factor in the persistence of anticontraceptive laws in Massachusetts and Connecticut is the high proportion of Catholics within these two states. Protestant churches differ in the way contraception is regarded. Some have come out with a definite stand in favor of the movement; others have taken a more qualified position; still others have remained silent.

Why do people voluntarily limit the sizes of their families? (1) In some cases there are biological reasons connected with the health of the mother or the heredity of the offspring. (2) More frequently reasons are personal and social, due to a distaste for pregnancy, a fear of childbirth, or a reluctance to be bothered with the responsibility of children. In this connection we can note that small families have become so much the norm that those who deviate are often made the objects of jokes and ridicule; concern over social approval, in other words, has become a motive for family limitation. Too, in a highly individualized culture such as this, pleasure patterns tend

---

[16] Planned Parenthood Federation of America, Inc., "The Legal Status of Contraception."

to crowd out concern over progeny. (3) Related to these just given, but more easily recognized and rationalized, is the economic factor in family size. Of all reasons, this is the one most likely to be named by the couple.[17] This is true even with those who are financially well off; as income goes up, so do the standards. It used to be that children were an economic asset and that those whose families were the largest were generally the most fortunate financially because of the greater labor force at hand. But times have changed. Child-labor laws, compulsory school attendance, the decline of a self-sufficient economy, rising costs and standards of living, all have made child-rearing more expensive than formerly. Because of this expense (which is much greater and less compensated for through family work than formerly) the child of today has come into competition with economic goods—though he may still be an asset when all values are considered, *he is no longer an economic asset.* Realizing this, modern parents frequently choose between having another child or a new car, or, as someone has put it, between having a new baby or a new baby grand.

How much does it cost to bear and rear a child to maturity? One method of estimation is to consider the federal income tax deduction figure as the average yearly expense. Tax payers are now allowed a deduction of $600 for each dependent. Figuring roughly, and on the basis of twenty years of dependency for each child, this would mean a cost of $12,000. Obviously, some children will involve the parents in less expense than this, and others more; actual cost will depend upon such things as purchasing power of the dollar, income level of the family, place of residence, and age at which the child becomes self-supporting.

But it isn't always just the cost which underlies the decision. During the early postwar years, when automobiles were scarce, there was a couple who faced this same dilemma—whether to have a new baby or a new car, and not being able to afford both they decided on the new baby "because we could get delivery sooner."

---

17 Cf. Christensen, *op. cit.,* pp. 274-75; also Hill and Christensen, *op. cit.* pp. 499-500.

Another aspect of family planning has to do with the spacing of children. In a Utah County study of the time-interval between marriage and the first birth, the author reached the following conclusions: (1) The modal interval between the marriage of parents and the birth of their first child was about ten or eleven calendar months. (2) The trend from 1905 to 1935 was toward a lengthening of this interval. (3) Heterogeneity between husband and wife, as to both age and premarital residence, was associated with the long time-intervals. (4) In general, the older the couple at marriage the longer was the interval between that marriage and the birth of a first child. (5) The occupations of farming and unskilled labor were associated with short intervals and the skilled and professional occupations with long intervals. (6) Relief work was associated with disproportionately short time-intervals. (7) Urban dwellers showed longer intervals than did the residents of rural communities.[18] It will be observed that the waiting period between marriage and a first birth is shorter in those groups which characteristically have the highest birth rates and the largest families. This suggests the possibility of predicting family size from a knowledge of the timing of the first birth.

Using a different approach, Anderson studied the spacing of all children in the completed families of former Cornell University students. He found that most of his couples had their first child during the second year of their marriage, which was not true in the Utah study cited above. This difference might be expected, for the Utah group was largely Mormon and the New York group was selected by the fact of college attendance. Anderson also found that the interval between marriage and the birth of the first child is shortest in the largest families, with one-child families showing the longest wait; that the average length of the intervals between successive births decreases as the size of family increases; and that for families of

---

18 Harold T. Christensen, "The Time-Interval Between Marriage of Parents and the Birth of their First Child, in Utah County, Utah," *American Journal of Sociology*, 44:518-25, January, 1939. Study based upon a sample of 1,670 marriages.

a given size the average length of the interval increases for each successive birth.[19]

There are both advantages and disadvantages in delaying children for a year or so after marriage. Advantages lie in the opportunity this wait affords husband and wife to make their first adjustments without the added strain of pregnancy and child-care; they can become accustomed to one thing at a time. Disadvantages lie chiefly in the fact that long delays tend to establish a pair pattern so firmly that the couple might grow reluctant to having children or find greater difficulty in adjusting when children come. There is also the fact that sterility increases with age, which means that some couples (those with low fecundity to start with) might give up their chances of ever becoming parents. It is usually considered advisable for there to be some delay in the starting of a family; how long this should be will depend upon the individuals concerned and the circumstances involved.

Medical men generally recommend that the interval between subsequent births be approximately two years. This is long enough to protect the mother's health and short enough to permit the children to grow up together and to afford companionship for each other. Also, planned spacing gives the mother a better chance to look after the health needs of earlier children; in families of closely spaced pregnancies, infant death rates are known to be higher than average.

REPRODUCTION

Nearly every married couple wants children. Powerful drives, both biological and social, make parenthood seem normal. Many people consider reproduction as the central or primary purpose of marriage. Consequently, most marriages bear fruit.

But not all. There is a minority of husbands and wives which either does not want or cannot have children. Fifteen

[19] W. A. Anderson, "The Spacing of Births in the Families of University Graduates," *American Journal of Sociology*, 53:23-33, July, 1947.

per cent or more of all marriages end childless. At least half of these are attributable to sterility and the remainder to choice.

Conception.—Life begins with the uniting of a sperm and an egg (ovum). This union usually takes place in one of the Fallopian tubes, after which the fertilized egg enters the uterus and attaches itself to the wall. Growth takes place by multiple cell division. Approximately nine months later the child is ready to be born.

The timing of conception is controlled primarily by the physiology of the female. Sperms can be released by the normal adult male at almost any time, while the releasing of an egg (ovulation) with the female is automatic and happens only once each month. Furthermore, there are upwards of 200,000,-000 sperms released in each ejaculation (any one of which is good for fertilization), while normally only one egg is involved in each ovulation. This means that conception can only occur at, or about, the time of ovulation.

Ovulation most generally takes place midway in the menstrual cycle. Since the cycle usually runs about twenty-eight days, this would place ovulation at approximately the fourteenth day from the beginning of each preceding menstrual period. Sexual intercourse which takes place within twenty-four, or even forty-eight, hours on either side of ovulation is that which is most likely to result in conception. The "safe period" from the standpoint of birth control is just before and just after menstruation. However, since women vary and are often irregular in their menstrual patterns, it is not always possible to predict the time of ovulation; hence the "safe period" may not be very safe. There is no exact knowledge as to how long a sperm or an egg can survive in the reproductive tract after it has been released. Medical opinion allows about twenty-four hours for the egg to survive and nearly twice that long for the sperm, though this latter estimate is less definite. Since less is known concerning the length of time that a sperm can survive, the time preceding ovulation is less "safe" than is the time following it.

Sterility refers to the inability of a couple to conceive. It is a factor in about one out of every ten marriages. Formerly there was the belief that involuntary childlessness was always the fault of the wife; in many earlier societies, barrenness was sufficient grounds for a husband to secure a divorce. But it is now known that in at least one third of all cases the sterile condition is with the male. Actually, with the majority of cases involving difficult conception there is something which needs correction in both husband and wife.

Sterility may result from one or more of many conditions. In the female there is likely to be a blocking of the Fallopian tubes or of the cervix; or the uterus may be out of place; or the ovaries may not be functioning properly. In the male there may be a blocking of the sperm duct; or the sperm count may be below normal; or the testicles may be impaired and producing an inferior quality of sperm. Sterility can be the result of an earlier infection, such as mumps in the male and gonorrhea in either sex. In rare instances sterility stems from an absence, underdevelopment, or malformation of some part of the reproductive system of one of the mates. Poor health, either physical or mental, is known to lessen the probability of conception.

Physicians and clinicians dealing with this problem report success in about one third to one half of the cases that come to them. There is little doubt but that even this record will be bettered through future advances in medical science. Sometimes conception is made possible by means of surgery; sometimes through hormone treatment; sometimes as a result of changes in the timing and technique of sexual intercourse. It frequently happens that a presumably sterile couple will conceive after mental tensions have been relaxed, or after the genral physical condition of one or both has been improved. Certainly all sterility is not absolute. Many cases are on the borderline and can be corrected by a relatively slight alteration of mental and physical conditions. As evidence of this, note the fact that adopting couples frequently find themselves pregnant with a child of their own sometime after they had given up and adopted another—the changed family situation had released mental tensions and improved general health sufficient to tip the balance in the direction of fertility.

Adoption is generally recommended for couples who want children but are unable to conceive. Many have testified that this substitute can be practically as satisfying as the experiences of blood-related families. Where children are selected through reliable child-placing agencies, and are taken when they are rather young, the risk is not great—even less great, some claim, than in bearing a child of your own.

Another substitute for normal conception is the employment of artificial insemination. This is only applicable in cases where the husband is sterile but the wife is not. By the use of an instrument, the physician will place some of the sperms from an anonymous male donor at the mouth of the wife's uterus, near the time she is expected to ovulate. Thus there will be normal pregnancy and childbirth, though the husband will not be the father. Children from such arrangements are popularly known as "test tube babies." Though there is still considerable reluctance about it, the practice of artificial insemination is gaining in acceptance. There remain a number of social and legal problems, however, such as questions concerning the child's legitimacy, the possibility of the male donor's becoming known, in which case he might interfere.

Pregnancy.—The normal period of human pregnancy is usually figured at 280 days (40 weeks). This is counting from the beginning of the last menstrual period. Since conception cannot take place until ovulation, it follows that the actual length of pregnancy is about two weeks shorter than this, or approximately 266 days. If the exact date of conception is known, the probable time of delivery can be determined rather simply by adding 266 days. A more usual method is to add seven days to the beginning of the last menstruation and then subtract three months. For example, if the first day of the last menstrual period were June 15, adding seven days and subtracting three months gives March 22 as the estimated date of confinement. These predicted dates are approximations; there is nothing abnormal in a pregnancy's running a few days under or over the expected time.

Usual early signs of pregnancy are: the missing of a menstrual period; an increasing fullness and tenderness of the breasts; a feeling of nausea known as "morning sickness"; and a greater frequency of urination. But none of these is absolute proof of pregnancy; each may be the result of other causes. If several of them occur together, however, it is a fairly good sign that pregnancy is under way.

Greater certainty is obtained through the physician's examination. This will not ordinarily take place until about two months have elapsed from the last menstrual period, for it is not until then that the positive signs become evident. If pregnancy is present the doctor will then notice certain changes in the vaginal lining, in the cervix, and elsewhere. Sometimes it is important to know concerning pregnancy without waiting for two months and the appearance of positive signs. To meet this need, there recently have been developed a number of tests whereby pregnancy can be determined with almost 100 per cent accuracy a few days after the missing of a menstrual period. Urine from the female is injected into a mouse, or rabbit, or frog, and if the woman is pregnant there will be a reaction set up within the animal which can be easily recognized.

The fertilized egg implants itself on the wall of the uterus about seven or eight days following fertilization. Already it has commenced to grow through a process of cell division. Continued growth in the same manner brings about an enlargement in size and a differentiation of body structures. The embryo, as this new life is at first called, receives its food and disposes of its wastes through the umbilical cord, which, in turn, reaches to the placenta attached on the wall of the uterus. There is no direct connection between the blood streams of mother and embryo; foods and wastes merely filter through the walls of the two separate systems of blood vessels within the placenta. Growth will necessarily follow the pattern laid down by heredity; once conception has taken place there can be no altering of sex, eye color, intellectual capacity, or anything else which has been dictated by the genes. Though prenatal environment is important from the standpoint of the baby's survival chances, there is no way by which a mother can influence or condition her unborn child along specific lines. (See page 63.)

The stages of prenatal growth follow a regular pattern. At first the embryo is scarcely distinguishable from those of other life forms. By the end of two months it will have grown to a little over an inch in length and most of its body features will be formed; after this it is called a fetus, and subsequent changes will have to do principally with an increase in size. By about the middle of pregnancy the heartbeat will have become strong enough for the doctor to hear it through a stethoscope, and movements will have become vigorous enough for the mother to feel them. If birth takes place during the first seven months, the child's chances for survival are rather small. These chances increase as the time of delivery approaches the date for normal termination of pregnancy.

Miscarriages, or spontaneous abortions (to use the medical term), mark the termination of about one out of every ten pregnancies. Most of these occur early; nearly three fourths of them happen during the first three months of pregnancy.[20] The great majority of these unplanned interruptions are due to defective germ plasm. Where the embryo or fetus is not developing normally, it is better for it to be aborted; that is nature's way of protecting itself. Severe illness during pregnancy and certain abnormalities of the reproductive organs are other factors conducive to abortion. All causes are not known. It is known, however, that if the egg is firmly lodged it will not be easily aborted by means of violent exercise, physical abuse, or the taking of special drugs designed to bring on menstruation.[21] Therapeutic abortions performed by qualified physicians are permitted under state law. For these to be legal it must be shown that the pregnancy is endangering the mother's life.

---

20 Alan F. Guttmacher, "Miscarriages and Abortions," chap. x of Part II in Morris Fishbein and Ernest W. Burgess (eds.), *Successful Marriage* (New York: Doubleday & Co., 1947), p. 207.

21 *Ibid.*, pp. 210-11; 216-17.

During recent years there have been phenomenal reductions in both infant and maternal death rates. This has been made possible by an enlargement of medical knowledge and the expansion of medical care. Today more is known concerning the needs of the mother during pregnancy and of mother and child following delivery. Of even greater significance, perhaps, is the fact that more and more parents are using the services of physicians and hospitals. There are fewer midwives in the business now than formerly, and fewer home deliveries. Death rates incident to childbirth are still highest in those groups and with those families that have been reluctant to take advantage of the newer knowledge and available services.

It is highly important that a competent physician be consulted early and frequently during pregnancy. Upon the kind of care the mother receives at this time will depend both her health and that of the child. Through periodic examinations the doctor is able to: (1) direct the mother in such things as diet, rest, and exercise; (2) correct any condition which might be unfavorable to the development or future birth of the child; and (3) anticipate and be prepared for any difficulties that could be present at the time of delivery. Physical comfort during pregnancy, ease of childbirth, general health and shape of the mother's body afterwards—to say nothing of survival chances for both mother and child—are all made more sure by and through the services of a specialist.

Unfortunately, these services are not equally available to all. Isolation and inadequate income sometimes serve as barriers. Proper care during and following pregnancy is not so easily obtained in rural areas and among poor people as it is in the cities and among the more well to do. The Children's Bureau of the United States Department of Labor, and the Public Health Departments of the federal, state, and local governments are making progress in the direction of correcting this situation. Under their sponsorship many communities now hold "prenatal clinics" and "well-baby clinics" free of charge. In addition, there is always the local health department that can be called, and public-health nurses who will visit the home.

Pregnancy is a family affair. There is more involved than the physical care of the mother, as important as that is. Routines of family living are likely to be upset, requiring adjustment on the part of *all* members. This is particularly true during the later stages of pregnancy or earlier if the mother experiences any unusual difficulty. The husband may need to "take over" at mealtimes and to assist more than formerly with younger children and with the housework. There will be certain personal and social inconveniences which require understanding and some sacrifice on the part of the husband. Doctors advise that sexual intercourse be practiced with more care at this time and that it be abandoned entirely during the last two months. Social activities may need to be curtailed. With a sympathetic husband, the pregnant woman is less likely to feel sensitive over her figure and is better able to bear the discomforts which are hers.

Pregnancy allows time to plan and prepare for the coming event. There will need to be material preparation in terms of purchasing supplies or getting together a layette. It may even be that the family will want to change residence if the present house is too small, or to find another job if the present income is too low, although usually such drastic measures will not be necessary. Psychological preparation is also important. If there are fears over childbirth, these can usually be eliminated by securing adequate information to eliminate ignorance, and by using the services of a competent physician. If there are regrets over the prospect of another child, as is sometimes true, these can be adjusted before the birth takes place. An unplanned pregnancy does not need to result in an unwanted child. When it does, the results can be unfortunate both for the child and the family.

Where there are children old enough to understand, pregnancy can be used as a valuable aid in sex education. With the family as the laboratory, and the mother as the central figure, children will be told exactly what is taking place. There will be open discussion within the family circle concerning the entire process of reproduction, including the role of the father and the birth experience. Told in this way, children will be more likely to see sex without the usual distortions—see it as something that is natural and acceptable; see it in the setting of love, marriage, and family.

Being Born.—After pregnancy has run its course, the fetus is expelled from the mother's body and is then ready to begin a new phase of development, this time as a child. The process by which birth takes place is known as labor.

Labor begins with rhythmic contractions of the uterus accompanied by a gradual dilation of the cervix so that the baby can come through. These contractions involve a certain amount of discomfort and are known as "labor pains." They start out rather mildly and widely spaced, but increase in intensity and frequency as time goes on. The length of labor varies with individuals. First births (averaging about sixteen hours) generally take longer than subsequent ones. After dilation has become complete, uterine contractions grow more severe so as to force the infant through the cervix and the vagina and into the outer world. It usually arrives head first. Almost immediately it starts to cry—and breathe. The doctor then cuts and fastens the umbilical cord. Within a few minutes the placenta (afterbirth) is also expelled. Birth is over. The mother's uterus now starts to contract and the muscles supporting it commence to return to their original positions.

If requested, most doctors will administer anesthesia during childbirth for the relief of pain. The practice has become rather general, though it remains controversial. Some doctors believe that the pain of childbirth is due entirely to fear; women in our culture expect it to hurt, so they enter labor all tense; if they could relax, the cervix would have a better chance of dilating and the birth process would be easy.[22] Though the claim that absence from fear can remove *all* pain from childbirth might be open to question, there is little doubt but that the general theory has merit. Medical men are agreed that it is the women who are relatively calm and who cooperate who have the easiest time in delivery. There is need, therefore, to educate women toward acceptance of childbirth as a normal process. With im-

---

[22] Cf. Grantley Dick Read, *Children Without Fear* (New York: Harper & Bros., 1944).

proved knowledge and facilities for handling maternity cases, there should be less cause for fear today than in earlier times.

It is important that mother and child keep close contact with the physician for some time after the delivery. This is both for general guidance and as a protection against infection and other complications which might set in (infant and maternal death rates are highest in the first few days and weeks following childbirth). The usual practice is to remain in the hospital for about a week, longer when necessary. Following that, the mother needs to take it easy for a while, making sure that she gets plenty of rest and turning back to former responsibilities only as rapidly as her growing strength permits. This is also a time when husband and older children will need to help. Sometimes it is important that a nurse or extra worker be hired for the matter of a few weeks. Approximately six weeks are required for restoring the mother's organs of reproduction to the size and strength of pre-pregnancy. This period is known as the *puerperium*. There should be no sexual intercourse between husband and wife during this period because of the danger of infection. The doctor will usually make an examination at the end of this time to determine whether or not conditions are normal. The wise mother will take herself and baby back for later examinations at times advised by her doctor.

PARENT-CHILD RELATIONSHIPS

Reproduction is only part of the story. After childbearing comes child-rearing. It is this second and longer-lasting phase of parenthood which requires the greater skill and responsibility. Being able to have children is no proof of one's ability to be a good parent.

When children come, husband and wife have to move over. Sociologically speaking, the marriage has now become a family, with three or more persons in interaction instead of just two. Established routines of the early period are now broken up. Couples who have grown used to each other on the exclusive basis of a pair relationship now find themselves forced into new and unaccustomed roles. They may feel, therefore, that the child is an intruder upon their privacy. For this reason the transition to parenthood is generally easier for couples who start their families during the early years of their marriage.

The initial excitements and thrills that go with having a new baby frequently degenerate into a partial disillusionment, though in time things settle down to the level of acceptance and pleasurable routine. The first stage of this adjustment sees congratulations, visitors, and the satisfaction that comes with a release from pregnancy and waiting. After returning from the hospital, however, these things slip into the background, to be replaced by night-crying, early-hour feedings, and daily diapers. Soon too, new parents come to realize that they are not free to leave whenever they want, for always there is the question of what to do with the baby. But after a while things begin to adjust; baby and parents alike come to accept the new routine and to grow in each other's affection. When this time arrives the pair has completed its change into a threesome and family solidarity has become a reality.

Developmental Stages.—Nature's process of growth and development is known as maturation. Within each newborn infant are a number of potentials, which, given time, will become actuals. When the child gets ready to cut his first tooth, it will be cut; ready to walk, he will walk; ready for puberty, puberty will take place. Such happenings are largely automatic. They are a part of one's original nature and they unfold according to nature's pattern. There is little that man can do to alter the schedule.

But paralleling this inevitable process of maturation is another phase of development known as learning. This is not automatic; there is much that parents and the person himself can do to alter it. Nevertheless, learning must wait upon maturation. It is a mistake to try to compel a child into a developmental performance before changes in his organism have made him ready. Trying to force a child to walk, for example, may actually result in delayed walking because of a dislike or fear built up within his mind. In teaching, it is important to understand the maturational level with which one is dealing.

Development follows a similar, though not identical, pattern for each child. Variations are explained by such factors as sex, intelligence, and socioeconomic opportunity. Girls develop more rapidly than do boys. Bright children develop at a faster rate than do dull children. Those who are well stay ahead in development of those who are undernourished or sickly. In addition, each child has its own timetable of development which in some respects may be unique. Yet there is enough uniformity to establish general patterns.

The first stage of postnatal development is known as infancy. It extends from birth until the child is one year of age. It is a period of rapid growth and decreasing helplessness. After losing a little during the first few days of life, the infant again starts to gain and by the end of the first year it will have about trebled the birth weight. This is a rate of growth more rapid than at any future time of life. The infant also gains a gradual control over the muscles of his body. He starts to smile and to raise his head a little at about the age of one month. By approximately five months he can roll over; six or seven months, sit up; seven or eight months, crawl; eight or nine months, pull himself up to things; nine or ten months, walk with support; ten or eleven months, stand alone; and eleven to thirteen months, take his first steps without help. The first tooth is likely to appear when the infant is six to eight months old. By one year the child has learned to imitate a number of things; he may play "peek-a-boo," or wave "bye-bye," or say "da-da."

After infancy, the one-year-old starts through a period known as early childhood. This will take him up until he is about six years old and ready to start school. During this time the child gains greater control over his body and its processes. He learns to feed himself and to put his clothes on and off. After a few bumps he becomes more sure-footed in his walking and running. Bowel and bladder control are usually mastered during the second year, except perhaps for the nights. Also during this year the child learns to speak; by two he is able to assemble simple words into short sentences. A little later he starts to ask all sorts of questions and to beg for nursery rhymes and bedtime stories. Early childhood is a period of great curiosity,

SEVEN STAGES IN BOY-GIRL RELATIONSHIP

INFANCY-BABYHOOD
Boy and girl
interested only in
themselves.

EARLY CHILDHOOD
Seek companionship
of other children
regardless of sex

ABOUT AGE EIGHT
Boys prefer to
play with boys,
girls with girls.

AGES 10 TO 12
Antagonism shown
between sex groups.

AGES 13 TO 14
Girls become
interested in boys,
try to attract their
attention;
boys aloof

AGES 14 TO 16
Boy group also shows
interest in girls; some
individuals begin to
pair off

AGES 16 TO 17, ON
"Going out in couples"
becomes general

FIG. 7.—(From *Women and Men,* copyright, 1943, 1944, by Amram Scheinfeld. Used by permission of Harcourt, Brace and Company, Inc.)

imitation, and exploration. Children at this time are continually getting into things or trying things out. Lacking experience and judgment, they are likely to take chances which put themselves and others in danger—such as running into a busy street without looking or striking matches without taking proper precautions. It is for this reason that preschool children need such close and constant supervision.

Late childhood extends approximately from ages six to twelve or thirteen; it parallels the period of grade-school attendance. Sometimes this is referred to as "The Gang Age." It is characterized by a strong desire for companionship with those of one's own sex, coupled with antagonisms toward the opposite sex. The influence of associates upon each other is great at this time. Learning proceeds at a new pace, due to added stimulation from the classroom. It is now that the child first learns to read; with reading, a whole new world of knowledge and interests opens up. Parents are relieved of a certain amount of responsibility during this stage, both because the children are in school and because they are gaining in independence and self-care.

Adolescence begins with the onset of puberty, which is around ages twelve or thirteen for the girl and thirteen or fourteen for the boy. It ends at about age twenty-one, the time of legal maturity. Puberty brings with it certain body changes: with the girl, menstruation starts, the breasts commence to enlarge, and hair develops under the armpits and at the pubic region; with the boy, nocturnal emissions make their appearance, the voice deepens, facial hair becomes more prominent, and hair develops under the armpits and at the pubic region. In both sexes physical growth takes place rather rapidly. Generally, also, there will appear such symptoms as loss of appetite, indigestion, headaches, fatigue, insomnia, and skin disorders, accompanied by daydreaming, restlessness, moodiness, and irritability. Early adolescence is known as the awkward age; new and strange changes are taking place within the body which the youth is not quite sure of, nor in control of, and which build up a feeling of self-consciousness. For a while, therefore, the teen ager is apt to pull within himself, to draw away from the crowd. In time he gains control of his body and builds up a new self-confidence. It is then that he starts to assert his individuality by showing off and rebelling against adult authority. Attractions for the opposite sex gain new strength and are surrounded by the glamor of romance. Love affairs tend to be intermittent, separated by periods of disillusionment. Decisions concerning one's lifework are likely to consume a large amount of mental and emotional energy. The adolescent boy or girl is no longer a child and not yet an adult; he is in transition between the two. It is from this fact that most of his problems are to be explained.

A Philosophy of Discipline.—It has been said that children can wreck a house but make a home. Someone has defined a child as "a noise with dirt on it." No one will deny that children cost money, are an inconvenience at times, and that they multiply the work of housekeeping. Furthermore, all children are "problem children" in the sense that sometime or other they spit out food, break dishes, are impolite to visitors, and in other ways break the conventions of adult society. But since they are not yet adults, such behavior needs to be judged by the standards of their own particular age level. Parents who understand this will make allowances for a few broken dishes, tipped-over lamps, frolics in the mud puddle, and the like. By accepting children for what they are and helping them to develop according to needs and potentialities, parents frequently discover that family life can be fun.

By discipline we do not mean punishment, though this latter may sometimes be involved. As used here, discipline refers to parental guidance during child development. It is our belief that guidance works best when it is more creative than restrictive, when parents lead more than they drive. In developing this thesis we shall want to examine four factors briefly: the home environment; consistency in treatment; meeting the child's needs; and the goal of self-discipline.

1. It has been shown how personality takes shape within the mold of early family experiences. Attitudes and habits formed during childhood are the ones which set the stage for later

adjustment or maladjustment, happiness or unhappiness. (See pages 74-78.)

Psychiatrists are continually discovering behavior problems in children which trace back to the fact of maladjusted and neurotic parents. Some even claim that unhappy homes constitute the chief cause of child and adult disturbances.[23] Generally speaking, children come to accept the example of their parents, to reflect the atmosphere of the home in which they grow. Family conflicts tend to be absorbed into the personalities of children, bringing frustration and disorganization to them during their most impressionable years. Similarly, happily married mates will radiate the love that is between them, bringing security and stability to the offspring.

Home environment also includes the manner by which parents and children interact. Strecker, a psychiatrist, has blamed "momism" for a large amount of the emotional instability found among young men. Too much sentimentality is attached to the concept of mother love in this culture, he claims. As a result, many women over-mother their sons—keep them dependent, won't let them grow up. Unprepared to face reality, boys who are reared like this may later rebel or become disorganized under the strain.[24] Sometimes this "mom"istic tendency is referred to as "smother love." It can be indulged upon daughters as well as sons.

Normal development requires the presence and participation of both parents. Yet some children seldom see their father. Where work keeps him away all day and most of the week there is little opportunity to become really acquainted. On top of this, many fathers spend all too little time with their children even when home. They reason that this is woman's work and so keep busy with other things. Many fathers are little more than animated spanking machines. There is need for a change in philosophy.

Margaret Mead feels that the modern father is taking more time to do things for his children than was true earlier. With

23 Cf. Walter R. Stokes, *Modern Pattern for Marriage* (New York: Rinehart & Co., 1948).

24 Edward A. Strecker, *Their Mothers' Sons* (Philadelphia: J. B. Lippincott Co., 1946).

the arrival of a five-day work week, Saturday morning is being cleared as a time when "dad" can be home with the family. She suggests that we use it that way, that we beat commercial interests to this time and set it up as a kind of national father's morning.[25]

2. Other things being equal, that discipline is most effective which is most consistent. Children need to know what they can count on. Growing up, at best, is difficult; it involves both the curbing of natural tendencies and the learning of a vast array of new behavior. Confusion results when the new roles expected of the child are themselves in contradiction. After confusion comes frustration, then rebellion. There is nothing that can get a child so mixed up as to "play fast and loose" with his emotions, to keep him continually guessing. If the child can come to know that the world about him is dependable and predictable, he feels secure and is able to organize his life and accept responsibility for his actions; otherwise he may grasp at anything or rebel against what he does not understand. This argument, however, is not to be taken as an excuse for parents to perpetuate a mistake once made—for the sake of consistency.

There are four types of consistent action which seem important: First, there is consistency between one occasion and the next. Parents who have the habit of punishing a child for a given act at one time and letting this same act go unpunished on another occasion, perhaps even thinking it cute, are making a grave mistake. They are encouraging the child to gamble on disobedience. Discipline based upon the moods of parents, rather than the efficacy of the act, is likely to backfire. Second, there is consistency between parents. Unless husband and wife are able to present a united front, their children will soon learn to play one parent against the other—to the detriment of the children and the possible weakening of the marriage. This does not mean that parents must always agree on the method of discipline to be used; only that their disagreements be discussed in private and that they be willing to support each other in front of the children. Third, there is consistency in treatment as

25 Margaret Mead, "What Is Happening to the American Family?", *Journal of Social Casework*, 28:323-30, November, 1947.

among the several children. Though a certain amount of sibling rivalry is to be expected, parents sometimes intensify the trauma involved by favoring one child over another, either consciously or unconsciously. In the long run this is to the disadvantage of both or all children. Fourth, there is consistency between words and actions. Children need to know that parents mean what they say; otherwise there is the temptation to disobey and gamble on the consequences. Most children are prone to test out their superiors, trying to see how far they can go, to determine how much is meant of what is said. This is only natural; children want to know where they stand. When parents don't follow through, children then know that the threats are merely bluffs. Instead of backing words with actions, some parents merely increase the intensity or the violence of the word-threats until in turn these are discovered as bluffs, after which the dose of verbal venom is again stepped up and the vicious circle is under way. Parents who complain of children never minding are usually those who have been too free with angry verbiage and too sparing on positive action. Obedience is born of respect. Respect without consistency is impossible.

Terman found that marital happiness is greatest with couples who, as children, were under a discipline that was "firm but not harsh." He also discovered marital happiness to be associated with an earlier parent-child relationship that was close and free from conflict.[26]

3. Discipline frequently misses its mark because of a failure to understand the child. Adult standards, arbitrarily applied, may be as far from the actual needs of children as it is possible to imagine. Unmet needs result in frustration.

As shown in Chapter 3, there are certain fundamental needs which are common to everyone: the need for physical sustenance; the need to feel safe and secure; the need to love and be loved; the need for esteem or ego-support; and the need to explore and create. Deprived of any one of these, the child will be unsatisfied and likely to cause trouble. Thus one child may be irritable because he is undernourished; another may be unco-

---

26 Terman, *op. cit.,* pp. 228-31.

operative due to inconsistent treatment or an unstable environment; still another may "act up" because he isn't loved or because he finds that that is the best way to get attention; and so it goes. For best results parents must go beyond the satisfying of mere physical requirements and make the child feel secure, loved, useful, and wanted. Also, realizing the need for new experience, they must encourage initiative and creativeness —even at the expense of a little trouble.

Within limits, the needs and capacities of children change according to the various levels of development which they go through (see above). Parents must be awake to this fact and aware of what takes place so that they are in a position to adapt. It is pointless to try to force a child beyond his present stage of maturation. Similarly, it is dangerous to apply childhood patterns of discipline upon a teen ager.

It is important to recognize that no two children are alike, even those of the same age group. For this reason it is impossible for parents to find answers for all of their problems in books; children cannot be reared by rigid formula. The books can help, of course, in building a general understanding; children are enough alike to permit the formulation of broad principles. But in the final analysis, each parent is an artist and every child a unique creation. This means that parents will need to study their children separately and to treat them somewhat differently—though equally.

A certain amount of negativistic behavior is to be expected as a part of the total process of growing up. Natural urges of the child must be curbed and his behavior molded in line with social acceptance. This means wish-frustration, which often leads to open rebellion. Negativism (such as temper tantrums, defensive lying, and uncooperative withdrawal) is simply the ego asserting itself against pressures from the outside which it feels it must resist. Mild tendencies in this direction will usually be outgrown.

It would be a mistake, nevertheless, to infer that all that parents have to do is sit back and let nature take its course. Many behavior difficulties are the result of unmet needs. When this is true. there is only one answer: find out what the child is lacking, then supply it. Some child problems require the assistance of a specialist.

The task of determining what a particular child's needs are at a given time, and then neither over- nor undersupplying them, is a difficult one. Parents sometimes err by giving too much protection, attention, and affection to the growing youngster so that he becomes self-centered and thwarted in social development. We have already referred to this as "smother love." Another mistake lies at the opposite extreme; whenever parents neglect or reject a child they cause him to develop deep-seated feelings of inadequacy which may stay with him for the rest of his life. The overprotected child feels insecure because of being socially immature and unable to cope with the world about him. The underprotected or rejected child likewise feels insecure, but because of being denied the love and attention his nature requires. In both instances there may be behavior difficulties growing out of the insecurities and anxieties which have been set up.

4. Ideally, discipline within the home is aimed at the development of self-control. Early restraints upon the child are necessary because of his immaturity. As he grows older, however, his judgment develops and he becomes capable of more and more responsibility. To accompany this process there needs to be a gradual lifting of external controls and an assuming of internal controls; discipline, in other words, needs to become internalized within the individual. Otherwise he will be left unprepared for responsibility in the adult world.

If self-control is to be developed, there must be allowed a certain amount of freedom and opportunity for self-expression. By insisting upon rigid obedience parents may be unconsciously crushing the child and destroying his initiative, making him weak and overdependent. Furthermore, they may be forcing him to repress feelings which need ventilation and which may then pile up and one day explode. Docility is no assurance that discipline has been successful. Many parents regard discipline largely in terms of restraint and use it merely to further their own ends. Actually, that discipline is best which contains a minimum of restraint and a maximum of constructive leadership adapted to the needs of the child. Obedience is justified as a means to an end but never as the end itself.

Some mothers and fathers make the mistake of extending a child freedom without responsibility, which can be disastrous. Constructive guidance implies that parents will give the child opportunity for self-expression, yes, but also give him training in responsibility. To recognize that extremes in discipline can be harmful is not to say that disobedience needs to be encouraged. There is no point in letting a child "run the roost" as is done in some instances; a child-dominated family is as undesirable as a parent-dominated family, perhaps even more so. Children need to be taught to respect the experience and maturity which are back of parental judgment. They also need to come to understand that acts have consequences for which people are responsible.

Insofar as possible, the leadership afforded by parents ought to be constructive rather than restrictive. Instead of "don't do that" it needs to be "let's do this." Generally speaking, rewards are more effective than punishment; they can accomplish as much and without the traumatic effects. Approval and praise are exciting rewards for most children and are generally sufficient.

Nevertheless there will be times when punishment seems to be the only way of impressing the child of his responsibility. In administering this kind of treatment, the following points need to be kept in mind: (1) Make sure that the offender understands what the punishment is for. (2) Choose a type of punishment that is commensurate with the offense. (3) Apply the punishment as soon after the act has taken place as possible. (4) Accompany the punishment with love, so that the child knows he is not being rejected, even though his actions are disapproved. (5) Guard against punishing in anger, too frequently, or out of habit.

Self-control is developed most effectively under conditions of democratic leadership. This means that children are given a voice in family matters just as soon as they are old enough to make their wants known. In progressive homes the family counsel system is often used. Under this plan husband, wife, and older children get together occasionally to talk over the affairs of the family and to make decisions regarding them. These meetings do not need to be regularly scheduled or to be conducted in any formal fashion, although some prefer it the formal way. Family meals are frequently used for this kind of business, since usually all members are together at those times. Sometimes a special gathering will be called to discuss a proposed purchase, plans for change of residence, advisability of the mother's working, or some other family project. Children can be brought in just as soon as they are old enough to understand. The advantage of including children is that it gives them a sense of oneness with the family and training in practical democracy. Though some views or requests may need to be rejected (a voice does not necessarily mean a vote), all should be heard. Talking things over in this way not only develops self-discipline, it builds for family unity.

In comparing democratic leadership with two other types, called the authoritarian and the *laissez faire,* Lippitt and White found the former as being productive of the highest morale and the most efficient realization of group goals.[27] Other studies have connected democratic leadership with the development of resourcefulness and self-reliance in the child.

"The Family as a Launching Center."—At about the time of legal maturity children commence leaving home, getting married, and starting families of their own. The parental family is the launching center; it serves as a place of preparation prior to the parting, and it stands by, ready to help in case of an emergency following the separation.

If the home environment and training have been favorable, the child will be in command of himself and ready for adult responsibilities when the time for separation arrives. He will have made a good start in "weaning" himself from the home nest. He will have achieved a certain amount of independence and initiative. He will have learned how to "stand on his own

---

[27] Ronald Lippitt and Ralph K. White, "The Social Climate of Children's Groups," in Roger G. Barker and others (eds.), *Child Behavior and Development* (New York: McGraw-Hill Book Co., 1943), pp. 485-508.

feet." In other words, he will be mature emotionally and socially as well as physically. This should make for a good launching.

Many family conflicts known to be common during the adolescent period are attributable to the launching process. Young people frequently complain of their parents being inconsiderate and bossy. The parents, in return, indict children for being disrespectful and rebellious. Undoubtedly evidence could be gathered in support of both claims; parents do sometimes think more of their own conveniences than of their children's needs, and children are sometimes thoughtless and impetuous in the things they say and do. There is room for improvement on both sides. But to a considerable extent, improvement is dependent upon a better understanding of what is taking place. Adolescence is a period of transition into adulthood; it is preparation for the launching. Naturally, therefore, there will be readjustments in family relationships which may be painful for the parents. Naturally, also, children will make a few mistakes as they feel their way along. Youth finds it difficult to grow up. Parents find it difficult to let go. Both are in readjustment, and each needs to understand the other. Adolescent boys and girls need to realize that the greater experience and maturity of parents qualify them for counsel. Parents need to realize that growing up requires an increasing amount of freedom and independence.

The most traditional launching pattern has been that of getting the daughter married off and the son set up in some kind of job or occupation. But parents are interested in whom the son marries also, though they have less responsibility there and are not concerned so directly or so extensively in the wedding preparations. Furthermore, with the equalizing of sex roles, more and more girls plan for employment in addition to marriage. Parental attempts to dictate either the occupation or the marital choice to a son or daughter frequently result in resentment and rebellion. Guidance in these matters is important, but it had better come somewhat subtly or by invitation. Where earlier parent-child relationships have been close and cordial there will already have been guidance, and there will exist a foundation for its likely continuance.

What happens when the launching goes contrary to plan? Perhaps it is a daughter who has made a bad marriage, a son who seems unable to establish himself on a sound financial footing, or a child who turns out to be a "black sheep" and disgraces the family. It is understandable that these things will bring disappointments and a certain amount of pain to the parents. But parents must realize that there are some things which are beyond their control. Misfortunes like this happen to the wisest of parents, and when they do, it is better to accept the situation as it is and make the best of it. Parents can usually find ways to help a married or departed child who is in trouble. But they must be careful not to interfere. Certainly there is no point in brooding over the matter in the spirit of self-blame.

Thus mothers and fathers frequently discover that they are not finished even after the formal launching. Marital troubles may bring a daughter home, financial difficulties may cause a son to ask for help, or other misfortunes may come to a departed child. It is in this way that the family serves as a stabilizing link between generations. And it is well that it can. The unfortunate thing is that this function is occasionally abused, that children sometimes overimpose upon parents at a time when these parents need to be conserving their strength and thinking about their own security in old age.

Problems and Projects

1. Describe changes which are taking place in the typical family cycle. Tell why. Explain the significance.
2. Give major reasons for the long-time decline in birth rate. For the rise in birth rate during the 1940's.
3. Explain the various fertility differentials which were described in the text. What are the eugenic and socioeconomic implications?
4. Examine the proposition that marital happiness is partially influenced by the presence and number of children in the home. Cite evidences and draw conclusions.
5. Give and defend your position on birth control.

6. Approximately how many children would you like in marriage? Give your reasons for not wanting more than this. For not wanting fewer.

7. Is it generally better for the married couple to start right off with a family or to delay a few years before the first child? Why?

8. From other sources, prepare a paper on sterility: extent, causes, treatment, and substitutions (such as by artificial insemination or child adoption).

9. Describe the process of human reproduction—starting with conception, continuing through pregnancy, and ending with childbirth.

10. What adjustments must the husband and other family members make during the pregnancy? After the child is born? Discuss various problems involved in having to "move over."

11. Why is competent care under the hands of a physician so important during pregnancy, delivery, and the puerperium? Is this kind of medical service available for all? Make suggestions.

12. Describe typical stages of child development from infancy through to maturity. Why is an understanding of the maturational processes important to successful parenthood? Discuss.

13. How can the average American father improve his family role? Why is this important? Discuss.

14. Why should parents strive to deal with their children consistently? Give examples drawn from personal observation of each of the types of inconsistency named in the text.

15. Discuss the pros and cons of spanking as a method of discipline.

16. "In the final analysis, each parent is an artist and every child a unique creation." Discuss.

17. How much obedience should parents insist on from their children? From instances you know, cite examples of common mistakes. Were any of these because the child was given too little freedom? Too much? How could they have been better handled?

18. How far should parents go in deciding with whom a son or daughter shall date? Where he shall go on the date? What time he shall be in at night? Whom and when he shall marry? Discuss.

19. How can parents adjust to the marriage of a child which took place without their consent? To a son or daughter who has turned out to be the family's "black sheep"? Discuss.

Selected Readings

ALDRICH, C. ANDERSON, and ALDRICH, MARY M. *Babies Are Human Beings*. New York: The Macmillan Co., 1938.

BABER, RAY E. *Marriage and the Family*. New York: McGraw-Hill Book Co., 1939. Chaps. x, xi, "Parent-Child Interaction."

BARUCH, DOROTHY W. *Parents Can Be People*. New York: Appleton-Century-Crofts, Inc., 1944.

BECKER, HOWARD, and HILL, REUBEN (eds.). *Family, Marriage, and Parenthood*. Boston: D. C. Heath & Co., 1948. Part IV, "Problems of Parenthood and Family Administration"; Chap. xxv, "Larger or Smaller Families for America?"

BOSSARD, JAMES H. S. *The Sociology of Child Development*. New York: Harper & Bros., 1948.

BRECKENRIDGE, M. E., and VINCENT, E. LEE. *Child Development*. Philadelphia: W. B. Saunders Co., 1943.

BROOKS, LEE M., and BROOKS, EVELYN C. *Adventuring in Adoption*. Chapel Hill: University of North Carolina Press, 1939.

CARRINGTON, WILLIAM. *Safe Convoy: The Expectant Mother's Handbook*. Philadelphia: J. B. Lippincott Co., 1944.

DUVALL, EVELYN MILLIS. *Keeping Up With Teen-agers*. New York: Public Affairs Committee, 1947.

———, and HILL, REUBEN. *When You Marry*. Boston: D. C. Heath & Co., 1945. Part III, "The Making of a Family."

FISHBEIN, MORRIS, and BURGESS, ERNEST W. (eds.). *Successful Marriage*. New York: Doubleday & Co., 1947. Parts III, "Conception, Pregnancy, and Childbirth"; IV, "The Child in the Family."

GESELL, ARNOLD L. *Studies in Child Development*. New York: Harper & Bros., 1948.

GROVES, ERNEST R. *Marriage*. New York: Henry Holt & Co., 1941. Chap. xxi, "The Birth Experience."

HARPER, ROBERT A. *Marriage*. New York: Appleton-Century-Crofts, Inc., 1949. Part IV, "Family Adjustment."

LANDIS, JUDSON T., and LANDIS, MARY G. *Building a Successful Marriage*. New York: Prentice-Hall, Inc., 1948. Chaps. xvii, "Family Planning"; xviii, "Reproduction"; xix, "When Children Come"; xx, "Bringing Up Children."

MAGOUN, F. ALEXANDER. *Love and Marriage*. New York: Harper & Bros., 1948. Chap. xi, "Parents and Children."

SMART, MOLLIE STEVENS, and SMART, RUSSELL COOK. *It's A Wise Parent.* New York: Charles Scribner's Sons, 1944.

STOKES, WALTER R. *Modern Pattern for Marriage.* New York: Rinehart & Co., 1948. Chap. viii, "Guiding Children Toward Sound Marriage."

UNITED STATES CHILDREN'S BUREAU. *Prenatal Care.* Washington, D. C.: Government Printing Office, 1942.

———. *Infant Care.* Washington, D. C.: Government Printing Office, 1945.

———. *Your Child from One to Six.* Washington, D. C.: Government Printing Office, 1945.

———. *Guiding the Adolescent.* Washington, D. C.: Government Printing Office, 1946.

WALLER, WILLARD. *The Family: A Dynamic Interpretation.* New York: Dryden Press, 1938. Part IV, "Parenthood."

YOUNG, KIMBALL. *Personality and Problems of Adjustment.* New York: Appleton-Century-Crofts, Inc., 1940. Chaps. xiv, "The Induction of the Child into the Family"; xv, "Other Aspects of Fundamental Training"; xvi, "Some Problems of Adolescence and Maturation."

Chapter 12

GROWING OLD GRACEFULLY

Until recently, very little attention has been given to the scientific study of old age—to either the processes involved or the problems presented. Especially neglected has been the area of family relationships as affected by the aging of husband and wife. Yet growing old is a part of the total family picture; marriage is generally followed by widowhood, and parenthood by grandparenthood.

Though many people grow old, not all do so gracefully. For a large number, old age means little more than disillusionment and anticlimax. This need not be. Changing it, however, will require a certain amount of social reorganization, plus better preparation of the personality during its earlier years.

Role of the Aged in Society

Not every culture provides the same kind of treatment for its aged. There are instances where elderly people are regarded with esteem and sought after for counsel. There are other instances where they are either abandoned or killed when it is thought that their usefulness has been outlived. In general, earlier societies have had fewer old people but have afforded those few a higher status than does our own. Note the following:

In contrast to modern civilization, old age is something of a rarity in primitive societies; most people die in youth or in middle age. Because of their rarity, those few who do survive the rigors of primitive life are usually awarded considerable distinction and prestige. Primitive culture succeeds to a great extent in utilizing the services of these few old people and so gives them an opportunity to be regarded as treasured assets. With far less medical knowledge, they entertain many efforts to find secret remedies for rejuvenation. *While modern civilization has added more years to life, it tends to leave less life in the years.*[1]

Numerical Trends.—There are approximately 11,000,000 persons sixty-five years of age or over in this country at the present time, and within a few decades this figure stands to be doubled. In terms of proportion, more than 7.5 per cent of the present population is sixty-five years of age or over, compared with only 2.6 per cent in 1850 and an estimated 13.1 per cent in 1990. All of this means that the population is getting older, that its balance is shifting in the direction of age.[2]

One explanation for the expansion in numbers of old people is that the population as a whole is on the increase. But this does not explain why the aged group is increasing at a more rapid rate and is coming to constitute an ever larger proportion of the total. One explanation for the latter is the declining birth rate, which reduces the proportion of young people in the population, thereby swelling the proportion in the older ages. But even this is only part of the answer. The main reason for an aging population is the declining death rate, which increases the average length of life, permitting more people to survive to old age.

Landis tells how length of life today compares with that of earlier generations:

Four hundred years ago our ancestors had an expectation of life at birth of less than 25 years; a hundred and fifty years ago, of only about 35 years. At the beginning of the twentieth century the prospect was for about 50 years. In 1945 it was for almost 67 years.[3]

Most of the reduction in the death rate has taken place with respect to the infectious and contagious diseases and has been with the younger age groups. What has happened is that more and more people have been permitted to live into the older ages.

---

[1] Leo W. Simmons, "Attitudes Toward Aging and the Aged: Primitive Societies," *Journal of Gerontology*, Vol. 1, No. 1, January, 1946, p. 72. Italics not in the original.

[2] Consult various population reports of the Bureau of the Census.

[3] Paul H. Landis, *Population Problems* (New York: American Book Co., 1948), pp. 216-17.

The average length of life is longer now than formerly because there are more old people, not because old people live longer than before; they don't.

The great challenges facing medical science today are in the field of constitutional breakdowns, those body ailments that chiefly affect the middle and older ages. Heart disease, for example, has been on the increase as a factor in death and is now the most common of all causes. Both history and fiction are replete with schemes to preserve youth, or to rejuvenate the body after it has commenced to wear out. Most of these reachings for the "fountain of youth" have been based upon either wishful dreaming or superstitious magic. Unless, or until, someone finds a way to check the degenerative processes, there will not be any pushing out of the upper limits of life. Though science may someday solve this problem, it hasn't yet. Recently there has come a report from a Russian scientist who claims to have developed a new serum that will strengthen or preserve the connective tissues in the body, and, in this way, add several decades on to the average life of man.[4] There has been no widespread testing of this claim, however, nor is it generally accepted in medical circles.

Characteristics of Age.—Census data supply an over-all picture of what the more mature part of our population is like. Following is a brief summary: [5]

Most of those who survive to the later years are only moderately old. This is demonstrated by the fact that about two thirds of the group aged sixty and over are in their sixties, and most of the remaining one third in their seventies, leaving extremely small numbers who survive to eighty years of age and beyond.

There is an excess of aged women over aged men, with the difference becoming greater as the groups get older. For example, 63.3 per cent of the centenarians in 1940 were females as compared with only 50.2 per cent of persons between the ages of sixty-five and seventy.

---

4 For a popular report of this claim see, William L. Laurence, "Tomorrow You May Be Younger," *Reader's Digest,* February, 1946, pp. 1-4.

5 Adapted from: Ruth Shonle Cavan and others, *Personal Adjustment in Old Age* (Chicago: Science Research Associates, 1949), pp. 40-46. Analysis based upon 1940 census data.

Fewer years of schooling were experienced by the older generation than for the present one. In terms of medians, those over sixty
years of age show only eight years of schooling, compared with ten
for those aged 25-29.

A disproportionately high percentage of old people are widowed,
especially the females, and widowhood for both sexes increases with
age. In the 60-64 age group, 11.1 per cent of the men and 31.3 per
cent of the women were widowed when the last census was taken.
Percentages for those eighty-five years of age and over were 58.3
and 85.1, respectively.

The majority (approximately three fourths) of aged men and
women live in their own homes. This is more true for men than for
women. With both sexes, the proportions who move in with children
or relatives or who enter an institution or become lodgers, increase
with age.

In round numbers, nearly one third of the group aged sixty and over
is working, another third is receiving some form of old-age allowance,
and the remaining third is being supported by savings, aid from children, and the like. More than two million persons receive federal Old
Age Assistance annually. For both men and women, the percentage
working decreases rapidly from one age period to another.

Up to this point we have been calling people old who have
passed a certain birthday, say the sixtieth or the sixty-fifth.
This is common practice, for it provides a simple means for
making statistical comparisons. There is error, however, in assuming that oldness commences with any given chronological
age. The process of growing old does not apply itself with equal
speed to every person. Some individuals become feeble and dependent even before sixty, while others remain active and able
to take care of themselves long after seventy. Furthermore,
culture has something to do with it—by either providing socially respected roles for the aged, as has been true in some
times and places, or by artificially restricting the activities of
older people, as is largely true today in our own culture.
Though in this society retirement is often arbitrarily prescribed
for a set age, usually 65, there is good reason for regarding
the aging process as being both gradual and variable.

Considered in this light, it is possible to describe four general characteristics of the aging process. Each of these is to be

understood as applying more to the later than to the middle years, and as starting earlier and developing farther with some individuals than with others:

1. There is a decline of physical health and vigor, which lets one know that the body is gradually wearing out. The skin becomes more wrinkled; the bones more brittle; joints stiffen; the hair turns gray or the head bald; hearing ability diminishes; the eyes grow less able to accommodate themselves according to distance; motor coordination declines; reproductive capacities decrease; chronic illness often sets in.

2. There is a similar slackening of mental ability. This starts long before the period of old age, however, as is shown by the fact that intelligence test scores are highest at about the end of the second decade of life, declining gradually thereafter. Old people generally learn more slowly, grasp new material with greater difficulty, show greater mental fatigue, and remember things less easily than do the young.

3. There is a shift of social role in the direction of less participation and greater dependence. Part of this is due to the decline of physical and mental powers within the individual and part to cultural prescriptions. Older individuals have more leisure time but are less active in community affairs; they have fewer companionable relationships either within the home or on the outside; they are less likely to be employed and more likely to be dependent upon others for support.

4. There is a greater tendency to worry, to lose interest in life, and to be generally less happy. Feelings of nervousness, of inadequacy, and of being unwanted are common. Old people tend to be more religious than those of the younger ages. They also tend to be more cautious and conservative. It seems likely that both of these are results, primarily, of the insecurity that surrounds old age in our culture.

Cultural Factors.—No problem of human adjustment can be completely understood without reference to its cultural setting. Behavior takes place within a societal framework and is influenced by the various forms of approval and disapproval which the culture imposes.

In our society old age is made more of a problem by the existence of two conditions: (1) the large, and increasing, proportion of old people in the population; and (2) the stripping from life's later years of much of the usefulness and dignity which once surrounded them. Let us examine each of these in turn.

One consequence of an aging population is a probable shifting among patterns of production and consumption. The market will be geared more and more to the needs and tastes of older people, less than now to the young and middle aged. Community planning along lines of recreation and housing will take increasing recognition of older citizens. Adult education will receive increasing emphasis. It has even been claimed that orphanages may be converted into infirmaries. Some of these changes are already under way. They will see further development with each additional increase in number of aged.

Closely related to the above is the larger and larger role that old people are destined to play in the political arena. As time goes on they will constitute an increasing proportion of the electorate and will operate more and more as a pressure group. Already this is taking place, with politicians recognizing the fact and making concessions. We can expect political platforms to continue to contain promises to the aged, and it seems probable that increasing amounts of public funds will be expended for their welfare.

As there come to be more old people, the burden of supporting them will get larger. Putting this another way, those in the productive years of life will be called upon to maintain an increasing number who have passed their period of self-support. This, for one thing, may have an indirect depressing effect upon the birth rate—having more dependents of the older variety, married mates may try to reduce the number of young dependents by bearing fewer children.

It is entirely possible that an increasing number of old people in society will cause the culture to become more conservative. Young populations are the ones that usually give birth to radical movements; age lacks the vitality and has too much invested in status quo. Though there is need for further testing of the claim that age is more conservative,[6] it must be recognized that old people generally have poorer health and fewer years to live than do others, which should make them less willing to risk the comforts and security they may have built up. If this be true, we can expect our national life to become somewhat less aggressive over the next half century or so and to emphasize programs more along lines of welfare and security.

Paralleling this trend toward an older population, with its consequences, has been a shift in the status and roles of elderly persons. The earlier condition in America is described by Cavan:

When American society was predominantly rural, there was little evidence of adjustment problems in old age. With advancing years, the older adults gradually decreased their farming or household activities. Their children assumed their responsibilities as they withdrew from them. Thus, as they grew older, they retained an economically productive, although decreasing, function until advanced years. The old parents also played a useful role socially. Often they were the connecting link between a new residence in the West and an earlier family residence in the East. They served as carriers of family traditions and culture and gave the family a sense of continuity. Often, also, they assumed much of the care of the young children, thus freeing the mother for more active duties and giving children needed personal attention, love, and informal teaching.[7]

It is clear that our earlier culture gave old people certain definite and useful functions to perform, which brought them respect and gave them comfort. But urbanization and industrialization have tended to change the picture. The impersonal relationships of the city have added to loneliness. Arbitrary retirement rules have, in many instances, resulted in idleness, restlessness, and dependency. So also has the reluctance of industry to hire older persons. Both of these innovations of the

---

[6] See *Ibid.,* p. 32. The authors say, "We cannot be sure that the supposition of conservatism among old people is true." Then they point out that even if it were true there is no proof that conservatism is a part of the aging process. To support this contention, they show how conservatism in the present old age group may have come from their greater rural background, plus present feelings of insecurity coming from inadequate treatment.

[7] *Ibid.,* p. 33.

machine age have meant a loss of status for older people. With that come feelings of uselessness and frustration.

Children feel less responsibility in the care of aged parents than formerly. For one reason, city apartments are small and there often isn't room for an extra person. Even if there were room, mobility has frequently added sufficiently to the cultural differences of the two generations to make living together in close proximity extremely difficult. Then, there is the matter of finance, which is a larger problem in an urban culture and under a wage economy than when families were mostly self-sufficient. Many children cannot afford to maintain a separate residence for their parents. And with fewer children and more old people per family, a proportionately greater burden tends to fall upon each child.

The point is, that old people in this culture find themselves forced to accept roles which they frequently do not want or which are incompatible with their needs and capacities. The pattern is defined by younger age groups in society and for the old there is little choice. Add to this the fact that there is often a great difference between the responsible roles previously held as an adult, and the new, but less respectable, ones which are imposed during later maturity. Thus, in our culture, the transition into the roles of old age comes as something that is both involuntary and radical.

Society has seemingly tried to compensate for its emasculation of the older ages by acting indulgently and protectively. An aged person might be helped across the street, or given a seat on the bus, or cared for in a county home, or allowed an assistance grant; but he is still "put on the shelf" whether he likes it or not. Maybe enforced retirement is inevitable in a technological era. But some way of helping people to keep productive and useful ought to be found, right up to the end.

The Old Folks Movement.—So great has been the interest and organized activity centering around old people recently that we can properly refer to it as a movement. Part of this concern over the aged is to be explained by a sheer increase in their numbers; part by a continuing dependency among them; and part by a growing group consciousness. At any rate, it would seem time for society to recognize the problem and to allow respectable roles for this large segment of its population. A start has been made.

One side of the movement comes from the old folks themselves. As their problem has grown greater, they have become more aware of it and more discontent. As their numbers have increased, they have come to feel a new sense of power. The result has been organization for political action, with the so-called "Townsend Movement" as the most notable example. Clubs started for the purpose of exerting political pressure have usually served a social function for members as well. With the trend toward an older population we can expect more agitation, or action, from the group itself; age is coming to use both self-help and pressure for its own cause.

The other part of the picture consists of attempts on the part of various outside agencies to promote conditions for the betterment of old age. This takes many forms, ranging from research on the physical and mental pathologies of aging to legislation establishing financial assistance for those in need.

Two terms have recently come into use: *gerontology,* which is the scientific study of the aging process, and *geriatrics,* which is the applied phase, or care of the aged. Medical groups, organized to study and treat problems of aging, are springing up all over the country. The United States Surgeon General has appointed a National Advisory Committee to deal with the subject. A unit on gerontology has been set up within the United States Public Health Service. The National Research Council has founded a Committee on Aging. State and county health departments are rapidly changing their programs so as to give better attention to the problem. Many hospitals are organizing special units along this line.

Scientific knowledge concerning the problems of aging is still meager. To date most research has had to do with the physical and mental disorders of old age, with relatively little attention being given to adjustment problems as affected by changes and conditions within society. This is the next step.

In the meantime there have developed numerous attempts to apply what is known and believed. One of these is the publishing of literature aimed at a better understanding of the problem; most of this has come within the last decade, showing that the movement is barely getting under way. Another is the setting up of a few special counseling centers for the aged; this too is new. A third is the organizing of special social clubs for the elderly. Churches, public welfare agencies, and city recreational departments seem to be taking an interest in the sponsoring of such clubs. For many of the aged no problem is greater than that of loneliness, no need greater than the need for companionship, and it is for this reason that the club movement merits encouragement.

But the problem can never be really solved until society finds a way to let people remain active and useful, so far as their health permits, throughout their later years. Cultural patterns will need to be changed. Cavan points out that, in our present culture, old people are expected to accept conditions as they find them and to do most of the adjusting themselves. She then says:

An alternative type of adjustment would be social adjustment, in which social norms, standards, and institutions would be adjusted to changed conditions in such a way that they would provide more fully for the satisfactions of the needs of the old. The only uniform social adjustment in the United States to the changed social world of the old has been in the provision for Old Age Assistance, Old Age and Survivors' Insurance, and Unemployment Compensation which old workers may secure for a limited period when they are unable to find work. The amounts of money granted are in general inadequate to meet present costs of living and hence represent an incomplete form of social adjustment. A widespread form of social adjustment is the provision of protective living arrangements; this adjustment takes the form of institutional homes and nursing homes or infirmaries. During the last war a form of social adjustment occurred when some plants employed previously retired workers, sometimes grouping them together with special modification of speed of work expected. A few centers for counseling old people have been established in some of the larger cities. In some large cities, also, individual social centers have been created to provide recreation for old people. *But in general, little*

has been done to change social conditions to fill the gaps left by the
disintegration of a primarily rural, handicraft society and the develop-
ment of an urban, mechanized society.[8]

It is to this end, largely, that the old folks movement is being
directed. Specific solutions to the problem must await development.

Processes and Problems Incident to Aging

But society adapts itself rather slowly, and not always successfully. It is wisdom, therefore, not to wait for utopia.
Though a part of the answer to the difficulties of age rests
upon social change, there is much that individuals can do within the present cultural framework.

It has been said that "life begins at forty." While the claim
is not entirely true, it does serve as a wholesome antidote for
the belief that age is something to be dreaded or feared. A
common tendency of middle age is to try to appear younger
than one actually is, to refuse to face the fact that one is getting
old. Women, particularly, are prone to understate their ages [9]
and to pretend perpetual youth by the use of make-up and the
like. We do not wish to imply that maturing individuals should
fail to keep themselves attractive; quite the contrary. But aging
is nothing to be ashamed of, or to dread, provided that one is
prepared, and is able to keep active and progressive as he moves
along. It is giving up or living low that should make one feel
embarrassed, not growing old. While there are difficulties involved, so are there at other levels of maturity; and the satisfactions people find, at whatever age, depend quite largely
upon their own attitudes and adjustments. Growing old is inevitable in the life process; maladjustment is not. In spite of
the problems which old age presents, many persons have discovered that life can become increasingly meaningful and enjoyable with each added year of experience.

---

[8] *Ibid.*, p. 29. Italics not in the original.
[9] See T. Lynn Smith and Homer L. Hitt, "The Misstatement of Women's
Ages and the Vital Indexes," *Metron*, Vol. 13, 1939, pp. 95-108.

The Climacteric.—As they grow older, both men and women experience a decline in reproductive capacity. This "change of life," which is often accompanied by other body disturbances, is know as the "climacteric."

In the female, the most recognizable sign of the onset of this crisis is the cessation of menstruation (known technically as the menopause). This usually occurs somewhere around the mid-forties, though it has been known to take place as early as the early-thirties and as late as the late-fifties. What happens is that the ovaries decline in their functioning and fail to produce sufficient growth on the walls of the uterus to result in bleeding. This decrease or absence of the ovarian function causes disturbances in other glands—notably the pituitary, thyroid, and adrenals—which in turn may set the entire body system off balance. Some women experience rather severe discomforts during this period, while others are bothered hardly at all. The length of the climacteric also varies considerably, ranging all the way from a few months to several years. Common symptoms are: headaches, hot flashes, vague pains, dizziness, insomnia, depressed feelings, nervousness, irritability. It is a time for patience and understanding on the part of other family members. Medical attention is sometimes needed. All women will at least want to consult a physician and have a check-up, though in many cases that is all that will be necessary. In time, nature will usually establish a new glandular balance within the body, and the climacteric is over.

The male climacteric generally commences later than with the female, is less severe, more gradual, and of longer duration. Just because the change of life is less spectacular with the male (does not include a menopause, for example), there is no reason for considering it any less real. It is glandular change that causes the climacteric in man, just as in woman, and the general symptoms are similar. As man grows older, both his desire and his ability for sexual intercourse decline. There are cases on record of men in their eighties and nineties becoming fathers; usually, however, man's reproductive capacity gives way before such extreme ages are reached. Along with this diminishing of the sex function comes a general but gradual decline of physical vigor. Hormone treatment, where needed, can usually bring relief.

It is the period accompanying the climacteric (from the early thirties to the late fifties approximately) that is the most crucial from the standpoint of health and well-being in old age. These are the years of greatest activity, responsibility, and strain. Diseases and disabilities commonly associated with later maturity have their beginning at this time—rheumatism, arthritis, heart trouble, glandular disturbance, diabetes, cancer, mental disorders. Unless checked they are likely to become chronic. One of the dangers grows out of the fact that these conditions often start without much warning and then develop slowly, so that much of the damage has been done before one becomes aware of the seriousness of the problem. Another difficulty lies in the highly competitive nature of our society, causing men and women to overforce themselves at the very time they ought to be slowing down.

There are a number of changes in social relationships which take place at this same time and which add to the personal problems just discussed. Cavan regards late middle age as a transitional period involving many cultural contradictions. After comparing it with the preschool and adolescent periods, also transitional, she says:

During the transitional period between adulthood and old age, conflicts again appear. The elderly person is expected to manage his personal affairs in a responsible manner, but is expected to retire from paid employment; he is expected to lead an independent social life without making demands upon relatives or friends, but often is ridiculed or frowned upon if in the loneliness of widowhood, he makes a second marriage; he is expected to support community institutions financially and personally, but not to be elected to a board presidency or staff position. Thus the person in late middle age finds that in some respects he is expected to behave like an old person. He is still young enough for certain types of adult activities but is considered too old for other types of adult activities. Therefore he cannot consistently be either adult or aged; social pressures force him to play both roles. Eventually the elderly person passes through this period of conflicting adult and old-age patterns and enters into a later period when he is no

longer expected to conform to the adult pattern. In this later period
the pressure of society is all toward his acceptance of the old-age
pattern.[10]

While the quotation is pointed particularly to the latest phase
of this shift into old age, it indicates the general nature of the
transition that commences at about age forty.

The forties and fifties are sometimes referred to as "the
dangerous age." One element of danger lies in the health problem, already discussed; another in the fact of new and emerging role conflicts. Sensing a decline in physical vigor, and feeling the growing pressure of social restriction, people of this
age frequently go to excesses in trying to demonstrate that
they are still young or in having a "last fling" before old age
overtakes them. In this attempted withdrawal from the aging
process younger persons of the opposite sex tend to seem especially attractive. With the children gone, or going, there are
likely to be fewer interests and responsibilities to tie to in the
home. The age is "dangerous," therefore, in the sense that it
brings an increased tendency toward infidelity.

In most families the climacteric comes to parents at about
the same time that children are marrying and leaving home.
This is the time, also, that society commences to define the
couple as getting old, and to impose restrictions. Thus a triple
adjustment is required: adjustment to personal discomforts
involved in the change of life; adjustment to lowered status
and restricted roles in society; and adjustment to a different
kind of family relationship. Regarding this latter, parents now
face the new task of "weaning" themselves from their children.
Each of these problems is made more difficult by the presence
of the others.

The Empty Nest.—We have already observed that modern
mates live together more than a decade, or about one fourth of
their entire married span, after the children have all married
and moved away. This is the period of the empty nest. Its increasing importance in the family cycle is due to both the declining birth rate, which lets the child-rearing state end sooner,

---

10 Cavan and others, *op. cit.,* pp. 20-21.

and the declining death rate, which permits husband and wife to live longer than before.

In the previous chapter we wrote of the need for young adults to emancipate themselves from the home. If marriage is to be successful, we noted, those who marry must overcome chronic homesickness and the tendency to lean excessively upon parents or to run to them every time trouble knocks. Here we are interested in the other side of the picture, in the readjustments required of parents.

Not only do parents need to "move over" when children first arrive in the family, but they must also learn how to "let go" when it comes time for these children to marry and leave home. This isn't always easy. Parents and children normally will have become adjusted to each other on an intimate and continued basis. Years of living together will have caused affections to grow deep and habits and ways of life to become established with respect to the total group. Any sudden severing of this relationship naturally brings some strain and pain to family members. While the children move on to a new life of expanding relationships, their parents are left by themselves and with frequent feelings of emptiness and loneliness at the loss.

Readjustment at this stage of family development is generally more difficult for the wife than it is for the husband. He is still active in his role as breadwinner; his big crisis will come later when he is faced with retirement. It is more the wife and mother who is left alone as the family contracts, for it is she who has been more active in the care and management of children up to this time. Furthermore, it is the woman who is more likely to live longer, which means that widowhood is a greater prospect for her than for her husband. These facts make it extra important for modern woman to prepare for the two or three decades at the end of life when she is to be deprived of her customary family contacts. For most women these changes in family interaction are inevitable. The crisis is less severe where there is a realistic acceptance of this fact and an honest attempt to fill the void with other kinds of productive activity.

Parents can be quite selfish in the matter of letting their children go. There are instances of children being kept from marrying so the old folks wouldn't be left alone. There are other instances of parents expecting or demanding too much of their married children, pushing themselves upon them without invitation and then acting hurt at the least sign of resistance. More than one marriage has been spoiled by the failure of parents to understand that married children, in order to establish a new home, need emancipation from the old one.

But the other extreme is equally serious. Married children who neglect or reject their parents are also selfish, and their actions contribute more to the sorrows of old age than perhaps anything else. One of the greatest hurts that ever come to aged parents is the discovery that their children no longer care, or that they want them out of the way. Public welfare records are replete with cases of old people unwanted by their children. Old folks homes and mental hospitals are full of forgotten men and women who seldom or never have visitors and whose letters go unanswered. The following is taken from a recent article in the *Indianapolis Star,* titled "Welter of Loneliness."

Once upon a time the man we'll call "Grandpop Smith" had relatives. Records show that back in 1914 his sister, three years his elder, had him committed to a hospital for the insane.

Maybe at first some of his relatives did visit the white-haired man. Records don't show and his memory has faded. But in as many years as records have been kept, there's nothing to show that "Grandpop" ever received a visit, a letter, a Christmas card from the "outside."

In the last few months "Grandpop" has been having trouble with his heart. Doctors listened and shook their heads. Officials of the colony started a search for relatives.

So far every effort has failed to turn up anyone claiming relationship to one of the state's "colony of lost men."

Ill and lonely, "Grandpop Smith" awaits death alone. If within thirty days of his death no relative wishing to claim his body can be found, state law requires that it be turned over to the anatomical board for research purposes.

The ideal relationship between parents and married children would seem to be midway between these two extremes. While the marriage of children requires a partial relinquishing of parental roles, it need not mean a complete severance of the family bond; normal cooperative interaction between parents and children can still go on, and to the benefit of both. Many married couples find that their parents can be a source of genuine companionship and helpfulness when given a chance. And many aging persons have discovered that their lives are made richer if they participate in the affairs of children only moderately, and supplement such family activity with something else. There can be emancipation without isolation or rejection. There can be interaction without interference.

The misunderstandings and conflicts that sometimes exist between parents and their married children are partly conflicts of two generations grown apart by social change. Dinkel claims that most disputes between aged parents and their children follow conflict patterns laid down during the early years of the family, and that these conflicts had their origin in the cultural setting of that time. Particularly significant, he found, was the dominantly rural background of parents, as contrasted with the newer urban culture which the children were following. He suggested that conflict between aged parents and their children may diminish in the future, due to certain shifts in the culture: a disappearance of rural pioneer mores which would make the cultures between generations less divergent; a further loosening of family ties and redefining of parental authority which would mean that the two generations would have less contact with each other than formerly, and the parents less control; and an improvement in the community interests and social status of the aged which would leave them less identified with their children and less concerned with their behavior.[11]

After parenthood comes grandparenthood. It is only natural for aging individuals to take an interest in their grandchildren, coming partly as a substitute for the time when they were surrounded by children of their own, and partly, perhaps, out of pride over an expanding progeny. A potential danger is for grandparents to interfere with the discipline set up by the

---

[11] Robert M. Dinkel, "Parent-Child Conflict in Minnesota Families," *American Sociological Review,* 8 :412-19, August, 1943.

parents, and to overindulge the children. Another tendency is for parents to overimpose upon the grandparents, using them as baby tenders and the like without adequate consideration for their needs and desires. With a cooperative attitude, these problems can be avoided. There may be occasions when one party or the other will need to explain what is happening, or even take a stand against the offending person, for the sake of the child, the marriage, or out of consideration for his own personal welfare.

Von Hentig has shown how the modern grandmother often plays a vital and effective role in family survival. Though not generally accepted as an active member of the group, she is always "standing ready in emergency, especially when there is a gap to be filled and missing members of intermediary generations have to be replaced." Here are typical situations into which she fits: providing shelter for divorcees, caring for illegitimate or neglected grandchildren, receiving children and grandchildren into her home when apartments cannot be found or when the man is out of work.[12]

The satisfactions and sorrows of elderly people are to a considerable extent related to the way their families treat them. On the one hand we have testimonies of unhappy persons in the later years of life who almost invariably complain of feeling unwanted, alone, and in the way. To counterbalance this, there are many others who tell of finding their greatest comfort from association with the children and grandchildren.

It seems right that elderly parents be permitted to associate with and enjoy their own progeny. But this is not to say that all of their activity and pleasure ought to come from this one source. Since in the parents' earlier years a large amount of attention was given to the family, it often seems natural for them to continue in much the same pattern after the children have married. This is a mistake, for it can lead to idleness, interference, and conflict. To put all of one's eggs in the family basket, so to speak, is to err, for it means being left stranded during the later years. Part of the art of growing old grace-

12 Hans Von Hentig, "The Sociological Function of the Grandmother," *Social Forces,* 24:389-92, May, 1946.

fully is to reserve interesting and profitable activities for the time of the empty nest.

With the children gone, husband and wife should be able to find more time for each other. There is opportunity now to rebuild some of the patterns that existed between them before their family started but which may have been sidetracked during the busy years of childbearing and child-rearing. More attention can now be given to the mate needs of one another; they can draw closer together in companionship.

There is also more time at this stage for nonfamilial activities. This is especially true for the wife. There may have been career or hobby interests that she found necessary to lay aside while the children were at home and needing care. Now is her chance to develop them. As a matter of fact, many women solve the dilemma of wanting a career and a family too by utilizing the postfamily state in this way. New interests can always be cultivated. Club and community work frequently provides an effective outlet for women without children; it keeps them busy, gives them a sense of usefulness, and opens up the way for new contacts and friendships.

Retirement.—The adjustment problems of later years are similar for men and women, though by no means identical. We have already noted that the loss of children presents a greater crisis for the female, as also does widowhood. This is because women, on the whole, depend more upon interpersonal affectional relationships for their satisfactions. It must also be remembered that women, as mothers, have more to do in caring for children, and that most wives outlive their husbands. Men, on the other hand, tend more to lose themselves in work activities outside the home. When the children marry, they are still active and interested in their job. Chances are more than even that they will finish their years without the necessity of living all alone. But they have become so habituated to their work that any sudden or forced cessation of this activity is apt to leave them feeling frustrated.

In our culture, retirement generally comes rather suddenly and is arbitrarily imposed. We have laws and regulations requiring that most workers step aside when they reach a certain age, usually sixty-five. It isn't a matter of gradually decreasing one's productive activity, but of suddenly stopping. Nor is it, except in some of the businesses and professions, a matter of free choice as to when one is ready to retire. Many of the disorganizing accompaniments of the aging process are attributable to these cultural impositions.

One of the most difficult aspects of retirement is loss of status. Up to about this time the individual will have been gaining in respect among his fellow men; he will have been building up, making a contribution. Now, suddenly, he is "put on the shelf" and told that his services are no longer needed. This, in a machine culture, means that others will no longer look up to him as they once did, for he is not producing. He may feel hurt and humiliated as a result.

Another difficulty in retirement is loss of significant activity. After one has spent a lifetime in being busy and useful, it isn't easy to turn suddenly idle or to engage in things that seem trivial and insignificant. Boredom is likely to set in. Life may become dull and montonous. There isn't much enjoyment in "just hanging around," seeming to be in the way of others, and waiting for the end.

Retirement could be made easier by the initiation of a few social changes: (1) permitting aging individuals to keep working on a part-time or reduced-load basis so that they would continue to feel useful and their transition into inactivity would be gradual; (2) varying the time of complete retirement according to the needs and abilities of individuals so that all who wanted could remain productive as long as they were physically and mentally capable; and (3) providing substitute roles and facilities so that the retired could continue to remain active, feel important, and have companions.

The most successful adjustment comes when the person retires *to* something worth while rather than *from* what he considers pleasurable and profitable in life. How well one can do this will depend upon both society and himself; social change is needed to give the aged more meaningful roles, but there is significance also in the attitudes and efforts of individuals.

Retirement makes it possible for one to do the jobs he may always have wanted to do but didn't have time for before. Places can be visited; books can be written; hobbies and avocations can be further developed. There will be more opportunity now for getting the diary or autobiography in shape and for working up the family genealogy. Memories can be relived, although one is usually happier if he doesn't try to stay too much with the past. Participation in club and community activities can prove both interesting and profitable from the standpoint of community service. All of these, together with others not mentioned, can help compensate for satisfactions previously derived from the workaday world.

There is much that a person can do by way of preparing for retirement. It is extremely important that one comes to accept the idea psychologically so that adjustment does not become blocked by feelings of resentment or hostility. Closely related to this, and of equal importance, is the necessity for getting practice in the enjoyment of leisure time as one moves along; those who tie themselves to their jobs too completely frequently find that they don't know how to use leisure when they get it. Then there is the matter of planning ahead, of storing up activities for the future, so that one never reaches the state of having nothing to do. Finally, preparation for retirement needs to take into account the fact that old people, too, have to eat.

Dependency.—Retirement is frequently the first step toward dependency. In earlier sociey, when familism was strong, it was not so necessary for working individuals to lay anything aside for old age—they could continue active as long as desired and after that their kinfolk would take care of them. Today it is different; not only are there many more persons in the upper ages than before, but children feel less responsibility for their parents, and society requires that they stop working. This wouldn't be too bad, perhaps, if people would and could save enough during their productive period to carry them over the later years. Some do this rather well; others accomplish it partially; still others not at all. It is safe to say that at least half of those sixty-five years of age and over need partial or complete support from sources other than themselves.

Some insight into the way children feel about taking care of aged parents can be obtained from a study by Dinkel. He found that the obligations which children recognize toward their parents differ by religion, by rural-urban residence, and by seriousness of the hardship involved:

Catholics more often than Protestants, and rural more often than urban residents, believe [that children have an obligation to the parents]. . . . Many more students accepted than rejected the obligation of children when the situation did not present unusual difficulties. The division of opinion was about even when the hardship was a severe one. Under extreme circumstances the balance swung sharply to the side opposed to the support of parents.[13]

This would seem to support our earlier contention regarding the effects of urbanization and industrialization upon familism. It also makes clear the modern tendency of children to decline responsibility for the care of parents whenever the difficulties involved are great.

Cavan has analyzed various types of living arrangements and shown how these relate to personal and family adjustments during old age. The majority of elderly persons, she found, live in their own homes as either head or wife of the family head. It is these individuals who are best adjusted and most happy; they have better health, higher economic position, more companionship, and a greater zest for living. Those who live with adult children, or who room out, or who enter an institution are distinctly less well adjusted, and in about that order. Yet with increasing age come increases in the proportions who are under one of these other arrangements. She concludes by saying:

Granting that it is often impossible for the old person to maintain his home until his death, what type of living arrangement seems best? Clearly, more institutions of the present type are not the answer; nor do rooming houses meet all the problems; homes with adult children

<hr>

[13] Robert M. Dinkel, "Attitudes of Children Toward Supporting Aged Parents," *American Sociological Review*, 9:370-79, August, 1944.

have both advantages and disadvantages. A new type of living arrangement is needed that will combine the economic and physical security provided by the institution, the personal contacts found in their own home or the home of adult children, and the activities and sense of usefulness of the person who is still living independently.[14]

One approach to the problem of old age dependency is for people to build up assets during their productive years so that they will have something to draw from when they want to retire. These savings can take the form of bank deposits, property investments, or annuity plans. The latter, especially, is coming into rather wide usage. It is a form of insurance wherein the purchaser pays in during his working years, and then, with retirement, receives certain calculated monthly payments for the rest of his life. Annuities can be purchased voluntarily, but there are any number of compulsory plans also where the employee accepts the system as part of his job and regular deductions are made from his pay check. Examples are: the railroad retirement system, the Carnegie retirement plan for college teachers, and arrangements for government employees. The "Old Age and Survivors' Insurance" feature of the Federal Social Security Act is of this same general type for it is built upon the insurance principle and involves forced savings. Various pension plans can likewise be placed in this category, for they operate on the principle of financing old age out of the surplus productivity of earlier years.

But most of the employed population does not operate under regular retirement plans. Furthermore, it isn't every worker that is able to save sufficiently for his later years. Inevitably, therefore, so long as society is organized the way it is, there will be people who grow old without accumulating the resources that would enable them to remain self-supporting. The recent swing toward public welfare is recognition of two things: greater need, and acceptance of the point of view that society is at least partly responsible. We are moving into an age of "social security." Applied to old age, we can note that more than two million persons in this country are now receiving

---

[14] Ruth Shonle Cavan, "Family Life and Family Substitutes in Old Age." *American Sociological Review.* 14:71-83. February, 1949.

Old Age Assistance that comes from tax funds. There are private programs in addition.

It seems to us that there are three sources of responsibility in this problem: (1) First and foremost is the couple itself. Its task is that of planning and saving for the future, of accumulating a surplus during the productive years. Insurance and annuities can help. (2) Then there is the family of the couple, notably the children. Their responsibility lies in the area of "return for services rendered." If the elderly couple is dependent, one reason might be that they have so worked and sacrificed for the children that they haven't been able to lay anything aside for the future. It is up to the children, then, to give them a return on their investment. (3) But there are many cases where the children of needy parents are themselves in need, or are in circumstances that permit them to render only meager aid. This is the time for society to lend a helping hand. After all, dependency is largely the result of social conditions. Furthermore, the over-all welfare of any social group is contingent upon the condition of its parts. The first aim of society ought to be for security through personal savings, insurance, and annuity. This can be government sponsored, as the "Old Age and Survivors' Insurance" part of the Social Security Act now is, but it need not be. Any substantial reduction in old-age relief rolls will undoubtedly require a further expansion of such plans, which encourage the working individual to lay something aside for his time of need. From whatever source help is given, it is well to be remembered that old people, too, have pride. There would be far less suffering if children and agencies made greater efforts to protect the independence and self-respect of those they help.

Infirmity.—As men and women grow older, it is inevitable that their body functions gradually slow down, lose power, and develop "knocks"; people wear out, as well as machines. The following is a summary from the *National Health Survey:*

The frequency of all types of illness among those over 65 is very high, about equal to that among children from 5 to 9 years of age. Moreover, illness in these later years is often prolonged; one estimate indicates that the average person 65 years of age and over will have about five weeks of disabling illness per year. Chronic illness and invalidism are common, due to the fact that deaths from degenerative diseases are often preceded by months or years of failing health, followed by illness that progresses toward a fatal termination. Diseases of the respiratory tract are frequent, and digestive disorders are more frequent than at any period except infancy. . . . The National Survey found that about 68 of every 1,000 persons surveyed among this age group were handicapped by some orthopedic impairment. The Survey also emphasized the increased frequency of blindness with advancing age. . . .[15]

The inevitability of some of this happening to everyone who grows old makes adjustment all the more necessary. There are three suggestions that we would offer: (1) Some things the individual can do to prevent, or at least delay, these various disabilities from afflicting him. He can learn how to relax along about middle age; he can slow down in his work when necessary; he can watch for early danger signals; and he can keep close to the counsel of his physician. (2) This last point warrants a little elaboration from the standpoint of therapy. Granting that certain disabilities will develop eventually, in spite of all that one can do, medical care is valuable both from the standpoint of easing discomfort and from the standpoint of preventing or slowing down further development of the difficulty. (3) But even the best in prevention and therapy cannot hold back all illness and discomfort during the aging process. The best thing, therefore, is to supplement these other efforts with a certain amount of psychological adjustment. To grow old gracefully, one has to learn how to live with his infirmities, to stop complaining about them, to accept the handicap.

Extreme cases of infirmity or senility require institutional care. After an individual has passed the point of self-help and responsibility, as happens to a few of the aged, it is only kindness to place him where he can be properly attended. To expect children to personally care for the bodily needs of parents, or to live through weeks and weeks of mental anguish trying to

---

15 National Resources Planning Board, *Human Conservation, The Story of Our Wasted Resources* (Washington, D. C.: Government Printing Office, 1943), pp. 92-93.

understand and please someone whose mind is failing, is perhaps asking too much. Besides, hospitals are better equipped to meet the needs of persons in this condition with regard to both comfort and therapy. It is unfortunate, of course, that so many of the institutions in which old people must be placed are substandard; this emphasizes the need for careful selection. Another and larger need is for an arousal of public interest in the problem, aimed at social action to improve the institutions.

SUMMARY AND IMPLICATIONS

Growing old is a slow-moving process involving gradual reduction in personal power and restriction in social activity. There is no one age that marks the time when a person is actually old, for people vary greatly in attitude, in physical and mental resilience, and in the rate at which they are willing to slough off activity. But, nominally speaking, one is old at the time society decides, usually at retirement. It is from this discrepancy between personal need and cultural definition that much of the adjustment difficulty of old age arises.

Studies in attitudes of old people reveal four major patterns of complaint: [16] (1) They dislike physical discomfort and ill health, particularly as these restrict their ability to work or care for the home. (2) They are unhappy about having to be alone so much of the time, of being denied adequate social contact and companionship, especially with their own children. (3) They are bored by inactivity and monotony, by not having anything to do that is interesting or that seems worth while. (4) They are resentful and disillusioned by dependency, with the lowered status and lost privacy and self-respect that are sometimes involved.

Though not entirely typical, the following account of an eighty-four-year-old bedridden woman illustrates many of the features listed above:

After she broke her hip and it became apparent she would not be able to walk again, she entered a nursing home in a remote suburb of

---

[16] Cf. Cavan and others, *op. cit.*, pp. 35-39.

the city where she had some relatives. She thus has the security of feeling near someone who would be responsible for her welfare; but by this move she has cut herself off from her many friends. She spends her time reading, listening to the radio, knitting, writing numerous letters, and reading the letters that come to her. She has made acquaintances among people who call upon other patients in the home, but regards her real friends as those of her earlier years whom she rarely sees.

She talks calmly about her handicap, laughs at old age, and asserts that she does not expect to live long. There is, in fact, an air of bravado in her attitude, as though she were forcing herself to view her situation objectively, not allowing herself to become emotional about it. The counterpart to this attitude comes in admissions that she feels "blue," often cries at night when no one can see her, feels that she has lived her life and would just as soon die as live, feels she is no longer useful. She looks back on a life that has been very useful and happy and talks about it with a certain nostalgia. But this life has ended; the next life has not begun. In the meantime she fills the time as well as she can and waits patiently for the transition period to end.[17]

Adjustment is a function of both the society and the personality. There are certain things that society can do to ease the process of growing old: it can, for example, allow for more flexibility in retirement rules, permit workers to let up gradually, encourage savings through annuity plans as preparation against dependency, provide better organization and facilities for the free time of elderly persons, and continue the development of gerontology and geriatrics, including the improvement of institutions having to do with care of the aged. Other things are up to the individual, such as: observing the laws of health, laying up savings during the productive years, accepting and planning for old age with some degree of pleasure, and actively seeking new friends and activities so that life can remain interesting right up to the end.

Adjustment is almost always more successful when it can take place gradually. Any sudden crisis, such as sickness, unemployment, or loss of a loved one inevitably complicates the problem. This is as true for old age as for any period in life,

---

[17] *Ibid.*, pp. 65-66. Taken from a longer sketch.

even more so. Elderly persons have less energy with which to meet a crisis. Furthermore, crises have a tendency to pile up during the later years; it is not easy to have to face retirement, ill health, and widowhood, all at about the same time.

Generally speaking, those persons who have proved themselves to be most adaptable during the early and middle years are the ones who are most effective in handling problems of later maturity. One advantage elderly people do have is experience. Old age is sometimes blamed for difficulties that are in the personality; at sixty or seventy people often have to face facts and problems that they previously were able to dodge. Those who have had practice in facing life and adjusting as they went along are the ones that are best prepared for these newer emergencies. Rigid and inflexible individuals have the most trouble. They are the ones who tend to become frustrated and to seek escape by continually dwelling on the past.

What has all of this to do with marriage and family relationships? The answer should be obvious: Old age is the last stage of a given family cycle. Most elderly persons will have first gone through the experiences of marrying and rearing children. This means that they will likely still belong to families, that they will continue to affect, and be affected by, interaction among descendants. In many instances they will still be married; in others, widowed (a subject to be treated in the next chapter). To grow old gracefully is to complete the picture of successful marriage.

Problems and Projects

1. "For a large number, old age means little more than disillusionment and anticlimax." List as many reasons as you can. Which of these are cultural? Which personal?
2. Assuming good health and financial independence, about how long would you like to live? Point out conditions that could change your mind, indicating how and why.
3. What are the likely social consequences of an aging population? Which of these do you consider desirable? Which undesirable? Why?

4. Should aged and dependent parents be taken care of by their children or by society? Discuss the pros and cons of each system, pointing out the specific arrangements which you think best.

5. Name ways in which you think society, or the culture, will need to change if old age is to be made more satisfying. Are any of these already under way?

6. Name ways in which elderly persons can increase their own satisfactions. When they are unhappy, is this their own fault or society's? Will self-effort solve the problem? Discuss.

7. From other sources, prepare a paper dealing with the health problems and necessary precautions incident to the climacteric —for both male and female.

8. What other changes, social and familial, usually take place at about this same time to complicate the problem of the climacteric? Discuss.

9. Why does the period of the empty nest demand more consideration today than in earlier times? Why is this period in the family cycle usually more of a crisis for the mother than the father? Make suggestions for the woman whose family has gone. Is her place still in the home?

10. What obligations, if any, do young married adults have toward their parents? Describe the type of relationship that you feel would be most productive of satisfaction on both sides.

11. Should a married couple consent to having an elderly or ailing parent live with them? Why or why not? Discuss the alternatives.

12. Visit a home for the aged and write a description of what you find, with special attention to the attitudes and feelings of the persons residing there. Make suggestions for improvement.

13. What useful family functions may grandparents still perform? Suggest ways for making grandparenthood more satisfying. To what extent should parents be permitted to indulge or spoil their grandchildren? Discuss.

14. Discuss the pros and cons of arbitrary retirement rules. What

social changes are needed to make retirement easier? What can the individual do to aid his own adjustment?

15. What has "growing old gracefully" to do with marriage and family stability? Discuss.

SELECTED READINGS

ARTHUR, JULIETTA K. *Jobs for Women Over 35*. New York: Prentice-Hall, Inc., 1948.

CAVAN, RUTH SHONLE, BURGESS, ERNEST W., HAVIGHURST, ROBERT J., and GOLDHAMER, HERBERT. *Personal Adjustment in Old Age*. Chicago: Science Research Associates, 1949.

ELMER, M. C. *The Sociology of the Family*. Boston: Ginn & Co., 1945. Chap. xxii, "Old Age."

FISHBEIN, MORRIS, and BURGESS, ERNEST W. (eds.). *Successful Marriage*. New York: Doubleday & Co., 1947. Part V, chap. v, "Sex Behavior and Problems of the Climacteric."

GROVES, ERNEST R. *Marriage*. New York: Henry Holt & Co., 1941. Chap. xxvii, "The Climacteric."

GUMPERT, MARTIN. *You Are Younger Than You Think*. New York: Duell, Sloan & Pearce, Inc., 1944.

JOHNSON, WINGATE M. *The Years After Fifty*. New York: McGraw-Hill Book Co., 1947.

LANDIS, PAUL H. *Population Problems*. New York: American Book Co., 1948. Chap. xv, "Changing Age Composition and the Population Structure."

LAWTON, GEORGE. *Aging Successfully*. New York: Columbia University Press, 1946.

——, (ed.). *New Goals for Old Age*. New York: Columbia University Press, 1943.

——, and STEWART, MAXWELL S. *When You Grow Old*. New York: Public Affairs Committee, 1947.

MARTIN, LILLIEN J. *A Handbook for Old Age Counsellors*. San Francisco: Gurtz Printing Co., 1944.

PITKIN, WALTER B. *The Best Years*. New York: Current Books, Inc., 1946.

POLLAK, OTTO. *Social Adjustment in Old Age, A Research Planning Report*. New York: Social Science Research Council, 1948.

POPENOE, PAUL. *Marriage Before and After*. New York: Wilfred Funk, Inc., 1943. Chap. xxxii, "Love After Forty."

STEINEROHN, PETER JOSEPH. *Forget Your Age*. New York: Doubleday & Co., 1945.

WINSTON, ELLEN. "Social Problems of the Aged," *Social Forces*, 26:57-61, October, 1947.

Chapter 13

LIVING WITHOUT A MATE

No analysis of marriage would be complete without consideration of the twelve million or more adult Americans who are living without a mate. A large proportion of these have never married; others have married but are single again through the death of a mate; the remainder have separated or become divorced. These are the unattached. Together they make up about one out of every seven adult persons in this country.

THOSE WHO NEVER MARRY

United States census figures reveal that nearly 10 per cent of our adult population never marries. Only about 90 per cent of all who reach the age of forty-five have had the marriage experience. Since very few of the remaining 10 per cent will marry after that age, it follows that about one tenth of all adults end their lives as single individuals.

The percentage that never marries is even greater when all ages are considered. This is illustrated by the fact that of every 100,000 females born, only approximately 78,000 ever marry (of these, only about 65,000 eventually become mothers).[1] This means that between one fifth and one fourth of all persons born never marry; some because of death before the time of marriage and others because they either choose it that way or lack opportunity on the adult level.

What Are They Like?—It would be both inaccurate and unjust to assume that the unmarried, as a class, are inferior to the married. Though some individuals remain single be-

---

[1] Paul H. Landis, *Population Problems* (New York: American Book Co., 1943), p. 238.

cause of personality deficiencies, others never marry in order to better express their personal talents. Though society encourages marriage, it is rapidly coming to accept the unmarried state as normal and to remove many of the handicaps which formerly surrounded it.

Single persons of every age group have higher death rates than do those who are married. This is particularly true of the male, but with certain exceptions during the childbearing ages it applies to the female as well. Reasons are two: (1) Marriage is selective as to health, the tendency being for those with serious constitutional weaknesses or deficiencies to remain single. (2) Marriage tends to favor the health of its members by encouraging a more settled and systematic mode of living.

There is a strong probability that unmarried men and women differ from each other in regard to quality. In an earlier chapter we referred to the commonly observed tendency of men to marry beneath themselves for the sake of ego protection—supported by parallel tendencies of many capable women to want a career, to delay marriage for it, and to be more particular than men in choosing a mate. This "marrying down" expresses itself in the areas of age, education, general socioeconomic status, and very possibly with reference to physical and emotional aspects of the personality. Folsom has used the term *mating gradient* to describe the tendency, claiming that it "would seem to leave an unmarried residue on the upper rungs of the female social ladder and on the lower rungs of the male ladder." [2]

This point finds reinforcement in the fact that of women who don't go beyond the sixth grade in school, about 95 per cent marry, while only some 70 per cent of those who graduate from college ever marry.[3] Apparently it is the more able and career-minded of the females that go on for higher education, and in going on they reduce their marriage chances, both by becoming older and by becoming too intellectual for the dominance-loving male. We should add parenthetically, however,

---

[2] Joseph K. Folsom, *The Family and Democratic Society* (New York: John Wiley & Sons, Inc., 1943), pp. 490-91.
[3] Metropolitan Life Insurance Company, "Marriage and Educational Attainment," *Statistical Bulletin,* August, 1945, pp. 4-6.

that though marriage after college graduation becomes slightly less likely for the girl, this does not apply while she is in school; the college campus has proved itself to be an extremely productive laboratory for mate selection. Furthermore, as studies reveal, college marriages, when they do take place, are less likely to end in divorce than are noncollege marriages.

Why Don't They Marry?—Some people remain permanently unmarried by choice, others due to circumstances. Major types are as follows: (1) Certain individuals are denied the right to marry by society. These are those who fail to meet the minimum requirements of the marriage statutes or who are under long-range custodial care in institutions. (2) Sometimes people remain single in the spirit of self-sacrifice and because of defects in heredity, health, ability, or character. These are likely to feel inadequate to the marriage situation—incapable of a normal sex life or of anything else that goes with marriage and family. (3) In certain cultures there are individuals who remain single out of devotion to a cause. A good example of this is religious celibacy, as in Roman Catholicism. (4) There are always a few persons who remain basically unresponsive to heterosexual love. These are frequently individuals who are autoerotic, or homosexual, or who have strong parent-fixations. Having been conditioned against marriage, they are likely not even to want it. (5) Then there are those who see marriage as something that is competing with other desires, and who consider the price as too great; they are reluctant to give up their independence or to accept this new responsibility. Men (more than women) sometimes seek arrangements whereby they can have sexual satisfaction without the obligation of marriage. Women (more than men) sometimes find love and marriage interests interfering with their plans for an education and career. (6) Finally, there are persons who never marry through lack of adequate opportunity.

This last point requires further elaboration. It seems likely that the majority of those who remain single do so out of circumstances rather than desire. This is especially true with the female, for she is less free in making advances. Yet choice is relative to the values and standards which people hold. Many of those who have gone through life alone could have married had they been willing to lower their sights and had they done it in time. But who is there to say which is better, no marriage, or marriage to an undesirable person? Judgment in such matters must be left to the people concerned. It is true, however, that single people as they get along in years frequently feel regret over having passed up earlier opportunities.

One's chances for marriage decrease with age. The middle-aged female is at a particular disadvantage, for men generally choose someone younger than themselves. Furthermore, the older men are when they marry, the greater is the age difference between them and the ones they marry. For this reason, older girls frequently get skipped and left out. By waiting too long—because of career interests, or extreme standards, or immaturity and indecision—young people sometimes let the opportunity slip away. Not only is the marriage market smaller as they get older, but they also become more set in their ways and harder to please.

Marriage opportunity is contingent upon situations which permit people to meet and associate with adequate numbers of the opposite sex. If the residential sex ratio is unfavorable, or if occupational activities keep the sexes apart, or if the culturally provided contacts are so formal or superficial as to make it hard for men and women really to get acquainted, marriage becomes difficult. The problem of the white-collar girl in this regard has already been described; surrounded by millions, she is nevertheless lonesome and without male companionship, or enough of it, or the kind desired. (See page 251.)

Sometimes people remain single because of not being able to attract a mate. It may be that they are immature, neurotic, or unmannered in personality; that they give evidence of being selfish and overindependent; that they are too shy to be sociable or even friendly; that they appear overanxious or aggressive (especially the girl); that they are unprepared for the responsibilities of marriage, such as the girl's being a sloppy housekeeper or a poor cook, and the boy's being lazy or unpredictable in the task of earning a living. Serious mate-seekers notice these things.

It is unfortunate, however, that the stigma of personal failure is so often applied to all spinsterhood, regardless of the causes or factors involved. Unmarried women are frequently made to feel that they are inferior or at fault. Actually, the condition may be out of choice, or else due to circumstances that are largely beyond the person's control. Furthermore, if there is to be a stigma it seems only just that men be made to bear a larger portion, since it is they who are most free to choose.

Problems of Adjustment.—The need for adjustment is not peculiar to those who never marry. Throughout most of this book we have been analyzing adjustment processes incident to preparing for and carrying out marriage. Here we turn to some of the special problems surrounding the permanently unmarried.

Single individuals face the same adjustments that are required of most people. Yet certain of their problems are unique. Note the following self-analysis of a forty-year-old college woman:

Like most normal girls, it was my utmost desire to have a husband, some children, and a home of my own. I have always been the home type, rather than a social climber. I love children very much and the sight of a sweet, clean little youngster will bring a lump to my throat faster than anything else. To be deprived of all this has been difficult.

Perhaps the thing which has been the hardest for me to face, and the thing I have cried myself to sleep over more than anything else, is the lack of love of both children and a companion. I have been fortunate in living near enough to married members of my family who have been kind to me in letting me share a little of their children's love. Realizing the pitfalls of this type of thing, I have tried to guard myself against interfering in any way or spoiling the children.

There are many, many times when loneliness overtakes a single person. There are places to go and types of recreation to participate in designed for couples only, or where society frowns upon the single woman's going alone. This need not be missed too much if she makes up her mind to the fact, and centers her interests on the kinds of activities that can be enjoyed alone or in the company of other girls.

Sometimes an unmarried girl gets to feeling that she is queer or without special charm. It is the way people regard marriage and the things they are apt to say that make her feel that way.

Not wanting this disappointment in life to make me the cynical "old maid" which society knows so well, I have tried to adjust and to make my work of primary importance. The thing which I desire most now is to be able to do my work in a pleasing and creditable manner. I want to live a useful life and to have the health and strength necessary for taking care of myself without becoming a burden to anyone.[4]

Though not entirely typical, this case illustrates some of the problems common to many women who fail to marry: there was a strong sense of loss at the lack of children and companionship; there was a feeling of social inconvenience in not being able to participate as freely in group functions; and there was a sensitiveness to being classed as peculiar or inferior. Adjustment, however, was reasonably complete and satisfactory; she had come to accept the situation and to rechannel her drives mainly in the direction of work activities.

It is understandable that failure to marry would bring disappointments to those who have planned and dreamed of love, home, and a family. The crisis is greater for some than for others, simply because people vary regarding goals and personality needs. Frequently there will be frustration due to a blocking of the sex drive. Many women experience their greatest loss in being denied motherhood and deprived of the opportunity to associate with and care for little children. Others miss most the companionship of a marriage partner. Frequently it is all of these.

A major difficulty facing unmarried persons is finding a sympathetic and reliable confidant. If mental health is to be maintained, there will usually need to be someone that the person can lean on, reveal secrets to, share worries with—for the sake of catharsis. Husbands and wives have each other.

Society is organized in favor of the pair. Many social events are planned for couples, and frequently the partnerless person

---

[4] Case study from the author's files.

is either not invited or is made to feel out of place. As a consequence there is the temptation to stay at home more than one should and to become a social recluse.

In other ways, too, society defines the situation to the disadvantage of the single individual. Those who marry are regarded as successful, while those who do not marry are viewed as failures in this regard. These latter are assigned a lower status. They are likely to be slighted, denied certain privileges, and sometimes even ridiculed.

Rose has called attention to inadequacies in living arrangements of the unattached.[5] Until recently, little attention has been given to the construction of housing units that are adapted to persons living alone. Though the problem is finally coming to be recognized, there are still large numbers of people without families who are forced to live in made-over or makeshift rooms which are often too small, too expensive, or in other ways unsuited to their needs.

There is always the danger that these various disappointments and disadvantages to which the permanently unmarried are put will cause them to become frustrated, cynical, and sour. They will have had a dream blacked out, and unless they are able to dream anew and along different lines, life may seem hollow. Feelings of loneliness, of inferiority at having failed, of resentment over having been short changed, of despair in having little left to work for: all are possible. Bachelor men and women are frequently very sensitive of their position, and restless, nervous, and irritable because of it. This is particularly true of the woman, for she is less independent, more the victim of circumstances, and more closely tied up with the reproductive process—which in this case has become blocked.

One pattern of reaction, therefore, is the development of an "old-maid type" of personality. Disappointed and partially rejected, the single person is inclined to turn his or her attentions inward. This makes the person appear odd or unsociable to others, which causes him or her to be further rejected, and the vicious circle is under way. Frustrated and resentful, such a

---

[5] Arnold M. Rose, "Living Arrangements of Unattached Persons," *American Sociological Review,* 12:429-35, August, 1947.

person is likely to become touchy and disagreeable. It must be remembered, however, that we are only describing a danger, not something that is inevitable. There are a great many well-adjusted single individuals; and there are poorly adjusted married persons, of both sexes, who reflect the "old-maid type" of personality.

Another kind of reaction is where the single person, almost in desperation, assumes an attitude of irresponsibility and commences to compete for the attention of married individuals. Since many more women remain single against their desire than is true of men, it follows that they more frequently let themselves get into this position of home-breakers. Sometimes the attempt is deliberate; at other times reluctant, though usually well rationalized. Frequently the job is made easy through constant association with married men at the office, plus the unconscious "cooperation" of nagging wives as competitors. Due to the higher male death rate, there is a larger proportion of women who are unmarried than of men. Furthermore, with the declining death rate being more noticeable among females than males, this difference is on the increase. Then, too, single men are usually that way out of choice, while with women it is more often a problem of frustrated desire. Some authorities have pointed out that the family might become increasingly threatened by this sort of competition from the outside.

It has even been suggested that polygamy be made permissible within the culture so that home-loving females could stand a better chance of realizing their desires. Another suggestion, sometimes heard, is that we legitimize unmarried motherhood so that single women (through artificial insemination, perhaps) could be privileged to bear and rear children of their own. Though the problems of the single woman are admittedly great, it is highly doubtful that our society is ready to accept either of these proposals as a solution.

Sexual adjustment is one of the most difficult problems to be faced by those who remain single. Though endowed with a strong sexual urge, unmarried individuals are nevertheless denied any culturally approved means of expressing it. Some succeed in rechanneling the drive and in finding substitute satisfactions along other lines. But others give themselves to a certain amount of overt sexual expression, regardless of society's disapproval. Undoubtedly the largest number of these engage in occasional masturbatory practices, with heterosexual stimulation coming next, and then homosexual contacts. (See Chapter 5.)

There is no ready answer to these problems of the permanently unmarried. Society can help by removing the stigma surrounding nonmarriage, and by accepting spinsterhood and bachelorhood as normal and in some cases even desirable. The signs of social change are already pointing a little that way. But it seems extremely doubtful that our society will soon accept nonmarital intercourse, unmarried motherhood, or polygamy as answers to the single person's dilemma. Since this is true, it is important that unmarried individuals themselves learn how to adjust. Part of such adjustment will lie in the realization that single life has its compensations, plus an attitude of acceptance and a determination to make the best of the situation. Here is how one woman looked at it:

I frequently decide that I would not change places with this and that married woman whom I know. When my married friends bring their difficulties to me for sympathy, I say to myself that I am spared that sort of worry, at least. So many of my intimate married friends are childless that I frequently think of the fact that in this respect I am as well off as they are. Many experiences, escapades, and pleasures, which come with freedom from responsibility for others, are possible when one is single, that are impossible for a married person. Since life is not finished and I enjoy its unraveling, I can contemplate my state of "single blessedness" (?) with full appreciation for the irony of it and dismiss it with a smile.[6]

Another important part of personal adjustment to the single life is learning how to sublimate the blocked desire by keeping busy and useful in some other line of activity. Idleness and brooding only make the matter worse. It is entirely possible to find satisfaction through substitution; though marriage is important, it is not everything. For example, many girls who

---

[6] Used by permission. From Case Study 84, in Ernest R. Groves, *Marriage* (New York: Henry Holt & Co., 1941), p. 622.

have been denied marriage and parenthood have found contentment in teaching, or nursing, or child-welfare work. In this way the experiences and satisfactions of other families become their own, vicariously. Others have lost themselves in a cause or a career so that they are too busy and interested to feel sorry for themselves. There is no medicine for discouragement like creative accomplishment. Though celibacy may not have been the choice, if it comes, uninvited, life still need not be sterile.

Finally, it must be remembered that some individuals are temperamentally more suited to a life alone than to marriage; some prefer to be single, are more happy that way. Certain of these marry out of social pressure and then fail.

WIDOWHOOD

There are approximately nine million widowed persons living within the United States. Most of these are elderly individuals, showing that widowhood is primarily a phenomenon of old age. Yet, in 1948 there were some two hundred and fifty thousand widows and widowers under the age of thirty-five, and over two million under the age of fifty-five.[7]

The great majority of widowed persons are women. Recent estimates give 6,725,000 widows as compared with 2,055,000 widowers, a ratio of more than three to one.[8] Furthermore, the average duration of widowhood is longer for women than for men—eleven years as compared with nine.[9] Reasons for these differences are three: (1) females outlive males on an average of about four years; (2) females usually marry persons who are two or three years older than themselves; and (3) after widowhood, females do not remarry as much as do males. Thus women are more likely to become widowed than men, to start it younger, and to carry on with it longer.

Readjustment.—The widowed individual experiences most of the same problems as the permanently unmarried, plus a few

---

[7] Bureau of the Census, *Current Population Reports: Population Characteristics* (Washington, D. C.: Series P-20, No. 23, March 4, 1949), p. 10.
[8] *Loc. cit.*   [9] *Ibid.*, pp. 3, 12.

extra. There are the same inconveniences attached to attendance at social functions. There is the same loneliness resulting from a lack of intimate companionship. There is the same sexual tension bound in by cultural restrictions. The difference is that while the single person must learn to do without certain things, the widowed person has to give up things to which he or she had become accustomed; the one is required to adjust and the other to readjust. It is frequently more of a crisis to have to give up what one has known than never to have known it in the first place.

But there are at least two advantages which the widow has over the spinster: (1) she is not stigmatized or made to feel inferior by society; and (2) she has the satisfaction of memories, and perhaps children, to help her adjust. It is likely that the majority of women would prefer widowhood to spinsterhood if they had to choose. During World War II the writer asked several large groups of college women to express themselves on this point; more than 90 per cent said that they would rather be widows—which, incidentally, helps explain the high marriage rate of that time.

Generally, widowhood presents less of a crisis if it doesn't come until old age than where it strikes the family during an earlier phase of the cycle. Aging mates will usually have realized the high probability of one of them dying first and will have made at least partial preparation. Furthermore, their sexual needs will have diminished by that time, which means less of a problem there. Even so, the loss of a mate by death is seldom easy. After a lifetime together there will inevitably be deep and lasting feelings of loneliness. If financial preparation has been incomplete, there may be the added problem of dependency. Then, too, adjustment at this stage of life is frequently complicated by the piling up of crises; failing health, retirement, and widowhood all come at about the same time, which makes each problem all the more difficult. (See Chapter 12.)

Young widowhood is complicated by the fact that it usually comes suddenly and catches the surviving mate unprepared. The following account from a woman who lost her husband fifteen

years ago, during the early years of their marriage, suggests
some of the difficulties:

The shock of losing my husband when we were both so full of
plans for the future, our son just a year old, and life seeming so good,
could well be compared with a shipwreck. Life seemed very empty
for the first few months and my thinking was all mixed up. Yet I
knew that I must go on, face the future bravely, make a living for
myself and son. New plans had to be made. If friends had not in-
sisted on my taking more time for major decisions, I am sure things
could have been worse.

It was the companionship of my husband that I missed most of all.
There was no one left to advise and counsel with, to show interest
and encouragement over my accomplishments, to share my intimate
joys and sorrows. Friends have compensated a great deal, but none can
ever take the place of a married companion. Social activities had to
change. This was not too serious in my case, since I could always find
congenial people to go places with—picnics, shows, musicals. Dances
and parties calling for partners had to be dropped. The problem of
supporting a family was a more serious one. It is still a man's world,
I find, and women who are often better qualified than men receive
less pay and much less recognition. But in spite of these difficulties,
one has only to look around to see others in much worse circumstances.
To feel sorry for oneself is unforgivable, I think. It is much easier
to be cheerful and friendly.[10]

Readjustment requires the alteration of fundamental habit
patterns. Marriage will have made the mates interdependent in
a number of ways; they will have become accustomed to each
other, habituated to a way of life. Death changes all of this and
leaves the surviving partner numb and bewildered for a while,
feeling as if he or she is only half there. Little habits of eating,
sleeping, dressing, conversing—to say nothing of the more
fundamental habits of sex and ego support—all have to be
changed. There are also disturbances in patterns of group participation which frequently require the making of new friends
and reducing and adjusting one's social activities to those events
which are permissible for the unattached. Habit reorganization

---

[10] Case study from the author's files.

is never easy and is frequently very painful. It means the mastering of frustrations resulting from blocked drives. It requires the focusing of consciousness upon just about everything that one does, for much of one's activity for a time will be new and unchanneled.

One of the most immediate problems following widowhood is the economic. This is especially true where there are dependent children, which is in about one third of all new cases. The problem is generally less severe with the widower, for he can continue with his job. However, he may have additional expenses, and certainly more inconveniences, over arranging for a nursery school or a housekeeper. In the case of the widow, there will often be the problem of finding work. If she has young children, there will be the added burden of caring for them and playing the new role of breadwinner, both at the same time. This may be further complicated by the fact that women still are not hired as easily or paid as much as are men. Occasionally, though, employers will favor widows as a gesture of social responsibility. The children of widows are sometimes forced by circumstances to take jobs while still very young, which may result in curtailing their education. In recent years widows have been able to ease their problem by drawing benefits under the Federal Social Security Act.

Sexual tension is another of the most difficult problems to be faced during widowhood. Having been accustomed to intimate intercourse in marriage, widowed persons frequently find it more difficult to control their erotic desires than do the permanently unmarried. A complicating factor is the intense loneliness and the reaching for companionship that are often expressed. This may be quite nonsexual, but it can be exploited by others for sexual ends. Too, society disapproves of the widow or widower remarrying before a "decent" lapse of time, even though there be considerable physical strain in the wait. Waller points out that unconventional sexual indulgences are more common with the divorced than with the widowed person, but says: "In order to effect a sexual readjustment, and also in order that he may satisfy his pressing sexual needs, the bereaved person, like the divorcee, must often make certain erotic compromises." [11]

Bereavement.—Readjustment during widowhood is in one sense made easier, and in another more difficult, by the fact of death. The widowed individual often finds support in memories of the past life. This is more than is possessed by those who never marry. It is also more than divorced persons have to help them readjust, for their recollections are more likely to be those of frustration and defeat. Yet, to have a loved-one die is an extremely traumatic experience. Generally speaking, the closer the marital adjustment, and the more sudden and unexpected the death, the greater is the immediate crisis.

Waller compares the death of a loved one with an amputation. The following brief analysis of the mourning process is adapted from his discussion.[12] (1) The primary source of bereavement is "the conflict between wish forces, which refuse to give up the object, and reality, which demands that it shall be given up. . . ."[13] (2) In the early stages of the process there are a number of protective mechanisms within the self which serve to shield it against the loss. There is a numbing effect incident to the catastrophe. The person is unable to realize fully what has happened. He struggles against reality, refusing to believe or accept the situation. He has "bereavement dreams" which tend to preserve the illusion; sometimes, in his waking hours, he is convinced that it is only a dream. His memory tends to be undependable and highly selective. At first he may have difficulty in thinking clearly about the deceased person at all; in time he is likely to forget past unpleasantries and to construct within his mind an idealized picture of the departed. (3) Mourning serves a socially useful function. Attention and sympathy focused upon the mourner tend to bring ego support at a time when part of him seems to have been taken away. By self-absorption, the mind is less likely to dwell upon the loss. In time the self can be freed (or nearly so) from the former

[11] Willard Waller, *The Family: A Dynamic Interpretation* (New York: The Dryden Press, Inc., 1938), p. 510; see also p. 520 and *passim*.
[12] *Ibid.*, pp. 491-522, 580-88.
[13] *Ibid.*, p. 498.

love object and made capable of attaching itself to another. Mourning provides a needed transition into an acceptance of the newer reality. When pretentious or overextended, however, its purposes may become perverted. (4) As much as anything else, adjustment requires a lapse of time. It is largely automatic. Though personal attitudes and the assistance of friends are undoubtedly helpful, each widow or widower must still go through the rather painful processes of love and habit reorientation. With the first shock there is likely to be the feeling that one doesn't care to go on, that life is meaningless; one may have to force oneself to respond. For a while the personality may be quite disorganized. But then, in time, reality becomes accepted, habits change, new interests appear, and life becomes normal again. This means the attainment of a new life organization. When it happens, adjustment is complete.

Since death is inevitable, one might expect more preparation for it than is usually the case. A few husbands and wives are spared widowhood by dying simultaneously (though this is rare and usually accidental); some others escape by way of divorce (though if they remarry they may yet be widowed); and half of those remaining never become widows or widowers because of dying before their mates. Widowhood is common enough, nevertheless, and the problems involved are grave enough to warrant very serious attention. There needs to be more preparation ahead of time—psychologically, so the happening will be less of a shock; and economically, so that the survivors can be self-supporting and have a better chance to readjust. One type of financial preparation consists of savings, annuities, and insurance. Another is for the wife to include some kind of job training in her premarriage experience, as "insurance" against such an emergency. Married mates need to discuss death as a possibility, and to lay out plans for such an eventuality.

Once widowhood has taken place, the important thing is to find and establish new habit patterns as rapidly as seems possible. Friends can help in this. The attitude needs to be one of acceptance and determination. Remarriage, as one possible solution, will be discussed at the end of this chapter.

Postdivorce Adjustments

Though the number of divorced persons in the population is not as great as either the unmarried or the widowed, it is nevertheless rather sizable and is growing. In 1948 there were estimated to be 1,027,000 male and 1,233,000 female individuals within this classification. This adds up to more than two and one-quarter million men and women, or better than 2 per cent of all persons fourteen years of age and over.[14] By way of time comparisons, earlier percentages were approximately 1.4 for 1940, 1.2 for 1930 and .7 for 1920. These figures are for the group reported as divorced at any one time; they do not include the uncounted millions who have divorced and then remarried. Furthermore, it is likely that these reported numbers of divorced persons are understatements, due to the stigma still attached to divorce and the reluctance of men and women within this status to admit it. It seems certain, therefore, that the number of living persons who have ever experienced divorce must be two or three times the number reported as having this status at any given time; this would mean a figure of between four and six million. In terms of probability, we can predict that one out of every four or five adult Americans, who live an average life span, will experience at least one divorce.[15]

Since monogamy is the only legal form of marriage recognized in this country, there are an equal number of men and women involved at the time of first divorce. The preponderance of females living in the divorced state, as shown in the above figures, is to be explained by a higher male death rate and a greater tendency for males to remarry.

The Divorce Trauma.—Certain of the problems which we have been discussing are common to all who live without a mate—whether they be unmarried, widowed, or divorced. One is the problem of loneliness and lack of affection. Another is the problem of social inconveniences within a society that is

---

[14] Bureau of the Census, *op. cit.*, p. 10.
[15] Cf. William J. Goode, "Problems in Postdivorce Adjustment," *American Sociological Review*, 14:394-401, June, 1949.

geared to the marriage pair. On top of these, however, the
divorced person is generally presented with a few others: in
common with the one who is widowed, he has the task of reorganizing his love life, rechanneling his habit patterns, and
reestablishing himself with social groups; in common with the
one who never marries, he is faced with a certain amount of
social disapproval or stigma connected with the status; and, in
addition to these, he has had to experience all of the disillu-
sionments and hurts that go with a lost love.

Waller has compared the divorce situation with bereavement,
pointing out symptoms and processes common to both—early
feelings of shock and numbness at the loss, the persistence of
old habit patterns, the need for gradual readjustment, and so
on.[16] But he went on to say that readjustment after divorce is
made all the more difficult by the absence of culturally approved
patterns; there are certain socially sanctioned means of working
out problems when a mate has died, yet there are practically no
approved means for the painful task of readjusting after a
marriage has "died." As a result, the divorcee is held in a
certain amount of scorn and is left with roles that are both un-
defined and contradictory.[17] Though this observation is undoubtedly correct, it is likely less true than at the time Waller
wrote it about two decades ago. Divorce is coming to be accepted within the folkways.

The divorce trauma is usually more severe for the unwilling
member, when there is such. Then there is added frustration and
wounded pride. The following case will illustrate:

During the months that Ray and I were separated I never got a
break. I saw him only a few times, and then the girl who got her
clutches on him was either with him or around the corner waiting
for him.

I didn't want the divorce. Even on the day I got it I thought of
refusing to go through with it. But I was afraid that if I did Ray
would go ahead and get it and I didn't want that.

Two or three days before the divorce, he came over and spent the
whole afternoon visiting with me. He said that I could have anything

16 Willard Waller, *The Old Love and the New* (New York: Liveright Publishing Corp., 1930).
17 *Ibid.*, p. 23 and *passim*.

I wanted in the house, if I needed any money he would be glad to give
it to me, and coached me in what to do at court.

After the divorce I felt numb, sick to my stomach, and thought of
suicide, feeling that I couldn't go on alone. Divorce was my funeral
and my witnesses were my pallbearers. I felt like going over in our
house and breaking everything, but, of course, couldn't and didn't
do it. If it hadn't been for that girl who got her hands on Ray, he
and I would be married today.[18]

But it must be recognized, also, that not every divorce is as
deeply disturbing to the persons involved as it is sometimes
thought to be. Frequently the couple are in mutual agreement
over separation. In the majority of cases the real break will
have come long before the formal court proceeding; there will
be trauma, but deriving more from the conflicts of prior married life than from the divorce itself.[19] This, of course, is not to
deny that almost inevitably there will be some pain connected
with the process of getting the divorce; in some instances,
court proceedings are quite disorganizing, especially where the
case is contested and the intimate details of earlier friction are
made public. However, here is an account from a woman who
feels that her divorce was a welcome release:

My feeling since separation and, later, divorce, has been one of
tremendous relief and release. We were incompatible from the beginning and as time went on things seemed to get worse. It has been
better to live alone than to live in an atmosphere of continual disagreement and tension, and I do not believe that I have known any real
sense of loneliness because of the separation. I am not cynical about
marriage (I have known too many happily married couples for that),
but I would not consider another marriage for myself unless I could
be very sure that it represented a harmony of ideals and was motivated by real love.

Naturally there have been problems in learning to live alone again
after eighteen years of marriage. It has been difficult for me to face
large social gatherings made up mostly of married couples, but there
has been no such feeling of awkwardness in smaller groups. My six-
teen-year-old son and many friends have helped to tide me over this

----

[18] Used by permission. From Ernest W. Burgess and Harvey J. Locke, *The
Family: From Institution to Companionship* (New York: American Book Co.,
1945), pp. 638-39.

[19] Cf. Goode, *op. cit.*, pp. 400-1.

initial period. In learning a new job and in maintaining a home for my son, I have kept too busy for excess worry. Most of all, I am being carried through by a faith in God. It would have been easy to have resorted to self-pity and bitterness, but I am trying, instead, to use the experiences of these past years—the successes and failures—as guides in the reconstruction of a new life for my son and myself. I am optimistic about the future! [20]

It is evident, here, that the real trauma came during an earlier period of estrangement, and that the divorce itself was merely a step in the direction of personal readjustment. She recognized certain difficulties connected with the separation, nevertheless, and pointed to her son, friends, work, and religion as sustaining factors helping her over the crisis.

A crisis is any situation which breaks the habit pattern and requires a fundamental change from one's accustomed line of action. Divorce does that. After having experienced the pair relationship, the divorcee, like the widow or widower, must now learn to be alone again. This means a reorganizing of the love patterns, including the sexual. It also means a severing of the many little dependencies which husbands and wives come to have with respect to each other. Furthermore, it usually means the reshuffling of friendship contacts and the reestablishing of status within the group. Sometimes former friends take sides or in other ways interfere. According to social definition, the divorcee is expected to feel bitter or at least indifferent toward the former spouse; actually he or she may feel more hurt and confused than anything, but is not supposed to show it.

There is frequently the question of economic support following divorce, particularly for the former wife. The problem is not usually as great here, however, as in the case of widowhood, for the reason that divorcees are usually younger, more capable of self-support, and less tied down with children. Employment statistics indicate that a disproportionately large number of divorced women do go to work. Others receive alimony, or return to the parental home, or go on relief. Alimony is more likely to be requested when there are children involved. More

---

women are granted alimony than men, but only the minority of either sex. Most of those seeking divorce don't even request it; they would rather be independent.

Typical Reaction Patterns.—Not all who are granted a divorce react in the same way. Some find it to be an extremely disorganizing experience; others are only mildly disturbed; still others feel a pleasant release. The intensity of the trauma will depend upon a number of factors: the sensitiveness of the personality involved, the amount of love that is still left, the rapidity and degree with which the divorcee is able to find compensatory adjustments within society, and so on.

Though not universal, the following reactions to the divorce experience are nevertheless rather common: (1) There will frequently be a feeling of shock, accompanied by self-pity and projected blame. The divorcee tries to rationalize the situation and to show an outward bravado as a cover up for inward disturbances. Thus the real emotional problems may lack adequate ventilation. (2) There is usually a feeling of restlessness resulting from disturbed habits and confused roles. As a result, the divorced person often tries to increase his or her social activities. Friends and relatives may help in establishing new contacts. (3) Not infrequently the divorced person will go through a period of unconventional behavior, trying to drown his sorrow in drink or to compensate for his loss by degrading sex.[21] (4) It is not uncommon for divorced individuals to experience ambivalent attitudes toward the former spouse; they may want revenge and feel affection both at the same time. Sometimes husband and wife continue with sexual intercourse for a time after they have been divorced. Occasionally they will remarry each other.

In spite of these many difficulties, divorce is sometimes preferable to staying married. (See pages 15, 22.) If the mates remain basically incompatible after serious and extended efforts to get along, there is little point in extending the misery. Staying together under such conditions can be productive of frustrated and neurotic personalities. Whenever adjustment within mar-

---

[21] Cf. Willard Waller, *op. cit.*, p. 56.

riage proves to be impossible, there needs to be a release in order that adaptations along other lines may be tried.

But divorce is no panacea. It, too, requires adjustments—which in most ways are more difficult than those of the married state. There are but two alternatives worth considering: learning to live alone and marrying again. We have already discussed the former.

THE QUESTION OF REMARRIAGE

This section might best be viewed as a postscript to the chapter. Technically, remarriage is not a part of "Living Without a Mate." But there is such a close relationship that the discussion would be incomplete without this next step's being treated. It is through remarriage that a great many widowed and divorced persons make their attempt at readjustment.

One out of every eight married persons in the United States, or about 13 per cent, has been married more than once. Of these who have married for the second or subsequent time, a considerably larger proportion comes from the group that is recently married than from those who entered marriage a longer time ago.[22] This would seem to indicate that the practice of remarriage is becoming more common, and that as time goes on an increasing proportion of the married population will fall within the category. Reasons for this trend are mainly two: substantial increases in the divorce rate, and cultural changes in the direction of greater acceptance of remarriage for the divorcee. Probably at least one half of all divorced persons remarry now.[23] With the remarried group constituting an expanding proportion of the total, we can expect interest and attention regarding this phase of the family phenomenon to grow.

There is little question but that the rate of remarriage is higher for the divorced person than for the widowed. One reason is that people sometimes get a divorce for the very purpose of marrying another, who is already selected. Too, the

---

22 Bureau of the Census, *op. cit.*, pp. 1, 11.

23 William Carlson Smith, "Remarriage and the Stepchild," chap. iv in Part IV of Morris Fishbein and Ernest W. Burgess (eds.), *Successful Marriage* (New York: Doubleday & Co., 1947), p. 339.

divorcee is generally more anxious to break with the past and
to demonstrate, by remarriage, that there is nothing wrong
with him or her; this is a reaction against the inference of
failure. Then there is the matter of marriage opportunity; divorce generally takes place at an earlier age than widowhood,
which leaves the person with greater bargaining power and
more time to work out another match. Also, children sometimes
interfere with one's chances for remarriage, and the divorcee—
because of being younger and married for a shorter length of
time—is not so likely to have as many. There is evidence that
the tendency to remarry varies inversely with the number of
children.[24] It has been estimated that the chances of eventual
marriage are 50 per cent greater for the divorcee who is thirty
years old than they are for the widow of the same age.[25]

Men tend to remarry at a faster rate than do women. In one
study Spiegelman found the annual remarriage rate (for widowed and divorced persons combined) to be 40.1 per 1,000 for
men, and only 14.4 per 1,000 for women.[26] Recent census estimates give less of a difference, but with the difference being in
the same direction—that is, with men showing higher rates.
According to this tabulation, 13.1 per cent of the men and 12.5
per cent of the women who were currently living with their
spouses had been previously married; for those under thirty-
five years of age, the percentage comparisons were 5.8 and 8.9,
while for those fifty-five years of age and over, they were 20.0
and 17.0, respectively.[27] This would seem to indicate that the
higher male rate is characteristic only of the later years of life,
and that the males then tend to select women somewhat younger
than themselves. The higher female rate in the younger ages is
to be explained partly by the fact that girls marry earlier, so that
by the age of thirty-five they have had a longer time in which
to become divorced and remarried. But it must also be remembered that the girl's chances for remarriage are substantially

---

[24] Mortimer Spiegelman, "The Broken Family—Widowhood and Orphan-
hood," *Annals of the American Academy of Political and Social Science,* 188:
117-30, November, 1936.
[25] Metropolitan Life Insurance Company, "The Chances of Remarriage for
the Widowed and Divorced," *Statistical Bulletin,* May, 1945.
[26] Spiegelman, *op. cit.,* pp. 121-23.
[27] Bureau of the Census, *op. cit.,* pp. 2, 11.

greater while she is young. The middle-aged woman, unless blessed with some unusual qualification such as money, social status, or outstanding personal charm, has a comparatively slight chance of ever remarrying. Though the man also experiences a decrease of marriage opportunity coming with age, the handicap is much less drastic with him; he is more free to choose and has an easier time reaching down into the younger ages for a partner.

When widowed and divorced persons decide to marry again, the tendency is for them to select persons who, like themselves, have been married before. Estimates from the Bureau of the Census indicate that nearly 60 per cent of all husbands and wives who have married more than once have a spouse who has also married more than once, and that this tendency toward homogamy in remarriage increases with age at the time of subsequent marriage.[28] From an earlier study, Bossard reached a similar conclusion; he also observed that: "Widowed persons tend to select the widowed; divorced persons, the divorced; and those both widowed and divorced seem to single out persons in similar conjugal condition." [29]

Are Second Marriages Successful?—As with all marriages, some are successful and some are not. In this respect, second marriages do not differ from the first: they involve human beings, require adjustments, and result in gradations of satisfaction extending from one possible extreme to the other. But are one's chances of adjustment and happiness greater or less in a remarriage? Very little research has been conducted on this point; that which has been reported tends to support the view that probability of success is less in a second or subsequent marriage than it is in the first.[30]

---

28 Bureau of the Census, *Current Population Reports: Population Characteristics* (Washington, D. C.: Series P-20, No. 21, December 19, 1948), pp. 3, 15.

29 James H. S. Bossard, "Previous Conjugal Condition," *Social Forces,* 18: 243-47, December, 1939, p. 247.

30 Cf. Paul Popenoe, "Divorce and Remarriage from an Eugenic Point of View," *Social Forces,* 12:48-50, October, 1933; "Remarriage of Divorcees to Each Other," *American Sociological Review,* 3:695-99, October, 1938; Harvey J. Locke, "Predicting Marital Adjustment by Comparing a Divorced and a Happily Married Group," *American Sociological Review,* 12:187-91; and Harvey J. Locke and William J. Klausner, "Marital Adjustment of Divorced Persons in Subsequent Marriages," *Sociology and Social Research,* 33:97-101.

Though there are no reliable data by which we can compare the relative success of widowed and divorced persons in remarriage, it seems reasonable to assume that failure is greater among divorcees. A higher percentage of the widows and widowers will have been happily married prior to the crisis, and hence a lower percentage will possess warped or neurotic tendencies in their personalities. By way of comparison, more of the divorcees will be embittered over the marriage experience and more of them will have unstable personality tendencies—which may be either a cause of the crisis, or a result, or both. With divorce coming to be more generally accepted, however, it is possible that the divorcee group is including more and more well-adjusted individuals who failed largely because of poor matching or extreme circumstances surrounding the prior experience. There is little reason to think that this type of person would be too much handicapped in a second or subsequent marriage. Yet it is highly probable that the divorced group still contains more than its share of neurotic individuals. Not all marriages fail because of the personal immaturities of husband and wife, but many do. When this type of person remarries, he usually has no better chance of succeeding the second time than the first. Some people marry to escape problems which they were not able to solve during courtship, then divorce to escape the deeper entanglements which enveloped them during marriage, and remarry to escape the still greater problems that can pile up after a divorce—when the real problem all the time was within themselves.

Support for the thesis that the divorced person is more likely than others to be unstable, and consequently a poorer marriage risk, is contained in recent figures from the Bureau of the Census. In April, 1948, it was found that 20 per cent of the divorced persons and 18 per cent of the married persons with spouse absent (deserted or separated) had been married more than once. By way of comparison, only 13 per cent of the widowed and 13 per cent of the married persons living with their spouse had been married more than once.[31] Since substantially larger

---

[31] Bureau of the Census, *op. cit.* (No. 23, March, 1949), pp. 1, 11.

proportions of persons who had been married more than once
were found among the divorced and the separated, it is evident
that these are the groups which are most unstable in marriage
behavior.

One of the most difficult problems of remarriage has to do
with the so-called rebound phenomenon. Frequently there is the
tendency to idealize the former mate. This puts the present mate
at a distinct disadvantage. Fixation upon a deceased spouse or
divorced partner acts to interfere with the newer adjustment.
There will be silent comparisons, if not subtle and open infer-
ences, which will antagonize the other member of the marriage.
The tendency is perhaps greater on the part of widowed persons
than divorcees because of greater happiness in previous marriages not broken by divorce. For this reason some people prefer
to marry a divorcee rather than a widow or widower; they
don't want to be in the position of being constantly compared
with a former "perfect mate." But even divorced persons are
far from being free of the rebound tendency. Some of them
were reluctant about separation in the first place. Not infrequently do divorcees remarry impetuously, as a demonstration
of their independence and ability, though remaining emotionally involved with the first mate. And with the divorcee the
situation may be further complicated by the presence of the
former mate, which will tend to perpetuate old memories and
in some instances result in competition or even actual conflict
between the former mate and the new spouse. If there are children from the first marriage, the former mate may try to turn
them against the new stepparent.

There may be other problems connected with children from
the first marriage. These children, especially if they are older,
frequently regard the stepparent as a stranger and intruder.
Sometimes they will have objected to their parent's remarrying
and will deliberately try to break up the match. The parent, in
turn, is likely to feel competing loyalties between his children
and the new mate. The problem of discipline comes in, with
the parent's often feeling that the new mate is being unkind
or harsh with his children. If there are children from both sides
by previous marriage, or from the new marriage too, the prob-

lem is further complicated by a tendency toward favoritism. Even when there is no favoritism present, certain happenings may be interpreted that way. Little mannerisms or habits of the children can prove to be quite annoying to a stepparent. The role of the stepmother is usually more difficult than that of the stepfather; also more crucial to the success of the new relationship. It is the stepmother who is most directly involved with the care and training of the children. Since men generally marry down in age, she is frequently handicapped by not being much older than the children she is trying to mother. Furthermore, she is often without experience. An additional handicap is the stepmother stereotype; people expect her to be cross and cruel. These are some of the tensions resulting from stepchild and stepparent situations which can wreck homes. It would be a mistake, however, to leave the impression that families involving stepchildren are invariably in conflict. By studying the problem together, and backing each other up, many parents and stepparents are able to keep the situation in a state of harmony. One device is to be even more considerate of the stepchildren than your own, as the following case illustrates:

We never resent correction by our stepfather because he is very just; he does not correct us as much as his own children. It always hurts us when we have to be corrected, not because of resentment, but because we admire him so much that we do not want to displease him.[32]

Something needs to be said in favor of remarriage. Those who have had an earlier marriage will now be older and more experienced. Presumably they will have learned a few things in the first round and will be better prepared to try again. They will be less dominated by romantic infatuation and should, for this reason, be able to make a more satisfactory mate choice. Second and subsequent marriages are more frequently business propositions than are the first ones—men want caretakers and women want breadwinners. But usually, also, they will hope for love and companionship. Many who remarry are more successful than they were the first time.

---

[32] Used by permission. From Smith, *op. cit.*, p. 352.

Things to Consider.—The question of remarriage hinges upon the relative advantages and disadvantages of this step as compared with other advantages and disadvantages involved in living alone. Most of these have been pointed out in the above discussions. Remarriage both solves problems and creates new ones. Decisions regarding the matter must be left to the individuals concerned, who should analyze the various pros and cons as applied to their own particular cases. Following are some of the most important things to be considered:

1. Are there unstable or neurotic tendencies that can be revealed by the previous marriage? If widowed, how happy was the marriage before bereavement? If divorced, was the break-up a result of personal deficiencies which might still be present? Has the earlier experience produced any attitudes or habits that will handicap adjustment in another marriage?

2. Is there likely to be a rebound, in terms of an emotional return to the former mate? Has there been a sufficient lapse of time to permit emancipation from the old love and establishment of the new? Is the plan for marriage being motivated by serious and legitimate considerations, or is it merely out of spite or desperation? What are the feelings toward one's former mate? Will he or she be around or likely to interfere?

3. Are there children involved? If so, how many and what ages? Do they approve of the marriage? Are other children contemplated in the new marriage? Do the prospective mates agree in general philosophy regarding child discipline and home management?

4. What are the relevant factors peculiar to you? Do you like living alone and is your adjustment to that mode of life satisfactory? Or are you excessively lonesome, economically insecure, or in other ways unadjusted? Would another marriage alleviate the problem? What are the likely number of years which you have left to live? Does this allow time enough to justify another marital experience?

In conclusion let it be said that remarriage is frequently the best possible answer to widowhood and divorce, especially where the individuals are young and personally well qualified. There will be problems of adjustment to be sure, but so are there among the first-married. For many, neither of these marital states presents so many difficulties as does living without a mate.

Problems and Projects

1. Do you agree with the adage: "It's better to have loved and lost than never to have loved at all"? Applying this thought to marriage, would you say that it is better to have married and failed than never to have married at all?

2. Some persons deliberately choose against marriage. List any reasons which you think might justify such a choice. Do you think one can ever be as happy without marriage as with it? Defend your position.

3. If it were a question of remaining single or "taking what you could get," how far would you be willing to lower your sights in order to get married? List the minimum qualifications that you would consider essential. Compare these with those of others in the class.

4. What advantages do men have over women in getting married? In remarrying, following widowhood or divorce? How do these differences vary with age? What are major personality differences between the unattached man and the unattached woman?

5. Describe the "old-maid" type of personality. How does it develop? How might it be prevented or corrected?

6. Name factors which are responsible for the problem of "the other woman." When this happens, who is to be blamed: the husband, the wife, or the other woman? Discuss.

7. Do you have any suggestions regarding sex adjustment among the unattached? Is complete sublimation possible? Give your reasons.

8. What are the ways in which you think society should change to better facilitate adjustment among the unattached? Should the stigma be removed from spinsterhood? From divorce? Would you make it permissible for the unmarried woman to become a mother as a partial answer to her problem? What about polygamy? Defend your position on each of these and make further suggestions.

9. Living without a mate breaks itself down into three types: the permanently unmarried, the widowed, and the divorced. Compare these in the following ways: (*a*) numbers and trends in the total population, (*b*) common and unique problems within each category, (*c*) advantages and disadvantages of each type, and (*d*) typical modes of reaction—adjustment or maladjustment.

10. Are people who have married more than once as likely to be as happy as other married couples? Discuss from the standpoint of the widowed, then the divorced. What are the factors making for success or failure in the second and subsequent marriages?

11. Interview a spinster or bachelor whom you know well, to get a picture of the problems and how they are being met. Do the same with a widow or widower. With a divorcee. With a stepmother. Write these up in the form of case studies.

Selected Readings

Baber, Ray E. *Marriage and the Family.* New York: McGraw-Hill Book Co., 1939. Chap. xv, "Divorce—(Continued)."

Becker, Howard, and Hill, Reuben (eds.). *Family, Marriage, and Parenthood.* Boston: D. C. Heath & Co., 1948. Chap. xxii, "Bereavement: Inevitable But Not Insurmountable."

Bowman, Henry A. *Marriage for Moderns.* New York: McGraw-Hill Book Co., 1948. Chap. iii, "The Permanently Unmarried."

Fishbein, Morris, and Burgess, Ernest W. (eds.). *Successful Marriage.* New York: Doubleday & Co., 1947. Part IV, chap. iv, "Remarriage and the Stepchild."

Groves, Ernest R. *Marriage.* New York: Henry Holt & Co., 1941. Chap. xxix, "Problems of the Unmarried."

Harper, Robert A. *Marriage.* New York: Appleton-Century-Crofts, Inc., 1949. Chap. ii, "Why People Do and Don't Marry."

Landis, Judson T., and Landis, Mary G. *Building a Successful Marriage.* New York: Prentice-Hall, Inc., 1948. Chap. iii, "Why People Marry Or Do Not Marry."

Mowrer, Ernest R. "Divorce and Readjustment," *Annals of the American Academy of Political and Social Science,* 160:191-96, March, 1932.

Truxal, Andrew G., and Merrill, Francis E. *The Family in American Culture.* New York: Prentice-Hall, Inc., 1947. Chaps. xxvi, "Desertion, Separation, and Death"; xxvii, xxviii, "Divorce."

Waller, Willard. *The Family: A Dynamic Interpretation.* New York: Dryden Press, 1938. Part V, "Family Disorganization."

WALLER, WILLARD. *The Old Love and the New.* Philadelphia: Liveright Publishing Corp., 1930.

YOUNG, KIMBALL. *Personality and Problems of Adjustment.* New York: Appleton-Century-Crofts, Inc., 1940. Chap. xxii, "Adjustment Problems of the Modern Woman."

PART IV
PROGRAMS

Chapter 14

TOWARD THE IMPROVEMENT OF MARRIAGE

All of the book has been directed toward the improvement of marriage. We started with the conviction that marriage and the family are useful social institutions, which, when successful, are productive of some of man's deepest satisfactions. But there was also the realization that these are not always successful, that in the association of the sexes misery often crowds out happiness.

Our problem was to analyze the various factors and processes involved so as to be in a better position to predict and control the results. Marriage has been regarded as the product of both social and personal factors, its success depending upon: (1) the amount of encouragement given it by the surrounding society; (2) the degree of personal maturity attained prior to marriage; (3) the amount of pair unity that develops out of matching and love involvement; and (4) the degree to which mates keep adaptable or adjustable as the marriage moves along. These factors have been viewed against the background of family dynamics, running all the way from early personality formation within the home, through courtship, into marriage, then parenthood, and finally to problems of the empty nest and living without a mate.

Why, then, another chapter? We have not, as yet, given any systematic examination to over-all approaches or broad family-oriented programs which bring support to marriage in this day.

THE RESEARCH APPROACH (INFORMATION)

Whenever one fails in something, it is not usually because of wanting to but of not knowing how to avoid it. Truth undis-

covered is of no avail. In any field, knowledge is the first prerequisite to accomplishment.

If one would be successful in marriage, therefore, the first
task must be that of discovering the principles back of marital
happiness.

How can this discovery be made? Must each person go
through the wasteful process of trial and error? How reliable
are old wives' tales and the various proverbs and bits of advice
that are passed on from generation to generation? What can
science contribute? These are the questions to which attention
is now directed.

From Folklore to Science.—The bases of marital bliss can
be discovered by both study and experience. But it is not necessary for one to burn his finger, so to speak, in order to know
how things operate. Personal experience, though valuable, is
sometimes the most wasteful and expensive way to learn. By
analyzing the experiences of others, and by studying good literature based upon solid research, trial and error learning can be
had vicariously and without the necessity of so many personal
mistakes. This not only saves time but also helps to avoid failure. Personal experiences in love will be had of course, and they
should be, but it is best that these be accompanied with as much
background of understanding from other sources as is possible.

Folklore has reference to the body of custom and tradition
that is handed down from the past. Science, on the other hand,
refers to the sum of present knowledge that has been discovered
objectively and verified empirically. The one is impressionistic
and tends to be self-perpetuating; the other is open to demonstration and is ready to yield whenever proof of its truth is
lacking. Early man built his lore. Modern man is trying to be
scientific.

It was only a little over a century ago that young men seeking mates were warned to:

. . . fly—as you fly from sin and death—fly from a philosopher. It
is very dangerous for weak minds examining (farther than is duly
delivered to them) what is right or wrong. . . .

All who find their minds superior to common rule and received opinion; value themselves on original thinking; talk politics; read Mary Wollstonecraft; or meddle with the mathematics; these are the unclean birds upon whom the protecting genius of honest men has set his mark, that all may know; and pray do you avoid them.[1]

And wives were admonished to:

Seem always to obtain information from him, especially before company, though you may thereby appear a simpleton. Never forget that a wife owes all her importance to that of her husband. Leave him entirely master of his actions, to go or come whenever he thinks fit. A wife ought to make her company so amiable to her husband, that he will not be able to exist without it; then he will not seek for any pleasure abroad, if she does not partake of it with him.[2]

Here are a few random bits of "wisdom" which have been repeated often as guides for love and marriage, but which need to be re-worked in the light of modern understanding:

Marriages are made in heaven.
Marry first and love will follow.
The female is the weaker sex.
All mankind loves a lover.
If you marry, marry a fool.
A nursing mother never conceives.
Spare the rod and spoil the child.
He that marries late, marries ill.
You can't teach an old dog new tricks.
Babies are brought by the stork.
Give a child his will, and he'll turn out ill.
Thoughts of the mother affect her unborn child.

Needles and pins, needles and pins,
When a man marries his trouble begins.

Traditional sayings and practices, though having in them much that is true, often also contain error and should be ac-

---

[1] *The American Chesterfield, or Way to Wealth, Honour, and Distinction,* being selections from the Letters of Lord Chesterfield to his son, and extracts from other eminent authors on the subject of politeness, with alterations and additions suited to the youth of the United States (Philadelphia: John Grigg, 1828), p. 210.
[2] *Ibid.,* p. 223.

cepted only with caution. Certainly everyone would want to listen carefully to those who have gone before, for there lies the wisdom of tested experience; but they should also remember that times change, as certain procedures and requirements do likewise, and they need ever to be on guard against errors and superstitions which tend to be perpetuated. Just as quack health remedies tend to persist in spite of scientific medicine, so superstitious and outmoded ways of handling marriage and family problems hang on, to some extent, in the face of change and newer scientific knowledge. Custom and tradition are worth while but only when measured by the changing times and tested against the most recent information as it develops.

But it is often more difficult to follow the ways of science than those of custom, to be rational than emotional. Furthermore, there is a great deal in our way of life that runs counter to science. Witness the barrage of sentimental and erotic stimulation that comes regularly from the radio, picture show, and popular literature. This emphasis tends to perpetuate folklore and interfere with the development of science. As a result, many individuals still marry a fantasy rather than a reality, and then, when disillusionment sets in, proceed to blame others for their failure, or the institution of marriage itself.

Our State of Knowledge.—If one were to judge wholly by what has been happening to marriage over the past several decades, the conclusion might be that man's research efforts, as applied to this problem, have been quite sterile. But perhaps it isn't science that is to blame for our marriage muddle so much as the failure of men and women to adequately apply what researchers are ready to teach. True, science has yet not given us all the answers; but it is on the way, and it has discovered enough to have established some reliable guides.

These guides from research have been background materials for all of this writing. Since it is presumed that the reader will be familiar with what has gone before, there is no point in attempting a summary here. Chapter 6 should prove especially valuable for purposes of review.

But what are the needs and prospects for the future? Here are the ones that seem most glaring: [3]

1. There is need for expanding the sources and refining the research techniques already in use; for re-testing some of the findings now accepted. Much of our present knowledge on the subject rests upon samples that are inadequate or unrepresentative. What applies to one group or level of society may not apply to another. With an increase in knowledge, and its validation on different levels, will come greater precision in prediction and greater power for control.

2. There is need for greater integration, more theoretical orientation, and further interdisciplinary cooperation among workers. To date there has been too much independent investigating and on scattered and often unrelated problems. This approach has resulted in a large quantity of material but has been without any over-all plan or framework and has left wide gaps in our fund of knowledge. It is time that family researchers decide together on a general frame of reference and on a series of problems that can be considered most important. Sociologists, anthropologists, psychologists, biologists, home economists, and others interested in this field are coming to recognize that they can learn from one another; the more these come to work together, the more their findings will "add up."

3. The "neglected areas" of family research need to be given more attention. One of these (receiving some emphasis but demanding more) is the phenomenon of child development and personality growth as related to marriage. Another is the bearing that certain sex patterns may have upon marriage; the possible relationship between chastity and frigidity, for example, or the long-time effects of premarital petting. Still another is the problem of matching between mates, of further determining which combinations make for compatibility and which for incompatibility in marriage. The whole field of in-

---

[3] The listing which follows draws heavily upon two recent articles: Ernest W. Burgess, "The Family and Sociological Research," *Social Forces*, 26:1-6, October, 1947; Leonard S. Cottrell, "The Present Status and Future Orientation of Research on the Family," *American Sociological Review*, 13:123-29, April, 1948. This latter article is discussed by Ernest W. Burgess, Ruth Shonle Cavan, and Mirra Komarovsky, pp. 129-36.

teractional or interpersonal dynamics needs better understanding—love involvements, role conflicts, adaptations to stages in the family cycle. An almost untouched field of study, and one that is looming larger in importance, is that of the aging family or period of the empty nest. Then there is need for better understanding the interrelationships existing between the family and society; how each influences the other.

4. Research must not only supply the raw materials out of which action programs are built, but it can also serve as a check on how effective these programs are. We need to know if our teaching methods are bringing results, if our marriage and divorce laws are accomplishing what they were designed to accomplish, if people who consult counselors or attend clinics become any more happily married than those with similar problems who do not ask for help. Evaluation research is far from adequate today.

5. Where important research is to be expected, adequate facilities must be provided. One need in family research is for funds sufficient to interest enough well-trained staff workers and to provide them with the necessary expenses and equipment. A related need is for some sort of organization, such as a research center, at the top—to solicit funds and stimulate and coordinate projects. Cottrell put it this way:

> It seems to me that the situation is ripe for a major next step in family research. There should be set up under the Social Science Research Council a carefully chosen, well-financed planning group who would devote full time for one or two years to a careful examination of what we know, what the critical problems for research are, the major hypotheses to be tested, and what research methods are available and what new ones are needed in the field.[4]

Following this recommendation, such a committee has been established.

The Educational Approach (Dissemination)

With the research point of view, man will be ever ready to probe into the unknown, searching out answers to his problems

---

4 Cottrell, *op. cit.,* p. 129.

and working out solutions to his difficulties. Applied to marriage, this will mean that the intellect can be called in to supplement the spirit of the home. Many people want to cooperate and do not know how; their attitude is good but their information and training are poor. While the spirit of cooperation is most essential to successful marriage, as will be seen below, an intelligent and mature understanding of the problems involved is important also. As the scientific method is increasingly applied to the study of the family, answers to our difficulties become more and more clear. Yet, without learning by the masses, all such newly acquired knowledge remains with the specialists. To be effective, information must be taken to the people. We turn, then, to the subject of family life education.

Two things have happened to increase the need of education for marriage and family life in our day: In the first place, society has become vastly more complex, and the family, because of it, has become less stable. It is not so easy to make a go of marriage now as at the time when living was relatively simple and the family had little competition. Hence the greater need for learning today. Secondly, in an earlier period, education for family life was likely to come naturally—because of large families, a rural habitat, and a self-sustaining economy where all family members contributed. Now, however, many of our children are reared much like hothouse plants, with little opportunity to observe complete family life or to adjust to its processes. (See pages 10-11.)

Quackery on the Loose.—So great has been the need for help on this subject of late that interest in it has greatly multiplied and discussions concerning it are broadcast far and wide. Rarely does one look through a magazine, or a newspaper, or a book without running into something about love, marriage, or children. The radio, too, has picked up this current of popular interest, as has also the picture show and nearly every other agency of entertainment and public expression. Much of this emphasis is helpful, for it spreads information and brings understandings that are needed.

But not all that one is exposed to can be regarded as productive of wholesome marriage and family relationships. Magazine stands are stacked high with cheap and questionable reading materials running all the way from lurid murder tales to glamourized love confessions. Newspapers portray the crimes and love failures of their subjects in all the sordid details. Advertising resorts to an overdisplay of the female form in order to attract attention. Novels, both short and book-length, relate the intimacies of sex as if they were public affairs. In all of this there is the danger of overstimulation and love-distortion.

Most harmful of all literature, from the standpoint of family welfare, is that which is actually obscene—known technically as pornography. Although there are laws to suppress the dissemination of such material, some does find its way around in an underground or bootleg fashion. Where this falls into the hands of immature adolescents, or adults either, for that matter, its lewd appeal can be devastating. As a matter of fact, one use to which such smuggled obscenity is put is erotic stimulation for the direct promotion of prostitution.

Just short of this illegal traffic in obscenity is the publication of materials which barely manage to stay within the law; the appeal is to passion but there is an attempt to be technically legal in making it. A large part of this business is carried on through pulp magazines of one sort or another, decorated highly with enticing pictures and captions. There is a constant battle between dealers in this kind of literature and the law— to see how far the publication can go without being stopped, to see how long a ban can be enforced. Sometimes it is bribery of law enforcement officials that permits the material to circulate; at other times, their indifference.

Another type of within-the-law pornography is the sensualized advertising and book circulating conducted by certain unreliable publishing houses whose purpose seems to be to capitalize for profit upon the sexual curiosity of man. Major features of this business are as follows: (1) Advertising and sales are usually taken care of by correspondence; and, as if to further insure the purchaser against embarrassment or discovery, promises are made that the book or books will be sent "in a plain wrapper." (2) The prestige of science is called upon as a guise; scientific men are quoted, but usually as pertaining to the subject being treated, or perhaps the author, seldom the book itself; scientific words and phrases are used, but as an opportunity in the flaunting of sex, seldom if ever to objectively impart information. (3) Titles, subtitles, and content descriptions are worded in such a way as to arouse the curiosity of the reader and stimulate him sexually; such as, "Picture Stories of the Sex Life of Man and Woman," "The Five Human Sexes," and "Truths in Connection with the Bridal Night." (4) When the books arrive they turn out to be disappointing; often the printing and binding are crude, and the chapters composed of unintegrated excerpts from other sources; the "pictures" prove to be diagrams and not too well done at that.

The various lovelorn columns and programs found in newspapers, magazines, and by way of the radio are difficult to classify. Some of these are conducted by individuals who are sincere and competent. But others, unfortunately, are put out by persons possessing a good voice, or a knack for writing, though unqualified otherwise. These latter frequently play upon the emotions of the lovesick and the unfortunate, exploiting their ignorance and their need. In this way sentimentality is often made the basis for a great deal of misinformation, and even well-adjusted individuals are sometimes stirred up emotionally and made problem-conscious unnecessarily. Lovelorn columns and similar programs on the air are effective means for reaching large numbers of people who need help, but their final worth must be decided case by case according to the professional training and good judgment of those who perform. There is value, certainly, in a symposium of marriage experts such as is occasionally heard on a national broadcast.

It is when the passions and troubles of people are exploited solely, or largely, for the sake of profit that quackery develops. Since the love and sex interests of men and women are strong and constant, and since most people need help of one kind or another, a vast literature on love and marriage has arisen. A considerable amount of this is sound and wholesome, but all is not. Every person needs to develop a sense of discrimination. There is enough reliable literature in the field of family life to permit everyone a well-rounded self-education, though to find it may require some sifting and selecting.

In short, it is education for better living that is needed, rather than erotic stimulation by charlatans for the sake of profit; and it is the facts of science that are to be disseminated, never the emotionalized impressions of the uninformed.

Formal Education for Marriage.—It is peculiar, but unfortunate, that man will study and work to the limit of his ability in order to raise a successful crop or to come out on top in the business world, and will at the same time take marriage, one of the greatest of all human enterprises, for granted. To assume either that man does not need training in family affairs, or that he will pick enough of it up informally and by himself, is to err. Bowman states it this way: [5]

Almost anyone may marry, may establish at least what passes for a home and becomes his castle even though he hates to live in it, and may, if he is biologically able, have children. Blindly, stupidly, or naïvely we assume that this "anyone" is prepared for these profound undertakings. How does he become prepared? Does he become prepared by reaching a certain age? By fulfilling the meager requirements of the law? By being subjected to a curriculum that includes little or nothing contributory to marriage and family life? By living in his own family, adequate or inadequate?

It is commonplace in discussing the family to mention its changing functions, to point out the shift from institutional functions to personality functions, and, to say that some of the functions have been taken over by outside agencies. Does this suggest that others of the functions, therefore, *must* be taken over by outside agencies? Has the laboratory been stripped of part of its equipment? If the family no longer does what it used to do, may we still assume that it can educate its members for family life? To some extent, of course, it does and probably always will. But must we not conclude that this intra-family education must be supplemented by that supplied by outside agencies?

---

[5] Henry Bowman, "Education for Marriage and Family Life," *Marriage and Family Living,* Summer, 1946, pp. 63-64.

As the family has moved from a producing unit toward a consuming unit economically, it has had to utilize goods produced by agencies other than itself. Hence the need for and importance of consumer education. Can a similar concept be applied to family personnel? Since the functions of the family have changed, the family is now composed, to a greater extent than formerly, of persons "produced" in part by outside agencies. Hence the need for education for marriage and family life.

Schools have recently been adding courses in courtship, marriage, and family life to the curriculum, together with a great many other subjects that touch upon this field either partially or indirectly. This is true whether we are thinking of the elementary, secondary, or college levels, though it is on the higher levels of learning that the greatest developments have come. High schools are doing it through courses in health, eugenics, home economics, and social science. Colleges have these also, and in recent years are supplementing them with special courses designed directly for marriage preparation. The first of these was offered in 1926 by Dr. Ernest R. Groves at the University of North Carolina. It proved to meet a growing need and to be exceedingly popular among the students. Other schools have followed suit and at the present time well over six hundred marriage and family courses are offered in the colleges and universities of the country.[6] Most of these are given by sociologists, with home economists coming second, and a few biologists, psychologists, and religionists entering in. The trend in emphasis is away from the study of the family as a social institution and toward the immediate personal problems of marital preparation and adjustment.[7]

Yet though the growth of marriage education within the schools has been tremendous, and the trend remains in that

---

[6] The 1945-46 Census conducted by the National Conference on Family Relations showed, from the 630 schools reporting, that 550 colleges were offering courses on marriage and family and that 657 courses were being offered. See *Marriage and Family Living*, May, 1946, p. 42.

Bowman's more recent study of 1,370 nontechnical colleges and universities during the academic year 1948-49 shows 661 courses in this field, with 632 schools participating. See Henry A. Bowman, "Marriage Education in the Colleges" (New York: American Social Hygiene Association, 1949), Publication Number A-770.

[7] Frances C. Thurman, "College Courses in Preparation for Marriage," *Social Forces*, March, 1946, pp. 332-35.

direction, present offerings are entirely inadequate for the needs that exist. Bowman, in pointing out that family life education is still frequently just a by-product of our educational system, insists that it touches too few students, that it under-emphasizes family relationships at the expense of domestic skills, that it neglects the education of the male, and that it lacks integration and is too academic.[8] Thurman, in summarizing his data on college courses, concludes by saying:

> With slightly over one fourth of the colleges offering practical instruction in marriage, and with only 6 per cent of the students enrolled in these colleges taking the courses offered, there remains much to be done by the colleges and universities toward laying a better foundation for modern marriage.[9]

The Family Life Movement.—Public concern over problems relating to children, parents, husbands, and wives has developed very rapidly of late, and in response to this concern has come a flood of local and national organizations and programs designed to strengthen family life. So rapid and definite has been this development that it can properly be referred to as a movement. While some of this new activity has to do with research, the sponsoring of legislation, and the offering of clinical services, much of it is directly educational and all of it bears some relationship to the teaching function.

Club and community projects for the improvement of family living are becoming more common. Sometimes it is a study club sponsored by a Y.M.C.A., a Y.W.C.A., a settlement house, or one of the civic groups. Sometimes, again, it is a special family life institute conducted by a local church, school, or other family-minded community group. Occasionally a community will organize its family life program around some central agency, with this agency acting as coordinator of other groups and supplying needed stimulation and professional as-

---

[8] Bowman, *op. cit.,* "Education for Marriage and Family Life," p. 64; "Marriage Education in the Colleges," p. 5.

[9] Thurman, *op. cit.,* p. 335. The more recent study by Bowman, cited in footnotes 6 and 8, shows nearly fifty per cent of the nontechnical colleges giving work in this field and estimates that approximately 50,000 college students, which is only about 1 in 50 of all college students, receive some sort of marriage instruction annually.

sistance. A good example of this is the Association for Family Living in Chicago.

Religious groups are shifting more and more attention to this important field in human relationships. This is made evident in the sermons delivered and the literature published on the subject, in the trend toward church-sponsored youth clubs and other discussion groups dealing with marriage, and in the newer emphasis ministers are giving to family counseling. Activities of the following church agencies are nation-wide:

> *Protestant:* Commission on Marriage and the Home, Federal Council of Churches of Christ in America, New York
> *Catholic:* Family Life Bureau, National Catholic Welfare Conference, Washington, D. C.
> *Jewish:* Jewish Institute on Marriage and the Family, New York

There are a great many national organizations, both public and private, that are now active in the field of family life education. Some of these deal with the family only incidentally; others have it as their sole and specific focus. Some of these organizations shape their programs to cover broadly the entire area of marriage and family relationships, while others specialize on one particular aspect. From the numerous national groups and agencies that are now functioning in the field, we list the following as being among the most prominent; students and community workers might consider the list as a source that can be readily tapped for useful materials and professional advice:

> American Association of Marriage Counselors, New York
> American Eugenic Society, New York
> American Home Economics Association, New York
> American Institute of Family Relations, Los Angeles
> American Social Hygiene Association, New York
> Children's Bureau, Federal Security Agency, Washington, D. C.
> Family Service Association of America, New York
> National Committee for Mental Hygiene, New York
> National Congress of Parents and Teachers, Chicago
> National Council on Family Relations, Chicago
> Planned Parenthood Federation of America, Inc., New York

The National Council on Family Relations was organized in 1938. It seeks "to bring together in one organization the leaders in research, in teaching, and in professional service in the field of marriage and the family. Its purpose is to advance the cultural values now principally secured through family relations for personality development and the strength of the nation." It "encourages the holding of regional, state and local conferences: (1) to foster acquaintance of people of diverse professional backgrounds and interests in marriage and the family; (2) to discuss points of view and experience; (3) to present important research findings; (4) to consider proposals for family welfare." [10] A large number of state councils are now organized; these affiliate with the national body. Finally, it publishes a quarterly journal called *Marriage and Family Living* which contains helpful articles, reviews, and notes of interest to family-minded persons.

The National Council on Family Relations holds annual meetings for its members at which times are reported the most recent in research findings and in teaching and counseling methods. In addition to meetings of this organization, there have been held each year for the last decade at the University of North Carolina what are known as The Groves Conferences on Conservation of Marriage and the Family. Attendance at the Groves Conference is limited mainly to professionals in the field and is by invitation.

Special impetus was given the family life movement by the holding of a National Conference on Family Life in Washington, D. C., during early May, 1948. The conference had the endorsement of President Truman, who offered the courtesy of the White House as a place for some of the meetings. It was attended by nearly one thousand delegates, both lay and professional, representing one hundred and twenty-five national sponsoring organizations having programs affecting American home and family life. Its chief purpose was "to arouse national consciousness of the adverse influence on American family life and to get thinking Americans thinking in terms of

---

[10] These purposes and aims are as found stated on the inside cover of any issue of *Marriage and Family Living*.

strengthening the position of the family in society." It was hoped that out of this conference would come increased local activity and the organizing of Community Councils on Family Life. This goal has been only partially realized.

The Clinical Approach (Consultation)

Marriage counseling is related to the field of family life education, though the two are by no means identical. In both cases the findings of research are given over to the individual, with the thought that solutions to problems are best found in an exposure to facts. But while education proper is primarily concerned with the dissemination of correct information, and is usually carried out on a group basis, counseling is concerned with the detailed application of information to a particular problem, and it is personalized. Though the teacher is oftentimes a counselor, and the counselor a teacher, the functions and procedures of the two are not entirely the same.

Who Shall Counsel?—People in trouble have always taken their problems to sympathetic listeners, hoping for understanding and help. Sometimes these listeners have been parents, relatives, or friends; at other times they have been religious leaders, school teachers, or other professionals. In recent years there have appeared a few specially trained, full-time marriage counselors—marking the emergence of a new profession.

In a broad, nontechnical sense each person at different times plays the dual roles of counselor and counselee; man in interaction both gives advice and seeks it, influences others and is influenced by them. There is a therapeutic effect, called *catharsis,* that comes from the unloading of one's burdens upon a confidant. Pent-up emotional states are likely to cause frustration and despair. They need release, and an understanding listener can frequently be the means of bringing this about. It is a mistake, of course, for anyone to unburden his troubles upon everyone, for such repetition only tends to exaggerate the problem in the minds of all concerned. Nevertheless, every individual does need at least one confidant. Under ideal conditions within marriage this will normally be the husband or the wife. It may be a friend, however, or a religious leader, or a professional.

But counseling implies more than passive listening; it includes understanding and guidance. The trend toward specialization in family guidance got its start in other professions. Church leaders, who have always been charged with "looking after the flock," have been turning more attention recently to training and practice in the field of marriage and family counseling as a means for more effectively carrying out their assignment. High school and college teachers, who have been accustomed to having problems of this nature brought to them for discussion, are finding now that young people feel less inhibited than formerly and seek counsel more often. This is particularly true of those teachers working directly with the new marriage and family courses.

The legal profession has also started to interest itself in family welfare: first, through the establishment of juvenile courts where delinquent children are taught and helped without the stigma or hardening experiences that accompany regular criminal procedures; and second, through the family court movement, or Courts of Domestic Relations, where emphasis is on the reconciliation of couples and the solution of marital difficulties rather than on divorce. Lawyers have a unique opportunity when consulted concerning the dissolution of a marriage. Those who are more public spirited than profit minded can and frequently do succeed in maneuvering a readjustment. But in fairness to the profession, the public must come to expect to pay for such services, if not the legal fee then a counseling fee, for time and technical skill deserve compensation.

Medical men likewise are becoming more and more interested in the social and psychological aspects of marriage. Their training now frequently includes courses in this field and they are coming to give counsel more freely, even though it takes them beyond the technical field of medicine. Counseling in conjunction with the premarital blood test, which is required by law in most states, or at the time of the complete physical examination that many modern couples voluntarily request prior to marriage, or at any other time at which physician and patient are in contact, is coming to be regular and recommended procedure. In addition, doctors are conducting various clinics on social hygiene, prenatal care, child development, and the like.

Welfare agencies are increasingly recognizing family backgrounds in the problems that concern them, and as a result are more frequently turning attention to education and counseling for the purpose of family reorganization. Child and family case work is becoming a specialized field, and many professionals are now being employed in it full time. Virtually all social case workers must deal with family problems in some degree, and most of them rather intimately and extensively.

There is need for a word of caution concerning lay counseling. Many of the problems which show up in marriage and family relationships are deep-seated within the personalities involved; they are complex and require the insight and skill of specialists. When well-meaning but uninformed individuals hand out advice, the results are often damaging instead of helpful. Church leaders, school teachers, attorneys, physicians, and social workers are better prepared to counsel in this field than are the nonprofessionals. Even so, their training is generally along only one line, which is not counseling; they frequently lack needed technical understanding concerning human nature, social relationships, or counseling techniques. The trend within these various professional groups toward greater training in the theory and practice of counseling is encouraging. Nevertheless, lay counselors will be wise if they limit their help to about three things: (1) sympathetic and intelligent listening for the sake of catharsis; (2) the imparting of factual information bearing on the problem, which they are capable of giving; and (3) referring the counselee to appropriate specialists for more advanced therapy, when needed.

In seeking out a specialist for help on marriage and family problems, one needs to beware of quacks. There is no license required of marriage counselors, and no powerful group to enforce minimum professional standards. As a result, the field is almost overrun with fortunetellers, advice-givers, and pseudo psychologists.[11] A good check on the competence of a counselor is to determine whether or not he has membership in one or more of the national professional organizations requiring training in this field.

Minimum qualifications for the professional marriage and family counselor might be outlined as follows: [12]

1. He will be well adjusted himself, both personally and socially. His personality will be attractive and his conduct above criticism. He will be genuinely interested in people, though able to remain objective in his dealings with them. He will be intellectually and emotionally mature. It is desirable, though not imperative, that he have a reasonably normal home life of his own.

2. His experiences and training will be such as to have given him a deep understanding of human nature and social behavior. Professionally, he will have studied such subjects as sociology, psychology, biology, economics, domestic law, medicine, and psychiatry. Not that he could be expected to master all of these, but to know the fields as they relate to the family and to be able to make intelligent referrals.

3. He will be informed and have some training in the technical skills of the profession—personality testing, interviewing, treatment of cases, and the like. Ideally his training will have included several years of graduate study and some experience in a clinical laboratory. Here again it is not expected that he will have a personal mastery of all skills in the profession, but he should know when they are to be used, understand their limitations, and be able to make proper referrals.

Thoughts on Counseling.—There is no "one way" for conducting a counseling interview. The good counselor is something of an artist, studying each client as a separate case and drawing upon his own personality resources in the way that works best for him. Since personalities differ, it is to be expected that there will be some procedural differences from counselor to counselor and from case to case. Yet there are certain broad principles that all need to follow.[13]

[11] Cf. Lee R. Steiner, *Where Do People Take Their Troubles?* (Boston: Houghton Mifflin Co., 1945).

[12] Adapted largely from Burgess and Locke, *The Family: From Institution to Companionship* (New York: American Book Co., 1945), pp. 740-43.

[13] Cf. John F. Cuber, *Marriage Counseling Practice* (New York: Appleton-Century-Crofts, Inc., 1948), Part I, pp. 1-117; also Henry Bowman, "The Teacher as Counselor in Marriage Education," *Marriage and Family Living,* 9:1-7, 12, February, 1947.

1. The counselor will want to establish rapport between himself and the person being interviewed. This will require that he stay friendly and cheerful; that he put the client at ease with the problem; that he pay attention, listen well, avoid interruptions or the appearance of being in a hurry; that he insure privacy and leave no doubt but that everything that transpires will be kept confidential; and that he show respect for the client and take the problem seriously.

2. The counselor will want to remain objective. He will not let his natural friendliness or sympathy becloud his judgment. He will keep emotionally detached, not feeling embarrassed or shocked at what he hears, and never using interviews to satisfy vicariously his own curiosities or desires. He will ask only pertinent questions, never pry. He will not solicit appointments. He will use standardized testing devices to aid in the diagnosis when these are available and practical, but will interpret them cautiously.

3. The counselor will want to bring his client to a better understanding of the problem and a greater willingness to do his part in its solution. He will not preach or moralize. He will examine carefully all relevant facts in the case, and will help the client to define the situation in the light of them. He will suggest but not force, working the problem through *with* the client but never *for* him.

4. The counselor will want to follow the case through to its logical conclusion. He will maintain suspended judgment during the analysis, avoiding premature solutions based upon incomplete data or preconceived notions that may not fit each particular case. He will face his own limitations, never pretending to know what he does not, and always being ready to make referrals to other professional sources whenever the need arises. He will close each interview with some plans or "next steps" that are to be pursued. But he will realize also that some problems are insoluble, or nearly so; that some marriages are like Humpty Dumpty and cannot be put together again. In such cases he will help the individual to adjust realistically to the situation as it is.

Marriage Clinics.—Clinical treatment of marriage problems is a relatively new idea. This is clearly demonstrated by the fact that literature on the subject is rather scarce even now, and prior to 1930 it was practically nonexistent; and also by the fact that 1922 marked the beginning of the movement in Europe and not until about eight years later were the first marriage clinics established in this country. The European experiment started in Austria where in 1922 its Department of Health opened a bureau for the treatment of marriage and family problems. The movement was apparently a success for it spread until there were soon several hundred such clinics on the Continent.[14]

In the United States the movement got under way with the opening of the Marriage Consultation Center under Abraham and Hannah Stone in New York City during 1929, the American Institute of Family Relations under Paul Popenoe in Los Angeles during 1930, and the Marriage Council under Emily H. Mudd in Philadelphia during 1932.

Marriage clinics are special counseling centers set up to deal specifically with problems of marriage and family interaction. Their work is primarily that of diagnosis and treatment through counseling, though often this will be supplemented with research and educational activities on the side. They differ from marriage counseling as a private practice in that they are organizations, usually incorporated, and employing the services of a number of specialists—psychiatrists, psychologists, sociologists, urologists, gynecologists, and the like. And since their full-time focus is upon family problems, they differ also from the many agencies, educational and clinical in nature, which devote only part time to the marriage and family field.

There are a dozen or more marriage clinics located in different metropolitan centers throughout the country.[15] Of these, the following are among the most active and most widely known:

> American Institute of Family Relations, Los Angeles
> Association for Family Living, Chicago
> Advisory Service, Merrill-Palmer School, Detroit
> Counseling Service, Boston
> Marriage and Family Council, Inc., Chapel Hill, North Carolina

---

[14] Paul Popenoe, "The Marriage Clinic," *Parents' Magazine,* April, 1932, p. 15.
[15] The exact number of marriage clinics functioning at any one time is never known, and for two reasons: (1) the activities of these agencies blend with those of private counselors and other types of organization so that classification is difficult; and (2) some clinics are short-lived, while new ones are almost continually coming into existence. Readers desiring names of reliable persons or organizations within their own communities might do well to contact, for suggestions, one or more of the national educational agencies listed in the section above.

Marriage Consultation Center, The Community Church, New York

Marriage Council, Philadelphia

Family Guidance and Consultation Service, Child Study Association of America, New York

Except that it is focused upon a special kind of problem, marriage counseling is little different from personal counseling in general. It is important, therefore, to note the emergence and probable future growth of mental hygiene clinics throughout the various states. These are staffed by what is coming to be known as "neuropsychiatric teams"—specialists representing such fields as psychology, psychiatry, psychiatric social work, and public health. Mental hygiene clinics are designed to function rather widely, encompassing virtually all problems of the personality, including those that relate to love and marriage.

THE LEGAL APPROACH (LEGISLATION)

One way of making marriage more successful is to improve the laws pertaining to it. While legislation can never be a proper substitute for adequate information, widespread education, competent consultation, or strong inward motivation, it can become a worth-while supplement.

Not all authorities are agreed as to what should constitute ideal family legislation. That we must have laws governing marriage, no one will deny; nor will they that present laws on the subject are far from satisfactory. When it comes to details as to what should be, however, there is a variety of opinion. This is one explanation for the great diversity found among laws and for the confusion that exists regarding them.

At this point the reader may wish to refer back to our earlier discussion of major legal provisions covering marriage and divorce. (See pages 279-85.)

Some Needed Reforms.—Among the many reforms that have been suggested, here are the ones that to the writer seem most pressing.

1. Most needed, perhaps, is a unification or standardization of existing marriage and divorce laws. Not only is legislation in this field needlessly complicated and confusing, but it permits easy evasion. States having blood test laws, for example, find certain couples dodging into neighboring areas for the ceremonies, and states that make divorce difficult find the same thing with reference to it. This not only makes for legal tangles but it defeats the very purpose of the law. Two methods for effecting legal uniformity have been proposed. One is the passing of a federal marriage and divorce law, authorized through a constitutional amendment. The other is the setting up of a model marriage and divorce law which would then, it is hoped, be adopted by all of the state legislatures. The first of these ideas has been promoted for several decades by Senator Arthur Capper of Kansas. Opponents of the proposal argue that it would be wrong to enforce a legal uniformity where little actual similarity in thinking or culture exists, and that the liberalizing of certain state laws for the sake of uniformity would actually increase the divorce rate. This plan has not made much progress. The second proposition seems to offer the most hope, although the model acts that have been drawn up for that purpose seem so far to be shunned by the majority of the states. A few, however, have been adopted, and the trend is unmistakably in the direction of such voluntary uniformity.[16]

2. There are a number of rackets that have grown up in connection with both marriage and divorce that ought to be abolished. One of these is "heart balm" growing out of breach of promise suits. Another is alimony. While there are situations that justify both of these, there are too many loopholes in the law and too many human leeches who are willing to take advantage of this fact. A third racket to be mentioned is that of the "marriage market" where the justice of the peace or some other licensed officiant, because he is on a fee rate and wants to make money, makes a brazen business out of marriage, with advertising, cut-rate offerings, and all the other sordid trimmings that go with it. The remedy would be to legislate

---

[16] Cf. Ray E. Baber, *Marriage and the Family* (New York: McGraw-Hill Book Co., Inc., 1939), pp. 137-40.

for a more careful selection of officiants and to place them on a salary basis. Finally, we shall point out that divorce itself is a racket for certain unscrupulous lawyers. Many a divorce has been encouraged and pushed through by them, for profit, when a reconciliation would have been entirely possible. If the law would more frequently provide for family courts, or courts of domestic relations as they are sometimes called, where experts bend their efforts toward effecting a readjustment rather than widening the breach, many such divorces could be avoided.

3. Marriage laws need to be revised in the direction of insuring better mate selection and better preparation before the wedding. If more attention were paid to the entrance of marriage, there would be fewer individuals seeking the exit. Legal prohibitions should be reexamined to see that they are based upon tested fact rather than just upon fancy or prejudice. Laws that protect against known hereditary defects, the venereal diseases, or other serious encumbrances should be encouraged. So also should the so-called "gin marriage laws" which protect against hasty marriage by providing for a waiting period between the application for the license and the performing of the wedding ceremony. In some states minimum age requirements should be raised to protect against unfortunate child marriages.

4. Divorce laws also need to be changed; not to make divorce more difficult necessarily, nor more easy either for that matter, but more consistent and less impetuous. In lieu of unification on a national scale, residence requirements should be sufficient in each state to insure against migratory divorce. Then too, because the majority of divorce suits are uncontested, with only one of the complaining parties appearing in court, some states are now providing for a court-appointed "divorce counsel" whose duty it is to investigate the real factors in the case, protest against perjured testimony, and thereby encourage a reconciliation. This trend is in the right direction. The interlocutory decree, which provides for a waiting period after divorce before the decree becomes final, actually saves some marriages and should be adopted more widely.

5. There is a type of legislation which, though not directed squarely at the family, nevertheless has an impact upon it. Such are child labor laws, social security statutes, housing acts, and the like. Space here will not permit an analysis of these. It will be sufficient for our present purposes to say that they are there, and that when properly designed and administered they can make real contributions to the family.

Recommendations of the Legal Profession.—It is encouraging to note that law-trained persons are among those urging legal reform. A committee of lawyers, writing for the National Conference on Family Life in 1948, observed that:

> Our divorce laws are thoroughly bad. They are universally condemned. They have failed of their objective. They constitute a threat to the stability of the home.
>
> They are based on a false premise. An entirely new premise must be substituted. That is the simplest way to correct a bad legal situation. The new premise of prevention should be substituted for the present premise of punishment.
>
> Divorce proceedings today are a farce. The truth is not in them. Hypocrisy is the order of the day. Nine divorces out of ten are secured by agreement of the parties. Everybody must pretend that is not so, but it is so.[17]

These are strong words. But they have the endorsement of the American Bar Association, as do also the following recommendations from the report, designed to help correct the situation.[18]

1. The President of the United States should be asked to appoint a commission of ten or more citizens drawn from the fields of religion, medicine, education, and sociology, as well as law. This commission would be assigned the task of reexamining our body of laws relating to marriage and divorce, of studying them in terms of their methods and results, and of recommending changes for the promotion of family stability.

2. There should be an entirely new type of procedure in divorce cases. The family court plan ought to be accepted and

---

[17] Taken from working papers on legal problems, prepared for the National Conference on Family Life (Mimeographed), pp. 1-5.
[18] *Loc. cit.*

made mandatory for all cases involving the family. This would be applying the juvenile court idea to a new area, that of marriage difficulties; emphasis would be upon diagnosis and care, not guilt and punishment; there would be psychiatrists, clinical psychologists, social workers, teachers, and other trained specialists assigned to the court. This would, in effect, be making counseling compulsory, but it would prevent a large number of divorces.

3. There should be an extension of the Legal Aid Movement, whereby the services of lawyers are made more readily available. There exists an abundance of law designed to protect the family and its members. But the law is complex and there are millions of persons who cannot afford to pay the usual fees for having it interpreted. The services of lawyers must be supplied, nevertheless—"freely to the poor and at low cost to persons of moderate means."

The Religious Approach (Motivation)

It is in the field of motivation that religion makes its greatest contribution to the family. Religion can provide a meaning for life, a purpose to justify man's effort. Men of learning very commonly make two mistakes, neither one of which is compatible with successful marriage: (1) They "hide their light under a bushel," so to speak, remaining indifferent and inactive. Many people are like this, not living up to the knowledge they have, lazy. Religion can give these the stimulation they need, the urge to action that will implement their progress. (2) Some, though informed and active, use their learning for selfish or destructive purposes. Many, too, are like this, lacking character and stooping to anything that seems to bring them personal gain. Real religion, by giving facts a moral orientation and man an incentive, spells the difference between sheer brilliance on the one hand and genuine intelligence on the other, between bare knowledge and mature wisdom.

Facts alone are sterile. It is a little bit like the farmer's son who came home from four years' college training to tell his father how to better operate the farm. After listening patiently to his boy's enthusiastic account of the newer and better methods of agriculture, the father said: "But what good is all of that? I am only farming half as well as I know how now!" By way of analogy, many people are only living half as well as they know how now, and this applies to family life too. Their problem is essentially lack of motivation, not information.

Thus we see that both information and motivation are important to family welfare. Intellectuality and spirituality are complementary, mutually reinforcing, processes. Without faith, facts become sterile; and without facts, faith degenerates into mere superstition. Science can provide the knowledge upon which successful family life may rest, but it is religion's opportunity to inspire participants to do their best.

Let it be understood from the beginning that religion, as used throughout this chapter, implies more than the institutional patterns it commonly follows. Defined broadly, and sociologically, religion can be regarded as the sum of man's beliefs and practices centering around his concept of the supernatural—it is man's effort to find ultimate meanings, values, and purposes in life and to live in accordance with what he finds; it is faith, it is the urge to bigger things. Institutional religion expresses itself in churches, rituals, and dogmas. Individual religion, on the other hand, finds expression in ethical living outside the controls of formal organization or prescribed pattern. Both give motivations to conduct and thus play vital roles in family stability.

The institutional variety, however, has the chief advantages of being systematized and of offering added fellowship and stimulation within the organization itself. Its main difficulty is the tendency toward institutionalism, where form becomes more important than spirit and personal welfare is made secondary to the perpetuation of established patterns. To the extent that this can be avoided, that blind conformity within the churches can be held less important than enlightened vitality, institutional patterns of worship will continue to give real strength and support to the family.

What the Figures Show.—From their study of 13,000 young people in Maryland,[19] the American Youth Commission found the following percentages of homes broken by divorce, desertion, or separation: Jewish, 4.6; Catholic, 6.4; Protestant, 6.8; mixed, 15.2; and no religion, 16.7. This suggests a relationship between church affiliation and successful marriage, especially when husband and wife are of the same faith.

Though accurate figures for the nation as a whole are not available, it is known that religious weddings are not followed by divorce so frequently as are those using a civil ceremony.[20] Why? There seem to be four possible reasons: (1) A slight effect may derive from the nature of the ceremony itself or from the mere fact of church affiliation. If this is as far as it goes, however, the influence on marriage is likely to be negligible. (2) The religious couple, because of group identification and pressure, may feel less inclined to get a divorce even though incompatible. This means that the divorce rate, considered alone, is an unreliable index of marital happiness. (3) It may be that there is a selective process operating in the direction of religious marriages, that those who are most mature and best prepared tend to prefer the church wedding. (4) It seems highly probable that, in addition to these others, religion contributes something by way of attitude and incentive.

Using adjustment instead of nondivorce as the criterion of successful marriage, Burgess and Cottrell also found religion and success to be positively associated. According to their data, married mates are best adjusted where they both: (1) had attended Sunday School beyond the age of eighteen; (2) had attended church on an average of two or more times each month; (3) had been married at a church or parsonage; and (4) had been married by a minister, priest, or rabbi. These

---

[19] Howard M. Bell, *Youth Tell Their Story* (Washington, D. C.: American Council on Education, 1938), p. 21. Cf. Judson T. Landis, "Marriages of Mixed and Non-mixed Religious Faith," *American Sociological Review*, June, 1949, p. 403.

[20] Cf. Paul Popenoe, *Modern Marriage* (New York: The Macmillan Co., 1940), pp. 216-17. Popenoe reports that approximately three fourths of all marriages are by religious ceremony, while only two thirds of all divorces come from this group.

authors conclude their analysis of this relationship by saying
the following:

> Whatever data were examined to test the relation to marital ad-
> justment of religious sentiments, interest, and activities—Sunday-
> school or church attendance, place of marriage, or official performing
> the ceremony—all agree in showing a positive association.[21]

Terman, though cautious in his interpretations, found higher
happiness scores for those married individuals who had had
"considerable" religious training within the home than for
those whose training in this regard had been either too strict
or negligible. He summed up as follows:

> The conclusion suggested, though by no means established, is that
> either very much or very little religious training is less favorable to
> marital happiness than a more moderate amount.[22]

Family and Church.—Religion and marriage have much
that they share in common. On the one side we find marriage
being sanctioned and promoted by the church—the wedding
ceremony has come to be regarded as a sacramental ordinance;
religious concepts are frequently couched in words of family
origin, such as "the fatherhood of God" and "the brotherhood
of man." On the other side we can note how prayer and other
forms of worship have been brought into the home, and how,
in the past at least, church attendance was largely by family
unit. The church gives support to the family, and the family
to the church. When one fails the other is weakened because
of it, and when one succeeds the other receives a lift in the
process. In both institutions personal rightness and brotherhood stand at the top of the value systems. In both, also, are
found such principles as trust, loyalty, unselfishness, justice,
and cooperation. These values which make up the core of
man's moral and religious code are also the principles upon
which successful marriage is built. In one sense, marriage
might even be regarded as spiritual, for, along with the church,

---

21 Ernest W. Burgess and Leonard S. Cottrell, Jr., *Predicting Success or
Failure in Marriage* (New York: Prentice-Hall, Inc., 1939), pp. 122-26.
22 From *Psychological Factors in Marital Happiness,* by Lewis M. Terman.
1938. Courtesy of McGraw-Hill Book Co., pp. 228-36. Quotation from p. 235.

it is dependent upon a certain amount of self-sacrifice and humanitarian interest.

It is neither cheapened marriage nor perverted religion that we are speaking of here, however. When we say that the Christian virtues are important to marriage, we mean successful marriage, the kind that makes people happy. Likewise, when we imply that the world is in need of a return to religion, we mean real religion, the kind that has life and power. Either marriage or religion may become perverted, departing from its real purposes, and when this happens the other is dragged down because of it. Family members, for example, such as in the case of a cruel father or a selfish mother, sometimes use religion as a cover-up, feigning piety and putting on a good front by going through the motions of worship. When religion sinks to that level, it is no wonder that it loses the support of those who are progressive, idealistic, and hopeful. Real religion stresses vitality and spirituality more than personal mannerisms or institutional conformity. Real religion carries over into the lives of its members, inspiring them to greater things and impelling them to live cooperatively and creatively. And such is the spirit that marriage must have if it is really to succeed.

A Motive for Living.—Thus religion, if it is the kind we refer to, may provide the motivation necessary for a happy home. Family failure is greatest among nonreligious people. While part of this may be due to selection, another and possibly larger part is due to the stimulation that is to be found in faith.

Reasons for this are not difficult to find. Chiefly they lie in the psychological adjustment values contained in such religious ideals as brotherhood and devotion to the right. Spirituality makes cooperation easier. A religious atmosphere in the home contributes toward understanding and harmony. While science gives us facts, religion stresses goals, purposes, and values; it gives a deeper meaning to life, a higher motive for living. Because of this, church people are inclined to take their marriage obligations more seriously and to try harder to make them succeed.

In addition to this, religion can help its participants keep their heads up in the face of family disappointments and sorrows. Bachelorhood, childlessness, ill-health, death of a loved one, these and other crises seem to be met better by those who have faith and who are living for eternity. Family life does not run smoothly for everyone in spite of all that is done. Religion can help people compensate for their inadequacies, giving meaning to their sacrifices and courage to carry on.

Home Atmosphere.—Personalities are invariably influenced by the environmental settings that surround them. To develop properly and to keep balanced, family members will need to maintain harmonious feelings and outward relationships toward each other. Attitudes are contagious. Most particularly is this true within the intimacies of family life. If home atmosphere is healthy and stimulating, the lives of members who breathe it will likewise be healthy and vigorous; but if, on the other hand, the atmosphere is clouded by pessimism and quarreling and hate, the lives of those who experience it cannot hope to be normal. All have seen examples of this very thing— lives made sweet or sour by the social climate in which they must live.

It is to religion that many families have turned for their most substantial aid in building the right home atmosphere. The spirit of the home is not unrelated to the spirituality of the church. Family worship frequently assists in the maintainance of family solidarity.

Applied to child development and training, all this means that religious education has a definite place within the home. As a matter of fact it is the home that can accomplish most in this regard because of its intensity and extensity of contacts during the impressionable years of childhood. Parents err who purposely keep religion out of the home so that the child can make up its own mind when it becomes an adult. So do parents who thoughtlessly neglect this important phase of child training. The difficulty is that it is almost impossible to remain neutral; those who are not religious are usually irreligious, not just unreligious. Furthermore, these early habits of thinking and acting usually carry through, so that instead of leaving the child's mind free, such parents unwittingly condition it against things spiritual. And since religion provides a strong support for ethics, children from such families are more likely to suffer from character defects.

Virtually all authorities on the subject support this point of view. One notable example is the White House Conference on Children in a Democracy, a conference of interested experts from throughout this country, organized to study problems in the fields of family life and child welfare. In its report this body recognized the importance of religion to character and character to democracy; it placed the primary responsibility for the child's religious development upon the parents; and it recommended a greater organized effort in both the home and the community to supply this need of spiritual values to the characters of children.[23]

It is entirely possible, of course, for religion to become a disorganizing factor within the home—where fanatical interpretations lead to unreasonable demands or differences in viewpoints make for quarreling and conflict. Home atmosphere may be unwholesome even when the mates lay claim to being religious. Up to now we have been examining religion's beneficial effects upon family life. If husband and wife are of different churches, however, or if their viewpoints are narrow, or if they differ greatly in them even though belonging to the same organization, there may be trouble ahead. Since the goals of life are so frequently tied up with religion, it follows that marriage can be either made or marred by the strength or weakness, unity or disunity, of the religious element that is there. Wise individuals will do well to consider these things before they marry, therefore, and in case religious friction develops after the home has become established they will show themselves to be both tolerant and patient. Unless they can come to see more nearly alike as time goes on, however, their family satisfactions will be either dulled or disrupted because of it.

---

[23] *Children in a Democracy,* General Report Adopted by the White House Conference on Children in a Democracy (Washington, D. C.: January 19, 1940) pp. 29-31.

Character Emphasis.—Family stability and moral integrity seem to be interrelated. Any deterioration in either will cause a breakdown in the other, which in turn will reinfect the first, so that the two may become locked in a vicious circle of disorganization. For the sake of character, society must preserve the family, and for the sake of the family, it must preserve character. Religion is a buttress to them both.

We have already referred to the home as the seedbed of character. It is there that personality takes shape and morality gets its start. Not only is the child most impressionable in his early years, when the home has him, but home influences have a greater effect upon his character than do other groups all the way through. Hartshorne and May, in testing the moral judgments of a large number of children and comparing their scores with those of their associates, found the highest correlation between children and their parents, and the next highest between children and their friends, with club leaders, school teachers, and Sunday-school teachers following on down in that order.[24] This shows that the moral judgments of children come largely from their parents. It also emphasizes the tremendous opportunity, and responsibility, that parents have. First impressions are the strongest; early habits are the ones that last; and both of these take place in the home. Juvenile delinquency is almost invariably related to unfortunate home conditions. Conversely, success in life comes almost exclusively to those whose parental homes were successful and whose childhoods were happy. These things are habits that start early and carry through. It has already been shown how happy home life conditions children for their own marital happiness later on.

As to husband and wife, we can observe how marriage both spreads the range and increases the intensity of their satisfactions. When successful, marriage and family life bring some of the greatest satisfactions that it is possible for men and women to know. When unsuccessful, however, they lead equally far

---

[24] H. Hartshorne and M. A. May, "Testing the Knowledge of Right and Wrong," *Religious Education*, October, 1926, pp. 539-54; as cited in William F. Ogburn and M. F Nimkoff, *Sociology* (New York: Houghton Mifflin Co., 1940), p. 181.

in the opposite direction, leaving misery, sorrow, and despair. While marriage is not a reform school, and it is risky indeed to gamble on making someone over after the wedding, yet when things go well marriage does provide a boost for ethical living. Successful mates give support and strength to each other. There is no discouragement like the rebuff or the betrayal of a loved one, however, and no temptation so strong as that which emits from the person for whom one most cares. If the standards of the mate are low, therefore, or if the relationships of marriage are going badly, marriage becomes a drag on character instead of a lift.

If marriage influences morals (and happiness), as has been seen, the reverse is also true. Character weaknesses have negative effects upon family stability. Some of these are as follows: egotism and selfishness, indifference and laziness, deceit and unfaithfulness, self-indulgence such as in gambling, drunkenness, and sexual impropriety.

The Community Approach (Activation)

By community approach we mean something that is a composite of these others, but on the level of self-help and group action. It is democracy at work. We have seen the importance of knowledge to successful marriage, noting its inception in scientific research and its social application through the fields of education, consultation, and legislation. We have seen the place of religion, as motivation. But being informed is not sufficient. Neither are legal controls superimposed from the outside. Nor is it enough to be inspired. Sometimes these conditions, though excellent starts, become aborted. Sometimes a marriage fails because it contains nothing much but good intentions; because it lacks "carry over"; because its potentials are never sufficiently activated.

Conflicts in Ideology.—The world today is torn between two philosophies: that of totalitarianism or dictatorship on the one hand, which promotes a powerful state made possible by force, and that of democracy on the other, which respects the individual and uses government for his protection and welfare. The first of these operates on the principle of might makes right; the second, right makes might. Under totalitarianism, war is generally glorified, brutality justified, and personal freedom regarded as a weakness. Under democracy the reverse is true, peace being the ideal and liberty and humanity of action being considered as imperative. The eighteenth and nineteenth centuries saw a partial victory for democracy. But the twentieth, so far, has given it a setback. Two world wars, the greatest mankind has ever had to endure, have been fought over this conflict of ideologies within less than a half century. Both have been won in the name of democracy. Yet the struggle goes on. The fighting has stopped but the issue remains—unsettled. It may well be, unless this time we can put democracy over and make it stick, that there will be another world war and a setback in civilization. With the atomic bomb in its hands, society must rapidly learn how to control itself or it will destroy itself. Democracy is the answer.

But democracy without morality is unthinkable. How could there be equality and justice if people were all the time hateful and selfish! How could there be self-governing if people were always grabbing and fighting and misrepresenting! There couldn't be. Brotherhood, a principle of both democracy and Christianity, is the only key that can unlock the door to world peace. But brotherhood requires understanding, self-sacrifice, and character.

Do we have these qualities in America? In the rest of the world? Only in isolated instances. There are individuals and groups who put principle above personal profit and general welfare above private interest. But there aren't enough of such. Too frequently man has allowed prejudice to crowd out love, and discrimination to take the place of equalization and justice. And this in America, too. Americans have talked glibly of their democracy, boasting of it to the world, while at the same time failing to apply its principles to the minority groups within their boundaries. It is time now for a housecleaning, both at home and abroad, before it be too late.

The Home as a Laboratory in Democracy.—Folsom, after analyzing this crisis in democracy, and the relationship of the family to it, concludes as follows: [25]

> The family is our most important primary group. In large measure it determines personality development. If we believe in Democracy we shall seek to promote freedom in and through the family and to help parents build young personalities which will not sabotage Democracy in the larger world through their frustrations and pent-up hostilities. This is the real significance of the family in modern society.

The rise of democracy within the political state has been paralleled by a similar trend within the home. As seen in Chapter 2, patriarchal patterns in family relationships have been yielding to individualism and equality. This presents both a problem and an opportunity. The problem grows out of the transitional nature of present family organization, the fact that traditional controls have been lifting and new ones are not yet here to take their place. The opportunity lies in the greater freedom for growth now afforded the individual. In total, this trend means only challenge—for through adjustment, problems can be solved, and with freedom, new progress can be made.

But not only did political and family democracy parallel each other in development; their survival chances are equally inter-related. If we would have peace and justice in community, national, and world relationships, therefore, we must first of all establish correct foundations within the home.

Among the contributions to democracy that parents can make are these: (1) They can cooperate with each other in the spirit of equality, fraternity, and justice. This will create an atmosphere favorable to growth and will demonstrate to children how democratic unity is possible. (2) They can respect the personalities of their children, giving them a certain amount of freedom and responsibility in the home, teaching them to make choices and to solve problems rather than to obey orders blindly. This will give young people a feeling for and practice

---

[25] Reprinted by permission from *The Family and Democratic Society* by J. K. Folsom, published by John Wiley & Sons, Inc., 1943, p. 251.

in democracy that should carry over into their relationships on the outside. Autocracy is not democracy, and if we would have the latter, we must cease using methods of the former in the home. Obedience in a democratic family is never an end in and of itself; but only a means to an end, the end of self-control. The humiliations and personality abuses that some wives must endure at the hands of selfish and domineering husbands, the crushed initiative in some children that comes from the lock-step training of parents who insist upon blind obedience—both are foreign to the highest ideals and needs of this day.

The home is the laboratory of society. Servility there will lead toward the exploitation and enslavement of peoples on the outside. But democracy in family relationship will do the reverse, building leadership in place of mere dominance or submission, and moral brotherhood in place of selfish egoism. If we would avoid a new onslaught of totalitarianism, therefore, we must train our youth to understand and love democracy; and the best place to start is in the home.

Though it takes self-sacrifice and effort to make democracy work, whether in family or society, the rewards are well worth it. Threats and coercions are the ways of a bully, and lead to either rebellion or crushed submission. There is a dignity about individuality that is offended by all such methods. Real progress and happiness are contingent upon freedom. And freedom in the home, motivated to mean responsibility rather than license, is the first step in the building of a free world.

Family Life and the Community.—The stability of the family is related to its social setting. We have already observed how family life could be strengthened by the elimination of war, by the establishment of economic security, by the raising of educational and cultural levels, and the like. Anything, as a matter of fact, that can be done to improve society will at the same time improve the family.

Here we should like to consider the democratic processes of the local community and what can be done there to build happiness in the home.

Every family is a part of the community in which it lives. If there are slum areas, certain families may be disorganized because of it. If parks and other facilities for wholesome recreation are inadequate, or if unwholesome commercial offerings are permitted to get out of hand, children and others might be tempted away from the home and become demoralized in character as a result. But if, on the other hand, communities are alert to family needs and active in the sponsoring of worth-while programs, family life is thereby made better.

Three errors in community organization come to our attention: (1) Sometimes, because of public indifference, coupled with the community's need for additional sources of revenue, and occasionally because of the bribery of public officials, unwholesome establishments are allowed to operate. Whether these be beer joints, "cheap" dance halls, gambling dens, or what not, they can have the effect of undermining character and destroying home life. So also can a lack of law enforcement regarding such matters as child labor laws, curfew hours, and closing times. (2) For reasons similar to those just given, economy and laxity mainly, many communities fail to provide enough of the right kind of recreational and cultural activities. When this happens, young people and others are tempted either to waste away their leisure time by loafing on the streets or else to dissipate it in the wrong kind of activity. (3) Frequently the various clubs, schools, churches, and other organizations devoted to community service are allowed to compete, or even fight, among themselves without any over-all planning or coordination of activity. When it is like that, there are likely to be some areas of community need left entirely neglected while others are overworked. Furthermore, with every organization promoting its own program without regard to others in the community, many individuals will become too active and many homes will be neglected as a result. The problem is one of both overorganization and lack of integration.

Whenever community organization is poor, in ways such as those just indicated, home life suffers, and with it character. We know that juvenile delinquency is often a matter of parental inadequacy of one sort or another. One of these inadequacies, that some parents give evidence of, is neglecting their duties as citizens and community members so that their children are left in an unwholesome environment. Morality and family can both receive either a build-up or a letdown on the community level.

Community organization can be improved, and family life with it, by following a course that is the opposite of the shortcomings listed above: (1) Citizens need to be on their toes to see that the proper officials are elected to public positions and that these do their duty in law enforcement and in other ways protect the community from influences destructive to the home. (2) Worth-while community projects, whether these be a new library, the building of a recreational and cultural center, the setting up of a community recreational program, or something else, need the enthusiastic support of all citizens. (3) The various community organizations must be willing to get together and cooperate for the good of everyone. For each group this may mean that it will need to give up certain of its functions or modify parts of its program, but the step will make for better unity and efficiency. A community council of some sort, representing the various groups in the community, is usually an effective technique for bringing about this desired coordination.

There are indications that the family is not generally reaching this ideal of internal democracy, and that the community is not sufficiently alert to the situation nor active in effecting improvement. Too many husbands and wives fall far short of real mutuality in their relationships, and too many children are denied the responsibility and the opportunity for self-expression that need to be theirs. Communities too frequently compete with families for the time and interests of members, rather than control situations and establish programs designed to add strength to the family structure.

Lyle, in her study of 120 rural families in Iowa, found: (1) that very few of the homes were furnishing the stimulation needed in preparing members to meet new situations with intelligence and foresight; (2) that there was little sharing in "joint planning and choice of the goals for family living";

(3) that there was too "little encouragement for the development of special talents of either parents or children"; and (4) that concern over either world affairs or community welfare was largely lacking. She felt that the home could do a much better job in democratic training than it is now doing, and that the most promising approach to this end would be the reorganization and revitalization on the community level of adult education for family life.[26]

Christianity, morality, and democracy have much in common. All of these, furthermore, impinge upon the family, and it in turn upon each of them. Brotherhood, for example, which is high among Christian virtues and has been advocated by moralists throughout the ages, is also basic to the concept of democracy. Another such value common to all is equality of opportunity. A third is personal freedom. A fourth is justice. And each of these adds strength to the family as well as drawing support from it.

Successful marriage does not just happen. One can never dream nor wish himself or herself into real family happiness, though many so try. And it doesn't do much good to merely read about what must be done if married mates are to be happy (even from books such as this), nor to talk about it (though discussion is a part of education), nor to make resolutions and promises. We need to get out of the armchair.

Community action is an important step in the building of marriage and family solidarity. This implies the development of active interest on the part of virtually all persons and groups within society, the resurgence of family-mindedness. Then, perhaps, marriage would come to be regarded more as a challenging job and less as a selfish right, and lovers would plan to put as much into the relationship as they expected to get out of it. If this can be, there is little question but that the enigma of marriage failure can be brought largely to an end.

---

26 Mary Stewart Lyle, *Adult Education for Democracy in Family Life* (Ames, Iowa: Collegiate Press, 1944), 160 pp.; as reviewed in *Family Life Education,* March, 1945, pp. 1, 2.

Problems and Projects

1. Make a list of traditional sayings and/or superstitions pertaining to love and marriage which you have heard. Which of these seem valid? Which need further testing?

2. How is science being applied to the problem of marriage failure? Show the value and limits of this approach.

3. Examine and analyze the worth of: (*a*) eight or ten current "pulp magazines" dealing with love, sex, and marriage; (*b*) one or two "lovelorn columns" extending over several weeks; and (*c*) several radio programs directed toward problems of marriage and family life.

4. Read and evaluate one or more novels using the family theme. What are the situations described? What are the insights or understandings to be derived from this reading? Are the books wholesome or unwholesome in influence? Illustrate your point of view.

5. Give examples of quackery in the field of marriage counseling. To whom should one turn when in need of help? How far can a lay counselor safely go? Discuss.

6. Analyze family legislation from the standpoint of needed reform. Should divorce be made either easier or more difficult? What are the pros and cons of uniform divorce legislation? Do you have other suggestions?

7. List as many reasons as you can for the lower divorce rate following religious weddings. Which of these do you think is the most significant? Why?

8. From married couples whom you know, show how religion can both add to and subtract from harmony in the home. Draw conclusions.

9. "The home is the laboratory of society." Show how. What are the implications of this statement for democracy? For world peace?

10. Give a brief but pointed evaluation of this book as an approach to better marriage. What should be stressed more than is here done? What less? Are there statements or points of view with which you disagree?

11. At this point the teacher may want to ask students to give an honest appraisal of the course. This can be done by means of either an oral discussion or a written assignment. If the latter, it may be advisable to have the papers unsigned as an invitation to complete frankness.

SELECTED READINGS

ANSHEN, RUTH NANDA (ed.). *The Family: Its Function and Destiny.* New York: Harper & Bros., 1949. Chap. xx, "Religious Values."

BABER, RAY E. *Marriage and the Family.* New York: McGraw-Hill Book Co., 1939. Chap. xviii, "The Conservation of Family Values."

BECKER, HOWARD, and HILL, REUBEN (eds.). *Family, Marriage, and Parenthood.* Boston: D. C. Heath & Co., 1948. Chaps. xx, "Religion in Family Life"; xxvi, "Plans for Strengthening Family Life."

BURGESS, ERNEST W., and LOCKE, HARVEY J. *The Family: From Institution to Companionship.* New York: American Book Co., 1945. Chap. xxii, "Family Reorganization."

CUBER, JOHN F. *Marriage Counseling Practice.* New York: Appleton-Century-Crofts, Inc., 1948.

DUVALL, EVELYN MILLIS, and HILL, REUBEN. *When You Marry.* Boston: D. C. Heath & Co., 1945. Chaps. xviii, "Family Life and Religious Living"; xxi, "Tomorrow's Family."

ELMER, M. C. *The Sociology of the Family.* Boston: Ginn & Co., 1945. Chaps. vii, "The Family and Religion"; xxvi, "Cooperation of Home, School, and Other Agencies."

FISHBEIN, MORRIS, and BURGESS, ERNEST W. (eds.). *Successful Marriage.* New York: Doubleday & Co., 1947. Part V, chap. vii, "Education and Family Life."

GROVES, ERNEST R., and GROVES, GLADYS H. *The Contemporary American Family.* New York: J. B. Lippincott & Co., 1947. Part IV, "Specialized Programs for the Conservation of the American Family."

HARPER, ROBERT A. *Marriage.* New York: Appleton-Century-Crofts, Inc., 1949. Chaps. xi, "Legal and Community Aspects of Marriage"; xv, "Family Unity in an Individualistic Society."

HART, HORNELL, and HART, ELLA B. *Personality and the Family.* Boston: D. C. Heath & Co., 1941. Chap. xvi, "Family Counseling."

MAGOUN, F. ALEXANDER. *Love and Marriage.* New York: Harper & Bros., 1948. Chap. xiii, "Religion in the Home."

SBARBARO, JOHN A. *Marriage Is on Trial.* New York: The Macmillan Co., 1947.

TRUXAL, ANDREW G., and MERRILL, FRANCIS E. *The Family in American Culture.* New York: Prentice-Hall, Inc., 1947. Chap. xxix, "The Reorganization of the Family."

APPENDIX

(Prepared by Harold T. Christensen and Evelyn S. Wigent)

DO NOT sign your name. This survey is entirely impersonal and anonymous.

Age_____. Sex_____. Purdue Classification_____.
Are you married?_____ Engaged?_____ Single and unengaged?_____

This is not a test but a survey of preferences. There are no "right" or "wrong" answers. Record what you actually feel rather than what you may think you ought to feel.

PART I.—A. Listed below are traits that are commonly looked for in choosing a mate. Consider them from the standpoint of the *kind of marriage partner you would like to have.*

Please indicate your preferences by a scale similar to the Purdue grading system. *First,* place a six (6) in front of the four or five items that you consider most important. *Second,* place a five (5) in front of the four or five items that you consider of next importance to you—above average, but not of most importance. *Finally,* continue in this same manner until all of the items have been rated—using a four (4) to designate average importance; a three (3), just below average; a two (2), of least importance; and a one (1), of no importance at all. *Note:* Use a one (1) *only if there are items that are totally irrelevant, unimportant, or undesired on your part. Do not leave any spaces blank.*

____ Rates Socially (Is prominent, popular, sought-after; has a good reputation).
____ Family-mindedness (Desire for home life and children).
____ Health and Vitality (Not ill, or delicate, or usually tired).
____ Good Financial Prospect (Will likely be a good provider).
____ Good Homemaker (Cooks well, knows how to keep house, understands home management).
____ Poised and Confident (Peace of mind, free from worry and moodiness, not nervous or rattled, not shy or self-conscious).
____ Ambitious and Industrious (Restless to achieve, to get ahead, not lazy).

____ Considerateness (Thoughtful, patient, understanding, kind, attentive, sense of fairness, respect for others, not overbearing, not stubborn).

____ Well-groomed and Mannered (Clean, neat, wears clothes well, conventional, refined).

____ Does Not Smoke.

____ Physical Attractiveness (Good looks, sex appeal, well-proportioned body).

____ Sociability (Meets people well; is able to mix well in most situations; is at home with the social arts such as conversation, dancing, sports).

____ Romantic Appeal (Emotional attraction, the "look in her (or his) eye," infatuation).

____ Does Not Drink.

____ Religious Nature (Attends church, has a spiritual outlook on life).

____ Fits Traditional Sex Role (Is masculine if a man, feminine if a woman).

____ Intellectual Stimulation (Intelligent, educated, thinks logically and deeply, has interesting ideas).

____ Normal Heredity (No serious family deficiencies or blights that might be passed on to the offspring).

____ Pleasant Disposition (Cheerful, agreeable, optimistic, sense of humor, good sport).

____ Conventional Sex Standards (Modest, doesn't pet, maintains chastity).

____ Similarity of Background (Religious, educational, economic).

____ Affectionate (Friendly, warm, lovable, sexually responsive).

____ Stable and Dependable (Sincere, honest, reliable, responsible, can be trusted, steady).

____ Emotional Maturity (Grown-up, adaptable, not temperamental, sulky, or otherwise childish).

PART I.—B. *For those who are engaged or married.* Please go back over the items above and *check* (∨) those that particularly apply to your fiancé(e) or marriage partner. These checks are in addition to your earlier ratings. Leave unchecked any items that do not coincide with the traits of your fiancé(e) or marriage partner.

PART II.—A. Below is the same list of traits (though rearranged) that you already evaluated from the standpoint of marriage choice. Here you are asked to study and rate them again, but this time *from the standpoint of what you most like in a date*—without any direct thought of marriage.

Please use the same device for grading as in Part I.—A, which is similar to the Purdue grading system. *First,* place a six (6) in front of the four or five items that you consider most important. *Second,* place a five (5) in front of the four or five items that you consider of next importance to you—above average, but not of most importance. *Finally,* continue in this same manner until all of the items have been rated—using a four (4) to designate average importance; a three (3), just below average; a two (2), of least importance; and a one (1) *only if there are items that are totally irrelevant, unimportant, or undesired on your part. Do not leave any spaces blank.*

____ Physical Attractiveness (Good looks, sex appeal, well-proportioned body).

____ Good Homemaker (Cooks well, knows how to keep house, understands home management).

____ Ambitious and Industrious (Restless to achieve, to get ahead, not lazy).

____ Conventional Sex Standards (Modest, doesn't pet, maintains chastity).

____ Sociability (Meets people well, is able to mix well in most situations, is at home with the social arts such as conversation, dancing, sports).

____ Emotional Maturity (Grown-up, adaptable, not temperamental, not sulky or childish).

____ Health and Vitality (Not ill, or delicate, or usually tired).

____ Rates Socially (Is prominent, popular, sought-after, has a good reputation).

____ Stable and Dependable (Sincere, honest, reliable, responsible, can be trusted, steady).

____ Pleasant Disposition (Cheerful, agreeable, optimistic, sense of humor, good sport).

____ Well-groomed and Mannered (Clean, neat, wears clothes well, conventional, refined).

____ Intellectual Stimulation (Intelligent, educated, thinks logically and deeply, has interesting ideas).

____ Considerateness (Thoughtful, patient, understanding, kind, attentive, sense of fairness, respect for others, not overbearing, not stubborn).

____ Normal Heredity (No serious family deficiencies or blights that might be passed on to the offspring).

____ Similarity of Backgrounds (Religious, educational, economic).

____ Poised and Confident (Peace of mind, free from worry and moodiness, not nervous or rattled, not shy or self-conscious).

____ Affectionate (Friendly, warm, lovable).

____ Fits Traditional Sex Role (Is masculine if a man, feminine if a woman).

____ Does Not Drink.

____ Romantic Appeal (Emotional attraction, the "look in her (or his) eye," infatuation).

____ Does Not Smoke.

____ Family-mindedness (Desire for home life and children).

____ Religious Nature (Attends church, has a spiritual outlook on life).

____ Good Financial Prospect (Will likely be a good provider).

PART II.—B. *For those who are not engaged or married.* Please go back over the items above and *check* (√) those that particularly apply to your last date. These checks are in addition to your earlier ratings. Leave unchecked any items which your date did not possess.

PART III.—A. The following list of traits is compiled from commonly heard criticisms of the dating process. You are asked to study each item very carefully and to decide, as best you can, which of the two sexes it more accurately describes. If there are any items that seem irrelevant or wholly unobjectionable to you, please leave them blank. Make your judgments in the light of all your observations and impressions derived from your total dating experience. Here are the rules:

(1) Go through the list and underline the *five* traits which seem most objectionable when present.

(2) Place the letter "M" in front of each statement that you feel *is more characteristic of males* than of females in dating.

(3) Place the letter "F" in front of each statement that you feel *is more characteristic of females* than of males in dating.

(4) Write the letters "M" and "F" in front of each statement that you feel is approximately the same for both sexes.

____ Is disrespectful of the opposite sex; makes slurring remarks; takes advantage.

____ Prefers to date only popular "numbers."

____ Is indefinite and indecisive in dating; indifferent about planning or carrying out the date; breaks dates for no legitimate reason.

____ Lacks "life" and energy; complains of being tired or is often sick.

____ Flirts with others or brags about other dates.

____ Asks stupid questions or makes trite and silly remarks; shallow interests; excessive frivolity.

____ Is too serious, jealous, and possessive; overly sentimental; "clinging-vine" type.

____ Sloppy appearance; carelessness in dress and mannerisms; unskilful make-up.

____ Is overbearing, stubborn, and impatient; always wants own way; complains, argues, is bossy.

____ Stays too late on a date; doesn't know when to say "goodnight."

____ Is prudish regarding matters of morals and sex.

____ Is too cold emotionally; lacks warmth; isn't lovable.

____ Wants too much necking or petting.

____ Lacks etiquette; is crude and unrefined in manners; forgets the common courtesies.

____ Unwilling to share spotlight with others; wants to be entire center of attention.

____ Never thinks to offer compliments or to say thanks; takes others for granted; inattentive and inconsiderate.

____ Is too staid and conventional; dull; lacks "sparkle" or glamour.

____ Uses dishonest flattery; "strings a line"; tries to get others to fall, to be a person of many loves.

____ Tells off-color jokes; uses vulgarity or profanity.

____ Is overtalkative and loud around others; a "show-off"; full of "smart" slang.

____ Is childish; lacks sense of humor; touchy or easily angered; sulks; a poor sport.

____ Is too self-conscious, shy; awkward in groups; difficult to engage in conversation.

____ Is late in calling or in being ready for a date.

____ Weak in the social arts, e.g., dancing, bridge, sports, etc.

____ Artificial dress and manners; putting on airs; trying to be a fashion plate.

____ Is a spendthrift; wants always to do expensive things or expects expensive favors.

_____ Acts nervous and rattled; isn't calm or at ease; lacks self-confidence and poise.

_____ Too dependent upon others; has no mind of his (or her) own; spineless.

_____ Overly self-assured; blind to own shortcomings; acts as if doing partner a favor; egotistical.

_____ Unwilling to enjoy other's friends or to associate with one's folks.

PART III.—B. Now go back over the list given in Part III.—A, and check (V) any items that you think apply particularly to yourself. These checks are to be in addition to your earlier ratings of the two sexes. They are to be assigned in the spirit of honest self-criticism and are to indicate those problem areas *in your own personality* that you feel are particularly great or need special attention. Check as many or as few as you like.

AUTHOR INDEX

Abrams, Charles, 50-51
Adams, Clifford R., 270
Aldrich, C. Anderson, 389
Aldrich, Mary M., 389
Anderson, W. A., 363-64
Angell, Robert C., 55
Anshen, Ruth Nanda, 25, 51, 55, 493
Arlitt, Ada Hart, 298
Arthur, Julietta K., 420

Baber, Ray E., 16, 25, 129, 168, 270, 305, 324, 347, 389, 449, 474, 493
Bacal, Jacques, 347
Bain, F. W., 6
Bain, Read, 40-41
Banning, Margaret, 149, 155, 168
Barker, Roger C., 385
Baruch, Dorothy W., 389
Bates, Alan, 244
Becker, Howard, 25, 55, 93, 133, 168, 206, 238, 270, 305, 347, 389, 449, 493
Bell, Howard M., 479
Bergler, Edmund, 93
Bigelow, Howard, 347
Bossard, James H. S., 75-76, 93, 246, 358, 389, 443
Bowman, Henry A., 107, 125, 129, 270, 275, 305, 449, 462-64, 470
Brav, Stanley R., 301
Breckenridge, M. E., 389
Brooks, Evelyn C., 389
Brooks, Lee M., 389
Buck, Pearl S., 130
Burgess, Ernest W., 8, 17, 30, 37, 43, 45, 55, 73, 79, 82, 88, 93, 101, 128, 130, 132, 144, 168, 171, 182, 183, 184, 187, 193, 195, 206-7, 208, 234, 238, 242, 263-64, 270, 289, 293, 296, 298, 305, 330-31, 347, 389, 420, 438, 441, 449, 457, 470, 480, 493
Burkhart, Roy A., 238
Butterfield, Oliver M., 166, 347

Caplow, Theodore, 232, 250
Carrington, William, 389

Cavan, Ruth S., 43, 55, 393, 397, 400-1, 403-4, 412-13, 416-17, 420, 457
Centers, Richard, 248
Christensen, Harold T., 98, 153, 221, 226-27, 247, 257, 353, 354, 362, 363, 495
Cooley, Charles H., 79
Cottrell, Leonard S., 17, 88, 128, 132-33, 171, 182, 183, 195, 234, 242, 289, 296, 330-31, 358, 457-58, 480
Crawley, Ernest, 6
Cuber, John F., 470, 493

Davis, Katharine B., 150
Dean, John P., 51
Dearborn, Lester W., 144
De Schweinitz, Karl, 166
Dewey, John, 79
Dickinson, Robert L., 101
Dinkel, Robert M., 407, 412
Duvall, Evelyn Millis, 55, 93, 101, 158, 168, 205, 209, 238, 292, 305, 319-20, 324, 347, 389, 493
Duvall, Sylvanus, 239

Eldridge, Hope T., 95-96
Elliott, Mabel A., 19, 25, 239
Ellis, Albert, 185
Elmer, M. C., 420, 493
Exner, M. J., 347

Faris, Ellsworth, 79
Farnham, Marynia F., 120, 130
Fishbein, Morris, 101, 130, 144, 168, 184, 195, 264, 298, 305, 347, 389, 420, 441, 449, 493
Folsom, Joseph K., 55, 130, 206, 422, 487
Ford, Mary E. N., 226, 239
Frank, Lawrence K., 56
Frank, Robert, 168

Gallup, George, 309
Gates, R. Ruggles, 61
Gesell, Arnold L., 389
Glick, Paul C., 109, 349
Goode, William J., 436, 438

SUBJECT INDEX

Abortion, 154-55, 369-70

Adjustment; *see* Mate adjustment

Adolescence, 137-38, 377-78, 386; *see also* Children; Parent-child relationships

Adoption, 154, 366-67

Affection; *see* Love

Age at marriage, 281, 288-93, 359, 424

Alimony, 284-85, 474-75

Ambivalence, 209-10

Animal contacts, 134-40, 145

Annulment; *see* Divorce

Assortive mating, 262-69; *see also* Homogamy

Autosexuality, 134-40, 144-45, 165, 429

Bachelors; *see* Permanently unmarried

Bereavement, 431-35, 437

Birth control, 359 ff.
acceptance of, 360-61
as a factor in sex ratio, 98
effectiveness of, 153
legal status of, 360-61
methods of, 360, 365
personal reasons for, 361-64

Birth process, 290, 372-74

Birth rates, 44-46, 351-54; *see also* Size of family

Blood test laws, 282, 285, 287-88, 468

Budgeting, 341-42

Careers for women, 109, 121-24; *see also* Women

Character emphasis, 484-85, 486, 491; *see also* Delinquency

Chastity; *see* Premarital sexual intercourse; Sexual behavior

Child, cost of, 362

Child spacing, 363-64, 373-74

Child training; *see also* Parent-child relationships; Sex education
achieving maturity, 83-92
discipline, 378-85

importance of early years, 57, 73-79, 91, 164
motivating factors, 80-83
"spoiling," 77-78, 89, 205, 383

Childlessness; *see also* Birth control; Birth rate; Sterilization
eugenic reasons for, 68
extent of, 364-65, 421

Children; *see also* Child training; Parent-child relationships
parental adjustment to, 373-74
parental influence on, 379-80
stages in development of, 374-78

Children and successful marriage, 34, 42-43, 356-59

Church; *see* Religion

Climacteric, 402-4

College students
birth rates of, 71, 353-54
marriages of, 290-92, 422-23

Common-law marriage, 279-80, 294

Community organization for family living, 488-91

Companionate marriage, 20

Complementary nature of the sexes, 5-8; *see also* Sex roles; Male-female comparisons

Conception, process of, 365-67

Conditioned response, 78-80

Contraception; *see* Birth control

Counseling, 467 ff.; *see also* Marriage clinics
agencies active in, 468-69, 471-73
catharsis from, 467-69
of old people, 400
principles of, 470-71
qualifications for, 469-70

Courtship, 211 ff.
charm and sociability, 233-35
cross-sex criticisms, 215-25
dating etiquette, 236
defined, 211-12
exploitation in, 228-30
"going steady," 231-32
jealousy during, 233
length of, 192
lovers' quarrels, 233, 276

505

Unattached, 421 ff.
Unmarried; *see* Permanently unmarried
Unmarried motherhood, 18, 429; *see
also* Illegitimacy

Venereal disease, 18, 44, 46, 50, 66,
151-52, 164, 282, 366
Virgin hospitals, 21

War and family instability, 45-48,
189, 351-52
Wedding, 294 ff.
as a sacrament, 296, 480
cost of, 297-98
etiquette of, 298-300
type of ceremony, 295-98
White-collar girl, 251, 424

Widowhood, 430 ff.; *see also* Remarriage
numbers in, 430
problems of, 430-35
sex ratio in, 96-97, 430
Wishes; *see* Motivation
Women; *see also* Male-female comparisons; Sex roles
adjustment to empty nest, 405, 409
careers for, 109, 121-24, 422-23
dilemmas faced, 116-24
discontentment of, 114-15
emancipation of, 108-11, 204-5
tendency to understate ages, 401
working wives, 340

Youth; *see* Adolescence